## MACMILLAN EXAMS

D1630247

# Ready for
# FCE

THE LEARNING CENTRE
HAMMERSMITH AND WEST
LONDON COLLEGE
GLIDDON ROAD
LONDON W14 9BL

## teacher's book

Hilary Thomson

Roy Norris

with

Andrew
Jurascheck

**Updated for
the revised
FCE exam**

HAMMERSMITH WEST LONDON COLLEGE

330788

Macmillan Education
Between Towns Road, Oxford OX4 3PP
A division of Macmillan Publishers Limited
Companies and representatives throughout the world

ISBN 978-0-230-02765-7

Text © Macmillan Publishers Limited 2008
Design and illustration © Macmillan Publishers
Limited 2008

First published 2008

All rights reserved; no part of this publication may be
reproduced, stored in a retrieval system, transmitted
in any form, or by any means, electronic, mechanical,
photocopying, recording, or otherwise, without the
prior written permission of the publishers.

Note to Teachers
Photocopies may be made, for classroom use, of
pages 158–222 without the prior written permission
of Macmillan Publishers Limited. However, please
note that the copyright law, which does not
normally permit multiple copying of published
material, applies to the rest of this book.

Designed by Andrew Jones and eMC Design
Illustrated by Mark Collins
Cover design by Barbara Mercer

Hilary Thomson and Roy Norris would like to thank
their spouses, Miguel Angel and Azucena for their
support. Hilary Thomson would also like to thank
Roy Norris for his helpful and constructive comments
and her teaching and training colleagues for their
inspiration.

The publishers would like to thank all those who
participated in the development of the book, with
special thanks to José Vicente Acín Barea, Coral
Berriochoa Hausmann, Javier Buendía, Sue Bushell,
Jacek Czabánski, Debra Emmett, Elena García,
Loukas Geronikolaou, Emilio Jiménez Aparicio, Roula
Kyriakidou, Juan Carlos López Gil, Arturo Mendoza
Fernández, Jackie Newman, Carolyn Parsons, Javier
Redondo, Lena Reppa, James Richardson, Yannis
Tsihlas, Malcolm Wren and Mayte Zamora Díaz.

The authors and publishers are grateful for permission
to reprint the following copyright material:
Extracts from 'A Male Enters the Nanny State' by
Cathy Comerford copyright © The Independent 1997,
first published in The Independent 22.10.97, reprinted
by permission of the publisher.
Adapted extracts from 'Career File' by Sian Flanighan
copyright © IPC Media Limited/Marie Claire 2001, first
published in Marie Claire UK February 2001, reprinted
by permission of the publisher.
Extracts from 'Love parties but dread dancing' by
Peta Bee copyright © Peta Bee/Sunday Times 1999,
first published in Sunday Times 31.10.99, reprinted by
permission of the publisher.
Extracts from 'Too clean for our own good' by
Simon Crompton copyright © Simon Crompton/N
I Syndication 2000, first published in The Times
04.04.00, reprinted by Extracts from 'Big Brother
Google is watching' by Robert Verkaik copyright © The
Independent 2007, first published in The Independent
24.05.07, reprinted by permission of the publisher.
Extracts from 'Around the World in Anything but a
Plane' first published in Evening Standard 05.03.07,
reprinted by permission of Solo Syndication Ltd.
Extracts from 'Some Psychiatrists See 'Shopaholic' As
a Diagnosis' by Shankar Vedantam copyright © The
Washington Post 2006. reprinted by permission of the
publisher.
Extract about Dame Ellen MacArthur, reprinted by
permission of A P Watt Ltd, on behalf of Dame Ellen
MacArthur.
Dictionary definitions on page 162 taken from
the Macmillan English Dictionary, second edition,
published by Macmillan Publishers limited, © A & C
Black Publishers Ltd 2007

These materials may contain links for third party
websites. We have no control over, and are not
responsible for, the contents of such third party
websites. Please use care when accessing them.

The authors and publishers would like to thank
the following for permission to reproduce their
photographic material:
Alamy/ Horizon International Images Ltd p 221b;
Image Source p 221t; Image State p 220r;
Superstock/ Prisma p 220l.

Although we have tried to trace and contact copyright
holders before publication, in some cases this has
not been possible. If contacted, we will be pleased
to rectify any errors or omissions at the earliest
opportunity.

Printed in Thailand.

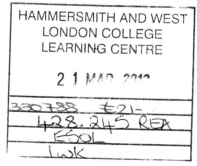

HAMMERSMITH AND WEST
LONDON COLLEGE
LEARNING CENTRE

2 1 MAR 2012

330788    £21-
428.245 REA
£001
Lwk

2015  2014  2013  2012
10   9   8   7   6

# Contents

# Contents map of the Coursebook

| Writing | Use of English | Listening | Speaking |
|---|---|---|---|
| Informal letters | Transformations (FCE Part 4) | Multiple matching (FCE Part 3) | Talking about photos (FCE Part 2) |
| 1 Letters: Asking for information (FCE Part 1)<br>2 Articles (FCE Part 2) | Word formation: Affixes<br>Word formation (FCE Part 3) | 1 Sentence completion (FCE Part 2)<br>2 Multiple choice (FCE Part 4) | |
| Essays (FCE Part 2) | Word formation: Suffixes -ful and -less<br>Word formation (FCE Part 3) | 1 Multiple matching (FCE Part 3)<br>2 Multiple choice (FCE Part 4) | 1 Collaborative task (FCE Part 3)<br>2 Further discussion (FCE Part 4) |

### Part 3: Multiple matching

| Writing | Use of English | Listening | Speaking |
|---|---|---|---|
| 1 Reviews (FCE Part 2)<br>2 Short stories (FCE Part 2) | Word formation: Adjectives ending in -ing and -ed<br>Transformations (FCE Part 4)<br>Word formation (FCE Part 3) | Preparing for listening: Focus on distractors<br>Multiple choice (FCE Part 1) | Talking about photos (FCE Part 2) |
| Letters: An application (FCE Part 2) | Word formation: Nouns and adjectives<br>1 Word formation (FCE Part 3)<br>2 Multiple-choice cloze (FCE Part 1)<br>Open cloze: Prepositions (FCE Part 2) | 1 True/False<br>2 Sentence completion (FCE Part 2) | 1 Talking about photos (FCE Part 2)<br>2 Collaborative task (FCE Part 3) |
| Descriptions (FCE Part 2) | Open cloze: Relative clauses<br>Transformations (FCE Part 4) | 1 Multiple matching (FCE Part 3)<br>Stated/Not stated | 1 Collaborative task (FCE Part 3)<br>2 Interview (FCE Part 1) |

### Part 3: Word formation

| Writing | Use of English | Listening | Speaking |
|---|---|---|---|
| Emails (FCE Part 1) | Open cloze (FCE Part 2)<br>Transformations (FCE Part 4) | 1 Sentence completion (FCE Part 2)<br>2 Multiple choice (FCE Part 4) | Supermarket psychology<br>1 Interview (FCE Part 1)<br>2 Talking about photos (FCE Part 2) |
| Essays (FCE Part 2)<br>Articles (FCE Part 2) | Word formation: -en suffix<br>Transformations: Future forms (FCE Part 4)<br>Word formation (FCE Part 3)<br>Multiple-choice cloze (FCE Part 1) | Multiple choice (FCE Part 1) | 1 Interview (FCE Part 1)<br>2 Talking about photos (FCE Part 2) |
| Informal letters (FCE Part 2)<br>Short stories (FCE Part 2) | Open cloze (FCE Part 2)<br>Word formation: Adjectives<br>Word formation (FCE Part 3)<br>Transformations (FCE Part 4) | Multiple choice (FCE Part 4) | 1 Collaborative task (FCE Part 3)<br>2 Further discussion (FCE Part 4) |

| Writing | Use of English | Listening | Speaking |
|---|---|---|---|
| 1 An article/A story (FCE Part 2)<br>2 Articles (FCE Part 2)<br>Short stories (FCE Part 2) | Multiple-choice cloze (FCE Part 1) | 1 Sentence completion (FCE Part 2)<br>2 Multiple matching (FCE Part 3) | 1 Collaborative task (FCE Part 3)<br>2 Further discussion (FCE Part 4) |
| Essays (FCE Part 2)<br>Formal letters (FCE Part 1) | Open cloze (FCE Part 2)<br>Transformations (FCE Part 4) | 1 Sentence completion (FCE Part 2)<br>2 Multiple choice (FCE Part 1) | Collaborative task (FCE Part 3) |
| 1 Reports (FCE Part 2)<br>2 Letters: Giving information (FCE Part 1) | 1 Multiple-choice cloze (FCE Part 1)<br>Word formation: Noun suffixes<br>2 Word formation (FCE Part 3)<br>Open cloze (FCE Part 2)<br>Transformations (FCE Part 4)<br>Word formation (FCE Part 3) | Multiple matching (FCE Part 3) | Talking about photos (FCE Part 2) |

### Part 3: Multiple matching    Part 4: Multiple choice

| Writing | Use of English | Listening | Speaking |
|---|---|---|---|
| Formal letters: An application (FCE Part 2)<br>Email (FCE Part 1) | Word formation: Miscellaneous nouns<br>Word formation (FCE Part 3)<br>Transformations (FCE Part 4) | 1 Sentence completion (FCE Part 2)<br>2 Multiple choice (FCE Part 1) | |
| 1 Set books (FCE Part 2)<br>2 Essays (FCE Part 2)<br>Essays (FCE Part 2) | Word formation: Adjective suffixes -ible and -able<br>Word formation (FCE Part 3)<br>Transformations: Hypothetical situations (FCE Part 4) | Multiple choice (FCE Part 4) | Collaborative task (FCE Part 3) |
| Articles (FCE Part 2) | Multiple-choice cloze (FCE Part 1)<br>Transformations (FCE Part 4) | Multiple matching (FCE Part 3) | |

### Part 3: Collaborative task    Part 4: Further discussion

Listening scripts
Page 218

# Introduction

*Ready for FCE* consists of the following components:

- Coursebook (with and without key)
- Teacher's Book
- Three CDs
- Workbook (with and without key)

## Coursebook

Each of the 15 units in the Coursebook provides a balance and variety of activity types aimed at improving students' general English level as well as developing the language and skills they will need to pass the First Certificate in English examination. At the end of every unit there is a two-page Review section, containing revision activities and exam-style tasks, which enable students to practise the new language they have encountered in the unit and, as the course progresses, in previous units.

The book also contains five supplementary 'Ready for-...' units, which provide students with information, advice and practice on each of the five papers in the First Certificate examination. These are situated after every third unit and may be used in the order in which they appear in the book: ie Ready for Reading after Unit 3, Ready for Use of English after Unit 6 and so on. However, they are intended very much as a flexible resource which may be exploited at such a time during the course as the teacher feels appropriate.

At the end of the Coursebook you will find a Wordlist and Grammar reference, each closely linked to the 15 units in the book. There is also an Additional material section, to which students are referred in certain units, and the Listening scripts. The Coursebook is available with or without the answer key.

The following boxes, which appear throughout the Coursebook, provide help and advice to students when they perform the different tasks.
- **What to expect in the exam:** these contain useful information on what students should be prepared to see, hear or do in a particular task in the examination.
- **How to go about it:** these give advice and guidelines on how to deal with different examination task types and specific questions in the unit.
- **Don't forget!:** these provide a reminder of important points to bear in mind when answering a particular question.

## Teacher's Book

The Teacher's Book contains teaching notes for each activity in the Coursebook. A typical unit of the Teacher's Book provides you with:
- a summary of examination task types contained in the Coursebook unit
- guidelines and ideas for exploiting the Coursebook material, including further suggestions for warm-up and follow-on activities
- classroom management ideas
- answers to exercises
- tapescripts for the listening activities
- sample answers for many of the writing exercises, together with the examiner's comments and the mark awarded.

At the end of the Teacher's Book you will also find the following:

### • Photocopiable vocabulary exercises
These are optional exercises which can be used to exploit the vocabulary in reading and listening texts. They are intended as pre- or post-reading and post-listening activities.

### • One photocopiable exercise for the Ready for Speaking unit
This exercise accompanies the recorded sample interview of two students performing the speaking tasks in the Ready for Speaking unit.

### • Five photocopiable Progress tests
These are intended for use after every three units and provide teachers with the opportunity to assess their students' progress on the course at regular intervals. They contain useful practice in examination task types as well as revision of the language that has been presented in the previous three or more units. Each test follows the same format:

    One FCE-style reading exercise
    Two or three Use of English exercises
    One FCE-style listening exercise
    One vocabulary exercise
    An FCE-writing task.

In each case the exam task types in the test will already have been encountered by students in the Coursebook.

### • One photocopiable Final test
This is a full First Certificate style examination, including all five papers. Paper 5 should not be photocopied. To make it similar to the real exam, the teacher should interview students in pairs.

# Workbook

The 15 units of the Workbook follow the same order and general topic areas as the Coursebook. They have been designed to provide students with further practice, revision and extension of the language presented in class, as well as examination practice and skills work. Each unit follows the same format:

**• Reading and follow-up vocabulary work**

To ensure variety, the reading task type in most units of the Workbook is different from that in the corresponding unit of the Coursebook. Students will, however, already be familiar with the reading task type they encounter in the Workbook and are thus provided with an opportunity for revision. In each unit there is at least one exercise exploiting the vocabulary which occurs in the reading text.

**• Vocabulary**

There is usually a combination of puzzle-type exercises (eg crosswords, word grids, wordsearches) and more familiar vocabulary exercises (eg gap-fills, multiple choice and matching exercises). Some exercises extend the vocabulary from the topic area by drawing on items from the Wordlist at the end of the Coursebook. On occasions students are given the opportunity to revise vocabulary presented in earlier units of the Coursebook.

**• Language focus**

This section contains further controlled practice of the grammar presented in class. None of the exercises contains grammar which students have not already encountered in the Coursebook.

**• Use of English**

There is a Use of English section in each unit. Most of the language tested in these exercises will already have been encountered by students in the corresponding unit, or previous units, of the Coursebook.

**• Writing**

The Workbook contains a complete writing syllabus to complement that in the Coursebook and to ensure that students are fully prepared for Paper 2 of the First Certificate examination. Extensive help is given in the form of useful language, model answers and/or planning guidelines. A feature of the Workbook's writing syllabus is that whilst the writing task in each unit is relevant to the topic area of the corresponding unit in the Coursebook, the task type is the same, in most cases, as that of the previous unit of the

Coursebook. This enables revision to take place and ensures that students are given the opportunity to practise the same task type with different topic areas.

At the end of the Workbook you will find the following:
- a list of phrasal verbs including the phrasal verbs encountered in both Coursebook and Workbook
- a list of lexical phrases, including the phrases presented throughout the Coursebook which contain the following verbs: *get, take, have, come, give, put, make, do*
- a list of irregular verbs.

The Workbook is available with or without the answer key.

# Using the course to prepare students for the FCE exam

Whilst *Ready for FCE* can be used as a general course for students at an upper intermediate level of English, one of its main aims is to prepare students for the Cambridge First Certificate in English examination. An overview of the examination can be found on pages iv–v of the Coursebook. A range of support is available in the various components of the course to help you prepare your students for the different aspects of the FCE exam.

## Vocabulary

In every unit of the Coursebook there is at least one section devoted to topic vocabulary, that is, words or phrases which are linked to the theme of the unit. This topic vocabulary is reproduced in the Wordlist at the end of the book, where it is grouped according to the unit in which it appears, together with further items which form part of the same lexical set. Vocabulary activities in the Workbook both revise the topic vocabulary presented in the units, and provide practice of the additional items from the Wordlist. This ensures that students build a sufficient vocabulary store to meet the requirements of the First Certificate examination.

As well as individual words, students are encouraged throughout the course to learn whole phrases, a key element in the Use of English paper (Paper 3), though also of importance in the other four papers of the exam. Attention is given to different types of collocation, and there are regular sections which focus on expressions with verbs such as *get, take, give* and *put*. These expressions are grouped for reference in the Lexical phrases list at the end of the Workbook.

In addition, the course contains work on dependent prepositions, words which are often confused, affixation (see Use of English) and phrasal verbs. A variety of different approaches is used to present phrasal verbs, which always appear in the context of a sentence or continuous text as a guide to meaning. An alphabetical list of all the phrasal verbs from the course is included at the end of the Workbook.

All elements of vocabulary are revised in the Review sections of the Coursebook as well as in the Workbook, both in the unit in which they are first presented and in later units, too.

## Grammar

Each unit of the Coursebook contains one or more Language focus sections, which generally use contextualized examples from a reading or listening text to present and illustrate a particular grammar point. Students at this level will already be familiar with the majority of the grammar areas which are required for the First Certificate examination. Most Language focus sections, therefore, do not simply give students the grammar rules, but encourage them instead to apply their existing knowledge to example sentences and work out the rules for themselves. To achieve this they may be invited to answer questions about the examples or perhaps match each example to a rule. Having checked their ideas in the Grammar reference at the end of the book, students then go on to perform written and/or spoken practice activities. Further practice is provided in the Review sections at the end of each unit, as well as in the relevant unit of the Workbook. This practice often takes the form of Use of English exercises.

## Reading

Authentic texts from a variety of sources (magazines, newspapers, novels, etc) are used to develop students' reading skills and prepare them for Paper 1 of the FCE examination. Help is given throughout the Coursebook on how to approach each of the four task types, with further advice on appropriate reading strategies contained in the Ready for Reading unit on pages 38 to 41.

In order to promote sound examination technique students are encouraged at all times to read through the text for gist (general understanding) first, before they go on to complete the FCE-type reading task. They may, for example, be required to answer one or more gist questions, or perhaps check predictions they have made in a pre-reading activity. Once all reading tasks have been carried out, the 'Reacting

to the text' sections provide students with the opportunity to discuss the content of the passage and express their own opinions on the issues involved. Further reading practice is provided in each unit of the Workbook.

### Vocabulary in the reading texts

It is not, of course, necessary for students to understand every word in the texts in order to complete the various reading tasks. However, the following support is available when dealing with vocabulary which is likely to be unknown to your students:

- Page 18 in Unit 2 of the Teacher's Book provides guidelines on how to decide which vocabulary, if any, needs pre-teaching before your students read or listen to texts.
- For some reading texts, key vocabulary is presented in the Coursebook before students read.
- The photocopiable vocabulary exercises at the end of the Teacher's Book provide the option to exploit the vocabulary contained in the texts, either before or after students read.
- Pages 38 and 39 of the Ready for Reading unit focus on the skill of guessing the meaning of unknown vocabulary from context.
- Some texts in the Coursebook are followed by 'Noticing language' exercises, which actively encourage students to focus on certain items in the texts.
- All reading texts in the Workbook are followed by exercises which exploit and/or extend vocabulary contained in the texts.

## Writing

All FCE writing tasks are covered, both in the Coursebook and the Workbook. The writing sections in both books prepare students thoroughly for each new task and may focus on one or more of the following features: planning answers; help with ideas; paragraph organization; useful language; appropriate style; checking work for mistakes. Model answers appear throughout the course and always when students encounter a particular task type for the first time.

In addition, the Teacher's Book contains authentic examples of students' answers to some of the writing tasks in the Coursebook, particularly for the earlier units. These are accompanied by comments from an examiner and a mark of between 1 and 5, where 3, 4 and 5 are considered to be of pass standard, 5 being the maximum mark attainable. An indication of the criteria for marking Part 1 answers is given on page 120 of the coursebook in the Ready for Writing unit, though the same general categories (content, range and accuracy of language, organization and cohesion, style and format, target reader) also apply when marking Part 2 questions. The Ready for Writing unit and Units 12 and 14 of the Workbook each contain a small bank of Part 2 questions which can be used for extra writing practice as the exam approaches.

Question 5 of Part 2 of the Writing Paper consists of a choice of two tasks based on the set reading texts specified in the Examination regulations issued each year. This option is intended to promote extended reading amongst students. Should you decide to study one of the set reading texts with your class, note that this is dealt with thoroughly in Unit 14 of the Coursebook.

## Use of English

The comprehensive nature of the Language focus and Vocabulary sections ensures that students receive the appropriate language input to enable them to deal confidently with the tasks in the FCE Use of English paper. In addition, they are provided with plenty of opportunity to practise all four task types of this paper, both in the Coursebook and the Workbook.

A key feature of *Ready for FCE* is the Word formation syllabus, which aims to teach rather than simply test. A systematic approach to word building is adopted, with a number of units each focusing on a different aspect of affixation. Word formation practice exercises test only those items which have been presented in the same unit as the exercise or in earlier units. The effect is therefore accumulative, so that by the end of the course students will have been exposed to all the major areas of affixation tested in Part 3 of the Use of English paper.

## Listening

Each unit of the Coursebook has either one or two listening activities of the type students will encounter in the FCE Listening Paper 4. A wide range of sources has been used for the listening texts and the recordings contain a variety of different accents. Again, information on listening in the FCE exam and guidance on how to tackle the tasks are given in the 'What to expect' and 'How to go about it' boxes, particularly in the earlier stages of the course, when students require most support.

The pre-listening stage is an extremely important one and can greatly influence how successfully students complete the listening task. *Ready for FCE* therefore includes a number of pre-listening activities intended to raise students' interest in, and activate their knowledge of the subject of the recording, as well as to suggest techniques which can be applied during the actual FCE examination itself. These activities include discussion questions on the topic, prediction of language and/or information which students are likely to hear, raising students' awareness of distractors, and a focus on intonation and its importance in answering certain questions. The Ready for Listening unit on pages 158 to 161 contains an example of each of the four parts of the listening paper, together with further help and advice.

As with the Reading paper, students are not expected to understand every word in the recordings in order to be able to complete the tasks. The listening scripts can be used in conjunction with the advice on page 18 in Unit 2 of the Teacher's Book in order to decide which, if any, vocabulary needs pre-teaching.

## Speaking

Guidance is given throughout the Coursebook on how to approach the four parts of the Speaking Paper. There are regular 'How to go about it' and 'Useful language' boxes, particularly for parts 2 and 3, where students need most help with procedure and technique. The Ready for Speaking unit on pages 196 to 199 contains further useful practice and advice, and includes a recorded interview of two students performing the different tasks in Paper 5.

Clearly, the more speaking practice students have in class, the faster their oral skills will improve and the better prepared they will be for the Speaking paper of the FCE examination. *Ready for FCE* provides regular opportunities for students to speak in pairs, in pre- and post-listening and reading activities, as well as in Vocabulary and Language focus sections. These are indicated by the special speaking icon, most usually found in the left-hand margin.

# 1 Lifestyle

## Content Overview

### Themes

This unit is concerned with clothes and different lifestyles. The vocabulary and grammar come directly from the reading and listening exercises and recur throughout the unit so that learners see each item more than once.

### Exam-related activities

| | |
|---|---|
| **Paper 1** | **Reading** |
| Part 2 | Gapped text |
| **Paper 2** | **Writing** |
| | Informal letters |
| **Paper 3** | **Use of English** |
| Part 4 | Transformations (Review) |
| **Paper 4** | **Listening** |
| Part 3 | Multiple matching |
| **Paper 5** | **Speaking** |
| Part 2 | Talking about photos |

### Other

Language focus 1: Habitual behaviour; general tendencies, frequency adverbs

Language focus 2: *Be/Get used to* and *used to*

Vocabulary: Clothes

Expressions using *get*

### Vocabulary 1: Clothes                    Page 2

**1** Refer students to the pictures in their book and the instructions below. Students discuss their ideas in pairs or small groups. Monolingual learner dictionaries could be used for the items of vocabulary that are not included in the box, or for any items the students are unsure of.

### Answers

People from left to right:
1 waistcoat, bow tie (shirt, shoes, trousers)
2 scarf, blazer (shirt/blouse, shoes, skirt, tie, tights)
3 trainers, dungarees (hat, jacket, T-shirt)
4 bracelet, cardigan, high-heeled shoes (dress, necklace, tights, watch)
5 jumper (jeans, shoes)
6 trainers, tracksuit bottoms (baseball cap, T-shirt)

Note: *dinner jacket* does not appear in the picture

**2** Students could work in the same groups as before to match the adjectives to the pictures. For some of the more positive descriptions you could encourage students to use other members of the class, eg *Maria's wearing a colourful jumper.* This is a good check that they have understood the vocabulary.

### Answers

Suggested answers
1 formal, plain, tasteful, smart
2 unfashionable, smart
3 casual, unfashionable, shabby, colourful (jacket), waterproof (jacket)
4 formal, colourful, tasteful, smart (shoes), tight-fitting (dress)
5 baggy (jumper), casual, colourful (jumper), plain
6 baggy (T-shirt/tracksuit bottoms), casual, colourful (baseball cap), plain (T-shirt), trendy (trainers/tracksuit bottoms)

**3** For some students this exercise will be a review. Others may be less familiar with it, so you may want to exploit the pictures in the Coursebook for the first group of verbs. Notice *to suit someone* but *to go with something*.

In the second group of verbs *wear* and *put on* are transitive whereas *get dressed* is intransitive. This information could be dealt with either before or after the activity. This type of exercise is useful preparation for the Paper 3 Use of English Part 1 Multiple-choice cloze test.

### Answers

| **A** | **1** go with/match | **2** match | **3** suit | **4** fit |
|---|---|---|---|---|
| **B** | **1** get dressed | **2** put on | **3** wearing | |

**4** Ask students to describe what the people are wearing in the photographs on page 2.

**5** Speaking: this gives students the chance to relate the vocabulary seen so far to their own experience and to express their likes and dislikes. If appropriate, before students start speaking, you may like to tell them about the clothes you most like wearing.

## Reading: Gapped text  Page 3
**FCE Part 2**

Photocopiable vocabulary exercise on page 158.

**1** If you have access to pictures of models this would provide a visual focus for the questions that students are asked to discuss. Alternatively, refer students to the picture in their books and the instructions that accompany it.

**2** Ask students to read the article on page 4 quickly and to ignore the spaces for the moment. Draw their attention to the gist question. (Answer: Yes, her comments in the last paragraph suggest she would recommend it.)

**3** Students read the instructions for the reading task. Draw their attention to the 'How to go about it' advice before they start the task. The parts in bold are designed to help students identify key elements of context. First go through gap 1 as an example with the class.

**Exam note:** Students need practice in being able to detect the linguistic 'clues' which will lead them to the correct answer. To make this task more challenging the texts usually include 'distractors': words and expressions that may lead the students away from the correct answer. In order to do the task successfully, students need to realize the importance of the context, ie the sentence(s) immediately before and after each gap.

### Answers

How to go about it
**a** they, them, theirs
**b** D

Reading task
**1** D  **2** B  **3** H  **4** F
**5** A  **6** C  **7** E

G is not used because:
- in many cases the pronoun *she* does not fit the grammatical context surrounding the gaps.
- it does not make meaningful sense in any of the contexts.

### Reacting to the text
This provides an opportunity for students to react to the content of what they have just read. It is a natural lead on from the activity and provides a

useful change of pace and skill focus. In Speaking Paper 5 Part 4 candidates take part in a discussion with the interlocutor based on the theme of Part 3 of the exam, so students have to get used to answering 'open' questions like this. They also have to be able to develop their answers and should be encouraged to do so at every opportunity. The questions can be discussed in pairs or with the class as a whole.

## Language focus 1: Habitual behaviour
Page 5

### A General tendencies
**1** Write the sentence on the board so that you have the students' attention. Elicit the answer (*use to* is not possible) and refer students to the Grammar reference on page 206.

**2** Stronger students could respond to these prompts orally in pairs or small groups. Weaker students may need to write their ideas down first. This should help them internalize the new item.

### B Frequency adverbs
**1** Students study the extracts from the text.

**2** Ask students to discuss the normal position for frequency adverbs in pairs, referring to the extracts in 1.

### Answers

| | | |
|---|---|---|
| a | main verbs | immediately before (or before the subject – see Grammar reference page 206) |
| b | | after the verb *to be* |
| c | aux. verb | after the auxiliary verb |

### Practice
**1** Students read the sentences and decide if the position of the adverbs is correct. Refer students to the Grammar reference on page 206.

### Answers

1 Correct (*or* Hardly do I get clothes for my birthday or for Christmas.)
2 I sometimes have breakfast in my pyjamas. (*or* Sometimes I have breakfast in my pyjamas.)
3 I always fold my clothes up before I go to bed.
4 Correct

5 When I go shopping for clothes I can rarely find jeans which fit me perfectly.

6 Correct (*or* I occasionally wash my own clothes, but my mum or dad normally does it.)

**2** Students work in pairs or small groups to discuss the sentences in exercise 1. Encourage them to use frequency adverbs and *tend to*. You may need to start students off by giving an example of your own, eg *I never fold my clothes up before I go to bed. I tend to leave them on the floor.*

### C *Used to* and *would*

| Answers |
|---|
| **1** a   **2** a   **3** b   **4** c   **5** a   **6** b   **7** b   **8** c   **9** c |

## Vocabulary 2: *Get* Page 6

This is the first and one of the most frequently occurring of the delexicalized verbs that we will see in the course. Verbs such as *get*, *give*, *have* and *put* often carry little or no meaning in themselves when used with other words, unlike verbs such as *read* or *jump*, whose meaning is constant. These delexicalized verbs are very common in English and are tested in the First Certificate exam.

### A Expressions with *get*

This section can be used first to test students' existing knowledge or you could leave it until after they have done the other exercises. Note that the exercise deals with both phrasal verbs and expressions.

| Answers | | | |
|---|---|---|---|
| 1 C | 2 D | 3 A | 4 A |
| 5 B | 6 B | 7 A | 8 C |

### B Meanings of *get*

**1** Students match the uses of *get* with the appropriate equivalent.

| Answers |
|---|
| **1** c   **2** e   **3** f   **4** d   **5** b   **6** a   **7** h (*or* a)   **8** g |

**2** Ask students to find examples of *get* in the text. They decide which of the meanings in 1 is appropriate in each case.

| Answers |
|---|
| Sometimes we had to console them even when they did get the job they wanted. |
| **a** receive/obtain |
| Kate Moss had to get to Paris. |
| **f** arrive at/reach |
| I flew with her to Brussels with the intention of getting the train from there. |
| **e** catch |
| Parents were usually encouraged to get involved in their daughters' careers. |
| **c** become |

**3** Students discuss the questions in pairs or small groups.

 **Listening:** **Multiple matching**
**FCE Part 3** Page 7

Focus students' attention on the exam instructions and the advice in the shaded box.

**Prediction**
Students do exercises 1, 2 and 3 as suggested in their books. Encourage students to record their vocabulary by grouping related words as below.

**Exam note:** In order to prepare students sufficiently for this kind of task, it is essential that they are given practice in predicting the content of listening exercises.

| Answers | |
|---|---|
| **1–2** possible answers | |
| A a wedding | guest, witness, priest, best man, church, registry office … |
| B a birthday party | guest, host, at home, at a disco … |
| C a job interview | candidate, interviewer, panel, in an office or other place of work |
| D a sporting event | spectator, competitor, star opponent, in a stadium, at a sports centre |
| E a film premiere | a star, audience, director, producer, at a cinema |
| F an examination | candidate, invigilator, in an examination hall |
| **3** There are many possible answers. | |

**Listening task**

Play the recording twice and let students compare their answers together between listenings.

Ask students what made them choose their answers to see if they could distinguish between the distractors and the clues. This will also follow up the prediction work done at the pre-listening stage.

The post-listening question provides a further opportunity for students to speak together as they are asked to respond to the content of the listening text.

| Answers | | | | |
|---|---|---|---|---|
| 1 A | 2 F | 3 D | 4 C | 5 B |

### Listening 1: Listening script 1.1–1.5

**Speaker 1**

After we got the invitation my mum and I kept having big rows about what I was going to wear for the big event. She's always criticizing me for my taste in clothes and she'd bought me this long, bright red dress to wear on the day. Of course, I refused. I went instead in a short black skirt, trainers and a sports top, thinking I'd look really cool and trendy. But, of course, when we got to the church and I saw all the other guests in their smart new clothes and expensive hats I just felt really, really stupid and embarrassed. The bride and groom looked quite surprised when they saw me so I spent most of the time at the reception trying to avoid them.

**Speaker 2**

We really had no other option but to send her home to get changed, dye her hair back and take out the nose stud. We have rules and the rules are there to prepare young people for the reality of the world of work. I don't know of many jobs where you could turn up with shabby old clothes, green hair and a pierced nose. We insist on uniform from the first day until the last, and that includes sitting your GCSE exams. It's unfair on other candidates who respect the regulations, and distracting for them at a time when they need maximum concentration.

**Speaker 3**

... Indeed, attitudes to women were already beginning to change. In 1919, the young French star Suzanne Lenglen caused a sensation at the British championships by wearing a calf-length, sleeveless dress. Her unconventional, yet practical clothing shocked spectators, who were used to seeing women play in the long, heavy dresses which were typical of that period. As a result, Lenglen attracted the kind of attention from the world's press which was normally reserved for the stars of the silent movies. She silenced her critics, however, by beating her opponents and going on to win several major titles.

**Speaker 4**

He clearly has ability. You only have to look at his examination results to see that. And he used to live in France, which means he probably wouldn't mind changing countries if we needed him to. No, what concerns me is his appearance. If he's prepared to turn up for something as important as this, wearing what can only be described as casual clothes, what would he be like with our clients? If he really is a serious candidate and we decide to take him on, then he will have to get used to wearing something a little more formal.

**Speaker 5**

They had to have their little joke, didn't they? 'Jane's having a little celebration at her house for her "coming of age" and she wants everyone to go in fancy dress.' That's what they said. So, I thought about it for ages, what I was going to go as and everything. I spent more time thinking about my costume than about what present I was going to get for Jane. Of course, when I turned up at the house dressed as Coco the Clown and everybody else was wearing normal clothes, I don't know who was more surprised, me or Jane.

## Language focus 2: *Be used to, get used to* and *used to*                    Page 8

**1** Refer students to questions 1a and 1b. Check their answers to these questions before moving on to question 2.

| Answers |
|---|
| **1**  1 a    2 b    3 a |
| **2**  This is a typical area of confusion for students. |
| *Be used to* + *-ing*/noun in the affirmative describes the state in which one no longer finds situations new or strange. |
| eg *I am used to the heat* means it is no problem for me now. |
| *Get used to* + *-ing*/noun in the affirmative describes the process of reaching normality with a new or strange situation. |
| eg *I am getting used to the heat* means it is less of a problem for me now than before. |
| **3**  the gerund |

**Common problems**

Using a version of *used to* to express present habits, eg *I use to get up early on Saturdays* instead of *I usually get up early on Saturdays*.

*I do not get used to …* rather than
*I can't get used to-…*
*I am used to cook for my little brother* rather than
*I am used to cooking for …*

and general confusion regarding when to use the infinitive and when to use the gerund. Oral drilling of short model sentences will help to 'fix' the structures more firmly in students' minds.

### Practice

**1** This is further practice, focusing on pronunciation. Drill the example sentence with special attention on the weak forms of the target structure. You will need to isolate that part of the sentence. Be careful that you yourself do not stress the weak forms.

Students continue in pairs. Other ideas are:

- you move to another city
- you become single again
- you start university
- you leave university

**2a** Find out if any of your students have been to Britain. Those who have could answer question 2a based on their own experience. If no one has been then they can imagine strange/new aspects of life there.

**2b** Ask students to read the whole text to compare their ideas before they try filling the gaps. Remember that students must be encouraged to read through and generally understand the whole text before they have to focus on details.

| Answers |
| --- |
| **2c 1** get used to having |
| **2** used to cook |
| **3** is/has got used to eating |
| **4** used to write |
| **5** get used to |
| **6** be/have got used to driving |
| **7** get used to driving |

### Further practice

At the beginning of the next lesson put the following unfinished sentences on the board:

1 I used to _____ but I don't any more.
2 Some people find it difficult to get used to _____ .

3 I didn't use to _____ but now I do.
4 When people visit my country they sometimes _____ because they aren't used to _____ .

Students individually complete the sentences with, as far as possible, information that is true for them. They then read out (in a random order) only the parts they have completed and their partner has to identify which sentence is being referred to. This tests whether they have understood and remembered the different meanings and grammatical patterns.

---

### Speaking: FCE Part 2 — Talking about photos
Page 8

This takes students through what is required in Part 2 of the oral exam and gives them practice of useful language which can be applied to different themes. Draw students' attention to the 'What to expect in the exam' box at the bottom of the page. For their one-minute task, candidates are given their instructions in both oral and written form. This is particularly useful for candidates who, because of nerves, do not pay full attention to what the interlocutor asks them to do.

### Lead-in

Ask students to close their books. Show them two flashcards/large pictures that show different lifestyles. Give the instructions mentioned in the student's book:

- Compare the photographs, and say what kind of lives you think these people lead.

You could try to elicit some of the prompts that are in their books. From the things your students tell you, try to feed in the language mentioned on page 8 by gently reformulating what they say where necessary.

Now refer students to their books. Let students read through the exam instructions and the 'How to go about it' section. If, in the first phase with you, they came up with other good language exponents to introduce similarities and differences, re-elicit or remind students of these, too.

In the exam, candidates have to speak for one minute and then briefly respond for about twenty seconds but in this classroom activity it is probably better to let them speak for as long as they productively can.

## Writing: Informal letters Page 10

**1** This section is intended as an introductory training exercise for writing informal letters in either Part 1 or Part 2 of the writing paper. The more open-ended nature of the task in exercise 6 resembles that of a Part 2 letter, whereas the fact that it is based on a piece of written input material (Mark's letter) is an element of Part 1 writing tasks. In addition, the language presented and information given is also relevant to writing emails.

As the course progresses, the distinction between Part 1 and Part 2 tasks will quickly become clear. One such difference is the number of words students are expected to write: 120–150 in Part 1 and 120–180 in Part 2. For this initial task, as well as that in Unit 1 of the Workbook, students are asked to write the latter amount.

Notice that students are exposed once again to areas covered in the unit so far: *get used to*, *get up*, *getting late*, *every morning*, *often*, *tend to*.

Once students have answered the question, you could elicit the above language by asking questions:

*How does he feel about milking the cows?*
*What does he say about the radio?*
*How do they normally spend their day after breakfast?*
*What time of the day did he write this letter?*

Do not spend too long on this: it is designed as a reminder of the language students have been working on. Alternatively, you may prefer to leave this until after students have finished the next stage.

| Answers |
|---|
| Mark wants to know how I am settling in to the new house. He wants to know if I can visit to help them in the summer. |

**2** Students generally have problems organizing their written work into paragraphs. This section ensures that the purpose of paragraphing and its importance is focused on from the start of the course.

| Answers | |
|---|---|
| Paragraph 2 | to describe how he spends a typical day |
| Paragraph 3 | to give news and invite you to visit |
| Paragraph 4 | to finish and ask for a reply |

**3** Students follow the instructions.

**Exam note:** It is important that students are aware of appropriate register or level of formality when they are writing. A common problem is for students to misuse or mix the use of formal and informal expressions. Candidates lose marks if they do this.

| Answers |
|---|
| **1** e    **2** a |
| **3** no, because this expression is too formal |
| **4** c    **5** g |
| **6** no, too formal |
| **7** no, too formal |
| **8** d    **9** b    **10** f |

**4–5** Students follow the instructions.

| Answers | | | | |
|---|---|---|---|---|
| **4** | **1** while | | **5** | **1** giving news |
| | **2** as | | | **2** asking for help |
| | **3** and, as well | | | **3** inviting |
| | **4** but | | | **4** refusing an invitation |
| | **5** so | | | **5** accepting an invitation |
| | **6** but, while | | | **6** apologizing |

**6** This exercise is designed to make students focus on the key elements of the question which they need to be aware of in order to answer the question fully. Make sure that students organize their writing into paragraphs.

| Answers |
|---|
| **Paragraph 1** |
| Thank Mark for his letter. |
| Make a friendly comment about his life on the farm. |
| |
| **Paragraph 2** |
| Mention what you have/haven't got used to. |
| Say whether you have made any friends. |
| Say two or three things about your daily routine. |
| Mention how long it takes to get to school/work. |
| |
| **Paragraph 3** |
| Accept or refuse the invitation and give a reason. |
| |
| **Paragraph 4** |
| Explain why you have to finish the letter. |
| Refer to a possible future meeting/letter. |

## Sample answer

Dear Mark,
I'm writing to you to tell you that I'm not going to go to your farm in summer because of my new work. However, I'll try to see you as soon as possible.

As you know, I moved to a new house six months ago and since then I've met new people.

I think that living there is better than I thought and with regard to my new surroundings I must say that they are excellent. I usually get up at half past seven and I went to work. Then I have a breakfast with my friends and I go to improve my English spoken in the afternoon in a specific classe. In the evening, I'm used to going to the cinema because here it's cheaper.

After all, I think is good have a new experience in your life and this is an example to explain it. As far as I'm concerned, I don't know if I'll have to return to my city, but it doesn't matter so much in these moments.

I hope you write me as you did.
All the best
Luis

186 words

**Examiner's comment**

**Content:** Adequate coverage of points.

**Accuracy:** The errors do not obscure communication but they may distract the reader – *I'm used to going to the cinema* is not appropriate here, the use of *went* instead of *go* in the third paragraph, the omission of the subject in *I think is good* are some examples of inaccuracies.

**Range:** Vocabulary is generally appropriate except for *a breakfast, a specific classe*.
Tenses are generally correct – *since then I've met new people*.

**Organization and cohesion:** An abrupt beginning but the letter is organized into paragraphs. Successful use of simple sequencing in the third paragraph – *then, in the afternoon/evening*.

**Register and format:** Awkward at times – *with regard to my new surroundings* (too formal for the context), and some confusion is evident in the use of *After all* and *As far as I'm concerned*.

**Target reader:** The overall effect would be reasonably positive: the information asked for has been provided and the tone, although inconsistent at times, would not cause problems.

**Mark:** good band 3

### Review 1 answers Page 12

**Use of English** **Transformations**
FCE Part 4

1 is slowly getting over
2 getting rid of
3 tend to buy
4 always borrowing my things without
5 we would often go
6 get used to sharing
7 got used to working
8 looking forward to seeing
9 'd/had better phone

## Vocabulary

**A Clothes**

| 1 | *afternoon* | 2 | baggy | 3 | waterproof |
|---|---|---|---|---|---|
| 4 | tight-fitting | 5 | long-sleeved | 6 | waist |

**B Expressions crossword**
Expressions for use in informal letters

| Across | | Down | |
|---|---|---|---|
| 1 | thanks | 2 | know |
| 5 | forward | 7 | better |
| 8 | way | 11 | hear |
| 9 | love | | |
| 12 | taken | | |

Expressions with *get*

| Across | | Down | |
|---|---|---|---|
| 3 | rid | 1 | trouble |
| 4 | on | 3 | ready |
| 10 | touch | 6 | dressed |
| 13 | paid | | |

**C People**

| 1 | e | 2 | f | 3 | a |
|---|---|---|---|---|---|
| 4 | b | 5 | d | 6 | c |

1 competitor, spectators
2 host, guests
3 bride, groom
4 audience, performers
5 doctor, patient
6 candidates, invigilator

## Workbook answers

### Reading: Gapped text   Page 2

1

| Name of star | Former possessions |
|---|---|
| Cher | white T-shirt, black shirt (also mentioned: top, dress) |
| Mel Gibson | denim shirt |
| Cary Grant | silver cigarette case |
| 'Dr McCoy' | tunic |

2   1   D   2   B   3   H   4   F
    5   A   6   C   7   E   G not used

3   1   celebrities   5   purchase
    2   pick up       6   shrank
    3   bargain       7   delighted
    4   memorabilia   8   fancy dress

4   1   up as   2   to pieces   3   my eye on
    4   my heart

### Vocabulary   Page 4

#### A Clothes

1   1   shabby      2   scarf     3   tracksuit
    4   waterproof  5   blouse    6   plain
    7   helmet      8   belt      9   bracelet
    10  blazer      11  slippers  12  baseball cap

2   Suggested answers
    1   a baggy jumper
    2   a pleated skirt
    3   a checked waistcoat
    4   a flowery dress
    5   tight-fitting jeans
    6   striped swimming trunks
    7   spotted socks

#### B Get

1   1   by    2   over    3   back    4   away
    5   on    6   off     7   out of

2   1   touch   2   trouble   3   paid    4   rid
    5   ready   6   mark      7   worse   8   dressed

#### C Word combinations

1   fashion/film industry
2   model/news agency
3   political/birthday party
4   television/job interview
5   social/sporting event
6   film/world premiere
7   news/bedtime story

### Language focus   Page 6

#### A Adverbs of frequency

1   correct
2   I have never been wearing
3   Her clothes are often quite tight on me/ Often her clothes are quite tight on me
4   I sometimes see/Sometimes I see
5   correct

#### B Used to and would

1   b (only used to)
2   c (neither used to or would)
3   a (both used to and would)
4   b (only used to)
5   b (only used to)

### Use of English   Page 6

#### Transformations

1   don't/do not usually eat much
2   hardly ever stay
3   always used to be
4   keeps (on) phoning me
5   's/is rare for Anna to
6   looking forward to going
7   not used to getting

#### B Multiple choice cloze

| 1 | B | 2 | D | 3 | C | 4 | A | 5 | D |
|---|---|---|---|---|---|---|---|---|---|
| 6 | C | 7 | A | 8 | B | 9 | B | 10 | A |
| 11 | D | 12 | C | | | | | | |

### Writing   Page 8

#### Letters and emails

1

| | Formal | Informal |
|---|---|---|
| Complaining | 7 | 4 |
| Asking for information | 1 | 10 |
| Giving information | 5 | 9 |
| Apologizing | 3 | 6 |
| Giving advice | 8 | 2 |

2

| Formal | | Informal | |
|---|---|---|---|
| 1 | inform me | 10 | let me know |
| 8 | We strongly advise you not to | 2 | You really shouldn't |
| 3 | the delay in responding to you | 6 | it's taken me so long to get back to you |
| 7 | Moreover | 4 | And |
| 5 | estimate | 9 | reckon |

#### Informal letters

2   Paragraph 1 a   Paragraph 2 c
    Paragraph 3 b

# 2 High energy

## Content Overview

### Themes

This unit deals with the themes of music and leisure activities. The listening and reading materials provide a contextualized source for the grammar and vocabulary which will be focused on.

### Exam-related activities

| | |
|---|---|
| **Paper 1** | **Reading** |
| Part 3 | Multiple matching |
| | |
| **Paper 2** | **Writing** |
| Part 1 | Letters: Asking for information |
| Part 2 | Articles |
| | |
| **Paper 3** | **Use of English** |
| Part 3 | Word formation (Review) |
| | |
| **Paper 4** | **Listening** |
| Part 2 | Sentence completion |
| Part 4 | Multiple choice |

### Other

Language focus 1: Indirect ways of asking questions
Language focus 2: Gerunds and infinitives A/B
Vocabulary:           Music
                              Sports
Word formation:    Affixes

## Vocabulary 1: Music                    Page 14

**1** Ask students to discuss the questions in pairs. In Paper 5 Speaking, students must show the ability to speak for extended periods as well as interact effectively with other people during a conversation. They must therefore be encouraged to develop and elaborate on what they say where possible.

**2a** Elicit the names of the musical instruments on to the board. You could refer students to the Wordlist on page 202 of the Coursebook.

**2b** Question 2b focuses students on common music-related collocations.

### Answers

**2a** Photograph 1: flute, trumpet, sousaphone (a type of tuba)
Photograph 2: violin, viola, cello, double bass, harp, flute, clarinet

---

| **b** 1 lead | 2 a song | 3 musician |
|---|---|---|
| 4 on | 5 play | 6 live* |
| 7 in | 8 instrument | |

*pronunciation /laɪv/

**3** This is a memory activity with an element of competition, although this aspect can be ignored if you (or your students) prefer. Try the same activity again at the end of class and/or at the beginning of the next class to see how many of the combinations students can remember.

**4** Ask students to discuss this task in groups of three or four.

---

### Listening 1:
**FCE Part 2**

### Sentence completion
Page 15

**1** The theme of this listening is discos and disc jockeys (DJs).

Students discuss their answers in pairs or small groups. Exploit the picture in the Coursebook in order to pre-teach essential vocabulary.

**Pre-teaching *key* or *essential* vocabulary**
Before listening and reading activities, decide what vocabulary your students may not understand. Remember that *not all* unknown vocabulary needs to be pre-taught.
To find out what vocabulary in a text is essential look first at the task the students will be doing. If there are words in the questions which students may not know, these need, of course, to be dealt with. Next, look at the tapescript. If there are unknown words or expressions which students will need to know in order to answer the questions, these too need to be pre-taught.

eg Listening 3 Sentences 1–10

*Possible unknown words in the questions*
'turntables' (number 2)

*Possible unknown words in the tapescript (essential for the completion of the task)*
'mixing tracks' (number 4)

In this case, by exploiting the picture in the Coursebook, both of these items of vocabulary can be taught before students listen by pointing and asking *What does the DJ put the record on?* and *What are all the buttons and switches used for?*

Remember that asking students first gives anyone who knows the answer the chance to respond. (If no one answers, tell them the word.)

**2** Draw students' attention to the 'What to expect in the exam' box. They should discuss the type of information they expect to hear and write down their final ideas. Encourage stronger students to use modal verbs of deduction, as in the example.

**3** Play the recording twice and let students compare their answers together between listenings.

### Answers

| | |
|---|---|
| 1 the seventies | 6 weekend |
| 2 three | 7 on a journey |
| 3 talented musicians | 8 (a form of) meditation |
| 4 mixing tracks | 9 computer programmes |
| 5 ten thousand | 10 a younger audience |

### Listening 1: Listening script 1.6

**I = Interviewer   B = Brad Andrews**

**I:** With us today in the studio we have Brad Andrews, one of the most famous names in dance music and club DJ-ing of the moment. Brad, why are club DJs so popular these days?

**B:** DJ-ing has changed an awful lot since the seventies. People used to go to discos and clubs to drink, talk or pick each other up. Now they come for the music, so whether you have a good time or not depends very much on the skills of the DJ.

**I:** Do you really need that much skill to put on a few records?

**B:** It's not that simple. I often operate three turntables at once, sometimes using one or two CD players as well. A lot of DJs are talented musicians, because you need a great deal of co-ordination to play with the records and use these huge decks we have nowadays. The job of DJ-ing is mostly about mixing tracks, using several records at once to create a totally whole new sound. On one record I might use just the high notes and sounds, and combine that with the bass on another record. Then I'll bring in a third one with the bass and treble turned off and use it to mix in vocals or another drum. It's a complex business.

**I:** And from what I hear, a well-paid one, too. Would you mind telling us how much you earn for a single gig?

**B:** There are probably about three or four DJs in the country earning up to ten thousand pounds for a three-hour gig, that much I can tell you. But you have to understand this is an extremely demanding job. People go to see their favourite DJs like fans go to see bands, except top DJs play live gigs every weekend and not just three or four weeks in the year. Dedicated clubbers will often follow a DJ around the country, or ... or even the

world. People come from Paris to London just to spend Saturday night in a club, before going back on the train on Sunday morning.

**I:** Does a gig require much preparation?

**B:** You're dead right it does. I arrange and build a set at a club like I would do in a concert on stage, or if I was recording a single in the studio. You're basically composing a three-hour piece of music. It's as if you're taking people on a journey, and you want them to enjoy it. I also need to clear my mind before I get out there and do my stuff, so I use a form of meditation to get myself ready for a gig.

**I:** Looking ahead now Brad. Could you tell us what the future of dance music is? How do you think it will develop in the next few years?

**B:** Well, it's interesting to think that here we are at the beginning of the twenty-first century, still using the old-fashioned vinyl records on old-fashioned turntables to create sophisticated sounds. But obviously computer programmes can now be used to put together a dance track in the same way that I described earlier, and of course much quicker. That could well be the way ahead for DJs. Another trend now is for established, big-name bands to ask DJs to rearrange their music in order to attract a younger audience.

**I:** A bright future indeed, then. We'll take a break now, but don't go away. Brad's going to do a bit of live DJ-ing for us here on Radio Perfect ...

**4** These two questions invite students to react to the content of what they have heard and round off the listening stage with an opportunity for speaking.

## Language focus 1: Indirect ways of asking questions          Page 16

This language item occurs at this early stage in the book because students may need to include indirect questions in the formal letter.

Students have the chance to put this into practice in the writing task immediately after this language point.

**1** The example sentences come from the listening activity so the context should be clear to the students.

### Answers

**2 a** word order – no inversion of subject/verb auxiliary verbs – in the present simple and the past simple *do/does/did* are not used.

Notice that some indirect questions do not need a question mark.

**b** Questions like this are commonly known as 'Yes/No' questions. They need *if* or *whether* in the indirect form.

I'd like to know *if/whether a gig requires much preparation.*

**Practice**

### Answers

Possible answers

1 Could you explain why dance music is so popular?
2 Would you mind telling us what a clubber has to pay to see you perform?
3 I'd be interested to know when you did your first gig.
4 Could you tell us if/whether you plan to work with any famous groups?
5 I was wondering if you could tell me what you like most about DJ-ing.
6 We'd like to know how you became a DJ.
7 Could you tell us if/whether anything has ever gone wrong at a gig?

## Writing 1: FCE Part 1
### Letters: Asking for information  Page 16

**1** Students may have to write a letter, formal or informal, in the exam. They must be able to identify which of the two registers is appropriate. A common mistake, which loses candidates marks, is to mix the two registers or styles.

**2** Students read the letter and discuss the answers in pairs. Notice that this activity shows students useful informal expressions, too.

### Answers

2 formal register is appropriate
   1 would like          5 indicate
   2 I would be grateful  6 I would be pleased
     for                    to receive
   3 I would            7 I look
   4 some queries        8 receiving your reply

**3** Refer students to the instructions in their books.

### Answers

**3a** Yes
   **b** ... *last week's edition of 'International Musician'* ...
      ... *interested in having violin lessons* ...
      ... *If you have a brochure with photographs* ...
   **c** (included in price?)  ... *whether the cost of excursions is included?*
      (ask!) ... *I would like to know the price of a one-month course* ...

**4** The work students have done on the model text will help them with their own writing. Refer students to the advice in the 'Don't forget!' box.

As before, ask students to identify the purpose of the letter (asking for more information) and the target reader (Tour Organizer). Therefore a more formal register or style is required.

Ask students to think about and decide on what relevant points of their own they could include, eg
- *We have to ... on Friday so will not be able to arrive until ...*
- *It would be very expensive for me if I missed my flight.*

Then ask them to rephrase the language from the notes in the question using the ideas in exercise 3 to help them.

The writing itself could be done for homework. Encourage students to keep a separate notebook in which to write compositions.

### Sample answer

Dear Sir / Madam
I am writing about your advertisement on the Saturday's edition of 'El Pais'. I am interested in the Rock Festival which will take place in Oxford in two weeks time. I would like to receive further information about some details of the festival.

Firstly, I would appreciate if you could indicate me the timetables of the transport you provide between Heathrow and Oxford. This information would be quite important for us, since we have to take the plane back to Madrid on Sunday at 9.15pm and we do not want to miss it.

Furthermore we can not come on Friday and we would know wether we can have a reduction if we only assist to the festival for two days. Finally, we would like to stay all in the same room, so we would be grateful if you could tell us if a room for three is available.

We look forward to receiving your reply
Yours faithfully
Elena García

159 words

**Examiner's comments**
**Content:** All major points covered, with good manipulation and development of information in the input material (eg second paragraph).

**Accuracy:** There are a number of inaccuracies but they generally do not impede understanding – *two weeks(') time, I would appreciate (it) if you could indicate (to) me, we would (like to) know w(h)ether, assist to (attend) the festival.*

**Range:** Good range of grammar and appropriate range of vocabulary eg *I would like to receive further information about, we would be grateful if you could tell us if a room for three is available.*

**Organization and cohesion:** The letter is clearly organized with suitable paragraphs and the linking devices used are used accurately: *Firstly, Furthermore, Finally, since we have to, so we would be grateful.* The opening and closing are appropriate, except for *on the Saturday's.*

**Style and format:** Entirely appropriate to the task.

**Target reader:** Would have a clear idea about the writer's questions.

**Mark:** band 4.

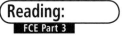

## Reading: FCE Part 3 — Multiple matching
Page 18

Photocopiable vocabulary exercise on page 158.

The theme of this reading is 'extreme' sports.

**1** Use the pictures and questions as suggested in the Coursebook. Additionally, before this you could ask students individually to write down three things:

- *a sport they enjoy or used to enjoy*
- *the most dangerous sport they have heard of*
- *a sport they would take up if they had the chance*

Students discuss their answers in pairs or small groups. If necessary, write *WHY?* on the board and point to it if you see that some people are not giving much information.

To encourage more speaking you could add these questions to the board:

- *Where do you think this sport originated?*
- *Which one do you think looks the most dangerous/ most enjoyable/most frightening?*
- *Which would you never try and why?* etc.

**2** Refer students to the instructions in their books. This matching exercise and comparing ideas stage ensures that students read and generally understand the whole text before they start on the exercise.

| Answers | | | |
|---|---|---|---|
| **A** Street luge 3 | | **B** Ice-climbing 2 | |
| **C** BASE-jumping 4 | | **D** Zorbing 1 | |

**3** Refer students to the instructions and the 'How to go about it' box, which is designed to help students with their first multiple matching exercise. The underlined sections in text A highlight the contextual clues, which students will have to find for themselves in texts B–D.

| Answers | | | | | | |
|---|---|---|---|---|---|---|
| 1 B | 2 D | 3 A | 4 C | 5 D | 6 A | 7 B |
| 8/9 A, D in any order | | 10 C | | 11 B | | 12 C |
| 13 D | 14 A | 15 C | | | | |

**Reacting to the text**
Now that students know more about each of the sports in the photographs they can exchange opinions to see if any have changed their minds!

## Language focus 2: Gerunds and infinitives A
Page 20

**1** Refer students to the instructions in their books. The language to be dealt with comes directly from the text students have been working on.

| Answers | | |
|---|---|---|
| **a** Zorbing | **b** Base-jumping | **c** Base-jumping |

**2** As this stage is designed to focus students on a specific language area, you may prefer to use the board as the main focus rather than the page. Write up the sentences in 1 (or the relevant parts of them), eg

*This sport involves **rolling** downhill ...*
***Gaining** access to the top ...*

Read out each of the explanations to elicit the correct answers (see below). These explanations could be written next to the appropriate sentence above.

### Answers

**2 a** 3     **b** 1     **c** 2

**3 a** infinitive  **b** gerund   **c** gerund
**4 b** *began*
(*Begin* can be followed by the
infinitive *to jump* with no change in meaning.)

**Practice**

**1** Draw students' attention to the verbs in italics and ask them to complete the sentences. Students can check their own answers on pages 206 and 207 of the Grammar reference.

### Answers

1  going, to meet
2  smiling, to hit
3  (to) improve, taking
4  to take, studying
5  to let, asking

**2** Ask students how they feel about different things which are relevant to them, eg the weather at the moment, their school subjects, the transport system where they live, parking facilities in the area, etc. Some students should naturally produce some of the verbs in the box. If the difference between *I don't mind* (+ gerund) and *I don't care* (+ *what/ where/who*, etc + clause) is a problem for your students, now is a good time to deal with it. *I don't mind* means that something is not a problem for you or that each of the choices offered to you is equally appealing. *I don't care* is dismissive, indicating that you are not interested in what you do or somebody else does.

Refer students to the box in their books. If your group is not too big you could put the exponents in the box onto large pieces of card and copy the line onto the board. Hand out the cards to different students and tell them to come up to the board and stick the cards in what they think is the correct place on the line.

### Answers

detest, hate, can't stand, don't like, don't mind, quite like, really enjoy, love, absolutely adore

**3** The following expressions should be familiar to students but they may not be using the dependent prepositions correctly or with confidence.

### Answers

interested ***in*** *        bored ***with***
fond ***of*** *            excited ***about***
good/bad ***at***

**Note:** Prepositions are very difficult to remember, as often they do not add any real meaning to the expression they are used with. Notice that in the expressions marked the adjectives themselves carry a clue as to the correct preposition.

**4** Students write sentences of their own using the language from exercises 2 and 3.

**5** Students practise interviewing each other about their likes and dislikes. This is extremely useful practice for Part 1 of the Speaking test.

### Listening 2:    Multiple choice Page 21
**FCE Part 4**

**1** The pre-listening questions preview some aspects of what students are about to hear and cover one of the possibly unknown items of vocabulary which students need to know in order to answer question 5. Other essential items (see page 18 for a procedure to help you decide what language is essential and what is non-essential) are:

*guys* – young men/males (Q 4)
*dry slope* – artificial slope (Q 6)

**2** Refer students to the information in the box and Q 1. Try to elicit from the students the fact that the answer is B and the key expression is *I haven't skied since then.*

## Answers

| 1 B | 2 C | 3 C | 4 A | 5 C | 6 A | 7 B |
|-----|-----|-----|-----|-----|-----|-----|

---

### Listening 2: Listening script 1.7

**I = Interviewer    L = Liz**

**I:** In today's edition of 'Sports Showcase' we talk to 19-year-old Liz Harris, one of the country's rising stars in the fast-growing sport of snowboarding. How long have you been into snowboarding, Liz?

**L:** I first did it when I was on holiday with my parents. When I was younger I used to go skiing every year with them and then one year I tried snowboarding, and I haven't skied since then. That was ... five years ago.

**I:** And what's the achievement that you're most proud of so far?

**L:** I suppose it has to be ... when I entered my first international competition this year. I came first in the Big Air event and won some money.

**I:** Well, let's hope you can go on winning! Would you say, Liz, that there are any particular qualities or strengths you need to have to be a snowboarder?

**L:** Good co-ordination and balance helps, but you don't have to be born with it. If you practise for a few days, you'll get it anyway, even if you're not naturally sporty.

**I:** And have you ever had any nasty falls?

**L:** I hurt my back a few years ago on a dry slope. I was doing a jump, and I fell really badly, but I didn't break anything. So far I've been really lucky, unlike my friends, who've all had bad injuries. Broken limbs, that kind of thing. No doubt I'll break an arm or a leg soon! It's just a question of time.

**I:** How many boys are there compared with girls who snowboard?

**L:** There are more guys, that's for sure, but it's a lot more even now. When I first started snowboarding you hardly ever saw any girls, but now there are loads of them. Not as many as the guys, but almost.

**I:** And how do the male snowboarders treat the girls?

**L:** Well, as far as my friends are concerned, they couldn't care less what sex you are. But there are certain people that think girls are rubbish, and that they shouldn't get paid as much as guys. On the whole, though, spectators have got used to seeing girls on the slopes.

**I:** You're professional, aren't you, but you don't get paid?

**L:** No, I get a few hundred pounds from some of my sponsors just to help me to pay for my lift pass. They also give me a few boards a year and then, you know, when I get photos in a magazine on the board it's basically a free advert for the company. So, yeah, all of my equipment is given to me and that's very useful, of course. But I usually just save up the money in the summer and then go and spend it all riding in the winter.

**I:** What sort of advice would you give to a girl who wanted to take up snowboarding?

**L:** If you can't get out to the Alps, then ... try going along to your local dry slope, where you can get lessons and hire equipment, or you could try the Cardiff Snow Dome, which is like a big indoor fridge with real snow. So wrap up warm because it can get quite cold in there. Anywhere in Britain, though, is fine really. There are dry slopes all over the place.

**I:** We hear you've been doing some modelling work as well. Is that right?

**L:** Yes, I have. I was on the cover of a fashion magazine a couple of months ago and I'm hopefully going to get some more work because of that. I didn't actually get paid for doing it. But, of course, it's great exposure, and any part-time modelling work now could be useful for the future.

**I:** You mean, you might go on to become a full-time model?

**L:** Who knows? If my luck runs out with the snowboarding, then why not? We'll just have to see.

**I:** Well, good luck for the moment with the snowboarding, Liz, and we'll certainly be looking out for you on the catwalk.

---

The questions following the listening are best answered in pairs or small groups but if this is not possible then you could ask individuals for their responses. Further prompts are:

*Which of the qualities or strengths do you feel you already have?*
*Which would you need to develop?*
*How could you do that?*
*Why are more people interested in these kinds of sports nowadays?*

## Word formation: Affixes          Page 22

This is the first in a series of exercises in the book aimed at exposing students to the different aspects of word formation.

**1** Before referring students to page 22 in their books, write the root words 1–4 on the board and ask students if they know how to form the words for people. Continue the same way with 5, 6 and 7. Students compare their answers with those in the Coursebook.

Refer students to the remaining root words in the box and deal with any comprehension problems. In some languages *assist* is a 'false friend', ie it looks the same as a word in the students' first language but means something different in English.

## Answers

| | | |
|---|---|---|
| 8 | instruct | instructor |
| 9 | eco**no**mic | e**co**nomist |
| 10 | **moun**tain | mountain**eer** |
| 11 | e**lec**tric | elec**tri**cian |
| 12 | entertain | entertainer |
| 13 | assist | assistant |
| 14 | **in**terview | interview**ee**/interviewer |

(The sections in **bold** type indicate a change in the word stress. Mark this on the board for students to copy by underlining the relevant section of the word.)

**2** Refer students to the relevant section in their books. Check that they have understood the fact that all three words in each group use the same negative prefix.

## Answers

**1** *un*  **2** in  **3** il  **4** im  **5** im  **6** ir  **7** dis

**Note:** In many words beginning with *l*, *m* or *r* the initial consonant is doubled after the *i*. Words beginning with *p* are usually made negative by adding *im-* but notice that the negative prefix for *pleasant* is ***un**pleasant* not 'impleasant'. These are guidelines rather than fixed rules.

**3** This exercise contains the most common affixes. To help students, you could write up example sentences on the board, omitting the target words from the box, eg
*If you ____ you will put on weight. (overeat).*

Ask the students to select the correct word from the box. This will help them contextualize each word and understand the meaning.

## Answers

| | |
|---|---|
| under | too little/not enough |
| over | too much/excessive |
| pre | before |
| post | after |
| hyper | very big |
| micro | very small |
| mis | wrongly |
| re | again |
| ex- | former |
| -ess | woman |

## Language focus 3: Gerunds and infinitives B
Page 22

**1** Refer students to the instructions in the Coursebook. (**1** a, **2** b).

**2** This is a confusing area of English for learners. Let students look through the sentences individually before eliciting their answers and ideas or putting them in pairs to discuss the differences. Essentially, the difference in numbers 1, 2 and 3 is in the *order in which the actions really happened.* Time line diagrams (see below) on the board can help students to visualize the sentences.

## Answers

**1**
**a** 1 **b** 2
**2**
**1 a**

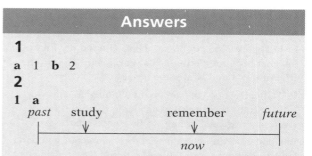

*I remember studying this piece of grammar last year.*

(First I studied it and later I remembered the action. = remember doing an earlier action)

**b**

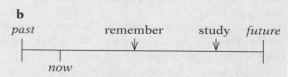

*I must remember to study my notes on gerunds and infinitives tonight.*

(First I need to remember and then I need to study. = remember to do a later action)

**2 a** First action – we regret
Second action – announce
**b** First action – I caught the train
Second action – I regretted it
**3 a** First action – I stopped what I was doing (eg walking, driving)
Second action – I bought a newspaper (infinitive of purpose)
**b** First action – buying newspapers
Second action – stop: I do not buy newspapers any more.
**4 a** This describes an experiment, doing something to see if it will solve the problem (s/he had lessons)
**b** This means that s/he made an effort (s/he did not have lessons)
**5 a** meant = entailed/involved
**b** meant = intended/planned

## Vocabulary 2: Sports     Page 23

**1** Refer students to the instructions in their books. Note that, in general,

- *go* is used with sports that end in *-ing*
- *play* is used with sports which use a ball
- *do* is used for other sporting activities

**Common mistakes**

In some languages it is correct to say *practise sport*. In English it is *do sport* or *play sport*. Draw this to your students' attention if necessary.

| Answers | | |
|---|---|---|
| **do** | **go** | **play** |
| athletics | skiing | volleyball |
| gymnastics | cycling | tennis |
| | swimming | basketball |
| | | football |

**2** Ensure that students use full sentences to give further practice of the appropriate verbs.

| Answers |
|---|
| You play volleyball, basketball and tennis on a court. |
| You go skiing on ski slopes. |
| You go cycling or do athletics on a track. |
| You do gymnastics in a gym. |
| You play football on a pitch. |
| You go swimming in a pool. |

**3** Students should also use full sentences here.

| Answers |
|---|
| volleyball player, tennis player, basketball player, skier, cyclist, swimmer, gymnast, footballer |

**4** Students choose the correct words. After you have checked your student's answers, you could ask them to write example sentences including some of the words. This will check understanding and provide further practice.

| Answers |
|---|
| 1  take part, take place |
| 2  win, beat |
| 3  play, practise |
| 4  spectators, audience |

## Writing 2:     Articles     Page 23
**FCE Part 2**

**1** Refer students to the instructions and the 'How to go about it' box. Ask them to read the model article and answer the questions on page 200 of the Coursebook.

| Answers |
|---|
| **2**  **Paragraph 1** c     **Paragraph 3** d |
| **Paragraph 2** a     **Paragraph 4** b |

**3** It is written for readers of *International Sports Weekly* magazine.

**4** The style is informal.
  a  Contractions: *doesn't, you've, you'll, I'm, you're, don't, they're*
  b  Informal linkers: *So, And, Also*
  c  Direct questions: *Have you ever seen a smile on the face of a long distance runner? So what is the attraction of running?*
  d  Phrasal verbs: *give up, take up, put off*

**5**  1  c     2  a     3  b

---

### Sample answer

In the world, as I know, there are a lot of sports that are very interesting and everyone can occupy with them like, for example, football, basketball, volleyball and so on, But in my opinion, the most famous and the most interesting, in the world, is football. Firstly I extremely fond of this kind of entertainment (I say this because for me and my friends, football is the same thing with the entertainment). We play football everyday and everywhere. We love it and anything else apart from football is boring for us. Once again I love it. Secondly, football has many particularities. Special equipment and special clothes are usuful. Although the professionals teams play in big football courts, the children play football everywhere. If you want to become a good and a famous football player you must go into training everyday with many efforts but because of the injuries you must be careful.

For all these reasons, I have the impression that this particular sport is lovely and I believe that there is nobody who watch this sport.
By Loukas Geronikolaou

178 words

**Examiner's comment**

**Content:** Adequate coverage of points 1 and 3 but point 2 (why do you like it?) not really dealt with. The question incites a personal response but the information given is mostly rather general again.

**Accuracy:** Reasonable. One missing verb (*I extremely fond of* – a slip?) one spelling mistake (*usuful*) one false agreement (*professionals teams*). The problem is awkwardness rather than pure inaccuracy (positive error). Final sentence doesn't communicate.

**Range:** Doesn't have all the vocabulary (*occupy with them, many particularities, big football courts*) though makes good attempts (*fond of, anything else apart from football, go into training, because of the injuries*). Some variety of structures, some complex sentences.

**Organization and cohesion:** Four paragraphs including an introduction and conclusion. Conventional paragraph links (*Firstly, Secondly*). Some sentence links (*although, if, because of*).

**Style and format:** Consistently neutral. Acceptable article format.

**Target reader:** Message not entirely clear; certainly some enthusiasm conveyed to the reader, but why does the writer like football so much? Some awkwardness of expression may distract target reader, and the final sentence is obscure.

**Mark:** borderline band 2/3

## Review 2 answers  Page 24

### Word formation

| | | | | | |
|---|---|---|---|---|---|
| **1** | **1** | undersleep | **2** | overlittle | **3** oversing |
| | **4** | missucceed | **5** | dislove | **6** doctoress |
| **2** | **1** | undercharged | **4** | misspelt/misspelled | |
| | **2** | overgrown | **5** | disappearance | |
| | **3** | overslept | **6** | waitress | |

### Use of English: FCE Part 3  Word formation

| | | | |
|---|---|---|---|
| **1** | impossible | **6** | underwater |
| **2** | Competitors | **7** | discourage |
| **3** | disappearing | **8** | unlikely |
| **4** | divers | **9** | misjudged |
| **5** | uncommon | **10** | director |

## Gerunds and infinitives

**1**

| | | | |
|---|---|---|---|
| **1** | to write | **5** | talking |
| **2** | getting | **6** | to study |
| **3** | tapping | **7** | to open |
| **4** | to have | **8** | putting |

**2**

**1** finish (takes the gerund, the others take the infinitive)

**2** begin (all of them can be used with the gerund or the infinitive, but *begin* is the only one for which the meaning remains the same)

**3** feel like (takes the gerund, the others take the infinitive)

**4** tend to (takes the infinitive, the others take the gerund)

**5** can't afford (takes the infinitive, the others take the gerund)

## Vocabulary
### Music

| | | | |
|---|---|---|---|
| **1** | on the radio | **5** | in tune |
| **2** | play a tune | **6** | mime a song |
| **3** | in the charts | **7** | on tour |
| **4** | session musicians | **8** | play a track |

## Workbook answers

### Reading: Gapped text  Page 10

**1**  **1** C  **2** G  **3** A  **4** E  **5** H
 **6** B  **7** F  D is not used

| | | | | | |
|---|---|---|---|---|---|
| **2** | **1** | head | **2** eye | **3** | foot |
| | **4** | arm | **5** mouth | **6** | face |

### Vocabulary  Page 11

**A Music**

| | | | | | |
|---|---|---|---|---|---|
| **1** | trumpet | **2** | flute | **3** | violin |
| **4** | tambourine | **5** | drum | **6** | saxophone |
| **7** | keyboard | **8** | accordion | | |

**B Sport**

| | | | | |
|---|---|---|---|---|
| **1** | **a** | athlete | **b** | basketball player |
| | **c** | cyclist | **d** | golfer |
| | **e** | gymnast | **f** | skier |
| | **g** | snowboarder | **h** | tennis player |

**2**  **1** *motor racing circuit*  **2** football pitch
   **3** athletics track  **4** ski slope
   **5** swimming pool  **6** golf course
   **7** tennis court  **8** ice-skating rink

**3**  **1** B  **2** D  **3** A  **4** C  **5** C
   **6** D  **7** A  **8** B

## Language focus  Page 12

### A  Indirect ways of asking questions

1 telling me what you have been doing recently?
2 where I can get something cold to drink?
3 what time you are coming to the party next week?
4 to me why you did not do the homework?
5 if you are interested in playing tennis on Friday.
6 what he does for a living.

### B  Gerunds and infinitives

1 looking, to have
2 learning, to speak, to think
3 to be, climbing, attracting, to wait
4 making, to concentrate
5 going, to stay
6 Giving, to lose/losing
7 to hear, seeing
8 to paint, forgetting, to buy
9 to live, to find, to pay
10 to work, going

## Use of English  Page 13

### Open cloze: Prepositions

**1** in  **2** on  **3** for  **4** into  **5** in
**6** in  **7** on  **8** on  **9** at  **10** out
**11** in  **12** in  **13** at  **14** with  **15** until

### Transformations

1 help laughing
2 to take up (playing) golf
3 'm/am not (very) keen on
4 can't stand being
5 's/is unusual for Andrea to
6 to take place
7 'm/am not very good at

### Word formation

**1** irrelevant  **2** disagreement
**3** misunderstood  **4** dishonestly
**5** unreliable  **6** immature
**7** overweight  **8** undercooked
**9** irresponsibly  **10** incapable

## Writing  Page 15

### A  Formal and informal style

**1** a  **2** a  **3** b  **4** b  **5** b
**6** a  **7** b  **8** a  **9** a

### B  An informal letter

**3** b, **8** a, **7** b, (new paragraph) **1** a, **6** a, **9** a, **2** a, (new paragraph) **4** b, (new paragraph) **5** b

Dear Nick

(3b) Thanks for sending me the advert about skiing in Nevis Range. (8a) It sounds just the sort of place I'm looking for. (7b) But before I book, there are a few things I'd like to ask you.

(1a) Firstly, as I'm not an experienced skier, I'd really like to know how many green runs there are. (6a) I wanted to ask you some questions about costs, as well. **I'm a bit broke at the moment, so the holiday needs to as cheap as possible.** (9a) Do you think I'd save much by getting the bus from London instead of the train? (2a) And can you remember if the skis cost a lot to hire? **If they're too expensive, I'll ask a friend to lend me hers.**

(4b) Finally, I'm only planning to go skiing for three days, so can you tell me if you think it's worth having classes. **I suppose it depends on the instructors – were they good?**

(5b) Thanks for all your help. Write back soon.

All the best

Caroline

### C  Building on the information given

1 between 6a and 9a
2 between 2a and 4b
3 between 4b and 5b

### D  Linking words and expressions

| Informal | Formal |
| --- | --- |
| as well | in addition |
| and | in addition (to this) |
| as | owing to the fact that |
| so | therefore |
| but | however |

# 3 A change for the better?

## Content Overview

### Themes

Machines, devices, the convenience society, mobile phones and computers are the themes focused on in this unit. As with previous units the vocabulary and grammar to be reviewed and practised are clearly contextualized and linked to the Listening, Reading and Speaking material.

### Exam-related activities

| | |
|---|---|
| **Paper 1** | **Reading** |
| Part 1 | Multiple choice |
| | |
| **Paper 2** | **Writing** |
| Part 2 | Essays |
| | |
| **Paper 3** | **Use of English** |
| Part 3 | Word formation (Review) |
| | |
| **Paper 4** | **Listening** |
| Part 3 | Multiple matching |
| Part 4 | Multiple choice |
| | |
| **Paper 5** | **Speaking** |
| Part 3 | Collaborative task |
| Part 4 | Further discussion |

### Other

| | |
|---|---|
| Language Focus 1: | Comparisons |
| Language Focus 2: | Articles |
| Vocabulary: | Machines and devices |
| | Linking devices |
| | *as ... as* expressions |
| Word formation: | Suffixes |

## Vocabulary: Machines and devices

Page 26

**Lead-in**

You could bring to class several small items of daily use for students to define to each other. If they know what the objects are called in English they must not use the name. Instead, working in pairs, they give definitions and explanations in any way they can. The 'listening' students can say the name in English if they know it or the name in their own language if you have a monolingual group.

**1** Refer students to the definitions given in the Coursebook. Writing down ideas should help students to maintain the conversation when

discussing the questions in class. You could refer students to the Wordlist on page 203 of the Coursebook.

**2** Ask students to look at and identify the objects in the pictures on page 27 (electric carving knife, electric pencil sharpener, electric/automatic curtains). Students then discuss the questions in pairs. If they need support, refer them to the Wordlist on page 203.

### Answers

electric carving knife – gadget or appliance, depending on the speaker's viewpoint: if it is considered indispensable then it could be called an appliance. If not, a gadget.
(adjectives – handy, labour-saving, etc)

electric pencil sharpener – gadget
(adjectives – handy, unusual, complicated, etc)

automatic curtains – gadget
(adjectives – clever, unusual, complicated, etc)

## Reading: FCE Part 1 — Multiple choice Page 26

Photocopiable vocabulary exercise on page 159.

**Lead-in**

Without referring to the Coursebook, write up some typically North American products or inventions, eg Coca-Cola, the hamburger, hot dogs, drive-in movies, the Internet, etc.

Ask students what these products have in common (they are from the United States) and what people did before they were invented (they drank tea and coffee, they ate at home or in restaurants rather than in the street, they went to the cinema, they wrote letters and sent faxes ... ).

Explain if necessary that the items on the board are designed to make our lives easier and save us time. They are part of 'the convenience society'. A *con* is a trick of some kind, as for example when you have bought something which does not work as well as you had imagined or been told. Elicit from students the meaning of the play on words in the title (that there is not much convenience in a convenience society).

**1** Refer students to the instructions in their Coursebook.

    **C** (the author's views are summarized in the last two sentences)

Ask students if they can identify if the author is using a serious or humorous style (humorous – he uses exaggeration).

**2** Students read the other questions and the text again to answer questions 2–7. Draw students' attention to the 'What to expect in the exam' box.

**Learner training**

Try to get students into the habit of marking in pencil where they have got their answers from as this makes the feedback stage more efficient. It also trains students to really find the answers in the text.

### Answers

2 **B** line 12 'The things that are supposed to speed up and simplify our lives more often than not have the opposite effect …'

3 **C** line 19 'they had come to expect machines to do almost everything for them.'

4 **C** in paragraph 5 the author is exaggerating for comic effect

5 **D** line 26 'and the whole thing (the knife is in his hands, not the turkey) flew out of his hands'

6 **A** line 35 'People are so addicted to convenience that they have become trapped in a vicious circle'

7 **B** 'it was full of gadgets … all of them designed to make life a little easier.'

8 **D** line 44 'We didn't go anywhere near them after the first week.'

**Reacting to the text**

Move on to the post-reading questions which students could answer in pairs or groups, or ask the questions to the group as a whole.

## Language focus 1: Comparisons  Page 29

The first exercise is designed to see how much the students already know or can remember.

### Answers

1 quicker (line 8)
2 speedier, more convenient (line 10)
3 more, than (line 13)

4 as, as (line 23)
5 less than (line 31)
6 with (line 32)
7 more, harder (lines 36–7)
8 easier (line 40)

**A Comparative and superlative adjectives**

This is revision and should not take too long.

### Answers

1 *quick-er, quick-est* one-syllable words
   eg older, louder, taller

   *speedi-er, speedi-est* two-syllable words ending in *-y* eg noisy, happy, silly

   *more convenient, the most convenient* words with two or more syllables
   eg modern, confident, comfortable

2 cleaner, the cleanest
   hotter, the hottest
   stranger, the strangest
   more clever (cleverer), the most clever (the cleverest)
   better, the best
   worse, the worst
   farther, the farthest or further, the furthest

3 big differences *far, a lot, significantly*
   small differences *a bit, slightly*

**Common mistakes**

• If necessary, remind students that the article is a necessary part of the superlative form and must be included.
• 'The biggest *of* the world.' instead of 'The biggest *in* the world.'
• 'Paris is bigger *that* Madrid.' Instead of 'Paris is bigger *than* Madrid.'

Students check their answers in the Grammar reference on pages 207 and 208.

**B Other comparative expressions**

Read through Other comparative expressions 1 and 2 with the students.

**Practice**

**1** This exercise exposes students to pairs of sentences with similar meaning but using different structures, rather like a completed transformation exercise. This way they should be more prepared for the real transformation exercise which follows in exercise 4.

### Answers

| | | | | | |
|---|---|---|---|---|---|
| **1** c | **2** a | **3** e | **4** b | **5** f | **6** d |

**2** Students follow the instructions in their books. Check what they have written by moving round the class if that is possible in your teaching situation. If you have a large group you could check a few pieces of students' work at random, varying whose work you check each time.

**3** Students complete the dialogues with common expressions which use the comparative form.

### Answers

| | | | | | |
|---|---|---|---|---|---|
| **1** d | **2** c | **3** a | **4** b | **5** f | **6** e |

**4** This exercise focuses entirely on the language of comparisons. Remember that contractions count as two words.

### Answers

1  was far worse than
2  as sad as she
3  the least enjoyable
4  you work now, the less
5  quite as much experience as

## Word formation: Suffixes -ful and -less

Page 30

This is the second in the series of word formation exercises.

### Lead-in

Write WORD FORMATION on the board as a title and to let students know what area of language is to be worked on. Before students open their books, write the words in the box on the board and give students one minute to write down as many adjectives as they can from their previous knowledge.

This could be done individually or in pairs. Get brief feedback from this (oral only) and let students know which of their words exist and which do not.

**1** Refer students to the box in their books. Ask them to form adjectives with a partner.

### Answers

| Root | Positive | Negative |
|---|---|---|
| success (n) | successful | unsuccessful |
| skill (n) | skilful (Am*: skillful) | unskilled |
| home (n) | — | homeless |
| cheer (n/v) | cheerful | **cheerless |
| delight (n/v) | delightful | — |
| thought (n) | thoughtful | thoughtless |
| harm (n/v) | harmful | harmless |
| pain (n/v) | painful | painless |
| end (n/v) | — | endless |
| power (n) | powerful | powerless |
| care (n/v) | careful | careless |
| price (n/v) | — | priceless |

*In the exam candidates must consistently use *either* British *or* American spelling.
** *cheerless* used mainly to describe the weather or a room

Note the following:

*endless* possible opposite – *finite*
*delightful* possible opposite – *awful*
the adjective 'homely' (simple and pleasant in a way that makes you feel comfortable and at home) also exists.

**2** Discuss the questions with the students.

### Answers

tasty – used to describe food with a strong and pleasant flavour
tasteful – used to describe clothes, decoration, etc which are attractive and show good taste.

1  helpful = useful
2  helplessly = unable to do anything
3  unhelpful = not willing/not wanting to help

**3** Before students start, ask them to go through the sentences and identify which part of speech is required in each one as this exercise practises adjective, adverb and noun forms. When you have checked this, students complete the exercise then compare their answers in pairs.

## Answers

| 1 | adv | skilfully |
| 2 | adj | unsuccessful |
| 3 | noun | carelessness |
| 4 | adj | thoughtful |
| 5 | adj | uneventful |
| 6 | adj | harmful |
| 7 | adj | painless |
| 8 | noun | cheerfulness |
| 9 | adj | pointless |
| 10 | noun | homelessness |

## Listening 1: FCE Part 3 — Multiple matching
Page 31

**1** Refer students to the Listening Part 3 instructions.

**2** Students discuss the questions in pairs. You could write the following prompts on the board: *cost, size, weight, expense, environment, convenience*.

Remember to let students hear the recording twice and compare their answers together between each hearing.

### Learner training
In these listening exercises there are usually both clues to the correct answer and distractors. Students need to learn to listen carefully until the end of each section before deciding.

When checking, ask students the reasons why they decided on their answers.

## Answers

| 1 D | 2 A | 3 E | 4 B | 5 C |

### Listening 1: Listening script 1.8–1.12

**Speaker 1**
They last for about eight hours, which is about all you need them for really, even during the winter months when the nights are much longer of course. They're absolutely marvellous. Each one has a solar panel, which stores energy during the day, and then they come on as soon as it gets dark. When we moved into the area, we were a little worried about security, so we put them all along the driveway. They certainly seem to keep the burglars away. They also help you to see your way safely back to the front door if you come back after a good night out.

**Speaker 2**
An amazing gadget. It's solar powered, so it doesn't need batteries. You just attach it to a box which has solar panels on top and leave it by the window. It'll charge itself in a couple of hours – as long as it's sunny, of course!

It's handy to have round the house for when you have a power cut and you can't see what you're doing, and it's ideal for camping, too. Just leave it outside the tent in the afternoon, and it's ready for you to use when you need it later on.

**Speaker 3**
We ordered it off the Internet. An American company. They said it was the latest in environmentally-friendly appliances. No batteries, no fuel, just sunlight. Take it on camping trips, they said, and enjoy delicious al fresco meals. Use it outside at home, they said, and keep the kitchen cool. What a waste of money. It keeps the kitchen cool alright, but … when you live in a country which hardly sees the sun all year, it keeps the food cool, too. It would have been better to order the fridge.

**Speaker 4**
This one looks good! Clockwork and solar-powered, and it comes in translucent red or blue plastic. There's a photo of one here. Cool! A bit expensive though – sixty quid. Anyway, it says here: 'As well as a handle to wind it up, it comes equipped with a solar panel which automatically takes over when the machine is placed in direct sunlight. Its waterproof beatbox is perfect for the beach.' It also says it's got headphones if you're worried about noise pollution. Can't see why you would be, though, can you?

**Speaker 5**
Solar-assisted, really. I mean, you still need batteries, but the tiny solar cell means you can use the playback without running them down. Cost an arm and a leg, mind you, but as far as I'm concerned it was worth every penny. I can plug it into my PC and the images are just fantastic. Really clear. Do you want to see where I went on holiday?

### Noticing language
**1** This section focuses on expressions formed with *as … as*.

## Answers

| 1 | as soon as = immediately(when)/once |
| 2 | as long as = if/provided/providing/ on condition that |
| 3 | as well as = in addition to/besides |
| 4 | as far as I'm concerned = in my opinion |

**2** Students complete the sentences.

## Answers

| 1 long | 2 soon | 3 many | 4 well |
| 5 far | 6 much | | |

**Further practice**

Ask students to write their own sentences with some of the expressions used in exercise 2. In the next lesson, write the expressions on the board and see if your students can remember their own example sentences. Try to ensure that they understand the importance of writing true sentences. If the sentences are not true then the exercise is not personalized and students may be less likely to remember the language.

 **Speaking 1:**
**FCE Part 3**

**Collaborative task**
Page 32

Refer students to the pictures and the exam instructions. The 'How to go about it' box contains advice about ideas and language. This task should be done in pairs, as in the exam.

### Answers

**a** past simple, *used to*, *would*
**b** present simple, adverbs of frequency, *tend to*
**c** to describe events which occurred at some time between the past and the present
**d** *used to*, *get used to*, *would* and comparatives

 **Speaking 2:**
**FCE Part 4**

**Further discussion**
Page 33

Parts 3 and 4 of Paper 5 Speaking are thematically linked. Refer students to the instructions in their books.

**Possible procedures**

• Students work in pairs as they will probably do in the real exam. (In special circumstances some students may be examined in groups of three) or

• students work in groups of three: one 'examiner' and two 'candidates', changing roles when instructed by the teacher (every two minutes) or

• the teacher leads the session, asking various students the questions given.

**Correction**

If you intend to correct students' mistakes, let them know what areas of language you will be specifically listening to. This serves two purposes:

• It's impractical to try to correct everything, even with a small group. This way you know what to focus on and what to ignore.

• The students know what you are listening out for and will focus their attention on that. This in itself tends to reduce the number of mistakes made in that area of language.

Language to focus on for correction: students' use of comparatives and superlatives, ways of describing past habits/situations and/or present perfect.

## Language focus 2: Articles    Page 33

This section is designed to let both student and teacher know which areas cause problems. The cloze test is followed by analysis of the use of the definite (*the*) and indefinite (*a*, *an*) articles and when no article is used.

**1** Refer students to the instructions and questions. The text is treated first for its content and then for its language, ie *what* it is saying before *how* it is saying it.

### Answers

**a** Many parents do not question the educational value of home computers although they themselves may not understand them.
**b** The Government is in favour of having more computers in schools in order to compete better with other countries.
**c** They believe that home computers cannot replace real teachers.

**2** Students complete the spaces in the text.

### Answers

| | | | | | | | | | |
|---|---|---|---|---|---|---|---|---|---|
| **1** the | **2** a | | **3** a | | **4** the | | **5** – | | |
| **6** – | **7** – | | **8** – | | **9** the | | **10** The | | |
| **11** the | **12** The | | **13** – | | **14** the | | **15** the | | |
| **16** – | **17** a (or *the* if he is the only lecturer) | | | | | | | | |
| **18** – | **19** – | | **20** – | | | | | | |

**3** Students discuss the reasons in pairs.

Ask students to highlight in their books which rules are different from their first language. This makes it easier for them to distinguish what is important for them personally and it will help them when they revise.

## Answers

| Question | Grammar reference section |
|---|---|
| The definite article | |
| 12 | A1 |
| 10 | A2 |
| 1, 4 | A4 |
| 11, 14 | A7 |
| 9, 15 | A5a |
| The indefinite article | |
| 0, 3 | B1 |
| 17 | B3 |
| 2 | B4 |
| No article | |
| 5, 20 | C1a |
| 7, 13, 16 | C1b |
| 6, 19 | C1c |
| 8 | C2 |
| 18 | C3 |

### Listening 2:
**FCE Part 4**

### Multiple choice
Page 34

Photocopiable vocabulary exercise on page 159.

**1** Draw students' attention to the pictures, headlines and definition in their books. These will help them to think about a wide variety of different robots when they answer the question.

Pre-teach *reveals* and *companion*.
*reveals* – makes something publicly known
*companion* – something or somebody that spends a lot of time with you

Students discuss the question in pairs and you could then ask some students individually for their answers.

## Suggested answers

domestic tasks
car manufacturing and other industries
dirty jobs, eg mining, cleaning toxic waste
the military, eg as soldiers, etc
space travel
as toys
providing companionship
operations in hospitals
house sitter
museum guide
drug detection

**2** Refer students' to the instructions and the 'Don't forget!' box in their books. Remind them that distractors may seem correct at first because they may contain words which are used in the tapescript. They must therefore check their answers carefully.

## Answers

**1** B   **2** C   **3** A   **4** A   **5** C   **6** B   **7** C

---

**Listening 2: Listening script 1.13**

**P = Presenter  K = Keith Wells**

**P:** My guest today is robot scientist Keith Wells. Keith's company, *ELA Robotics,* hit the news last year with their *Home Help* robot, the first of its kind to be able to perform more than one domestic task. What are you working on now, Keith?

**K:** I can't really tell you that, I'm afraid. It's not that I don't want to, it's just that we've all been given our instructions and signed an agreement not to give anything away until it actually comes on to the market. I don't quite know when that will be, but probably some time early next year.

**P:** OK, well we'll look forward to that. In the meantime, perhaps you could tell us what you think are the most important applications of robots in our lives. Why are they useful?

**K:** Well, they help us to do what we call 'the 3 Ds'. That's anything which is dull, dirty or dangerous. They can be used in the home or in the car manufacturing industry, to do dull or monotonous work; they're used for doing dirty jobs like mining or cleaning toxic waste; and then they have applications in the military or in the dangerous business of space travel. Of course, that's not an exhaustive list, but it gives you an idea of the range of different uses they have – and also of the variety involved in my line of work.

**P:** Yes, indeed. Let's talk if we may about one area in particular, though, the more humanoid robots, the ones with a recognizable human form. What are the latest developments there?

**K:** Yes, the ones being built now are able to see, hear, touch and even smell and taste. In the future they should also be able to display a range of emotions. They might feel happy for example that they have carried out a domestic task particularly well, or sad and guilty because they haven't. That way they will have a reason to go on doing the same task in the future, either to match their last performance or to improve on it. A robot with emotions is a robot with goals.

**P:** Amazing. But isn't all this a little bit worrying – robots with emotions? Isn't there a danger of science fiction becoming science fact, with robots taking over?

**K:** Yes, unfortunately, robots do get rather a bad press sometimes, don't they? Particularly in films and video games where they're either objects of humour and ridicule which we laugh at or else they're menacing characters which threaten to destroy the whole human race. But no, there is actually an ethical code which sets out what we can and can't do in robot design – and one thing we won't do is allow ourselves to lose control over our creations.

**P:** Don't you think, though, that robots will make us lazy, that we'll no longer want to do anything that requires any effort?

**K:** I think the car's already done that to us. It's made us physically very lazy. We don't walk so much as we used to and our bodies have suffered as a result. I think robots could well have the same effect on our brains. If we let intelligent robots do all of our thinking for us, there is a danger we won't be able to make any of our own decisions, that we'll become mentally lazy. And that, I think, is just as worrying.

**P:** Do you really think that the day will come when most homes have their own robot?

**K:** If you think back to just twenty-five years ago, few of us then would have predicted that we'd soon have a personal computer in our home, be logging onto the Internet and downloading hundreds of songs on to a thing called an MP3 player. So why shouldn't we all have robots? The truth is that we've been talking about robots for nearly a century and their development hasn't been quite as fast as we thought it would be, but now with advanced computer technology available, that should all change very soon.

**P:** How soon?

**K:** Well, it's changing already. The first humanoid robots at the end of the 1990s could do very little, then later models learnt to sit down and stand up, then talk, walk around, dance and so on. It's rather like watching a child grow. Through television and other media, the public is slowly growing accustomed to the idea of robots as a reality, and when they eventually become widely available, people will be ready for them.

**P:** Thank you, Keith. It's been fascinating having you on the programme.

## Writing: FCE Part 2 — Essays Page 35

**1** Students are introduced to one way of dealing with a discursive essay. The emphasis here is on giving a balanced argument.

Before students start analysing the model answer, ask them to read the question.

**2** Students identify the purpose of each paragraph. Let students work individually first before comparing their answers with their partner. This individual work gives them time to think and concentrate.

### Answers

| | |
|---|---|
| Paragraph 1 | a general introduction |
| Paragraph 2 | positive aspects/advantages of mobile phones |
| Paragraph 3 | negative aspects/disadvantages of mobile phones |
| Paragraph 4 | conclusion/summary of opinions |

**3** Students read the examples of linking devices in **a** and add more to the groups in **b**. Draw students' attention to the linkers for organizing ideas.

### Answers

**Expressing contrasts**
On the one hand/On the other hand
Some people feel that, Others argue that

**Adding information**
In addition (to this), What is more, Another disadvantage is, Besides this, Furthermore

**Concluding**
To sum up, On balance

**4** Students often fail to transfer the skills they have in their first language to second or subsequent languages and repetition is one example of this. If repetition is a problem with your students and they are a monolingual group, copy out or read out a text in their language repeating vocabulary. Students will quickly realize that the text sounds strange and will be able to identify why this is so. This is one way of making the reason for working on avoiding repetition clear.

### Answers

they, them, models, the mobile phone, (drivers who use) one, (what for many people is a) useful device, (for others is) a nuisance

**5** Students read the instructions in the 'How to go about it' box. For some students the most difficult thing about writing First Certificate essays is getting ideas together. For this reason, it is often a good idea (especially at this stage in the course) for students to do at least the preparation for writing in class time.

**Ideas for the essay**
**Positive aspects:**
- increase the speed of global communications, eg email, the Internet
- the Internet: a source of information, eg for work or study, a source of pleasure
- reduce the time to do work

- enables you to communicate cheaply via chats with people from other countries
- enable you to store information – no need for paper
- enable people to work from home
- a more independent way to learn English
- generally not controlled by governments – freedom of expression

**Negative aspects:**

- can spend too long on them
- can lose social skills
- people refer to books less often
- can affect your health, eg eye strain, backache … can go wrong and cause stress
- because it is capable of doing so much it can in fact create more work
- can expose children to violence and pornography

---

### Sample answer

Nowadays the computer has become a tool which, is in all kinds of jobs. Children learn to handle with them since they are very little. It has brought the chance to get a lot of information but many disadvantages too.

On the positive side, it helps us to keep a great deal of information in very little space. In addition to this, with Internet we can communicate with any other inhabitant of the world in seconds. Moreover, you can be informed about any subject you are interested in, thanks to the huge variety of websites you can find on the Net. Finally, our jobs have become easier if you have to deal with information in your office.

On the other hand, children are too obsessed with computer games and it makes them lose their social skills. Another point is that many activities which help us to develop ourselves such as doing sports or reading books have been replace by the computer.

In conclusion, I think the computer could help us to increase our skills and to improve our lives but I don't think most people use it in a good way.
By Javier Redondo

---

191 words

**Examiner's comment**

**Content:** Good realization of the task. An appropriately balanced approach to the question.

**Accuracy:** Some awkwardness/inaccuracies – *which is in all kinds of jobs, learn to handle with them,*

*has brought the chance to get, have been replace(d) by* but these do not cause misunderstandings or obscure communication.

**Range:** Generally the candidate shows good control of both vocabulary and grammar – *a great deal of, very little, thanks to the huge variety of, deal with information, such as doing sports …*

**Organization and cohesion:** Clear organization helped by good use of linking devices – *On the positive side, Moreover, Finally, On the other hand,* etc.

**Style and format:** Consistent, appropriate to the task.

**Target reader:** The reader would have a clear understanding of the writer's opinion based on a balanced evaluation of the advantages and disadvantages of computers.

**Mark:** band 4

---

### Review 3 answers  Page 36

## Vocabulary: Word partnerships

**1**  **1** food    **2** knife    **3** oven    **4** machine
**5** sharpener  **6** steamer  **7** control  **8** device
**9** appliance  **10** toothbrush

**2**  Student's own answers.

## Comparisons

**1**

**1** *d*    **2** e    **3** a    **4** b    **5** h
**6** c    **7** f    **8** g

**2–4** Student's own answers.

## Articles

**3** in **the** home        **10** on **the** train
**4** spend ~~the~~ more      **11** watched **a** young couple
**5** killed **the** art      **12** not just **the** young
**6** write ~~the~~ emails     **13** **a** high percentage
**7** **the** less            **14** into ~~the~~ your phone
**8** **the** mobile phone     **15** I'm **the** one
**9** put in **a**            **16** to **the** mountains

## ( Use of English: )  Word formation
**FCE Part 3**

The writer is clearly an older person, possibly middle-aged or older.

**1** painless    **2** thoughtful    **3** ungrateful
**4** cheerfully  **5** disadvantages **6** embarrassment
**7** careless    **8** effortlessly  **9** wonderfully
**10** fortunate

## Workbook answers

### Reading: Multiple matching   Page 18

**1**  **a**  A, B, D, F        **b** C, E

**2**  **1** A    **2** C    **3** B    **4** E
   **5/6** A, F in any order    **7** D
   **8** C    **9** A    **10** E    **11** B
   **12** A    **13/14/15** D, E, F in any order

**3**  **1** e    **2** a    **3** c    **4** d    **5** b

**4**  **1** get by        **2** came out    **3** take up
   **4** brought, up    **5** took over

### Vocabulary   Page 20

**Technology**

| Across | Down |
|---|---|
| **1** handy | **1** headphones |
| **3** DVD | **2** dial |
| **7** laptop | **4** disposable |
| **9** out | **5** remote |
| **10** surf | **6** IT |
| **11** on | **8** portable |
| **12** log | **10** system |
| **13** satellite | |

### Language focus   Page 20

**A  Articles**

**1** The, a, –, the
**2** –, –, –, a, a, The, a, the, –, the
**3** –, the, a
**4** a, a, the, The, a
**5** the, –, a, an

**B  Comparisons**

**1** hard    **2** hottest    **3** more careful
**4** better    **5** soon    **6** most boring
**7** more tired/tireder    **8** earlier
**9** fastest    **10** quieter/more quiet

**C  Comparative expressions**
   **1** b    **2** d    **3** e    **4** a    **5** c

**D  Correcting mistakes**

**1  Walkman**
   This invention which completely changed
   But however its creator
   the portable device, more smaller than
**2  Compass**
   This device was the most of important
   to can know
   the most significant of event

**3  Video**
   significantly very cheaper
   nearly as most common
   as more often as they like
**4  Space blanket**
   a type of the plastic
   It is used to, for example
   as a result of the Man's efforts
**5  Radar**
   and is used for to detect
   as an instrument as of war
   In addition to,

### Use of English   Page 22

**Transformations**

**1**  not nearly as/so difficult
**2**  not as many girls
**3**  least comfortable chair in
**4**  I smoke, the more
**5**  lives further/farther (away) from
**6**  did much worse than
**7**  not earn as much as
**8**  the cleverest person I have/I've

**Open cloze**
**1**  b

**2**  **1** used    **2** it    **3** The    **4** well
   **5** be    **6** on    **7** later    **8** from
   **9** The/These/Such    **10** an
   **11** that/which    **12** as

**Word formation**
**1** skilful/skilled    **2** technological
**3** tasty    **4** helpless
**5** inventor    **6** later
**7** appearance    **8** electrician
**9** successful    **10** widely

### Writing   Page 24

**2**  **Essay:**    **1** e    **2** g    **3** b    **4** d
   **Article:**    **1** f    **2** a    **3** h    **4** c

**3**  **Essay**
   Formal linkers (However, On the one hand/On
   the other hand, In addition, Moreover)
   **Article**
   Phrasal verbs (couldn't do without, get by)
   Informal linkers (And, But, So)
   Direct questions (Can you imagine an object in
   your house which you dislike having to use but
   which you know you couldn't do without?)

## First Certificate Paper 1

### Reading

**Part 1**     Multiple choice
**Part 2**     Gapped text
**Part 3**     Multiple matching

This is the first of five 'Ready for …' units which focus on the five different skills areas tested in the First Certificate exam: Reading, Writing, Use of English, Listening and Speaking.

In each of these 'Ready for …' units there is a clear explanation of the different kinds of exercise types students can expect to find in the exam. This serves to give the students a useful overview and summary of each paper. Students are also provided with and reminded of useful strategies that they should use in the exam to help improve their performance.

### Possible approaches to using the 'Ready for …' unit material

Although the material is designed for classroom use it is suitable for individual study and the Reading, Writing and Use of English units can also be set for homework.

The material in these units can be worked through step by step, as indicated in the Coursebook, or you may decide to select from the suggested guidance exercises depending on your particular class and the time available.

Whatever approach you decide to use, encourage students to justify their answers.

No guidance is given to students in the Progress tests which start on page 175.

### Lead-in

Write the following on the board under the title 'Reading strategies' and ask students to think about how we read each of them. Students 'pair' them depending on how we read them and justify their answers.

1   instructions for installing a computer program
2   a telephone directory
3   a novel
4   a dictionary
5   a letter from a friend
6   reading about how to play a new video game

### Answers

1 and 6   require very careful reading and detailed understanding of every word (intensive reading).

2 and 4   require reasonably fast reading and looking for only the information you need while ignoring the rest. It is not necessary to start at the beginning of the text and read all the way through to the end (scanning).

3 and 5   require you to start at the beginning and read through – general understanding of the text is needed but understanding of every single word is not (mainly skimming). If you are expecting a particular item of news from your friend then you may use a similar technique to that in 2 and 4.

### Part 1: Multiple choice     Page 38

**1**   Refer students to the explanation in their books regarding the multiple choice questions. Tell them to read through the article fairly quickly and then answer question 8.

### Answer

**8**

**A**   Mountains are mentioned but the text is not exclusively for mountain walkers. See paragraph 3: 'Better still then if you can plunge into a river or the sea fully-clothed.'

**B**   Not stated – the first sentence says, 'and if you're not very fit …' but this is not the main aim of the article.

**C**   Correct answer

**D**   There is no indication that the people who go walking in summer do not also go walking at other times of the year.

**2**

**Definitions**

*pump* (verb) – move liquid or gas in a particular direction, e.g. blood around the body
*intake* (noun) – the amount you eat or drink
*raging* (adjective) – very strong or severe
*swig* (noun) – a quick drink of a liquid
*palatable* (adjective) – having a pleasant or acceptable taste

**3**

**Vocabulary in italics (paragraphs 5, 6 and 8)**

| | |
|---|---|
| *swell* (verb) | to become bigger |
| *blister* (noun) | a swelling on the surface of the skin, which contains a clear liquid |
| *leak* (verb) | (in this case) the water gets into your boots |
| *rash* (noun) | lots of red spots on your skin |
| *breeze* (noun) | a light wind |
| *deceptive* (adj) | from the verb 'deceive' – something which tricks you, which makes you believe something which is not true |

**4** Tell students to decide why the incorrect answers are incorrect.

### Answers and rationale

**1**

**A** Not stated. The writer says that 'The majority of mountain rescue statistics are made up from summer walkers suffering heart attacks' but this does not mean that heat is the main cause of heart attacks in general.

**B** Correct answer – 'The answer is to keep up your water intake' and 'keep taking regular swigs from your water bottle'.

**C** Not stated.

**D** Not stated. The writer implies merely that if you are not fit you will suffer the effects of heat even more.

**2**

**A** Not stated

**B** No – it replaces the body salts lost through sweating, but it doesn't prevent their loss.

**C** No – it is a treatment for diarrhoea, not a prevention.

**D** Correct answer – 'Dioralyte will do the job just as well.'

**3**

**A** illogical

**B** Correct answer

**C** when the hat dries off, so will the head

**D** 'water' does not dry off: when a hat (or anything else) dries off, the water disappears

**4**

**A** No – 'cool water … reduces swelling and helps … comfort'.

**B** Your boots become tight because of the heat.

**C** Correct answer – 'Extra sweating makes the skin softer and increases the chance of blisters forming, in the same way as when water leaks into your boots and gets to your feet.'

**D** Not stated – 'Cool water from a stream reduces swelling' may distract students. In addition, boots may be waterproof and not leak.

**5**

**A** Not stated – 'The answer, if this does develop, is to try and stay cool' is a distractor.

**B** The writer says walkers should ideally wear 'lightweight and loose-fitting' clothing. Being light is not the reason the author gives for wearing loose-fitting clothing.

**C** Correct answer – 'Tight clothing … may even lead to the formation of an irritating rash known as 'prickly heat' on your skin.'

**D** Not stated

**6**

**A** Correct answer – 'It's understandable to want to remove any extraneous clothing when it's extremely hot …'

**7**

**A** Correct answer – '… deceptive. It might not feel so hot, so you probably won't notice the damage being done.'

**B** Not stated – '… a good strong sun cream should therefore be applied' is a distractor.

**C** 'breeze' is not a strong wind – 'an apparently harmless breeze'

**D** Not stated – 'harmless' and 'damage' may distract students.

## Part 2: Gapped text       Page 40

Refer students to the information and advice which comes before the reading in their books.

Note: students may not predict accurately sentence 5, but this will serve to show the reality of the situation in the exam: some sentences/paragraphs are more predictable than others.

### Answers

| | | | |
|---|---|---|---|
| **1** G | **2** E | **3** C | **4** F |
| **5** D | **6** A | B not used | |

## 4 A good story

## Part 3: Multiple matching

Page 40

Refer students to the information which comes before the reading task including the 'How to go about it' and 'What to expect in the exam' boxes.

### Answers for text A:

**10** You can select under subject and age group.

**13** each link has a five-line description so you know exactly where you are going.

### Answers

| | | | |
|---|---|---|---|
| 1/2 | B, D in any order | 3 | F |
| 4/5 | A, B in any order | 6 | C |
| 7/8/9 | B, E, F in any order | | |
| 10/11 | A, C in any order | 12 | F |
| 13 | A | 14 D | 15 F |

## Content Overview

### Themes

The common link throughout this unit is stories: films, an extract from a novel and embarrassing moments leading to students writing their own stories. Students work on aspects of language after reading or listening for meaning. In this way, the contexts for the language are clear. Students are actively encouraged to keep their vocabulary notebooks up to date.

### Exam-related activities

| **Paper 1** | **Reading** |
|---|---|
| Part 2 | Gapped text |
| | |
| **Paper 2** | **Writing** |
| Part 2 | Reviews |
| Part 2 | Short stories |
| | |
| **Paper 3** | **Use of English** |
| Part 3 | Word formation (Review) |
| Part 4 | Transformations (Review) |
| | |
| **Paper 4** | **Listening** |
| Part 1 | Multiple choice |
| | |
| **Paper 5** | **Speaking** |
| Part 2 | Talking about photos |

### Other

Language focus 1: *So* and *such*
Language focus 2: Past tenses
Vocabulary:      Films
                 *Take*
Word formation:  Adjectives ending in *-ing* and *-ed*
Pronunciation:   *-ed* endings

## Vocabulary 1: Films

Page 42

**1** You could either put students into small groups to discuss the film posters and what type of films they are or ask students yourself.

### Answers

*Night at the Museum* – comedy
*Pride and Prejudice* – historical drama/romance
*Spiderman* – science fiction/action film
*Pirates of the Caribbean* – action film/comedy/historical drama/romance

**2** This section aims to clarify some words which many students frequently misuse. If necessary, ask your students to write their own sentences using the words. The context of the sentence must make it clear that they have understood the word they are using in each case.

| Answers | | |
|---|---|---|
| **A 1** terrific | **2** terrifying | **3** terrible |
| **B 1** review | **2** critic | **3** criticism |

**3** Tell students to ignore the underlining as they read the review for the first time.

**4**

| Answers | |
|---|---|
| **1** set | **5** performance |
| **2** cast | **6** plot |
| **3** stars | **7** main characters |
| **4** role | **8** special effects |

## Language focus 1: *So* and *such*     Page 44

Refer students to the two examples from the text.

| Answers |
|---|
| Both words intensify the adjective or (adjective +) noun that follow. |
| *so* + adjective (or adverb) |
| *such* + (article) + (adjective) noun |

**Practice**

Students have the opportunity to use *so* and *such* correctly in transformations.

| Answers |
|---|
| **1** were so good (that) |
| **2** was such bad weather |
| **3** was such a boring |
| **4** were so many |

## Word formation: Adjectives ending in *-ing* and *-ed*     Page 44

In some languages, the same word can be used to describe both feelings and the thing or person that produces those feelings. Consequently, students often have problems using these adjectives correctly.

Refer students to the sentences and explanations in their books or copy the sentences below on to the board. If you use the board for this, ask students first to close their books.

I got *bored* very quickly during the film.
I'd be *interested* to hear what you think.

It was an extremely *boring* film.
He is a very *interesting* man. I could listen to him for hours.

Instead of telling them when the different types of adjective are used, ask the following questions:

*Which pair describes the thing or person that produces feelings?* (the second)
*Which pair of sentences describes feelings?* (the first)

**1–4** Students now follow the instructions in their books.

**Common problems**
This aspect of English pronunciation causes problems for many students, as the combinations of sounds produced (consonant clusters) may not exist in their own language. Pronunciation of the *-ed* ending depends on the pronunciation of the final sound (not letter) of the infinitive.

The general rules are:

**1** Is the final sound of the infinitive voiced? (See *surprise* and column 1 below.)
**2** Is the final sound of the infinitive unvoiced or voiceless? (See *embarrass* and column 2 below.)
**3** Is the final sound /t/ or /d/? (See *excite* and column 3 below.)

If it is hard to tell if a sound is voiced or unvoiced, try covering your ears with your hands and saying the sound. If you can hear the sound amplified, it is voiced. This technique often works better than putting a finger to your throat to detect movement in the vocal chords.

Provide pronunciation practice by modelling the pronunciation and getting the students to repeat together a number of times. Then ask individuals to repeat, varying who you ask each time. This stage should not take long.

## Answers

1 **Adjectives:** entertaining, complicated, confusing, stunning, disappointed
   **Adverbs:** surprisingly, convincingly

2
| **1** /d/ | **2** /t/ | **3** /ɪd/ |
|---|---|---|
| surprised | embarrassed | excited |
| annoyed | astonished | frustrated |
| tired | impressed | disappointed |
| amused | relaxed | disgusted |
| bored | | fascinated |
| frightened | | |
| terrified | | |

3  **1** impress      impressive (adj)

4  **Suggested answers**
   | 1 tiring | 5 fascinating |
   |---|---|
   | 2 amused | 6 disgusting |
   | 3 annoying | 7 Astonishingly |
   | 4 disappointingly | |

## Writing 1:
**FCE Part 2**            Reviews  Page 44

Students read the instructions in the 'How to go about it' box.

## Answers

| 1 c | 2 a | 3 d | 4 b |
|---|---|---|---|

## Sample answer

The last film I've seen on DVD was 'The Holiday' and it was alright. It is supposed it is a romantic comedy with Cameron Diaz, Kate Winslet, Jude Law and Jack Black and it is nice to watch but it is not a type of film that it makes you to laugh a lot.

The film is about two women very different. They are Iris, who is playing by Kate Winslet and Amanda (Cameron Diaz) and they decide to change houses for a holiday. Iris's house is a small one in England and Amanda's is enormous in Hollywood. Amanda falls in love to Iris's brother, who is widower, and Iris falls in love to Amanda's neighbour, who is componist. Kate Winslet is a bit disappointed in the role of Iris because she is normally very good actress. I like very much the photography and the music.

I would recommend the film to people who they are tired and they do not want to watch a complicate film. It is also very good for a rainy afternoon on Sunday of winter.

by David Benoa

180 words

**Examiner's comments**

**Content:** Reasonable realization of the task though rather a large section of the review is devoted to a simplistic summary of the plot.

**Accuracy:** A large number of distracting errors eg *it is supposed it is a romantic comedy, two women very different, who is playing by Kate Winslet* and use of relative clauses. *Disappointed* is used incorrectly *(disappointing)*, and it is not clear what is meant by *componist* (composer?).

**Range:** Very limited range of structures and vocabulary, particularly when expressing opinions eg *very good* (twice) and *nice to watch*.

**Organization and cohesion:** Adequate paragraphing. Some sentences poorly organized eg second sentence of first paragraph.

**Style and format:** Appropriate to the task.

**Target reader:** Reader may have some difficulty following the review due to the number of errors.

**Mark:** band 2

## Speaking:
**FCE Part 2**            Talking about photos
                         Page 45

Refer students to the 'Don't forget!' and 'What to expect in the exam' boxes before they look at the instructions and the pictures in their books.

In the exam one candidate speaks for a minute and the other has about 20 seconds to answer the question. However, as this is a practice, allow them a little more time to complete the task, but emphasize the need to keep speaking all the time, using fillers if necessary. This activity should be repeated with different pictures now and again.

## Preparing for listening: Focus on distractors                        Page 46

This section prepares students for what to expect in Listening Part 1. Each of the eight situations contains clues to the correct answer, as well as words and expressions which are designed to distract students from it. If students are not aware of this, they are more likely to be misled by the distractors. Explain this to the students as it is important that they realize both what they are going to do and why they are going to do it.

**1** In this exercise students have to understand and be aware of the words in bold as they provide clues to the other half of each sentence.

### Answers

1 c   2 d   3 a   4 e   5 b

**2** This exercise checks students' understanding of the linking words in 1.

### Answers

1 B   2 B   3 A   4 B   5 B

## Listening:
**FCE Part 1**

## Multiple choice Page 47

Refer students to the instructions and the 'Don't forget!' box in their books. Tell students to write down or try to remember any clues and/or distractors that they hear. This will be useful later when you check the answers.

### Answers

1 C   2 B   3 C   4 A   5 B   6 A   7 B   8 C

---

**Listening: Listening script 1.14–1.21**

**One**

I used to think he was so good looking – those sparkling blue eyes and that sexy smile – although now of course the wrinkles have taken over and he's lost it completely. Call me old-fashioned, but I really don't think that somebody of his age should be wearing tight trousers and flowery shirts. It's obscene. And the way he talks to the press! I mean, 'politeness' is just not a word he understands. I'm not surprised they get upset and give him bad reviews.

**Two**

**Man:** So, have you decided which film we're going to see, then?

**Woman:** Well, I really wanted to see the new Fiona Miller film which everyone is raving about.

---

**Man:** Oh, please, no! I couldn't stand another costume drama.

**Woman:** No, this one's very different from her others. She plays the part of an out-of-work spy who decides to turn to crime and begin a life as a jewel thief. But anyway, Katie says it's not her cup of tea, so I'm afraid it's 'get your handkerchief ready for another tear-jerker'. You know the plot already: boy meets girl, girl meets another boy, first boy gets upset – all that kind of nonsense.

**Three**

**Shop owner:** I'm afraid I'm going to have to ask you to pay an extra £3.

**Customer:** Why?

**Shop owner:** Well, you're only supposed to have the video out for two days: it says on the box – 48 hours only.

**Customer:** Right, and I took it out on Saturday.

**Shop owner:** And today's Tuesday, so that's one day overdue. Hence the extra £3.

**Customer:** But, you're not open on Sundays, so that day doesn't count. Saturday to Monday, one day, and Monday to Tuesday, two days.

**Shop owner:** I'm very sorry, sir, but that's not how we work.

**Four**

Drained, darling, absolutely drained. And have you read what the critics wrote about it? I don't know how anyone could say it was 'disappointing'. I mean, OK, so it's not the most exciting part I've ever had to play, but I gave it my all, absolutely everything. One look at my face will tell you just how utterly exhausted I am. I could sleep for a week.

**Five**

What do you think we should get him? ... An atlas! That's not very much ... I know he's interested in geography, but he's been with the company for nearly 25 years ... huh ... I really don't think an atlas would express our appreciation for all he's done for the firm. He's been like a father to us all ... bah ... I don't know, something that will remind him of us in his retirement, something he can use every day. How about a palm top or something?

**Six**

**Man:** What was it like?

**Woman:** Oh, don't ask. I certainly wouldn't recommend it to anyone.

**Man:** Too violent for you, was it?

**Woman:** Quite the opposite. I mean, at first there was the usual dose of gratuitous violence – basically what you'd expect from that type of film, and partly why I went to see it. After that, though, not a great deal happened. From what I can remember – when I wasn't falling asleep, that is – the script seemed to focus on an analysis of the protagonist's inner self.

**Man:** A kind of 'non-action film', then.

**Woman:** Exactly.

**Seven**

Hello, yes, it's about a book I bought in your shop last week. A Katharine Adams novel. I just wanted to point out that there were one or two pages missing ... No, no, there's really no need to apologize. I mean it's not as if it was the last page or anything. And I got the gist of what was happening without the pages. I just thought you ought to know so you can check the rest of your stock, or talk to the publishers or something ... That's OK ... Yes, pages 60 to 64 ...

**Eight**

Well, we were born in the same month, but I'm a Leo, as you know, whereas her birthday's at the beginning of July, which makes her a Cancer. I don't know if that's good or bad. We certainly seem to laugh at the same things; the same jokes, the same comedy programmes ... Sorry? ... Oh, next Friday. We're going to a jazz concert, although I can't say it's my favourite type of music. She's really into it, and she wanted me to go, so ...

## Vocabulary 2: *Take* Page 47

This section looks at different meanings of *take* and some common expressions that use *take*. The emphasis is on groups of words rather than on individual words. This exercise also revises the use of gerunds and infinitives, and other verb forms.

### A Phrasal verbs with *take*

The grammar of phrasal verbs is dealt with explicitly in the Workbook (Unit 6) whereas the Coursebook concentrates on meaning, and the presentation of phrasal verbs in context. See Workbook page 45 for information on which verbs are separable and which are inseparable.

**1**

| Answers | |
|---|---|
| take out | hire or rent |

**2** Refer students to the short story and elicit the possible title.

**Alternative approach**

- With books closed, tell the story on page 45, bit by bit, using the phrasal verbs, eg
'I take after my father in many ways ... we *both* love good food and we both tend to eat more than we need to.'

- Check students understand as you go along by asking them questions such as 'What do you think *I take after my father* means?'

- Once students have understood each expression, drill it to help with their pronunciation and 'fix' the expressions in their memories.

- Recap after every second or third sentence, eliciting as much as possible from the students – not just the expressions but other details from the story, too, eg

Teacher:   *What did I decide to do?*
Students:   *You decided to take up karate.*
Teacher:   *Why?*
Students:   *Because your clothes no longer*
            *fitted you.*

- When the story is finished, elicit or write up the phrasal verbs in the same order as in the story. Students work together to retell the same story to each other. Then take the verbs off the board and refer students to the instructions in their books.

This technique needs clear contexts and frequent recapping to help students remember. Once you feel confident, it is enjoyable, challenging for the students and memorable.

| Answers |
|---|
| Possible titles – *Karate changed my life* or *How I became a karate fanatic* |

**3** Students should do this exercise in pairs.

| Answers | | |
|---|---|---|
| **a** | take after | resemble |
| **b** | take up | start doing |
| **c** | took to | start to like |
| **d** | *taken me on | employ |
| **e** | take over from | replace |
| **f** | takes up | occupy |
| *note position of pronoun | | |

### B Expressions with *take*

**1** Ask students to ignore the lettering for the purpose of this exercise.

| Answers |
|---|
| **1** take     **2** 'd/would take   **3** taking/having taken |
| **4** to take   **5** took |
| **6** had taken/had been taking |
| **7** takes     **8** are taking/have taken |

**2–4** Here, students are encouraged to notice which words make up these expressions. Ask the students to record each expression as it appears in the sentence. The process of copying from their Coursebooks into their notebooks may also help them to remember the expressions.

### Answers

1  take (me) to (school)
2  take (them) back to the (shop)
3  taking (his) advice
4  take (any of) the blame
5  take (more) interest in (the children)
6  taken pity on (it)
7  takes (a great deal of) courage
8  taking so long to (do this exercise)

Note: the words in brackets can be substituted for others, depending on the context.

**3**  1 D   2 A   3 C   4 B

**4**  to take pride in something    C (3)
       to be taken to hospital       A (2)
       to take a joke                B (4)
       to take the infinitive        D (1)

**5** Students could write their own short story in class or as homework.

## Reading  FCE Part 2    Gapped text   Page 48

Photocopiable vocabulary exercise on page 160.

In the Reading paper there will almost certainly be items of vocabulary which students have not met before. If students wish to know the meanings of these words, encourage them to look at the context and to try to decide for themselves.

**1** Refer students to the photo in their books. This is a situation that most will be able to identify with. Either ask students the questions yourself or put them into pairs or small groups to answer them together.

**2** Students read the text and compare their ideas. The candidates are probably sitting for the First Certificate exam: 'The candidates were now on the third paper, which tested English grammar and vocabulary'.

**3** Refer students to the instructions in their books and the advice in the 'Don't forget!' box.

### Answers

1 H   2 C   3 B   4 E   5 A   6 G   7 D
F not used

The questions contained in 'Reacting to the text' are designed to open up the possibility of younger learners talking about cheating. Many adult learners will have a lot to say and usually enjoy talking about this.

## Language focus 2: Past tenses    Page 49

**1** Students name the underlined past tenses.

### Answers

**1**  1  past continuous
       2  past perfect
       3  past continuous + past simple
       4  past simple (x 3)
       5  past perfect continuous

**2**  1 d   2 b   3 e   4 a   5 c

**3**  1 a  He felt ill *during* the exam. (past continuous)
       1 b  He felt ill *after* the exam. (past perfect)
       2 a  I heard about it *while* I was listening to the radio. (past continuous)
       2 b  I heard about it, and *as a result* I listened to the radio. (past simple)
       3 a  I no longer live in Oxford. (past simple)
       3 b  I had been living in Oxford for six years *when* … (past perfect cont. – the speaker may or may not live in Oxford now)

**4**  *While* can be used in place of *when* in 1a and 2a. It emphasizes that the two things happened at the same time, but does not change the meaning. *As soon as* can be used in place of *when* in 1b and 2b. It emphasizes that the action in the main clause happened immediately after the action in the clause introduced by *as soon as*.

### Practice
**1** Refer students to the instructions.

### Answers

1 A   2 C   3 B   4 C   5 B   6 C

**2** Students should read through the texts before putting the verbs into the past tenses.

## Answers

**Bus blush**

| | | | |
|---|---|---|---|
| 1 | was travelling | 6 | sat |
| 2 | were having | 7 | had never seen |
| 3 | saw | 8 | smiled |
| 4 | was sitting | 9 | didn't stop |
| 5 | ran | 10 | (had) got |

**Mobile control**

| | | | |
|---|---|---|---|
| 11 | had been going on | 16 | (had) got |
| 12 | agreed | 17 | had taken |
| 13 | took | 18 | arrived |
| 14 | went | 19 | kept |
| 15 | had phoned | 20 | had had |

## Writing 2: FCE Part 2 — Short stories   Page 50

**1** Refer students to the exam instructions.

**2** In this section, students are led to an understanding of what makes a successful story at FC level. Students should be encouraged to say why one composition is better than the other.

## Answers

**B** is the better entry because:

- it ends with the required words exactly
- it is organized into clearly defined paragraphs
- it is not repetitive (unlike A)
- it uses a variety of past tenses appropriately.

**3** Encourage students to find the answers to these questions. It is vital that students know the criteria that examiners use when marking.

## Answers

**Content:**

**B** Yes, see point 1 above. The length is fine.

**A** No, the story does not end correctly.

**Range:**

**B** Tenses: Yes, past perfect simple and continuous, past simple and past continuous.

**B** Vocabulary: *Yes, thrilled, sparkling, blanket of snow, set off on foot, freezing, exhausted, could hardly make out,* etc.

**A** Tenses: Not really, the writer uses only the past simple and past continuous.

**A** Vocabulary: No, the vocabulary is repetitive: *went, went, went, went … they didn't have them, they didn't have them,* etc.

**Organization and cohesion:**

**B** Yes, use of tenses helps organize events.

**B** Linking devices are: *when, although, however, by the time, unfortunately, so, after, just as.*

**A** The events are organized chronologically so the telling of the story is not particularly interesting.

**A** Linking devices are more limited: *So* and *At last*

**Style and format:**

**B** Yes

**A** This story is rather informal – use of contractions and exclamation mark.

**Target Reader:**

**B** Yes, the reader would probably want to know what happened in the end. For all of these reasons, this entry would have a chance of winning the competition.

**A** No

**4** The 'What to expect in the exam' and the 'How to go about it' boxes aim to help students focus on what they need to do.

Having done most of the necessary thinking in class, students could write their story for homework. Remind students if necessary to write in their composition notebooks and remember to refer to the examiner's criteria when you respond to their work. If you give students only a very brief general comment they may not be aware of what aspect of their writing they need to work on and what aspects are improving.

### Sample answer

The Incredible Girlfriend

This is a story which may be very insignificant for the reader, but for me was one of the most surprising moments in my life.

It happened two years ago, when my friend Antonio phoned me to make a date. He wanted to introduced me his girlfriend. At the first moment, I was very surprised; I had never seen him with a woman. He has always been very timid with girls. He used to say that he was not successful among women because he was short and ugly.

> The day of the date arrived and I was waiting for my friend sitting at the closest table to the entrance of the pub. I was very impatient to know my friend's girlfriend. My impatience changed into amazement when I saw my friend entering the pub with one of the most beautiful girls I had ever seen. I became petrified when I realised that she was one of most famous top models in Spain. I had never been so surprised in all my life.
>
> By José Vicente Acín Barea

171 words

**Examiner's comment**

**Content:** The task is achieved in that the writer has written a story ending with the words given.

**Accuracy:** Good control of a variety of narrative tenses shown in the second and third paragraphs. Some minor inaccuracies, eg *He wanted (to) introduce(d) me (to) his girlfriend*, *At the first moment* instead of *At first*, the word order of *closest table*.

**Range:** The writer uses some ambitious language – *I was impatient to know*, *My impatience changed into amazement when …*

**Organization and cohesion:** Clear progression through the story indicated by tense use and time references – *It happened two years ago*, *The day of the date arrived*.

**Style and format:** Natural language use. Friendly tone.

**Target reader:** Very positive. The reader can easily follow the storyline.

**Mark:** good band 4

## Review 4 answers  Page 52

### Use of English:  Transformations
**FCE Part 4**

1 soon as the meeting had
2 the time we got to
3 once he had/was
4 leave until he (had) put
5 took to him
6 not to take him on
7 takes pride in

8 take much interest in
9 was so disappointed
10 was such a tiring

## Correcting mistakes

1 *had, during*
2 part, As for ~~as~~
3 that, of
4 when he ~~had~~ came, was
5 took ~~to~~ your advice, a

## Vocabulary: Cinema

| R | T | U | S | C | E | N | E | N | B |
|---|---|---|---|---|---|---|---|---|---|
| A | O | P | H | O | R | R | O | R | C |
| C | C | L | O | M | D | I | R | E | H |
| T | A | R | E | N | C | R | A | H | A |
| R | W | E | I | A | U | B | N | A | R |
| E | A | V | M | T | C | L | T | G | A |
| S | T | I | E | X | I | S | O | H | C |
| S | N | E | Y | F | A | C | R | F | T |
| A | C | W | M | C | P | L | O | T | E |
| S | B | T | H | R | I | L | L | E | R |

### Use of English:  Word formation
**FCE Part 3**

1 increasingly          6 motivated
2 disappointing         7 impressed
3 amazingly             8 surprised
4 Interestingly         9 astonishing
5 tired                 10 fascinating

## Workbook answers

### Reading: Multiple choice   Page 26

1  1 B        2 D        3 C        4 D
   5 A        6 C        7 C        8 B

2  a unequivical
   b seminal
   c dismissive
   d chilling
   e clumsy
   f literate
   g trendy
   h lofty

## Vocabulary, page 28

**A** Cinema and films

| | | | | | |
|---|---|---|---|---|---|
| 1 | cast | 2 | plot | 3 | make-up |
| 4 | scene | 5 | comedy | 6 | effects |
| 7 | part | 8 | stuntman | 9 | office |
| 10 | remake | 11 | soundtrack | | |

**B** Expressions with *take*

**1**
| | | | | | |
|---|---|---|---|---|---|
| 1 | interest | 2 | offence | 3 | pity |
| 4 | blame | 5 | care | 6 | notice |
| 7 | advice | 8 | joke | 9 | courage |
| 10 | risk | | | | |

**C** Phrasal verbs with *take*

| | | | | | |
|---|---|---|---|---|---|
| 1 | after | 2 | up | 3 | to |
| 4 | over | 5 | on | 6 | up |

## Language focus, page 29

**A** Tenses

**1**
1 had been living, started, was training, met
2 heard, phoned, had got, told, had taken
3 were watching, went, had forgotten
4 got, had eaten, had already left, were still dancing

**2**
| | | | | |
|---|---|---|---|---|
| 1 | told | 2 | had passed |
| 3 | took | 4 | were waiting |
| 5 | went | 6 | had finished |
| 7 | started | 8 | was holding |
| 9 | had got | 10 | had, driven |
| 11 | was sitting | 12 | was |

**B** *So* and *such*

1 so much homework
2 so few people
3 such delicious food (that)
4 such a good
5 so interested in the book

**C** Linking words

| | | | |
|---|---|---|---|
| 1 | for | 2 | As |
| 3 | In the end | 4 | at last |
| 5 | After | 6 | afterwards |

## Use of English, page 30

**Word formation**

| | | | |
|---|---|---|---|
| 1 | frightening | 2 | embarrassed |
| 3 | increasingly | 4 | tiring, exhausted |
| 5 | uninteresting | 6 | surprisingly |
| 7 | confused | 8 | annoying, unconvincing, impressed |

**Multiple-choice cloze**

| | | | | | | | |
|---|---|---|---|---|---|---|---|
| 1 | C | 2 | A | 3 | C | 4 | B |
| 5 | B | 6 | C | 7 | D | 8 | B |
| 9 | C | 10 | A | 11 | D | 12 | B |

## Writing, page 32

**1 b** **Advantages of book:**
Can read anywhere and at anytime/more entertainment from a book – lasts long time
**Advantages of a film version:**
Visual – makes story more memorable
Special effects – all scenes in book are possible
**Disadvantages of film:**
Film not always good interpretation
Film cuts and changes to story
**Disadvantages of book:**
Too much effort needed

**2 b**
1 Many people prefer going to **the** cinema
2 On the one hand,
3 books help **(to) develop** your imagination
4 You can decide what ~~do~~ the characters
5 the characters and places in the story **look** like
6 the enjoyment from a book lasts ~~more~~ longer
7 they **sometimes** cut
8 the most **interesting** parts
9 special effects are **so** good
10 ~~the~~ most scenes of a book
11 a book can ~~to~~ be shown
12 less effort **than** reading
13 it is **always** better
14 **Afterwards/After that** you can see it
15 if you want **to** compare

# 5 Doing your duty

## Content Overview

### Themes

This unit concerns itself with education at home or at school, household chores, being a parent and the world of work.

### Exam-related activities

| | |
|---|---|
| **Paper 1** | **Reading** |
| Part 3 | Multiple matching |
| | |
| **Paper 2** | **Writing** |
| Part 2 | Letters: An application |
| | |
| **Paper 3** | **Use of English** |
| Part 1 | Multiple-choice cloze |
| Part 2 | Open cloze (Review) |
| Part 3 | Word formation |
| | |
| **Paper 4** | **Listening** |
| Part 2 | Sentence completion |
| | |
| **Paper 5** | **Speaking** |
| Part 2 | Talking about photos |
| Part 3 | Collaborative task |

### Other

| | |
|---|---|
| Language focus: | Obligation, necessity and permission |
| Vocabulary: | Recording prepositions |
| | The world of work |
| Word formation: | Nouns and adjectives |
| Listening: | True/False |

 **Speaking: 1** FCE Part 2
### Talking about photos
Page 54

The first theme in this unit is home education. Refer students to the instructions in their books and elicit useful language for comparing photographs, eg
*Both pictures show ....*
*In the first picture .... whereas in the second one ....*
*There are some similarities, such as .... although .... etc*

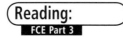 **Reading:** FCE Part 3
### Multiple matching
Page 54

Photocopiable vocabulary exercise on page 160.

**1–2** Encourage students to make a list of the advantages and disadvantages. Students then read the text quickly and compare answers as a class.

## Answers

### Advantages of home education
those mentioned in text

- no need to travel to school
- child receives more attention from teacher/parent
- child can learn at own pace
- more fun in certain subjects
- possibility of flexible timetable

Others
- more comfortable learning environment

### Disadvantages of home education

- child is isolated from other children
- child does not learn to work/play with others
- may suffer from overexposure to parents (and vice versa!)
- too many distractions at home (eg TV, toys, music, etc)
- parent may not be as knowledgeable/well qualified as teachers

### Disadvantages of learning at school
those mentioned in text

- have to travel to get to school
- can get bored
- slower learners can hold back stronger students
- child may be bullied
- timetables can be too rigid

Others
- quality of teaching not the same in all schools
- the school may be poorly resourced

### Advantages of learning at school

- school has better resources
- a variety of different teachers, each specialized in a particular subject
- child learns to work and play with others
- child learns discipline
- school is a preparation for the world of work

**3** Now, refer students to the exam task in their books and the 'Don't forget!' box.

## Answers

1 B  2 D  3 A  4 B  5 C  6 D  7 A
8/9 B, C in any order  10 D  11 A
12/13 B, C in any order  14 C  15 D

**Reacting to the text**
Students could work in pairs or groups for this stage or you could ask the questions to the group as a whole.

## Vocabulary 1: Recording prepositions
Refer students to the instructions in their books. To ensure that you have their attention and can reinforce how to record the expressions, copy the headings on to the board and add the expressions that students are asked to look for in the appropriate place (see below). Make sure that students also copy the relevant parts of sentences from the text as this will provide a useful guide to the meaning of the expressions.

## Answers

**Adjective + preposition**

Although she rapidly became bored *with* everything …

Home schooling is increasingly popular among parents fed up *with* bullying, etc.

Further examples: *critical of, necessary for, ahead of*

**Verb + preposition**

Cassie approves *of* this flexible regime.

Rhiannon … switches *to* maths.

Further examples: *opt for, withdraw from, work with*

**Noun + preposition**

… responsibility *for* ensuring that alternative arrangements are satisfactory does lie with local authorities.

Rhiannon may carry on with a subject she enjoys or is having problems *with*.

Further examples: *keep a check on, reason for, lack of, end of, package of*

**Preposition + Noun**

*On* average, home-schoolers are two years ahead of their schooled counterparts.

Now I can learn *at* my own pace.

Further examples: *on health grounds, at home, at work, at school*

## Language focus: Obligation, necessity and permission          Page 56

**1**  Refer students to the sentences (**a–h**) and the questions (**1–4**).

## Answers

**1**

1  g – can … listen

2  f – is not allowed to do        g – can't watch
   h – mustn't distract

3  a – have to catch     b – had to stay

4  c – do not have to follow
   d – do not need to tell       e – need not be

**2**

a  a teacher (to students)

b  one student to another

- *Must* expresses the authority of the speaker, ie the obligation comes from the teacher and it is the teacher who is imposing the obligation (the speaker's internal obligation).
- *have to* is used to show that the authority does not come from the speaker but from someone else ie the teacher (the speaker's external obligation).

**Common problems**

*Children have not to follow the …* instead of *Children **do** not have to follow the …*

This mistake is due to the fact that students often confuse *has/have* as main verb and *has/have* as auxiliary verb.

**Compare**

| | |
|---|---|
| *I **do** not **have** a car* | *have* as main verb, *do* as auxiliary verb |
| *I **have** not **seen** him* | *have* as auxiliary verb, *seen* as main verb |

**3**  This exercise contains many examples of common mistakes. Let students work through the sentences individually before comparing their answers together. Then refer students to pages 209 and 210 of the Grammar reference to check.

## Answers

1  I don't have to/don't need to tidy

2  Do you have to … ?/Must you … ?

3  Last week I had to go …

4  Were you allowed to watch … ?

5  Now I have to start

6  we don't have to wear a tie

7  you need to prepare

8  You really should go/You really must go

**4**  Before students attempt the two transformations ask them to tell you how the passive is formed. (The appropriate tense of the verb *to be* + past participle.)

This grammar area is fully dealt with in Unit 10.

## Answers

a  1  made to sound
   2  allowed to ('let' is not possible in the passive)

49

**b**
  **1** allowed to
  **2** let
  **3** makes/made

**5** This exercise provides a chance for students and teacher to find out if students have understood and can use the different forms correctly.

### Answers

**a**
| | | | |
|---|---|---|---|
| **1** | don't have to | **5** | must do |
| **2** | have to | **6** | mustn't |
| **3** | don't have to | **7** | have to |
| **4** | need to/have to | **8** | need to/have to |

**b** *Be supposed to* = should do because it is a rule or because it is expected.
*Had better* = should do because it is a good idea.

**6** Refer students to the instructions in their books.

### Answers

**1** wouldn't/didn't let me watch
**2** was made to
**3** can never do
**4** aren't we allowed to
**5** parents should smack
**6** don't need to hand
**7** had better tell
**8** are supposed to do

**7** To ensure that students have enough ideas you could elicit typical obligations and quickly put them on the board.

Other topics could include *in English classes, doing a favourite sport* (students could relate the language point to the rules of the game), *and visiting relatives.*

## Word formation: Nouns and adjectives
Page 58

Refer students to the introduction in their books or write up the nouns and elicit the adjectives.

**1** Students work in pairs or small groups, completing the table from previous knowledge then checking in their dictionaries. Alternatively, divide the class into groups and assign each group two or three of the verbs only. They fill in those parts of the table relating to their verbs, then work with

other students who have researched the other verbs and the students 'teach' each other.

### Answers

**1**
| Verb | Noun | Adjective |
|---|---|---|
| ignore | ignorance | ignorant |
| signify | significance | significant |
| appear | appearance | apparent |
| please | pleasure | pleasant |
| *confide* | *confidence* | *confident* |
| differ | difference | different |
| obey | obedience | obedient |
| depend | dependence | dependent* |

Note: *dependant* is a noun; your *dependants* are the people you support financially, usually your children.

**2 Opposite adjectives**
| | |
|---|---|
| intolerant | impatient |
| insignificant | disobedient |
| unpleasant | independent |

*Indifferent* can also be formed, but this is not the opposite of *different*.
Adverbs are formed by adding *-ly* to the adjective, eg *impatiently, obediently.*

Use of English 1: | FCE Part 3 | **Word formation**
Page 58

Before students start, write the following gist question on the board and ask them to read through quickly, ignoring the gaps, to answer it:

*Has the boy changed for the better or for the worse in the writer's opinion?* (Answer – for the better)

Then ask students to read through again and decide what part of speech is necessary for each gap, before completing the text with the correct word.

### Answers

| | | | |
|---|---|---|---|
| **1** | pleasantly (adv) | **6** | appearance (n) |
| **2** | significantly (adv) | **7** | confidence (n) |
| **3** | disobedient (adj) | **8** | resistance (n) |
| **4** | pleasure (n) | **9** | Apparently (adv) |
| **5** | importance (n) | **10** | independence (n) |

Listing 1: **True/False** Page 59

**1** Students discuss the questions in pairs.

**2** Play the recording twice, pausing between listenings to give students time to compare answers together before they listen for the second time. Note that this is one of only two non-exam-style listening tasks in this book (the other is in Unit 6.) There is no true/false task in Paper 4 of the First Certificate examination.

| Answers |
|---|
| 1 F  2 T  3 F  4 F  5 T  6 T  7 F |

### Listening 1: Listening script 1.22

**Richard:** Right, let's see, jobs and duties. Where shall we begin?

**Louise:** Let's talk about washing up first. Now that's something I really can't stand. My mum makes me do it after every meal at the weekend, and she won't let me go out with my friends until I've done it. I just think that's so unfair. I mean, none of my friends have to do it. I bet you don't either, do you?

**Richard:** No, you're right. In fact, no one in my family does. The most I have to do is get the plates out of the dishwasher.

**Louise:** Oh ... Lucky you! I wish we had one. And what about cleaning shoes? You have a machine to do that as well, I suppose?

**Richard:** Unfortunately not. If it was left up to me, I wouldn't bother. But my dad says that shoes tell you a lot about a person, so he has me brushing and polishing every other day. It's such a pain.

**Louise:** Oh ... Same here. I'm not made to do it that often, but I still dread having to do it.

**Richard:** Right, so that could be one of our three. What's next?

**Louise:** Well, I honestly can't understand why clothes shopping is there. That's no chore for me. I mean I could spend all day popping in and out of shops. But going to buy food – now that's completely different.

**Richard:** I can't bear doing either of them. In fact, even talking about them makes me feel funny. Shall we move on?

**Louise:** OK. What do you feel about ... visiting relatives?

**Richard:** Oh that's not so bad. I've got a pretty small family so it doesn't happen that often. And I get on really well with my grandparents, the ones that are still alive, that is. In fact, one of my granddads is a real laugh, and I think he enjoys my company when I go to see him, now that he's on his own. How about you?

**Louise:** Well, I suppose I'm a bit lazy really. My parents both say I should go and see my grandparents more often, but they live so far away ... I always make sure I'm in when they come to see us, and they come round quite a lot, so I don't feel as though I need to go and see them. I don't think my mum and dad agree, though.

**Richard:** Oh well, that's relatives for you. Let's have a look at the next one.

**Louise:** What about looking after animals? Have you got any pets?

**Richard:** I've got a couple of fish, but they're not really that much trouble. You just have to change their water once a week, and drop some food into their tank every now and then. But you've got a dog, haven't you?

**Louise:** Ugh ... Yeah, don't remind me. Every morning he's there by the front door with his lead in his mouth, looking up at me with his big eyes, as if to say; 'Come on, it's that time again'. And if I ignore him, he starts barking, and my dad gets angry and says, 'He's your dog, no one else wanted one, so you've got to take responsibility for him'. Thanks, Dad. You're a great help.

**Richard:** Bad luck. Get a fish next time.

**Louise:** Oh, I love him really. Anyway, what have we decided so far?

**Richard:** Well, we both seem to agree on cleaning shoes, and neither of us likes shopping for food. So that leaves one more. I can't talk about cleaning the car, 'cause we haven't got one.

**Louise:** And my dad won't let any of us go anywhere near his. I think he's frightened we might scratch it, or something, so he takes it to the local car wash. That's fine by me.

**Richard:** And if you tell me you like tidying your room, I just won't believe you.

**Louise:** Well I think we've found the third one ... I absolutely ...

## Speaking: FCE Part 3 — Collaborative task
Page 59

Refer students to the instructions and the information in the box but do not let them start talking until they have read the tips in the 'How to go about it' box.

### In future speaking activities
Whenever possible and appropriate, remind students to use these expressions when they are speaking together. At first, they may be reluctant to do so but insist. Only by using the expressions will they become part of the students' active language.

| Answers |
|---|
| The expressions heard in the recording are: |
| *Where shall we begin?* |
| *Let's talk about ... first.* |
| *So, that could be one of our three.* |
| *Shall we move on?* |
| *Let's have a look at the next one.* |
| *What have we decided (so far)?* |
| *We both seem to agree on ...* |

## Vocabulary 2: The world of work Page 60

**1** Much of this vocabulary comes up in Listening 2 and the Multiple-choice cloze. The emphasis is on expressions rather than individual words.

Point out to students that the uncountable word *work* can also be used with the verbs in 1a. Refer students to the instructions in their books.

Ask your students questions to check that they have understood the differences in meaning, eg:

Q: *One of these verbs means it is your decision to leave. Which one?*
A: *Resigned*
Q: *Which verbs means you have done something wrong?*
A: *Sacked*

| Answers |
|---|

**1a**

| | | | |
|---|---|---|---|
| **1** | *be out of a job* | **4** | go for an interview |
| **2** | look for a job | | for a job |
| **3** | apply for a job | **5** | get a job |

**b**

**1** made redundant
**2** resigned
**3** sacked

**2** The noun *career* is a false friend in some languages. This means that it looks the same as a word in the student's own language but it has a different meaning in English.

| Answers |
|---|

**a** *study* a career is **not** possible
**b** *earn* a competition is **not** possible

**3** You could ask the group as a whole if anyone knows the differences in meaning or you could give a definition (see below) and see if the students can identify the expression being defined.

| Answers |
|---|

*to work shifts* – work for a set period (eg 12am to 8am) before workers replace you for the next set period (eg 8am to 4pm)

*to work long hours* – work for many hours each day

*to work overtime* – work supplementary hours for which you are paid extra

*to work flexitime* – work with a flexible timetable: within limits you decide when you start and when you finish as long as you work the required total number of hours each month

*to work full-time* – when you are contracted to work the entire time appropriate to that job, eg 35 hours per week (a full-time job)

*to work part-time* – when you are contracted to work fewer hours than the entire time appropriate eg 21 hours per week (a part-time job)

**4–5** Refer students to the photographs in their books and the instructions.

| Answers |
|---|

waitress, hairdresser, surgeon, dustman, hotel receptionist

 **Listening 2:**
**FCE Part 2**

**Sentence completion**
Page 60

Photocopiable exercise on page 161.

Refer students to the instructions in their books and to the sentences in the 'Don't forget!' box.

| Answers |
|---|

- You *don't need* to write more than three words for each answer.
- You *should* write a word or phrase that you actually hear.
- You *don't need* to rephrase.
- Minor spelling errors *can* be made, but the words you write *need* to be recognizable so you *should* check your spelling.
- You *can* expect to hear the answers in the same order as the questions.

Before students start listening, give them 30 or 45 seconds (as in the exam) to read through the sentences they have to complete. When they have finished refer them to the instructions in their books. Encourage them to predict what kind of information they are likely to hear.

Play the recording twice and let students compare their answers together between each listening.

## Answers

1  academic qualifications
2  minimum height
3  back and legs
4  four
5  four days off
6  wear full uniform
7  fire engines
8  the evening
9  several hours
10 very satisfying

### Listening 2: Listening script 1.23

**I = Interviewer**
**AN = Allan Nicholls**

**I:** With us today on 'All in a Day's Work' we have Allan Nicholls, station officer at Hove Fire Station, who's here to talk about the job of the much-respected firefighter. Allan, the first thing I'd like to ask you is about the selection procedure. What do you have to do in order to become a firefighter?

**AN:** Well, as you can imagine, it's a fairly rigorous process, with a variety of different tests. Whilst we don't insist on any academic qualifications, potential recruits do have to undergo a short educational test, aimed at assessing … basic literacy and numeracy, or in other words, reading, writing and arithmetic.

Surprisingly for some, you no longer have to be a minimum height. Instead, there are a series of physical tests, designed to measure such things as how tightly they can grip things, or whether their back and legs are sufficiently strong. If they get through this stage, they go on to the next one, the practical awareness day, which involves fitness tests, checks to see if claustrophobia is a problem, and practical tasks such as ladder climbing.

**I:** And are women accepted into the force?

**AN:** Ah yes, indeed, though they are still very much in the minority. At the moment here at Hove we have four women on the workforce.

**I:** Now, firefighters are obviously on call 24 hours a day, but perhaps you could tell us how the shift system operates?

**AN:** Well, there's an eight-day rota. A firefighter works two nine-hour day shifts, followed by two 15-hour night shifts. And then of course we get four days off before … starting again. It's a continuous cycle.

**I:** And what characterizes a typical shift?

**AN:** We always begin with the Watch Parade, which is where one shift finishes and the next begins. This is a fairly formal affair and it's compulsory for everyone to wear full uniform. And then once the various jobs have been detailed for the shift, there are equipment checks. The breathing apparatus, for example, is a vital piece of equipment and lives can depend on it, so, it's essential that this and everything else is maintained in perfect working order. Nothing escapes attention, including, of course, the fire engines which also have to be checked from top to bottom. And then after that, if we're not called out to a fire there's the routine work which is programmed into the day. That can be anything from training to the more everyday jobs of cleaning and maintenance. Fitness, of course, is extremely important, so we also have a kind of mini gym where we work out every day.

**I:** Many listeners have phoned in saying they would like to know when your busiest period is.

**AN:** Well, we don't really have a 'busiest period,' despite the fact that most people might think it's November 5th, Guy Fawkes night. We do, however, tend to be busier in the evening, rather than during the day. That's the time when shops and other business premises are left unattended and also when most people are at home, cooking and so on, and, as you might expect, the majority of fires are domestic ones.

It's worth pointing out that the fires themselves often take only minutes to put out, whereas clearing up afterwards can take several hours. We have to do everything necessary to prevent the danger of a fire re-igniting, so that means taking all the floors up, getting flammable things like carpets out of the building, and so on.

**I:** Fire-fighting is obviously dangerous work, Allan. Do you ever feel fear?

**AN:** Any firefighter who said that he had never felt frightened would be fooling himself and you. But it's all a matter of control. It's what we've been trained for, and we learn to control feelings such as fear. But rather than the danger and the drama of the job, it's very satisfying being out on the street, knowing that you're helping the public. There's also the camaraderie which goes with working as part of a team. I certainly don't think I'd be able to do any other job.

## Use of English 2: Multiple-choice cloze
**FCE Part 1**  Page 61

Refer students to the instructions in their books, the example and the general comprehension question. Tell students to cover up the choices below when they read for the first time.

### Answer

Despite the stress, he is proud of his new career and achievements.

**A possible approach to the Multiple-choice cloze**

Students use a sheet of paper to cover the choices in numbers 1 to 12. As they read, they note down what word they would put without referring to the choices. For those gaps that they do not know, they leave a blank. When they have finished, they remove the paper and reveal the choices given. If one of the choices corresponds with what they have already thought of, it may well be correct. For those that they did not know, they should make a guess.

## Answers

| 1 | D | 2 | B | 3 | A | 4 | C |
|---|---|---|---|---|---|---|---|
| 5 | A | 6 | C | 7 | B | 8 | C |
| 9 | B | 10 | A | 11 | A | 12 | C |

## Writing: FCE Part 2

### Letters: An application Page 62

Before referring students to the information in their books, write the first part of the advertisement on the board:

> We are looking for
> Camp Helpers
> to work in the UK on one of our
> International Summer Camps

Elicit from the students the kind of person that would be suitable for the job and any other information they think would be important to consider, eg relevant experience, duties and activities, age, etc.

**1** Refer students to the advertisement in their books and compare their ideas with the ones contained here.

## Answers

**2** The applicant satisfies the requirements for the job and seems very suitable. He addresses all the points in the advertisement (and the exam question) and 'sells himself' very well. The effect on the target reader (ie camp organizer or personnel officer) would be very positive.

**3**
a I would like to apply for the job of Camp Helper
b I like working with children very much and I would enjoy the challenge of organizing activities

for them on one of your camps and I am therefore very keen to improve my language skills in an English-speaking country before I go to university.
c I like working with children and I feel I have the necessary patience and energy to make a positive and enthusiastic contribution to your camps
d For the past seven years I have attended summer camps in my country with the scouts and last year I helped to run a number of events, including an orienteering competition and a kite-making workshop.
e In October I will be starting a degree course in English.
f Sports – basketball, tennis, Outdoor pursuits: – orienteering, Other – guitar
g I have just finished school
h I hope you will consider my application favourably. I am available for interview at any time and look forward to hearing from you soon.

**4–5** Refer students to the Writing task instructions and the questions on page 200 and 201 of the Coursebook.

## Answers

**1** The register of the letter is not consistently formal, and the degree of informality of some of the language would have a negative effect on the target reader. The tone of the direct questions sounds rather rude.

**2** Revised letter with suggested paragraphing.
**Paragraph 1:** Reason for writing
**Paragraph 2:** Relevant skills
**Paragraph 3:** Relevant experience
**Paragraph 4:** Reason for applying and questions about the work
Closing comments

Dear Sir or Madam,
**c) I am writing to express an interest in** the job I saw advertised in the publication 'Summer jobs in the UK'.

**h) I am 25 years old** and I (have) recently completed a short course on garden design. My level of English is intermediate and **f) I have a good knowledge of gardening**. I am particularly interested in the cultivation of roses and the use of trees in lanscape design.

**a) As you will see from my curriculum vitae d) I have a great deal of experience. j) This includes a temporary position** on a campsite similar to those mentioned in your advertisement. **g) I enclose a reference from my previous employer.**

I like being part of a team and **i) I would enjoy the experience of working abroad.** I would be interested to know how many hours I would be expected to work each day. Could you also tell me how long the contract would be for? **e) I will be available to work from** the beginning of June.

**b) I look forward to receiving your reply.**

Yours faithfully

**6** Refer students to the instructions and the advice in the 'Don't forget!' box. When you are marking, pay special attention to, and comment on, how well or otherwise students have taken into account the advice given. The writing could be done for homework.

---

### Sample answer

Dear Sir

I would like to apply for the post of reception assistant for the coastal campsite as advertised in ABC on 25 April.

After reading the advertisement I feel I have the qualifications and relevant experience to work at the campsite.

As you can see in my CV I have studied phychology and I speak English and French fluently. In addition to this I have been working 5 years in a hotel. Moreover I have a great deal of experience with customers and I am acostumed to work very hard. I enclose a reference from my previous employer, the hotel manager Pepe Pérez.

Besides I would like to you to provide me more details about the date I would start to work, how long the contract is and how much a reception assistant earns at the campsite.

Finally I'm available for an interview at any time and look forward to hearing from you soon.

Mayte Zamora Díaz

156 words

---

**Examiner's comment**

**Content:** No reference made to 'working hours' but all other points covered. In a Part 2 task such as this, failure to cover all points in the question is not penalized quite so heavily as missing out elements in a Part 1 task. However, other factors in the candidate's writing must be dealt with reasonably well for the candidate not to lose marks.

**Accuracy:** Generally accurate. Minor spelling mistakes, eg – *phychology* (slip?), *acostumed*, as well as in more complex language attempts, eg *I am acostumed to work* instead of *accustomed to working* and in the fourth paragraph *I would (to) like you to provide me* (with) *more details*.

**Range:** Quite a good range of vocabulary and structures relevant to the task – *qualifications and relevant experience*, *I enclose a reference*, and correct word order in the indirect questions (fourth paragraph).

**Organization and cohesion:** Generally appropriate with the exception of the position of *Besides*.

**Style and format:** Appropriate, although should avoid the use of contractions in this kind of writing.

**Target reader:** The reader would understand why the writer thinks she is suitable for the job.

**Mark:** borderline band 3/4

### Review 5 answers  Page 64

**Use of English:** FCE Part 2  **Open cloze: Prepositions**

How does talking to babies and young children benefit them? (*It increases their intelligence.*)

What is one of the main obstacles to a child's progress, according to the text? (*television*)

| 1 about/on | 2 with | 3 without | 4 in |
|---|---|---|---|
| 5 on | 6 on | 7 of | 8 of/about |
| 9 for | 10 with | 11 of | 12 on |

### Word formation

1 **differ (v)**

different (adj)    differently (adv)
difference (n)    indifferent (adj)
indifferently (adv)    indifference (n)
differentiate (v)

**2 appear (v)**
apparent (adj)          apparently (adv)
appearance (n)          disappear (v)
disappearance (n)

**3 frequent (adj)**
frequently (adv)        infrequent (adj)
infrequently (adv)      frequency (n)
infrequency (n)

**4 please (v)**
pleased (adj)           pleasing (adj)
pleasingly (adv)        pleasant (adj)
pleasantly (adv)        pleasure (n)
displease (v)           displeased (adj)
displeasing (adj)       displeasingly (adv)
displeasure (n)         pleasurable (adj)

**5 tolerate (v)**
tolerant (adj)          tolerantly (adv)
intolerant (adj)        intolerantly (adv)
tolerable (adj)         tolerably (adv)
intolerable (adj)       intolerably (adv)
tolerance (n)           intolerance (n)
toleration (n)

## Vocabulary: The world of work

| | | | | | |
|---|---|---|---|---|---|
| 1 | get | 2 | sack | 3 | career |
| 4 | sense | 5 | company | 6 | apply |
| 7 | shift | 8 | devote | 9 | skills |
| 10 | running | 11 | wage | 12 | earn a living |

## Modal verbs

**1** C   **2** B   **3** B   **4** C   **5** A   **6** B   **7** A
**8** C

---

## Workbook answers

## Reading: multiple matching   Page 34

| 1 | 1 E | 2 B | 3 A | 4 D | 5 F |
|---|-----|-----|-----|-----|-----|
| | 6 C/E | 7 C/E | 8 B | 9 E | 10 A |
| | 11 C/D | 12 C/D | 13 E | 14 C/F | 15 C/F |

**2**  1  player
      2  computer
      3  simulator
      4  supervisor
      5  manager
      6  instructor

**3**  1  scanner          6  demonstrator
      2  calculator       7  competitor
      3  adviser/advisor  8  photocopier
      4  inventor         9  researcher
      5  presenter       10  spectator

## Vocabulary, page 36

**A Jobs crossword**

| Across | | Down | |
|--------|--|------|--|
| 1 | dustman | 2 | teacher |
| 6 | baker | 3 | waitress |
| 8 | hairdresser | 4 | lawyer |
| 9 | chef | 5 | butcher |
| 11 | accountant | 7 | surgeon |
| | | 10 | vet |

**B Questions and answers**

| 1 | 1 e | 2 g | 3 a | 4 c |
|---|-----|-----|-----|-----|
| | 5 f | 6 h | 7 b | 8 d |

**2**  judge, politician, company director
      (other answers may be acceptable)

**C Expressions with *work***
1  worked, overtime
2  worked for myself
3  to work long hours
4  working part-time, working full-time
5  to work flexitime
6  works shifts
7  working my way up

## Language focus   Page 37

**Obligation, necessity and permission**
**1**  1  should/need to
      2  have to/need to
      3  need to
      4  must
      5  Do we have to/Should we
      6  had to
      7  must, to have to
      8  must/should

**2**  1  *can, must*
      2  shouldn't, must
      3  can, can't
      4  needn't, must
      5  can, should
      6  can't, must

## Use of English   Page 38

**Transformations**
1  are not/aren't allowed to smoke
2  are they supposed to
3  had/'d better not drink
4  ought to have/show more
5  won't/don't let me stay
6  used to make me tidy
7  was made to clean

## Word formation

| | | | |
|---|---|---|---|
| 1 | assistant | 2 | exciting |
| 3 | advertisement | 4 | patience |
| 5 | ability | 6 | annoyed |
| 7 | carefully | 8 | being |
| 9 | confidence | 10 | learner |
| 11 | Unfortunately | 12 | intolerant |
| 13 | angry | 14 | satisfying |

## Open cloze

| | | | | | | | |
|---|---|---|---|---|---|---|---|
| 1 | as | 2 | a | 3 | made | 4 | had |
| 5 | our | 6 | take | 7 | up | 8 | us |
| 9 | get | 10 | at | 11 | there | 12 | as |

## Writing    Page 40

**1 a** No – apart from *A woman was speaking* and *they wouldn't know*, everything is in the past simple.

**b** No – basic vocabulary and some words (*couldn't, nice, phone, speak*) are repeated.

**c** No – only *and* (6 times), *then* and *but*. Most sentences are very short.

**d** No – the story is written as only one paragraph.

**2**

I was beginning to feel a little nervous. It was my first day **(1)** <u>as the personal assistant to a company director</u>. I **(2)** <u>had claimed at the interview</u> that I could speak French but **(3)** <u>it wasn't true</u>. I hoped they wouldn't **(4)** <u>find out</u> that I **(5)** <u>had been lying</u>.

**At first** everything went well. My boss was very **(6)** <u>helpful</u> and he **(7)** <u>explained to</u> me what I had to do. **Then** he introduced me to **(8)** <u>my colleagues</u>, **who** were all very **(9)** <u>friendly</u>. **Just as** I was sitting down at my desk the phone rang.

**As soon as** I **(10)** <u>picked up the receiver</u> I started to panic. A woman was speaking to me in French and **naturally**, I couldn't understand **(11)** <u>a word she was saying</u>. **When** the boss saw **(12)** <u>how upset I</u> <u>was</u>, he took the phone from me.

**To my surprise** he **(13)** <u>answered</u> the woman in English and then he **(14)** <u>burst out</u> laughing. **Afterwards** he told me it was his mother. She **(15)** <u>had just been to</u> the dentist's and **(16)** <u>was having</u> difficulty speaking properly. She **(17)** <u>had been talking</u> to me in English not French!

**3** The answer to all four questions, **a–d**, is now Yes.

## Content Overview

### Themes

This unit is about relationships within and outside the family. Students also review and extend their vocabulary related to describing people.

### Exam-related activities

| | | |
|---|---|---|
| **Paper 1** | **Reading** | |
| Part 3 | Multiple matching | |
| | | |
| **Paper 2** | **Writing** | |
| Part 2 | Descriptions | |
| | | |
| **Paper 3** | **Use of English** | |
| | Open cloze | |
| Part 4 | Transformations (Review) | |
| | | |
| **Paper 4** | **Listening** | |
| Part 3 | Multiple matching | |
| | | |
| **Paper 5** | **Speaking** | |
| Part 1 | Interview | |
| Part 3 | Collaborative task | |

### Other

Language focus 1: *Too* and *enough*
Language focus 2: Defining relative clauses
Language focus 3: Non-defining relative clauses
Vocabulary:    Phrasal verbs
            *Have* including causative *have*
            Describing people
Listening:    Stated/not stated
Reading:    Rock of Ages

**Reading:**
FCE Part 3

### Multiple matching
Page 66

Photocopiable vocabulary exercise on page 161.

Refer students to the picture in their books and ask some questions to get the students thinking about the theme, eg

*What do you think the relationships are? How do they feel? Why?*

Write the title *Family mealtimes* on the board and elicit students' associations.
Here are some ideas:
*conversation, television, arguments, food, drink, table manners, asking permission to leave the table, telephone ringing ...*

Now refer them to the instructions and the first piece of advice in the 'How to go about it' box. When students have finished reading, ask them if any of their associations were in the text and if so, which ones. Now, refer students to the rest of the advice.

| Answers |
|---|
| **1** A  **2** B  **3** E  **4** A  **5/6** A, C in any order |
| **7** D  **8** B  **9/10** A, E in any order |
| **11** C  **12** D  **13/14** C, A in any order   **15** B |

### Reacting to the text

Depending on your group and their ages, you may like to write up the first two questions in the past tense or simply tell students to adapt the questions to their own situations. If you have any students in your class who have studied English abroad or who have experience of living with a family abroad ask them to tell their group or the class any differences they noticed at mealtimes.

## Language focus 1: *Too* and *enough*

Page 68

### Common problems

- Some students confuse *too* with *very/really*, eg 'The film was too good', 'The book was too interesting'.
  *Too* has a negative connotation, as can be seen from the examples in the Practice transformation exercise in the Coursebook.
- 'I don't have money enough' is a common word order mistake, which the analysis and practice in the student's book should clarify.

**1–3** Students work individually, looking at the sentences and choosing the correct alternative in the rules in exercise 2.

| Answers |
|---|
| **2**  **a** adjectives and adverbs |
|     **b** nouns |
|     **c** before |
|     **d** after |
| **3** The structure of the sentence after *too* and *enough* is (+ *for* + object) + infinitive with *to*. |

### Practice

**1–2** Students work individually. Encourage them to write sentences that are true for them.

| Answers |
|---|
| **2** |
| **1** too quietly for me to |
| **2** not tall enough to |
| **3** are not enough eggs to |
| **4** is too much sugar |
| **5** there were too many |

## Vocabulary 1: Phrasal verbs

Page 68

### A Romance

**1** Students at this level may recognize some of these verbs. Refer students to the instructions in their books.

| Answers |
|---|
| **1** |
| **1** c  **2** e  **3** a  **4** b  **5** f  **6** d |
| **2** |
| **1** to fall out with somebody |
| **2** to split up with somebody |
| **3** to be going out with somebody |
| **4** to get on with somebody |
| **5** to fall for somebody |
| **6** to get over somebody |

### B Family

**1–2** Refer students to the instructions. Let students work individually and then compare together once they have finished.

| Answers |
|---|
| **1**  **1** to raise a child |
|     **2** to become an adult |
|     **3** to do things you know you shouldn't |
|     **4** to reprimand somebody |
|     **5** to respect somebody |
|     **6** to disappoint somebody |
| **2**  **1** to bring somebody up |
|     **2** to grow up |
|     **3** to get up to something |
|     **4** to tell somebody off |
|     **5** to look up to somebody |
|     **6** to let somebody down |

### Common problems

Point out to students that *bring up* is a transitive verb and can be used both in the passive and the active.

eg Active    *Rachel brought the children up.*
   Passive   *The children were brought up by*
             *Rachel.*

*Grow up*, on the other hand, is intransitive and cannot be used in the passive.

eg Active    *I grew up in Brighton.*
   Passive   (not possible)

Also point out *bring up* does not mean educate.

## Speaking 1: FCE Part 3    Collaborative task
Page 69

In the First Certificate exam candidates are allowed approximately three minutes for this. Ideally, students should work in pairs or groups of three for this activity. Give them time to think of which phrasal verbs they want to use. Then ask students to look back at Unit 5 as indicated in their instructions in order to choose useful expressions.

## Listening 1: FCE Part 3    Multiple matching
Page 70

Photocopiable vocabulary exercise on page 162.

**1** Refer students to the pictures and questions in their books. When students are discussing the pictures, encourage them to use the following expressions and verbs by putting on the board:

… *look(s) as if* …
… *look(s) like* …
… *must be* …
… *can't be* …

eg
'They *look as if* they get on well.'
'They don't *look like* each other.'
'They *can't be* twins because …' etc.

**2** Refer students to the instructions for the listening in their books and the advice in the 'How to go about it' box.

Note that students are told to listen carefully *both times*. Emphasize this point and tell them to:

• write down what they think the answer is on the first playing of the recording
• check their answers on the second playing, listening to all of what the speaker says and making sure they are not being misled by distractors.

**Note:** The word *teased* may be unknown by students and may therefore need to be pre-taught.

## Answers

1 D   2 F   3 E   4 C   5 A

---

### Listening 1: Listening script 1.24–1.28

**Speaker 1**
My sister was always going out alone on her bike and she'd spend hours cycling along the country lanes. She'd come home with blackberries she'd picked and tales of wild rabbits she'd seen. I couldn't understand how anyone could get so excited about a rabbit. She went on to live on a farm and milked cows for a living. I left home when I was 16 and moved into a flat with a boy who played drums in a punk band. My parents were really upset. I had my hair cut really short and wore clothes that got all the neighbours talking. We're still both like chalk and cheese.

**Speaker 2**
She'd do anything just to be different. That often caused a lot of friction in the family, and I know our parents had a really hard time. If the atmosphere got a bit tense I'd try to smooth things over. I was always there for my sister. Mum and Dad used to get really mad about the way she lived her life, but I'd always make excuses for her. And if she ever got into trouble I never told them the whole truth. I don't think they know half of what she got up to.

**Speaker 3**
When we first started school my sister used to get teased a lot because of her skin colour. It was never anything unpleasant or spiteful – just silly name-calling, mostly. In fact, it never seemed to affect her and she just ignored it all. She's always been very tough, my sister – determined to get on with her life without letting anyone or anything else bother her, and I've always looked up to her for that. I'm far too sensitive, by comparison. Even then, when we were at school, instead of rushing to protect her, I used to burst into tears every time someone started making fun of her. Silly, really.

**Speaker 4**
We might be twins but our characters are very different – I'm much more confident and outgoing, for one thing, and she's fairly quiet and shy. We don't share the same taste in music, we have different interests, and we also argue a lot, but then I think most brothers and sisters do, don't they? In our case it's because we want to be better than each other, at sports, at school and even at getting boyfriends. When people see us fighting they immediately think we don't get on with each other, but nothing could be further from the truth

**Speaker 5**
She always liked dressing up and putting on loads of make-up. When we were kids she always wore the shortest mini-skirts and she smelt like a perfume factory. She used to make fun of me because I was so plain and unconcerned about my appearance, and she laughed openly at my clothes. It never bothered me though. I knew I couldn't compete with her looks so I just laughed back. I called her 'Alexis' after that woman in one of those 70s soap operas on the telly.

**3** Refer students to the question below their listening task. This task is designed to stimulate discussion and so there is not a clear match for all of the speakers.

### Possible answers

Speaker 3: the girl on the left of the first photo
Speaker 4: one of the girls in the second photo
Speaker 5: the woman on the right in the third photo

## Speaking 2: Interview Page 70
**FCE Part 1**

Refer students to the instructions and advice in their books. Encourage students to ask further follow-up questions.

## Language focus 2: Defining relative clauses Page 71

**1–3** Refer students to the sentences in their books and/or write the sentences on the board.

### Answers

**1** in the first sentence – *that*
in the second sentence – *which*

They cannot be omitted because they are the subject of the verb in the relative clause.

**2** 'She'd come back with **blackberries** (that/ which) **she**'d picked and tales of **wild rabbits** (that/which) **she**'d seen.'
Note: In these sentences, the subject of the verbs *in italics* is **she**; the underlined relative pronouns are the object of the verbs in italics in the relative clauses. They can be omitted.

**3** The first sentence is more formal.
The relative pronoun can be omitted in the second sentence.

**4** Students complete the sentences individually and then compare their answers in pairs.

### Answers

**a** where **b** why **c** when **d** whose

**Practice**
Students complete the sentences in pairs.

### Answers

| | | | |
|---|---|---|---|
| **1** where/in which (formal) | | **2** that/which | |
| **3** whose | | **4** that/which/ – | |
| **5** who/that | | **6** that/which | |
| **7** that/which/ – | | **8** when/ – | |

## Reading Page 71

Students read the text quickly and answer the questions. Students could answer the follow-up questions in small groups or you could ask the questions yourself.

### Answers

Parents and children. They go dancing.
**a** You have something in common with your parent, you can talk about it.
**b** It brings back memories of his own youth. He probably understands his son better.

## Vocabulary 2: *Have* Page 72

**A Expressions with *have***
**1** Refer students to the example in their books and the instructions.

### Answers

to have:  some fun
a relationship with someone
something in common
a(n) (unique) insight into something

**2** Refer students to the instructions and prompts in their books which all contain expressions using *have*. Give students time to work individually and think about their answers. Encourage them to use full sentences when they speak together. Remind students to give reasons for their answers.

**3** This exercise gives practice of expressions with *have* and also introduces some natural uses of causative *have*, which will be focused on in section B. Ask students to work individually or in pairs to complete the exercise.

## Answers

1 a scarf/a book
2 a scarf
3 a tooth (causative *have*)
4 hair (causative *have*)
5 something private
6 a headache

**4** Discuss sentences **1–6** with the group. Give students five minutes to think up a short dialogue.

### B Causative *have*

## Answers

1  1  **a** She wants to dye her hair red (by herself).
    **b** She wants to have her hair dyed red (by someone else).

   2  **a** He took a photo of his daughter (himself).
    **b** He had a photo taken of his daughter (by someone else).

'To use this structure we need the appropriate form of the verb *to have* + the object + the past participle of the main verb.'
Grammar reference for more information.

2
1  *to have, shaved*
2  having, taken
3  to have, pierced
4  had, filled
5  having, cut
6  has had, broken

**3** Refer students to the instructions in their books. Encourage them to develop their answers.

## Language focus 3: Non-defining relative clauses
Page 73

**1** Refer students to sentences **a** and **b** in their books. Give students time to read through the explanation in their books.

## Answers

The correct alternatives are:
**a** *who* or *which* cannot be replaced by *that*
**b** the relative pronoun cannot be omitted
**c** commas are used

**Practice**
Students work individually. Remind them to add commas.

## Answers

1  We spent the weekend in York, where my mother was born.
2  My best friend, who always said she wanted to stay single, has just got married.
3  My oldest sister, whose husband is Greek, lives in Thessaloniki.
4  We're having our holiday in September, when everywhere is a lot less crowded.
5  His daughter borrowed the car, which he wasn't very happy about.

## Open cloze: Relative clauses
Page 73

Refer students to the instructions.

## Answers

| | | |
|---|---|---|
| 1 which | 2 that/which | 3 who |
| 4 that/which/ – | 5 whose | 6 where |
| 7 when/ – | 8 which/that | |

## Vocabulary 3: Describing people
Page 74

### A Personality
**1** Students work in pairs to divide the adjectives into positive and negative groups.

## Answers

**Positive:** sociable, reliable, sincere, cheerful, polite, tolerant, patient, decisive, mature, sensible, adventurous, practical, sensitive

**Negative:** bad-tempered, lazy, selfish, moody, mean

**2** Students could work on this together, sharing their knowledge and using dictionaries or the teacher as a resource.

## Answers

**-un:** unsociable, unadventurous, unselfish/selfless, unreliable
**-in:** intolerant, insincere, indecisive, insensitive
**-im:** impatient, impolite/rude, impractical, immature

different word: mean/generous, cheerful/miserable, sensible/silly *or* foolish, bad-tempered/sweet-tempered *or* calm, lazy/hard-working, selfish/selfless, moody/even-tempered

**3** Refer students to the instructions in their books. Stress that they should give examples to illustrate their descriptions.

**B Appearance**
Refer students to the pictures in their books. To find out what kind of language your students naturally use when describing people, ask them to describe one or two of the people, either in pairs with you monitoring closely to listen or in front of the group so that the others can hear and contribute.

**1** Students work together or individually. Elicit answers to the question below from the group as a whole so that you can deal with problems as they come up.

### Answers

**1** *bald  **2** pierced  **3** thinning  **4** well-built
* We can say *he is bald* but not *he has bald hair*.

**2** Students discuss the differences in connotations.

### Answers

**a**  All the adjectives describe weighing too much.
*Fat* has negative connotations in many parts of the world.
*Plump* is more positive and can mean either weighing a little too much or can be used as a 'polite' way of describing someone who is fat.
*Overweight* is descriptive and of the three, is the most neutral.
**b**
*Thin* means having little fat on the body; it is descriptive and neutral.
*Slim* means being attractively thin and has positive connotations.
*Skinny* means being unattractively thin and has negative connotations.

---

**Writing:** **FCE Part 2**   **Descriptions**   Page 75

**1** Refer students to the writing task instructions.

**2** You may need to remind students that they are listening for things which are said or not. The words they hear in the recording are different from the words written in their task.

This is the second of only two non-exam-style listening tasks in this book (the first is in Unit 5). There is no stated/not stated task in Paper 4 of the First Certificate examination.

### Answers

**1** ✓  **2** ✗  **3** ✗  **4** ✓  **5** ✗  **6** ✓  **7** ✗

---

**Listening 2: Listening script 1.29**

**M = Marion   S = Steven   K = Karen**

**M:** Oh well, that's easy. I know who I'm going to write about.

**K:** Already?

**M:** Yes, the mysterious Eilean.

**S:** Go on then, Marion. What happened?

**M:** Well, it was last summer. We were driving down to the coast to spend a week with my relatives. All my dad's family live down in Brighton, about … a five-hour drive from here. Anyway, just as we were coming into the outskirts of the town, all this steam started coming out of the engine. So we all got out of the car, and Mum and Dad had a look under the bonnet, but all they could do was scratch their heads. They hadn't the faintest idea about cars.

**K:** So what did you do?

**M:** Well, fortunately this other car stopped and the driver offered to help. And that's how I met Eilean, his daughter. She was ready to sort out the problem herself but her dad told her she'd get herself dirty, so he did it. I suppose the first thing I noticed about her was her clothes. They were 'hippy-style' – all long and flowing with lots of bright, cheerful colours. And that's how she was really – bright and cheerful – and we had a real laugh together there on the side of the motorway, and on the one or two other occasions we met as well. She was also incredibly tall, with long flowing hair that seemed to go down as far as her knees.

**S:** She sounds a bit like one of my ex-girlfriends, Marcia.

**K:** One of the thousands, no doubt.

**S:** Actually, come to think of it, I could write about her. We were both watching this street entertainer, a magician he was, and he asked for two volunteers to come out onto his 'stage', which was this low wall. So …

I went out and so did Marcia, and that's how we met. I remember thinking how soft her features were, and when I looked into her eyes I realized I'd fallen for her in a big way.

**M:** How romantic!

**S:** And then the magician asked us to focus on this rabbit he had in a box, but I just couldn't keep my eyes off Marcia, so I didn't have a clue what was going on and the magician got quite angry. That's when she smiled at me and I got so nervous I nearly fell off the stage! Brought together by magic, we were.

**M:** That's almost what Eilean said, only she believed in Destiny, and according to her, that's what caused us to meet. She was a bit strange, but I'd still like to have kept in touch with her. I have written a few times, but the most recent letters have gone unanswered and she seems to have disappeared off the face of the Earth.

**S:** Probably that magician again! How about you, Karen?

**K:** Well, it looks as if I'm going to have to make something up. Nothing like either of your two stories has ever happened to me. But … I often go walking in the mountains, so I'm going to write about a rescue when I was trapped in the snow with a broken leg.

**M:** Sounds good.

**K:** It gets better. The man who rescued me was a gorgeous, well-built hunk with piercing blue eyes and a beautifully dark complexion, let's say … a … Mediterranean type.

**S:** Oh dream on!

**K:** And his gentle manner and soft spoken voice comforted me in the freezing cold and almost made me forget my pain. The best bit though was when he picked me up in his arms and carried me down the mountain – that can be my last paragraph, leaving the reader wondering what happened next.

**S:** I've just thought of another story – the one of how Marcia and I split up with each other. We were at the theatre one night and one of the actors kept looking at her …

**3** Students can discuss the factual differences in pairs.

### Answers

Marion wrote it.
There are three factual differences:
- In the recording the breakdown occurred near the destination.
- In the recording Eilean's hair was long and flowing.
- In the recording Marion says they are no longer in touch with each other.

**4** Students work individually to identify the spelling mistakes.

### Answers

The correct spellings are in brackets.

holliday (holiday), mecanics (mechanics), extremly (extremely), noticeing (noticing), wich (which), colourfull (colourful), cheerfull (cheerful), chating (chatting), misteriously (mysteriously), moterway (motorway)

**5** Refer students to the instructions in their books.

### Answers

Organization
Paragraph 1
The background to the meeting
Paragraph 2
The meeting in unusual circumstances
Paragraph 3
What has happened since then
**a** paragraphs 1 and 3
**b** paragraph 2

Narrative elements
**a** past continuous (*my parents and I were driving*), past simple (*our car broke down*), past perfect simple (*we had been on the road*), present perfect simple (*We've kept in touch*)
**b** *broke down, pour from, pulled over, stretch her legs, spiky green, bright, cheerful*
**c** *while, after, when, but, who, which*

Descriptive elements
All of these aspects are mentioned except 'interests'
- *That and her colourful 'hippy' clothes were as bright and cheerful as she was …*
- *… was her spiky green hair, which seemed to grow out of her head like grass …*
- *I couldn't help noticing … and Perhaps her most striking feature was …*

Other ways of expressing a strong impression are:
*The first thing I noticed about her was …*
*The first thing that struck me about her was …*
*What struck me first about her was …*
*What I most liked/admired about her was …*

## Sample answer

Last week I went to the bank to ask a loan to buy a new car. I had an appointment with the branch's director. She was a woman very smartly-dressed, she had a shoulder-length hair, almond-shaped eyes and a smooth complexion.

While we were talking in her office we heard a very hard noise and someone shoutting. Suddenly, a man carrying a gun in his hand got into the office's director saying that that was a robbery. Then we had to get out of the office and lie down on the floor with the other people that was in the bank.

There was three armed robbers, two of them were keeping an eye on the hostages while the other was trying to get the money from the cashier's desk. In that moment, the cashier pushed the alarm and a very loud noise begun to sound. The robbers didn't know what to do and then the director hit one of them in the head with an extinguisher. When the other was turning to see what was happening she also hit his head. The third one runned away and it was impossible to catch him.

Since that day I fall in love with her (the director). I admire her bravery and her calm in that situation. By the way, I'm still trying to get the loan.
By Juan Carlos Lopez Gil

224 words

**Examiner's comment**

**Content:** Both parts of the question covered, with description of the person given through her actions, as well as her appearance and personality.

**Accuracy:** Frequent errors, none of which obscures meaning. The existence of so many errors distracts the reader – missing preposition (for), word order, *(a) shoulder-length hair* in the first paragraph, spelling mistakes *shout(t)ing … keep(p)ing*, patchy control of past simple verb forms *begun, runned* and subject verb agreement problems.

**Range:** Suitable structural range and good vocabulary – *were keeping an eye on the hostages*, *cashier's desk*, *an extinguisher*.

**Organization and cohesion:** Clear. Use of a variety of time references.

**Style and format:** Appropriate to the task.

**Target reader:** The writer fulfils the task with a reasonably well told story but is penalized because of the number of errors.

**Mark:** band 3

### Review 6 answers Page 76

## Relative clauses

1 *Jennifer Aniston, who is perhaps best known for her role as Rachel in 'Friends', has also appeared in several major films.*
Non-defining (the name itself defines the person)
2 *What's the name of the village where you got married?*
Defining – *where* cannot be omitted
3 *He hasn't given me back the book that I lent him.*
Defining – *that* can be omitted
4 *She told me that Vasilis had failed his driving test, which didn't surprise me at all.*
Non-defining (*which* refers to the whole clause)
5 *That song always reminds me of the time when I was working in Brazil.*
Defining – *when* can be omitted.
6 *He's the only person in this class whose first name begins with 'Z'.*
Defining – *whose* cannot be omitted.
7 *Emma received a phone call from the Managing Director, who had been impressed by her sales performance.*
Non-defining (there is, we assume, only one Managing Director)
8 *Few written records have survived so it is a period of history about which we know very little.*
Defining – *which* cannot be omitted as it follows a preposition. The sentence could be changed to:
*Few written records have survived so it is a period of history* **which** *we know very little* **about**.
In this case, *which* could be omitted.

## Vocabulary

### A Phrasal verbs

| | | | |
|---|---|---|---|
| 1 | let down | 5 | get on |
| 2 | told off | 6 | fell for |
| 3 | brought up | 7 | falling out |
| 4 | looked up | 8 | got over |

**B Describing people**

**Across**
| | | | |
|---|---|---|---|
| **1** unsociable | **3** greenish | | |
| **6** generous | **8** ear | **9** in | **10** selfish |
| **11** skinny | **12** bad | **14** pale | |

**Down**
| | | |
|---|---|---|
| **1** un | **2** cheerful | **4** hair |
| **5** mean | **7** sensible | **10** slim | **11** shy |
| **13** dis | | |

## Use of English: Transformations
**FCE Part 4**

1 no difficulty (in) making
2 has nothing to do with
3 a strong influence on
4 have (got) the strength
5 are having the roof repaired
6 had his tonsils (taken) out
7 to have it done by

## Workbook answers

### Reading: Gapped text   Page 42

1
| | | | |
|---|---|---|---|
| 1 G | 2 B | 3 F | 4 A |
| 5 E | 6 H | 7 C | D not used |

2 Words for male relatives: *nephew*, uncle, son, father/Dad, brothers, husband, grandfather

Words for female relatives: *sister-in-law*, aunt, daughter, Mum, sisters, wife, nieces

Words for both male and female relatives: *grand-parent*, cousin/second cousin, children, parents, (nearest and dearest)

3
| | | |
|---|---|---|
| 1 | close | Different **a** /kləʊs/, **b** /kləʊz/ |
| 2 | too | Same |
| 3 | live | Different **a** /lɪv/, **b** /laɪv/ |
| 4 | mean | Same |
| 5 | matches | Same |
| 6 | used | Different **a** /juːst/, **b** /juːzd/ |
| 7 | book | Same |
| 8 | fair | Same |

### Vocabulary   Page 44

**A Adjectives of personality**
| | | |
|---|---|---|
| **1** fussy | **2** bossy | **3** clumsy |
| **4** stubborn | **5** dull | **6** reserved |
| **7** ambitious | **8** affectionate | |

**B Compound adjectives**
| | | |
|---|---|---|
| **1** broad-shouldered | **2** left-handed | |
| **3** fair-haired | **4** round-faced | |
| **5** heart-shaped | **6** brown-eyed | |
| **7** shoulder-length | **8** well-known | |

**C Expressions with *have***
| | | |
|---|---|---|
| **1** an operation | **2** a look | |
| **3** the strength | **4** difficulty | |
| **5** influence | **6** a go | |
| **7** common | **8** sympathy | |

### Language focus   Page 45

**A Causative *have***

1 We had our car repaired yesterday.
2 I want to have my photo taken.
3 She has (*or* had) never had her ears pierced before.
4 I'm having (*or* I'm going to have) my hair cut at 5 o'clock tomorrow.
5 They'll probably have (*or* They're probably going to have) their house painted next month.
6 I always have my suits made in Milan now.

**B Phrasal verbs**

1 a I'm very fond of my grandmother. I've always **looked up to her**.
2 a I think I **take after my father** rather than my mother.
3 b I don't earn a great deal but **I get by**.
4 a I blame the parents. They haven't **brought him up** very well.
5 b He looked so lovely in the pet shop; I **fell for him** immediately.
6 b These meetings **take up** too much time.

**C Relative clauses**
| | |
|---|---|
| **1** who, which | **2** who/that, whose |
| **3** where, which/that | **4** why, when |
| **5** which, where | **6** who/that, which/that |
| **7** which/that, which, whose | |

**Commas are required in the following sentences:**
1 after *Mr Jones* and *15 years*
4 after *January*
5 after *The fox* and *shy animal* and *residential areas*
7 after *on Friday* and *my eldest sister*

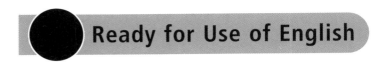

## Ready for Use of English

### Use of English   Page 47

**Multiple-choice cloze**

| 1 B | 2 D | 3 D | 4 B | 5 C | 6 D |
|-----|-----|-----|------|------|------|
| 7 A | 8 C | 9 D | 10 A | 11 B | 12 B |

**Transformations**

1  not tall enough to be
2  there was too much
3  had our house broken into
4  to have my hair dyed
5  for whom I have
6  whose cat I rescued
7  look up to
8  let them down

### Writing   Page 48

2  **1** g   **2** b, f, a, d   **3** h, j   **4** c, i   **5** e
3  **a** sincerely   **b** faithfully

## First Certificate Paper 3

### Use of English

**Part 1**     Multiple-choice cloze
**Part 2**     Open cloze
**Part 3**     Word formation

As stated in the Coursebook, information on the content of Part 4 Key word transformations appears at frequent intervals throughout the book.

As with the other 'Ready for ...' units, the emphasis in this unit is on teaching students rather than testing them. The unit starts with a True/False activity about the content and mechanics of the various exercises in Paper 3. This serves to give students an overall picture of the paper.

The exercises are designed to be done in the classroom but they could also be done at home.

### What do you know about the Use of English Paper?   Page 78

Students follow the instructions in their books.

| Answers |
|---|

1  **False** All except Part 4 (Key word transformations) for which the eight questions are unrelated.

2  **True** Students should read for gist first. Looking first at the title and predicting the content of the text will help their overall understanding.

3  **False** There is one mark for each correct answer except in Part 4 (Key word transformations): in this part, two marks are given for a completely correct answer, one mark if it is partly correct.

4  **False** Parts 1 and 2 each contain twelve gaps, but Part 3 (Word formation) contains ten.

5  **True**

6  **True** Unfortunately, some students do this in the exam. If they write the answer to the example where the answer to the first question should go, all their answers will be in the wrong space.

**7 False** If students are unsure of an answer, they should eliminate any alternatives they consider to be clearly wrong and then, if they still cannot decide on the correct answer, make a sensible guess.

**8 False** Only one word. Note that contractions (eg *can't, won't, I've*) and hyphenated words (eg *one-way*) count as two words.

**9 True** No half marks are given in this paper (although one mark out of a possible two can be given in Part 4 – see 3 above)

**10 True**

## Part 1: Multiple-choice cloze   Page 78

**What to expect in the exam**
Students follow the instructions in their books.

| Answers |
| --- |
| 1 A   2 C   3 a D   3 b C   4 B   5 D |

**Multiple-choice cloze task**
Either elicit their ideas onto the board, ask students to write down their ideas individually or after discussion with a partner, or conduct this prediction activity orally.

You could ask students to cover the multiple-choice answers and first try to identify the part of speech for each space. Students may be able to complete some spaces. They should then uncover the answers and work through them.

| Answers | | | | |
| --- | --- | --- | --- | --- |
| 1 B | 2 A | 3 B | 4 D | 5 D |
| 6 A | 7 C | 8 C | 9 D | 10 B |
| 11 B | 12 C | | | |

## Part 2: Open cloze   Page 80

The first text gives students an example of a completed cloze and asks them to think about the kinds of words that are omitted in this type of exam exercise. They then do an exam-style cloze test.

**1** To lead them into the content of the article and provide an opportunity for speaking practice students first of all discuss question 1.

**2** Students follow the instructions in their books.

Refer them to the information in the 'What to expect in the exam' box. (Answer: Blue door)

| Answers | | | |
| --- | --- | --- | --- |
| **Type of word** | **Number and example** | | |
| Articles | 1   an | 4 | the |
| Prepositions | 3   for | 10 | to |
| Auxiliary verbs | 11   was | | |
| Personal pronouns | 2   it | | |
| Possessive adjectives | 5   their | 9 | his |
| Relative pronouns | 6   who | 8 | that |
| Intensifiers | 7   so | 12 | such |

**3** If you feel your students need more practice in identifying the grammar of the missing words, tell them to read the text three times:
- once to get an idea of the general meaning of the text
- a second time to write down the grammar of the missing words
- a third time to decide what the missing words are.

| Answers | | |
| --- | --- | --- |
| 1   who/that | 2   which/that | 3   does |
| 4   it | 5   his | 6   The |
| 7   been | 8   on | 9   was |
| 10   for | 11   such | 12   for |

## Part 3 Word formation   Page 81

**1** Students follow the instructions in their books. Refer them to the information in the 'What to expect in the exam' box.

| Answers | | |
| --- | --- | --- |
| 1   humorous | 2   employees | 3   tighten |
| 4   increasingly | 5   uncomfortable | 6   heat |
| 7   saucepan | 8   extraordinary | |

**2** Refer students to the instructions and the example given.

| Answers |
| --- |
| 1   adjective; spelling change required (the 'u' in 'humour' is dropped)   2   noun in the plural |
| 3   verb   4   adverb   5   negative adjective |
| 6   noun; spelling change required |
| 7   compound noun   8   adjective |

**3** Students follow the instructions in their books. Point out that text headings are a useful indicator of the general theme and content of a text.

**4** Refer students to the instructions and the information in the 'Don't forget!' box.

| Answers | | |
|---|---|---|
| **1** magicians | **2** interested | **3** ability |
| **4** independent | **5** energetic | **6** physically |
| **7** strength | **8** easily | **9** careless |
| **10** disastrous | | |

# 7 Value for money

## Content Overview

### Themes

Shopping, buying things and living in different places are the themes in this unit.

### Exam-related activities

| **Paper 1** | **Reading** |
|---|---|
| Part 2 | Gapped text |

| **Paper 2** | **Writing** |
|---|---|
| Part 1 | Emails |

| **Paper 3** | **Use of English** |
|---|---|
| Part 2 | Open cloze (Review) |
| Part 4 | Transformations (Review) |

| **Paper 4** | **Listening** |
|---|---|
| Part 2 | Sentence completion |
| Part 4 | Multiple choice |

| **Paper 5** | **Speaking** |
|---|---|
| Part 1 | Interview |
| Part 2 | Talking about photos |

### Other

| | |
|---|---|
| Language focus 1: | The present perfect |
| Language focus 2: | Contrasting ideas |
| Language focus 3: | Expressing preferences |
| Vocabulary: | Shopping |
| | *Come* |
| | Towns and villages |
| Speaking: | Supermarket psychology |

## Vocabulary 1: Shopping                    Page 82

**1** Students will meet this vocabulary in the Listening exercise. Check their pronunciation of *aisle* /aɪl/ and *receipt* /rɪsiːt/.

| Answers | | |
|---|---|---|
| **1** out-of-town | **2** corner | **3** brands |
| **4** own-brand | **5** convenience | **6** range |
| **7** foodstuffs | **8** value | **9** aisles |
| **10** trolley | **11** checkout | **12** till |
| **13** cashier | **14** receipt | |

**2** These questions provide a chance to express opinions about the theme, practise the vocabulary from exercise 1 and round off the exercise.

## Speaking: Supermarket psychology

Page 82

Refer students to the instructions and questions in their books.

Either mix the groups so that students are speaking to people from other groups to compare their ideas or groups could nominate speakers and the comparison could be done across the class. The second option avoids the need for students to move.

## Listening 1: FCE Part 2     Sentence completion

Page 83

Refer students to the instructions and the advice in the 'Don't forget!' box. At this stage in their learning it is a good idea to allow students a little more time to read the questions.

Students listen to complete the sentences in their books. Three words is normally the maximum necessary for sentence completion and incorrect spelling is not penalized as long as the intention is clear. (Correct spelling is necessary if the word in the answer has been spelt out letter by letter.)

### Answers

| | | | |
|---|---|---|---|
| 1 | as many aisles | 7 | five times higher/ |
| 2 | an outdoor market | | greater/more |
| 3 | children | 8 | bakery/bread |
| 4 | fresh meat | 9 | shopping |
| 5 | the animal/animals | | experience |
| 6 | (the) well-known brands | 10 | buy on impulse |

---

### Listening 1: Listening script 1.30

**Announcer:** And next on 'Consumer Watch' I have with me Matthew Brereton, UK Head of the Safebuy supermarket chain. He's here to give away a few secrets on the psychology of supermarkets, and how the big companies design their shops. Matthew ...

**Matthew:** Thanks Barbara. Well, the layout of most major supermarkets is roughly the same, and for more or less the same reasons. You'll notice that the entrance, for example, is usually situated to one side of the building. This is to ensure, of course, that shoppers walk down as many aisles as possible before they leave the store. Ah ... if we had it in the middle, then they might visit only one half of the supermarket and as a result only buy half as much.

The first thing you often see as you come through the entrance is the fruit and vegetable area. As well as being pleasant to the eye, er, this also gives customers the impression they are coming into an outdoor market.

Fresh, colourful products are far more attractive than tins of convenience food, so the customer is put in a good mood from the start.

**Announcer:** A good mood to buy things, you mean?

**Matthew:** Exactly. And next to the fruit and vegetable area is the confectionery; umm, crisps, chocolates, sweets and so on. Parents often come shopping with their children and we need to ensure that they are kept happy and interested so that they don't disturb mum and dad from the business of spending money.

Then at the back of the supermarket in the corner you'll probably find the fresh meat counter. This is partly to make sure that as little room as possible is taken away from the main display areas by the staff who are serving. But it's also there so as not to distract customers when we have deliveries. Er, they really don't want to see us bringing big carcasses of meat through the store, so, er, it's brought in through the back door.

And very close to the fresh meat you can expect to see the pre-packed meat. Ah, people who are put off by the sight of blood and um ... dead animals prefer to buy their meat in the form of convenience food to prevent them having to make the connection between the product and the animal. Er ... they buy a lamb chop, but they don't think of a baby lamb in the field.

The freezer goods are nearby. There's a limited amount of space so the smaller suppliers often find it difficult to get room for their products. Ah ... that's why you only tend to see the well-known brands here.

**Announcer:** And how about those areas at the end of the aisle? How do you decide what to put there?

**Matthew:** Yes, these are key selling sites, and sales of goods at these points can be as much as five times higher than other areas. So we generally move goods to the end of aisle areas when we want to sell them quickly: goods which have not been selling well, and especially those which are nearing their sell-by date.

Bread, too, needs to be sold quickly, but we put the bakery section in the far corner, as far away from the entrance as possible, next to other basic foodstuffs such as milk. This is so that customers have to walk past hundreds of products to reach it. Um, it's expensive to run a bakery but it increases sales of other products. The smell, too, is an important factor as it helps to create a warm, homely atmosphere in the store.

**Announcer:** And the alcoholic drinks. They're often at the far end too, aren't they Matthew?

**Matthew:** Yes, very near the exit. Er, by this time the shopper is beginning to enjoy the shopping experience, so he or she will buy more alcohol if it's here than if it's by the entrance. Er, the same is true for those products we put at the checkouts; er, more sweets and chocolates, usually. The kind of things people buy on impulse as they wait to pay – er, a reward they give themselves for doing the shopping.

**Announcer:** Thank you very much, Matthew, for taking us through that shopping experience.

**Matthew:** Thank you.

**Announcer:** Next week the department store and we'll be talking to ...

Refer students to the instructions and questions which follow the listening. Students discuss their answers in their groups of three.

## Reading: FCE Part 2 — Gapped text    Page 83

Photocopiable vocabulary exercise on page 162.

Lead in briefly by eliciting from students the following answers:

A person addicted to alcohol is an ... alco**hol**ic.
A person addicted to work is a ... worka**hol**ic.
A person addicted to shopping is a ... shopa**hol**ic.

Now refer students to the cartoon in their books. Ask them how seriously the cartoonist regards this condition (not very seriously). Find out if your students have heard about this addiction and if so what they already know.

Refer students to the questions and ask them to read through the first time quite quickly to find the answers and get a general idea of what the text and missing paragraphs are about.

### Answers

What type of people are shopaholics?
Mostly women; increasingly men. People with low self-esteem.
What do they buy?
Women tend to buy items such as clothes, shoes, make-up and jewellery. Men tend to buy power tools and car accessories.
What effect does it have on them?
At first they feel happy, but they get into debt and feel very unhappy afterwards.

Remind students, or elicit from them, the need to look carefully at the context for this reading task. In this particular reading it is especially important that students look ahead to what is coming up in the next paragraph.

Students now complete their task individually and when finished compare their answers with the person next to them before open feedback.

### Answers

| | | | |
|---|---|---|---|
| 1 E | 2 B | 3 G | 4 D |
| 5 H | 6 A | 7 F | C not used |

**Reacting to the text**
Students discuss their answers in groups of three. Further questions:

*How and why do people become shopaholics?*
*Do shops themselves in any way encourage people to buy even when they do not need the things or cannot afford them?*
*How do you feel towards this disorder? Sympathetic? Sceptical? Other?*

## Language focus 1: The present perfect
Page 85

### A The present perfect simple
This is a review of an area of English that can cause confusion. In some languages the same tense form exists and the tense is used similarly to its uses in English in some contexts but differently in others.

**Common mistakes**
*I **have seen** him yesterday ...*
instead of *I saw him yesterday*

*It is a long time **since I don't see her** ...*
instead of *I haven't seen her for a long time*

*I **live** here for 12 years ...*
instead of *I have lived here for 12 years*

Refer students to the example sentences and explanations. Make sure they have enough time to read before they move on to the Practice.

The most important point to make is that the present perfect connects past time with present time as is shown in explanations 1–4.

**Practice**
**1** Refer students to the instructions.

### Answers

| | | | |
|---|---|---|---|
| 1 e | 2 a | 3 b, f | 4 c, d |

**2** Students could work on this in pairs or you could go through the examples on the board with the whole class.

### Answers

**To describe something that started in the past and continues until the present:**
'I've been doing it *since I was 12* when my father would give me his credit card,' she said.

*Until now*, few psychiatrists have regarded the problem as worthy of serious medical attention.

People have *always* used shopping as a way of cheering themselves up.

*Since the announcement* of his test programme, Koran's office has been inundated with hundreds of calls from shopping addicts clamouring to become his guinea pigs.

Silicon Valley ... has seen some of the fastest wealth creation in America's history.

**To give news of recent past events which have some relevance to the present:**
Professor Lorrin Koran of Stanford University in California believes he has found a cure for shopaholics.

**3a** This should be revision.

**A possible approach to the time expressions**
Having copied the expressions on to separate cards or strips of paper, write the two tense names on the board, hand out the cards and students come up to stick them in the appropriate column.

| Answers | |
|---|---|
| **Present perfect** | **Past simple** |
| yet | last summer |
| so far today | in September |
| in the last few days | two weeks ago |
| for the last two years | before I came here |
| over the last week | on my 10th birthday |
| already | when I was younger |
| this month | |
| since I got up | |

**3b** Stress that students should use the expressions in the appropriate tense in sentences which are true for them. Students write individually then compare sentences with a partner and ask more questions to find out more information.

Focus on any mistakes you have heard students make in their use of tenses or time expressions.

**B The present perfect continuous**
Refer students to the information in their books.

**Practice**
**1** Students work on the sentences in pairs so that they can discuss their ideas together.

| Answers | |
|---|---|
| **1 a** | incompleteness – the book is not finished |
| **b** | completed action – the book is finished |
| **2 a** | temporary nature – he is not staying with her on a permanent basis |
| **b** | long-term – she has lived there for a long time and will probably continue to live there |
| **3 a** | repetition – on a regular basis |
| **b** | one occasion – they are not here now |
| **4 a** | duration – the speaker considers all day to be important |
| **b** | focus on completed action – the finished product rather than the duration is important to the speaker (and listener!) here |

**2** Students complete the conversation in pairs.

| Answers | | | |
|---|---|---|---|
| **1** | 've/have just heard | **6** | have (you) made |
| **2** | have you been | **7** | 've/have been saving |
| **3** | proposed | **8** | 've/have both been working |
| **4** | kept | **9** | 've/have already saved |
| **5** | were | **10** | have (you) been doing |

**Vocabulary 2: *Come***                           Page 86

**A *to come as***
Refer students to the examples and instructions.

| Answers |
|---|
| **1** D *pleased* is not possible |
| Note: *pleasant* would be acceptable |
| **2** C *permanent* is not possible |

**B *to come to***
**1–2** Students discuss the sentences in **1** with a partner.

## Answers

Possible answers

1 *came to power* – see example
2 *come to any harm* – kidnappers talking to their hostage's mother or father
3 *come to a decision* – Trade Union representatives speaking to management
4 *coming to an end* – people who wanted to watch the film again without paying
5 *came to the conclusion* – girl speaking about a potential boyfriend
6 *came to nothing*– people at work discussing why their company did not win a big contract *or* bank robbers discussing why the robbery ended in failure

### C Phrasal verbs with *come*

**1–3** Refer students to the instructions.

## Answers

1 1 found by chance
  2 visit me/come to my house
  3 was mentioned *or* discussed
  4 getting
  5 think of
2 *come down with* a mysterious illness
  *come across* my old school reports
  *came up* in the exam
  *come round* to my flat
  *come up with* a solution to the problem

## Language focus 2: Contrasting ideas

Page 87

Students at this level have probably met these expressions before but some will have problems using them correctly. Students check their answers on pages 211 and 212 of the Grammar reference.

## Answers

Although the weather was bad, she enjoyed the trip.
She enjoyed the trip although the weather was bad.
The weather was bad. However, she enjoyed the trip.*
The weather was bad. She enjoyed the trip, however.*

Despite the bad weather/Despite the fact that the weather was bad, she enjoyed the trip.
Despite the weather being bad, she enjoyed the trip.

*Notice the use of the comma in the two examples with *however*.

### Practice

Students first complete the sentences on their own before comparing with a partner.

## Answers

| | | | | | |
|---|---|---|---|---|---|
| 1 | Although | 2 | in spite | 3 | despite |
| 4 | However | 5 | but | 6 | whereas |

## Listening 2: Multiple choice
**FCE Part 4**
Page 87

Photocopiable vocabulary exercise on page 164.

**1** Put the following categories mentioned in the listening on the board:

  *noise*      *crime*      *neighbours*
  *dangers*    *amenities*   *transport*
  *entertainment*

When answering the pre-listening question, students should refer to these categories.

**2** Refer students to the instructions and questions. Give them enough time to read through before the listening begins.

## Answers

1 B   2 C   3 A   4 C   5 A   6 B   7 C

---

**Listening 2: Listening script 1.31**

**I = Interviewer**    **R = Rebecca**    **G = Greg**

**I:** What made you go and live in the countryside, Rebecca?

**R:** I suppose my priorities had changed with age. When I first went to London, I used to love the hustle and bustle of the place. But then I gradually became more aware of the planes roaring overhead, car horns beeping all the time, music blaring out at strange hours. I needed a break.

**I:** Greg, I can see you're smiling.

**G:** Yes. I remember when I first moved out with my family, we all found it a little too quiet. But we quickly got used to it, and now we prefer living with less noise. We also like the fact that you don't have to worry about the kids so much if they go off on their own.

**R:** Hmm, I'm not so sure. Some people drive like maniacs on those narrow roads. I feel I have to keep an even closer eye on my two kids than before. And there are lots of wide open spaces for them to get lost in, too.

**G:** But that's where the neighbours come in. Everyone seems to know everyone else's business in the village. That could be seen as an intrusion, but it's very handy if your kids go wandering off, or you're worried about burglars breaking into your house.

**R:** You're right there. In fact, we leave everything unlocked, and the neighbours sometimes just come into our house without even knocking on the door. We don't mind, though. It's like having a big extended family.

**I:** What about the amenities where you live?

**G:** The basics are within walking distance from us; the school, the shops, even a couple of tennis courts.

**R:** I wish I could say the same. We have to get the car out just to go and buy a loaf of bread. And you really do need to be able to drive to live where we do; the bus service is just too infrequent.

**G:** It's better than not having one at all. We're actually trying to get the local authorities to put on at least one bus a day, particularly for the older residents who don't have a car and who sometimes need to go into town.

**R:** Yes, and I'm actually wondering how my two are going to find it when they become teenagers. Well, they'll want to go into town, too. They'll probably complain of boredom and want us to go and live in the city again.

**G:** And who can blame them? I know at that age I would have been bored out of my mind! No cinemas, no decent shops, no cafés to sit in, no discos to go to …

**I:** Do you think either of you will ever go and live in the city again?

**G:** Naturally, I'd prefer to stay in the village and work at home rather than do a nine-to-five job in an office. I have my computer, email and the phone, and a wonderful working environment. However, anything can happen, and we'd be prepared to move back to London if we felt it was to our advantage.

**I:** Rebecca?

**R:** I'll be going back to work just as soon as my youngest child starts school. Obviously I've thought about it a lot, and the fact that living where I do now will mean spending two hours driving to and from work every day. But I'd rather do that than give up my life in the country.

**I:** Well, thank you both for coming all that way to speak to us today. We'll have a break for music now and then it's competition time once again …

## Language focus 3: Expressing preferences                     Page 88

Refer students to the examples taken from the listening and elicit the differences in form. If you have access to different colour pens or chalk, use different colours to highlight the differences.

*I would prefer* + infinitive with *to … rather than* + base form
*I would rather* + base form … *than* + base form
*prefer* + gerund + *to* + gerund

At this stage you could elicit a couple of preferences which many in your class may share and drill them.

**Common mistakes**
Students often say 'I'd rather prefer (to) do X …' and may use *that* instead of *than*.

**Practice**

| Answers |
| --- |
| 1  rather watch than take |
| 2  buying books to borrowing |
| 3  to phone him rather than |
| 4  not go out |

## Vocabulary 3: Towns and villages

Page 88

**1**  Refer students to the instructions, the example and the lists of vocabulary.

| Answers |
| --- |
| 1 *e, f*  2 a, e  3 d  4 a, c, d  5 a, d  6 b  7 c 8 b |

**2**  If possible, hand out dictionaries for this exercise. Alternatively, if you and your students know the area you are in well enough, you could use real examples of areas of the city to teach the vocabulary.

| Answers | |
| --- | --- |
| Positive: | lively, bustling, pleasant, picturesque, prosperous, quaint |
| Negative: | dull, run-down, shabby, depressing |

**Speaking 1:**     **Interview**   Page 88
**FCE Part 1**

In the first question, students are asked *Whereabouts … do you live? Whereabouts* is common in conversational English and the interlocutor in the exam may use this term. When students are asking and answering the questions in pairs, remind them to develop their answers where possible.

## Speaking 2: FCE Part 2 — Talking about photos
Page 89

Refer students to the instructions, advice and photographs in the books. In the exam, students have one minute to speak about their pictures individually, and about 20 seconds to comment on their partner's photos.

## Writing: FCE Part 1 — Emails

**1** Refer students to the instructions and questions in their books. They should discuss and compare answers with a partner.

**2** Refer students to the questions and the information in the 'What to expect in the exam' box.

### Answers

Yes: friendly and informal

**3–5** Refer students to the instructions.

### Answers

**3**

Paragraph 2: *Describing the positive and negative aspects of the house*
Paragraph 3: *Describing the positive and negative aspects of the flat*
Paragraph 4: *Stating a preference and giving reasons.*

**4**
**a**

| Input material | Email |
|---|---|
| *properties* | *places* |
| *residential area* | *neighbourhood* |
| *overlooking the … river* | *by the river* |
| *within walking distance of the city centre* | *you can walk to the centre* |
| *in the heart of historic York* | *central* |
| *with shops and all amenities nearby* | *really close to everything* |

**b**

*I looked on the map*
*so we wouldn't have to get up early for class*
*that could be a bit noisy for me*
*the walk to school would be good for us*

**5**

**a** *great, alright, really, a bit, let me know, all the best*

**b** *I've, there's, it's, wouldn't, it's, I'd, it's*

**c** *exclamation mark in final paragraph*

The email also includes examples of the following language features which will be useful when students tackle the writing task:

- **Hypothetical language**
  *might be alright*, **wouldn't** *have to get up early*, **could** *be a bit noisy*, **would** *be good for us*
- **Language of comparison**
  *more central, it's* **quieter** *and £75* **cheaper** *than the flat*
- **Language of contrast**
  **though** *I looked on the map*
- **Language of preference**
  **I'd rather** *live in the house*
- **Other language:**
- Describing a positive point: *which is an advantage*
- Introducing a negative point: *The problem is that*
- Summarizing: *All in all.*

Write these bullet points on the board and ask students to find the examples in the email. You will probably need to help them with some items, for example by suggesting a key word. You may also want to suggest further alternatives such as *whereas* for the language of contrast and *on the whole, on balance* for summarizing.

**6** Refer students to the instructions and the information in the 'Don't forget!' box.

### Sample answer

Hi Ricardo
I'm really interested about going on a shopping trip and I've found two alternatives.

The first one is to Boulogne in France for just £21. That would be interesting as it would give both us a chance to practise our French and also we can buy things like wine and cheese in the hypermarket – delicious! Unfortunately, though, the coach leaves at 6 in the morning and I know you hate getting up early.

The other one is to Oxford Street in London and costs just £7 return. The clothes they sell there are fantastic and I really need to buy some new ones.

However, I think if you don't mind to pay a bit more, the one to Boulogne will be better because it takes three hours to get to London. That's a total of 6 hours in the coach, which I would find extremely tedious.

Let me know what you think
Best wishes
Jan (Ruber)

154 words

**Examiner's comments**
**Content:** All points covered and the writer builds on the information given eg *I know you hate getting up early, I really need to buy some new ones.*

**Accuracy:** Generally accurate and errors do not impede understanding eg *interested about going, give both us a chance, if you don't mind to pay.*

**Range:** A good range of structure and vocabulary eg *it would give both us a chance to practise, which I would find extremely tedious.*

**Organization and cohesion:** Good paragraphing and use of cohesive devices (*The first one, The other one, Unfortunately, though, However, That would be interesting as it would* etc).

**Style and format**: Appropriately informal email.

**Target reader:** Would be informed of the nature of the two options.

**Mark**: borderline band 4/5

## Writing: Reports
FCE Part 2

The topic area of shopping lends itself well to a report writing task. For work on report writing, including exercises focusing on linkers and the use of formal/informal language, see the photocopiable worksheet on page 163 of this book.

## Review 7 answers   Page 92

### Vocabulary: Shopping

1  *walking*    2   range   3   value   4   corner
5   meat      6   out-of-town   7   convenience
8   own-brand  9   brand  10   goods

## Use of English:  Open cloze
FCE Part 2

1   of          2   the         3   than
4   to          5   One         6   came
7   despite     8   was         9   for
10   rather/sooner   11   as      12   to

## Use of English:  Transformations
FCE Part 4

**A The present perfect**
1  1   c and e   2   b and d   3   a and f

2  1   last time I spoke to
   2   first time I have/'ve eaten
   3   has/'s been playing tennis since
   4   ages since he (last) saw/has seen
   5   haven't/have not been swimming for
   6   biggest supermarket I have/'ve (ever)

**B Language of contrast**
1   being able to speak fluent
2   the fact (that) his behaviour
3   she performed well, she lost
4   in spite of/despite the/an increase

## Workbook answers

### Reading: Multiple matching   Page 50

1  1 B       2 D        3 A       4 C
   5/6 A, D in any order         7   B
   8/9 A, C in any order        10   B
   11 A        12/13 C, D in any order
   14/15 C, D in any order

2  1 d    2 f    3 e    4 b    5 a    6 c

3  1   turned into        2   put up with
   3   moved out          4   springing up
   5   cut down, cut out

4  1   I've had words with them
   2   came to an agreement
   3   I've got my eye on
   4   put (our flat) up for sale
   5   I'm on first-name terms with
   6   it's getting beyond a joke

## Vocabulary, page 51

### A Wordsearch

| T | T | T | S | I | R | O | L | F | G |
|---|---|---|---|---|---|---|---|---|---|
| F | R | T | I | I | E | A | E | R | C |
| R | O | N | G | L | L | A | O | G | H |
| E | L | E | O | F | L | C | E | R | E |
| T | L | G | O | I | E | H | L | E | C |
| N | E | A | D | R | W | E | S | H | K |
| U | Y | S | S | S | E | C | I | C | O |
| O | H | W | A | H | J | K | A | T | U |
| C | H | E | M | I | S | T | A | U | T |
| C | N | N | I | A | G | R | A | B | T |

### Shopkeepers:

baker, butcher, chemist, florist, grocer, jeweller, newsagent

### Things in shops or supermarkets:

aisle, bargain, checkout, counter, goods, till, trolley

### B Multiple choice

| 1 | B | 2 | C | 3 | C | 4 | A | 5 | B |
|---|---|---|---|---|---|---|---|---|---|
| 6 | D | 7 | A | 8 | D | 9 | B | 10 | A |

### C Phrasal verbs with *come*

1 down  2 across  3 up  4 up  5 round

### D Expressions with *come*

1 come in handy  2 come on
3 come into fashion  4 come to terms with
5 come true  6 come to

### E Word formation: Nouns

| | Verb | Noun |
|---|---|---|
| 1 | try | trial |
| 2 | cure | cure |
| 3 | like | liking |
| 4 | split | split |
| 5 | consult | consultant |
| 6 | announce | announcement |
| 7 | behave | behaviour |
| 8 | create | creation |
| 9 | assist | assistant |
| 10 | appear | appearance |
| a | liking | |
| b | announcement | |
| c | trial | |
| d | behaviour | |
| e | creation | |

## Language focus   Page 53

### A Contrasting ideas

| 1 | B | 2 | B and C | 3 | A |
|---|---|---|---|---|---|
| 4 | C | 5 | A and B | 6 | A and C |

### B The present perfect and past simple

| 1 | has just published | 2 | has changed |
|---|---|---|---|
| 3 | has increased | 4 | (were) expected |
| 5 | lived | 6 | has risen |
| 7 | has doubled | 8 | have been |
| 9 | disappeared | 10 | has become |
| 11 | was | 12 | has taken |
| 13 | had | 14 | were |
| 15 | stood | | |

### C Correcting mistakes

1 My father's been working/has worked
2 I've broken my leg
3 Charlie Chaplin was one of the greatest
4 how long I've been waiting
5 the first time I have seen this film
6 known each other for many years
7 since I last played football
8 I have cleaned three rooms

## Use of English   Page 55

### Transformations

1 come to a decision
2 although he is unable
3 despite the train being
4 to walk rather than catch
5 not leave yet
6 has been learning French for
7 last time we saw
8 since I (last) had

### Word formation

| 1 | picturesque | 2 | inhabitants |
|---|---|---|---|
| 3 | beautiful | 4 | neighbourhood |
| 5 | peaceful | 6 | pleasant |
| 7 | disadvantages | 8 | infrequent |
| 9 | dependent | 10 | unfriendly |

### Open cloze

| 1 | a | 2 | to | 3 | than |
|---|---|---|---|---|---|
| 4 | a/each/every/per | 5 | are | 6 | more |
| 7 | for | 8 | how | 9 | what |
| 10 | If/Should | 11 | not | 12 | which |

# 8 Time travel

## Writing, page 56

**A Structure**

**Paragraph 1** d  **Paragraph 2** a
**Paragraph 3** c  **Paragraph 4** b

**B Language analysis**

a adjectives: *competitive*, fast, efficient, useful, informative, handy

modifiers: *extremely (competitive)*, particularly (useful), very (informative), fairly (good), especially (handy)

adverbs of frequency: *normally*, always, sometimes, usually, often

b **1** about  **2** fact  **3** Personally  **4** anyone

## Content Overview

### Themes

Holidays in space, as well as more down-to-earth travel and holidays are the themes in Unit 8.

### Exam-related activities

| | |
|---|---|
| **Paper 1** | **Reading** |
| Part 1 | Multiple choice |
| Part 2 | Gapped text |
| | |
| **Paper 2** | **Writing** |
| Part 2 | Essays |
| Part 2 | Articles (Review) |
| | |
| **Paper 3** | **Use of English** |
| Part 1 | Multiple-choice cloze (Review) |
| Part 3 | Word formation (Review) |
| Part 4 | Transformations (Review) |
| | |
| **Paper 4** | **Listening** |
| Part 1 | Multiple choice |
| | |
| **Paper 5** | **Speaking** |
| Part 1 | Interview |
| Part 2 | Talking about photos |

### Other

Language focus: The future
Vocabulary:    Phrasal verbs
               Travel
Word formation: Verbs ending in *-en*

## Reading 1: Gapped text  Page 94
**FCE Part 2**

Photocopiable vocabulary exercise on page 164.

Before students open their books, write the word *HOLIDAYS* on the board and ask them to write down reasons for going on holiday and what people's expectations often are. They could do this individually or in pairs. With a confident group, elicit their ideas directly onto the board.

**Ideas**

Reasons – to relax, for a change of scene, to escape from 'normal' life for a while, to see how other people live, for a change of climate, to meet up with people you see only once a year, to feel refreshed, etc …

Expectations – good weather, friendly people, night life, peace and quiet, time to think, time to read, etc …

**1** Now refer students to the picture of a 'space hotel' in their books and together decide which of the reasons and expectations they mentioned would be satisfied by this kind of holiday.

Students then discuss the questions in their books in pairs or small groups.

**2** Students now read the text to find out how many of their ideas are mentioned. Don't deal with unknown vocabulary at this stage and ask students to ignore vocabulary problems when they read the text for the first time.

**3** Refer students to the 'Don't forget!' box and the sentences which have been removed from the text.

### Answers

1 C   2 G   3 A   4 F   5 H   6 B
7 D   E not used

**Reacting to the text**
Refer students to the questions in their books.

## Vocabulary 1: Phrasal verbs

Students may already recognize some of these verbs. In this exercise they are encouraged to deduce the meaning from the context. Students can look up any other words they do not understand at home.

### Answers

1  think about and plan
2  compensate for
3  tolerate
4  provide with everything that will be needed
5  go towards

## Language focus: The future   Page 96

This is a review of ways of expressing different levels of certainty and different types of future: an area of particular confusion for students.

### A Making predictions
Refer students to the sentences from the text and the instructions.

### Answers

a 1   b 2, 3 and 4   c 5 and 6

**Negative forms**

| | |
|---|---|
| will definitely | definitely won't/will not |
| are likely to | are not/aren't likely to |
| will probably | probably won't |
| may well* | |
| might | might not |
| could | could not (but note that the |

negative form changes the meaning to 'certainty' or 'logical impossibility')

* may well not exists but may well is normally only used in the positive

**Practice**
Refer students to the practice activity. They should complete the exercise individually then compare and discuss with a partner. Answers will vary depending on their opinions.

**B Other futures**
In this section, students are asked to match a sentence with a description. Make sure they read through all of the descriptions before starting.

### Answers

1 a   2 d   3 e   4 c   5 i
6 h   7 f   8 b   9 g

**C Time linkers**
Students should complete the sentences individually.

### Answers

1 before        3 until
2 By the time   4 when/as soon as

**Practice**

**1** Ask students to work in pairs for sections A–D. A reference to the relevant explanation from section B is given on the right of each answer below.

### Answers

| A | 1 | is going to rain | b |
| | 2 | we're going | f |
| | 3 | we'll have to | first conditional |
| B | 4 | takes off | c |
| | 5 | I'll get up | i |
| | 6 | we'll be driving | d |

| C | 7 | I'm seeing | h |
|---|---|---|---|
| | 8 | will last | expresses a personal opinion and is often used with *I think, I suppose, I believe* and their negative forms |
| | 9 | are only going to sign | f |
| | 10 | will have/be finished | e |
| D | 11 | shall we meet | *shall* is often used when asking for or making a suggestion |
| | 12 | don't open | c |
| | 13 | will/'ll get | i – a decision made at the moment of speaking |
| | 14 | will/'ll probably see | a fixed expression, part 'prediction' (*probably*) and part future fact |

**2** A strong group will probably not need any preparation time before they start discussing the questions with their partner. However, you may prefer to give students two minutes to formulate their answers either on paper or in their heads. If necessary, remind students that the correct structure is
*I don't think I'll* … rather than *I think I won't* …

## Vocabulary 2: Travel                     Page 97

**1** Students often confuse these words. Let them complete the sentences individually before checking with the whole class.

| Answers | | |
|---|---|---|
| **1** flight | **2** journey | **3** trip |
| **4** travel | **5** voyage | **6** cruise |

**2** You could discuss these questions with the whole class, or divide the students into groups of three.

**3** Refer students to the instructions. You may wish to spend some time discussing the difference in use between each pair of easily confused words.

| Answers | | |
|---|---|---|
| **1** holiday | **2** campsite | **3** stayed |
| **4** relax | **5** funny | **6** excursion |
| **7** crowded | **8** package | |

## Speaking 1:  Interview   Page 97
**FCE Part 1**

Refer students to the 'examiner's' questions. They should try and give full answers when they are the 'candidate'.

## Speaking 2:  Talking about photos
**FCE Part 2**    Page 98

Students follow the instructions in their books. You could do this as suggested in the Coursebook or, by using a different picture, you could preview the language in the box by doing the following:

- Using a 'holiday scene' picture that is big enough for all students to see, elicit from the students their descriptions.
- Ask questions if necessary, eg
  *What kind of holiday destination is this?*
  *What kind of people would go there?* etc.
- When appropriate, reformulate what your students say, using the expressions from the box.
- When you feel that they have said enough, either elicit the reformulated sentences on to the board or refer students to their Coursebooks and ask them which of the expressions in the box you used.

## Listening:  Multiple choice
**FCE Part 1**    Page 99

Refer students to the information in the 'How to go about it' box before they listen. Ask students to give reasons for their answers.

| Answers | | | |
|---|---|---|---|
| **1** A | **2** B | **3** C | **4** A |
| **5** B | **6** C | **7** B | **8** C |

> **Listening: Listening script 1.32–1.39**
>
> **One**
> We really didn't expect this. We thought it'd be the typical economy type hotel. You know, nothing special, just a bed, a wardrobe and a shower in the room if you're lucky. Well, the en suite bathroom was a big surprise, I can tell you. It's twice the size of ours at home. And as for the view from the balcony, it's unbelievable. We really can't complain.

**Two**

... and I think that although my experience running a restaurant may not seem very relevant, it's still a people-orientated job. I am definitely a 'people person'. I like dealing with the public. So whether it's listening to customers and giving them advice on the best places to go, or talking on the phone to tour operators and trying to get the best deal, I think I'd be well suited to the job. I have good people skills and I think that's an important strength.

**Three**

**Tour Guide:** Are you sure you had it when you left the hotel?

**Woman:** Positive: I didn't want to bring it but my husband made me put it in my bag. He said you should never leave your money or your passport in your room. And then when we were having a drink and I went to pay, it had gone. Well, someone must have put their hand in when I wasn't looking.

**Tour Guide:** We'll have to report it straight away.

**Four**

We went there because we wanted to see the stained glass windows. They say they're among the finest in Europe and the colours are supposed to be incredible when the sun shines through them. Unfortunately we couldn't go in because we weren't properly dressed – they won't let you in if you're wearing short trousers. And the next morning when we went back it was Easter Sunday. So of course, we couldn't get to the part where the windows are because there was a special service.

**Five**

**Man:** Yes, your skin is quite badly burnt. How long were you out in the sun for?

**Boy:** About an hour, maybe. It was after lunch and I fell asleep on the beach.

**Man:** Do you have any other symptoms – dizziness, a temperature?

**Boy:** No, it just really hurts.

**Man:** Well, it doesn't sound like sunstroke. This cream should take away the sting, but if you start to feel sick or dizzy, get yourself to a doctor straight away.

**Boy:** Thanks. How much do I owe you?

**Man:** I'll just check. One second.

**Six**

I shouldn't complain really. I mean, the whole economy of this town is based on tourism and if they stopped coming, then a lot of people would be out of work and on the dole. But I do wish they'd show a little more respect. There are a lot of them who have music blaring out of their cars during the day, and then at night you get big groups coming into the centre for the pubs and clubs. And they don't seem to care that we can't sleep with them making such a racket. Most of them drunk, I shouldn't wonder.

**Seven**

**Boy:** Where are we going?

**Mother:** Well, we picked up a leaflet for a nature park just outside the town. They've got all sorts of wild animals and you can drive through and see them in their natural habitat. It looks very good.

**Boy:** But you said we were going to go to the Aqua Park.

**Mother:** We can't go in this weather. And besides, your father and I want to do something different.

**Boy:** But that's not fair. You can't just change your mind like that.

**Mother:** Don't be selfish, Steven. It's our turn today.

**Eight**

No, the 14th ... That's right, Saturday the 14th ... Well my plans have changed and I'm not going to Bristol any more. I couldn't get anywhere to stay there, so I had to find somewhere in the city of Bath ... But I don't see why I have to pick it up two days before. Surely you could just give me the new one the day I travel, on the 14th ... Yes, I appreciate that's the procedure, but it's very inconvenient.

## Reading 2:  Multiple choice
### FCE Part 1
Page 100

Photocopiable vocabulary exercise on page 165.

**1** Refer students to the pictures in their books and the questions. (If your students come from an area popular with tourists tell them that they will have the chance to give their opinions fully after the reading.) You might also ask them to consider the possible effects of tourism on historic monuments (eg graffiti, erosion to stones, etc) and the positive or negative effect on the culture and traditions of native people.

**2** After they have discussed their opinions refer them to the exam rubric and the information in the 'How to go about it' box. Give them three minutes to read the text for the first time. Time the students carefully and stop them when three minutes is reached. In this way they can begin to have an idea of how quickly or slowly they read. When everyone has finished reading the text, elicit students' answers to the gist reading questions.

| Answers | | | | |
|---|---|---|---|---|
| 1 B | 2 B | 3 A | 4 B | 5 D |

**Reacting to the text**

These questions could be discussed as a class or students could work in pairs or groups of three.

Further questions:
*What is your favourite holiday destination?*
*What would happen if tourists stopped coming to your country or region?*

## Word formation: *-en* suffix   Page 102

**1** Students work on this in pairs or groups with a dictionary if possible.

## Answers

| Adjective | Noun | Verb |
|---|---|---|
| *broad* | *breadth* /e/ | *broaden* |
| *wide* | *width* /ɪ/ | *widen* /aɪ/ |
| deep | depth | deepen |
| high | height | heighten |
| long | length | lengthen |
| short | shortness | shorten |
| strong | strength | strengthen |
| weak | weakness | weaken |
| deaf | deafness | deafen |

**2** Students first work on this individually and then compare their answers in pairs.

## Answers

| | | |
|---|---|---|
| **1** lengthen | **2** weakened | **3** widening |
| **4** strength | **5** deafening | **6** height |

## Writing: FCE Part 2    Essays    Page 102

**1–2** Refer students to the instructions and the model article in their books. Students should read the essay quickly for the first time.

## Answers

The writer agrees with the statement.

**3** Students look at the organization of the essay.

## Answers

The writer gives three main reasons introduced by *Firstly*, *Secondly* and *Another benefit is*. Further supporting ideas are introduced by *Consequently*, *It seems to me* and *As a result*. The purpose of the first and last paragraphs is to state the writer's opinion, ie to agree with the title.

**4** Students look back at the model and find the linking devices, then add some more of their own. (The words and expressions in italics are not contained in the model article.)

## Answers

| 1 Introduce the writer's opinion | 2 Indicate the order of points |
|---|---|
| Personally, I think | Firstly |
| It seems to me that | Secondly |
| I strongly believe | Another benefit is |

| | |
|---|---|
| In my opinion | Another drawback/disadvantage is |
| To my mind, | Lastly |
| | First of all |

| 3 Show the result or consequence of something | 4 Bring the essay to an end |
|---|---|
| Consequently ... / ... lead | To conclude |
| to ... / ... owes a great deal | *To sum up* |
| to ... | *In conclusion* |
| As a result | |
| *Therefore result(s) in ...* | |
| *thus* | |

**5** Refer students to the exam instructions.

**6** Assign different types of transport to different groups of students. Students discuss and write down three or more advantages of this type of transport when travelling in a town or city.
To help students with ideas write up the following prompts:

*possible effects on the environment*
*cost*
*time*
*stress*
*convenience*
*comfort*

**7** Remind students to organize their ideas using the structure given here. Refer them to the 'Don't forget!' box.

## Review 8 answers  Page 104

### Use of English: FCE Part 4    Transformations

**1** **1** *c*  **2** a  **3** f  **4** b  **5** e  **6** d

**2** **1** are you planning to spend/planning on spending
**2** on the point of saying
**3** is likely to rise
**4** probably won't/will not
**5** will probably (all) have died/may well (all) have died

### Use of English: FCE Part 3    Word formation

| | | |
|---|---|---|
| **1** unpleasant | **2** widened | **3** deafening |
| **4** sleepless | **5** Unable | **6** politely |
| **7** successful | **8** worsened | **9** shorten |
| **10** broadens | | |

## Use of English: FCE Part 1 — Multiple-choice cloze

| 1 C | 2 B | 3 A | 4 B | 5 D |
|-----|-----|-----|-----|------|
| 6 C | 7 A | 8 C | 9 B | 10 A |
| 11 C | 12 B | | | |

## Writing: FCE Part 2 — Articles

### Sample answer

Natal

Where to go and put your feet up in winter's days without worring about catching a cold? Natal, in the North-east of Brazil, has the same warm temperatures during all over the year.

Natal is one of the emergent places for a new kind of tourists interest – beaches throughout there are included in the route of called 'Ecological Tourism'. Travel agents orient you how to enjoy your holiday without damaging the environment. You can stay in hotels, in Youth Hostels as well as in the local people's house: Natal inhabitants are very kind and hospitable.

Besides relaxing in different beaches each day, you can go to the city centre to enjoy 'frevo', a kind of dance in the street, conducted by a carnival band. But if you are a sort of shopaholic, there are a lot of craft markets in addition to conventional markets and shopping mals.

Moreover, if you have some extra time and want to know about their culture you can see the sight of the town, constructed by Portuguese, Dutch and English conquerors. Afterwards you still can eat fishes only just caught and grilled on the seashore. You should go and see!

By Nicola Veret

195 words

### Examiner's comment

**Content:** Good realization of the task set. All points covered and different interests catered for.

**Accuracy:** The first two paragraphs contain numerous mistakes but these do not impede understanding although they may distract the reader – *in winter's days, worring, during all over the year, tourists interest,* etc. Otherwise, it is generally accurately expressed.

**Range:** Appropriate with some examples of natural language use – *if you are a sort of shopaholic, craft markets, without damaging the environment, grilled on the seashore …*

**Organization and cohesion:** Good use of appropriate linking devices in the third and fourth paragraphs – *Besides relaxing, in addition to, Moreover, Afterwards.*

**Style and format:** Informative and friendly, appropriate to the audience.

**Target reader:** Would be suitably informed.

**Mark:** band 4

## Workbook answers

### Reading: Multiple choice   Page 58

1

| 1 C | 2 A | 3 C | 4 D |
|-----|-----|-----|-----|
| 5 B | 6 B | 7 D | 8 A |

2
a   took up
b   catch up on
c   put off
d   used up
e   picked up

### Vocabulary   Page 60

**Confusing words**

| 1 fun | 2 crowded | 3 campsite |
|-------|-----------|------------|
| 4 holiday | 5 stay | 6 resort |
| 7 souvenirs | 8 views | 9 trip |
| 10 cruise | | |

## Language focus    Page 60

**The future**

**1**

**1**  I'll put
**2**  you're going to have
**3**  We're meeting/We're going to meet
**4**  you leave
**5**  I'll get/I'm going to get
**6**  we'll be sitting
**7**  are you doing/are you going to do
**8**  I'll have spoken

**2**

**1**  'll/will carry
**2**  'm/am having
**3**  ends, 'll be
**4**  'll be watching, will/'ll have finished
**5**  'm going to get
**6**  gets
**7**  will/'ll have been travelling, 'll/will want
**8**  'll be/'m going to be

## Use of English    Page 61

**Transformations**

**1**  am/'m (really) looking forward to
**2**  are/'re likely to take him
**3**  by bus makes up
**4**  to set up
**5**  if they get on
**6**  come up with
**7**  to give up smoking
**8**  split up with

**Open cloze**

| | | | |
|---|---|---|---|
| **1** | in | **2** | a/each/every/per |
| **3** | off | **4** | well |
| **5** | than | **6** | with |
| **7** | not | **8** | is |
| **9** | as | **10** | which |
| **11** | whose | **12** | one |

**Word formation**

| | | | | | |
|---|---|---|---|---|---|
| **1** | loosened | **2** | lengthen | **3** | worsened |
| **4** | sharpening | **5** | depths | **6** | thickens |
| **7** | deafness | **8** | reddened | **9** | brightened |
| **10** | tightening | | | | |

## Writing    Page 63

**A Model**

**a**  congratulate you on    **b**  with regard to
**c**  you could also perhaps mention
**d**  it is true    **e**  it is worth
**f**  you claim that    **g**  no longer the case

**B Analysis**

**1**  However, but, although
**2**  Firstly, In addition, Finally
**3**  a  with regard to
     b  it is true that
     c  no longer the case

**C Adding relevant information**

**the gifts:** *the handmade knives for which the area is famous*

**the restaurant:** *the portions are usually very large*

**the river:** *It has recently been cleaned and in some places it is possible to swim.*

# 9 Fact or fiction?

## Content Overview

### Themes

Topics included in this unit are ghosts and tips on how to tell ghost stories, Hallowe'en old and new, and other festivals, including Bonfire Night.

### Exam-related activities

| | |
|---|---|
| **Paper 1** | **Reading** |
| Part 1 | Multiple choice |
| Part 2 | Gapped text |
| | |
| **Paper 2** | **Writing** |
| Part 2 | Informal letters |
| Part 2 | Short stories (Review) |
| | |
| **Paper 3** | **Use of English** |
| Part 2 | Open cloze |
| Part 3 | Word formation (Review) |
| Part 4 | Transformations (Review) |
| | |
| **Paper 4** | **Listening** |
| Part 4 | Multiple choice |
| | |
| **Paper 5** | **Speaking** |
| Part 3 | Collaborative task |
| Part 4 | Further discussion |

### Other

Language focus 1: Modal verbs of speculation
Language focus 2: Question tags (including intonation)
Vocabulary: *Give*
Word formation: Adjectives

---

 **Reading 1:** **Multiple choice**
Page 106

Photocopiable vocabulary exercises on page 165.

**1** Elicit students' opinions for a class discussion on the questions, or divide them into groups of three.

**2** Refer students to the instructions, and give them three minutes to read the text and answer question 1.

**3** Students follow the instructions for the remaining questions.

| Answers | | | | | | | |
|---|---|---|---|---|---|---|---|
| 1 C | 2 A | 3 C | 4 D | 5 C | 6 B | 7 A | 8 B |

---

**Reacting to the text**

Students could discuss these questions in small groups. Ask them to choose the best story to tell the class.

## Language focus 1: Modal verbs of speculation
Page 108

Refer students to the extracts from the text.

| Answers |
|---|
| **1a** a and c    **1b** b |
| **2** *have* + past participle |
| **3** could, may |
| **4** No |

**Practice**

**1** Students work on this in pairs.

**2–4** Refer students to the instructions.

| Answers |
|---|
| **2** 1 b   2 d   3 e   4 a   5 f   6 c |
| **3 a** present, continuous infinitive without *to* |
| **b** present, infinitive without *to* |
| **c** past, *have* + past participle |
| **d** past, *have* + past participle (continuous) |
| **e** past, *have* + past participle |
| **f** present, infinitive without *to* |

---

 **Multiple choice**
Page 108

**1** Refer students to the picture and the questions in their books. These could be discussed in pairs or as a whole class. Students could answer the question beginning *Have you or anyone you know-…?* now or after the listening exercise. Leaving it until later could mean that students are warmed up to the theme. Check students know the meaning of the word *haunt* as this comes up in the listening exercise.

**2** Give students enough time to read through the questions.

| Answers | | | | | | |
|---|---|---|---|---|---|---|
| 1 C | 2 A | 3 C | 4 B | 5 C | 6 A | 7 B |

## Listening: Listening script 1.40

**I = Interviewer  A = Alastair Agnew**

**I:** We have in the studio today Alastair Agnew, Chairman of the Ghost Club in London. He's here to give us some advice on how to correctly identify ghosts. Alastair, a see-through figure in white that walks through walls. That's a fair enough description of a ghost, isn't it?

**A:** Well, only one out of three correct, I'm afraid Jean. Far from having the translucent appearance they do in the films, ghosts look solid, just like real people. The only thing that gives them away is the fact that, as you rightly say, they can walk through walls. And the only reason they do that is that when they were alive the wall may not have existed. Indeed, what's interesting is that in many cases you may only see them from the knees upwards, due to the fact that the ground level was lower in their day.

**I:** And how about the noises we usually associate with ghosts? The footsteps and the moaning sounds we all make when we imitate one …

**A:** … and the sound of laughter, crying and even the noise of music. Yes, these have all been heard when ghosts have been sighted. In fact, in a study carried out in England it was revealed that in 39 per cent of hauntings people claimed to have heard ghostly footsteps. One popular explanation for these sounds is the 'stone-tape theory'.

**I:** And what does that say?

**A:** That the brickwork or stones of a building can somehow absorb sounds and later play them back, rather like a tape recorder. And the same theory is used to explain some of the smells which are given off when ghosts are around. Er, smells such as decaying flesh, baking bread or animal odours are supposedly absorbed into the walls and then later released. So a building that was once used as a church, for example, may give off the smell of incense.

**I:** And as Chairman of the Ghost Club you would not agree with that explanation, would you?

**A:** It may account for some of the phenomena, but it certainly does not prove that ghosts do not exist. Sceptics have yet to put forward a theory to explain why, for example, some people have their hair stroked or sometimes feel a sharp poke in the side of their body when no one else is around.

**I:** And are there any places where ghosts are more likely to occur than others?

**A:** Er … if your house is on or near a crossroads, you may well be haunted. That's because these used to be burial places for suicides and many criminals who were hanged nearby. Er … the number of car crashes at crossroads is also presumed to raise the spirit count. And even if you don't live on a crossroads, if you wait at one for a bus, there's a good chance a spirit will follow you and give you a bit of a surprise.

**I:** And finally Alastair, are we all able to see ghosts?

**A:** Certainly, yes, though some people are more likely to attract paranormal attention than others. Er, similarly, some household pets are also good indicators that there's a spirit in the vicinity. Dogs, for example, may stubbornly refuse to enter one part of a room or start growling without explanation if they sense a ghost. Cats may hiss and spit, while a budgie or a hamster will look on wondering what all the fuss is about.

**I:** Thank you Alastair. So then, if you or your dog think you might have spotted a ghost, the Ghost Club would love to hear from you. We'll be giving out their address at the end of the programme. Now it's over to …

## Language focus 2: Question tags

Page 109

**1** Refer students to the instructions and example sentences in their books.

### Answers

The subject and the auxiliary verbs are repeated and the order is reversed. If they are affirmative in the sentence they change to negative in the tag. Notice that the demonstrative pronoun *that* in the first sentence becomes *it* in the tag.

**2** Play the example sentences again and draw student's attention to the intonation. Note that the examples have been recorded separately after the listening.

### Answers

**a** sentence 1 is a real question
**b** in sentence 2 the speaker expects agreement
The difference is in the intonation:
rising intonation ( ⟶ ) = real question
falling intonation ( ⟶ ) = asking for confirmation

### Listening: Listening script 1.41

**2** That's a fair enough description of a ghost, isn't it? And as chairman of the Ghost Club you would not agree with that explanation, would you?

**3** **1** You don't believe him, do you?
**2** You won't let me down, will you?
**3** You went away for the weekend, didn't you?
**4** He's not playing very well, is he?
**5** He's already passed First Certificate, hasn't he?
**6** I'm right about that, aren't I?
**7** You can play chess, can't you?
**8** Let's phone Paul, shall we?

**3–4** This exercise checks students' ability to form question tags. Ask students to complete the statement with an appropriate tag. Students listen to check their answers, then listen again to identify the intonation patterns on the tags and mark the intonation pattern with an arrow.

**Common problem**

It is often easier to recognize intonation patterns than to produce them and students may have particular difficulty producing falling intonation. The tendency is to make the intonation on *all* question tags rise.

It is difficult for students at First Certificate level to use question tags naturally but is it important that they know of their existence and know how to form them. A lot of exposure to the natural use of question tags, as well as practice and assimilation time, are necessary for students to be able to produce them with any degree of confidence and naturalness.

---

**Answers**

1 You don't believe him, do you?

2 You won't let me down, will you?

3 You went away for the weekend, didn't you?

4 He's not playing very well, is he?

5 He's already passed First Certificate, hasn't he?

6 I'm right about that, aren't I?

7 You can play chess, can't you?

8 Let's phone Paul, shall we?

Note: these intonation patterns are the more typical patterns in a given situation. Other patterns are possible when one is expressing surprise, and with imperatives, etc.

---

**5** Students repeat the sentences with the same intonation. They could do this as a whole class.

**6** Once students have written their sentences, go round to them each quickly checking that they have used the question tags correctly

**7** Students take turns to ask and answer each other's questions.

## Vocabulary: *Give*  Page 110

**A Phrasal verbs with *give***

**1–2** Students follow the instructions in their books, working in pairs or individually and then checking their answers in pairs.

---

**Answers**

1 1 b  2 a  3 c

2 1 revealing *or* betraying
  2 stop a habit
  3 distribute
  4 submit/hand to the teacher, return
  5 yielded/agreed (usually after a long argument)

---

**B Expressions with *give***

**1** The contexts of each of these sentences will help students to decide on the suitable ending. Check that students understand *broad* (similar to wide), *piercing* (penetrating) and *sigh* before they start.

---

**Answers**

**Part A**
1 d  2 c  3 e  4 a  5 b
**Part B**
1 e  2 d  3 f  4 a  5 b  6 c

---

**2** Students follow the instructions and match the expressions, checking their answers in pairs.

---

**Answers**

a 3 give great pleasure, 4 give someone a nasty shock

b 5 give an impressive performance, 6 give a lengthy speech

c 1 give your best regards, 2 give full details

---

**3** Refer students to the explanation of 'collocations' in their books. Explain that collocations are words that are often used together in language. Ask students to 'test' each other in pairs, taking it in turns to remember.

**Note:** students usually enjoy these 'memory' activities. They are challenging and the students themselves are often interested to learn how much they can remember. By their nature they should be quick and can be repeated easily in subsequent lessons.

**4** Refer students to the example in their book. To provide variety, put students into small groups for this or, with a confident class, ask the students yourself. In either case, tell students to use the expressions in their answers, as in the example.

## Use of English: Open cloze    Page 111
### FCE Part 2

**1** Elicit on to the board students' ideas for the essential ingredients of a ghost story. At this stage you could pre-teach the words *chill* (v) and *unnerving* (adj) which come up in the text, or you could leave them until students have completely finished and deal with them if they have not been able to deduce their meaning from context. Refer students to the 'How to go about it' box before they start the cloze.

| Answers | | | |
|---|---|---|---|
| 1 | been | 7 | in |
| 2 | whose | 8 | lot/number |
| 3 | but/though/although | 9 | sort/kind/type |
| 4 | over | 10 | the |
| 5 | make | 11 | be |
| 6 | Without | 12 | their |

## Reading 2: Gapped text    Page 112
### FCE Part 2

Photocopiable vocabulary exercise on page 166.

**1** Refer students to the pictures in their books and the questions. After students have discussed their answers in pairs or small groups, elicit their answers onto the board. They then look at the answers on page 201 of the Additional material section.

Ask students:
*How many did you guess correctly?*
*Do any of the real answers surprise you?*

**2** Refer students to the instructions and the advice in their books which focuses on grammatical and lexical links.

| Answers |
|---|
| 1 F   2 H   3 D   4 A   5 E   6 G   7 C |
| B not used |

### Reacting to the text

The whole class, with the teacher asking the questions, could discuss these questions. If about half of the students think Hallowe'en is a good idea and the other half don't, you could organize a debate. Students put together their reasons for or against Hallowe'en and then give their views to the class.

Reasons some people give for not liking Hallowe'en are:

- it is not safe for unaccompanied children to go out in the dark
- children could frighten old people by dressing up as witches and ghosts
- some youngsters commit acts of vandalism if they are not given sweets or money
- it is not an authentic British tradition. Guy Fawkes night is – see Writing model on page 115 of the Coursebook.

## Word formation: Adjectives    Page 113

**1–2** Elicit the answers for exercise 1 with the whole class, before letting students work in pairs to do exercise 2.

| Answers | |
|---|---|
| 1 *foggy* (adj) | *fog* (noun) |
| numerous (adj) | number (noun) |
| contro**ver**sial (adj) | contro**ver**sy (noun) or **con**troversy |
| impressive (adj) | impress (verb) |

**2**  1  ambit<u>ious</u>, religi<u>ous</u>, infecti<u>ous</u>, cauti<u>ous</u>
(remove -*on* and add -*ous*)

2  occupation<u>al</u>, profession<u>al</u>, emotion<u>al</u>, sensation<u>al</u>
(add -*al*)

3  cloud<u>y</u>, wind<u>y</u>, rain<u>y</u>, ic<u>y</u>*
(add -*y*) *no *e* in the adjective

4  deci<u>sive</u>, inclu<u>sive</u>, explo<u>sive</u>, offen<u>sive</u>
(remove -*de/d* and add -*sive*)

5  biolog<u>ical</u>, geograph<u>ical</u>, econom<u>ical</u>*, histor<u>ical</u>*
(remove -*y* and add -*ical*)

6  dange<u>rous</u>, disast<u>rous</u>, humo<u>rous</u>, poison<u>ous</u>
(add -*ous*) note further changes:
disaster – disastrous, humour – humorous

7  compar<u>ative</u>, imagin<u>ative</u>, compet<u>itive</u>, sens<u>itive</u>*
(remove final *e* and add -*ative/itive*)

8  anx<u>ious</u>, var<u>ious</u>, cur<u>ious</u>, gene<u>rous</u>
(remove -*ety/ity* and add or incorporate -*ous*)

9  benefi<u>cial</u>, influen<u>tial</u>, residen<u>tial</u>, finan<u>cial</u>
(remove final *ce* and add -*cial/-tial*)
note further change:
benefit – beneficial

10  healthy, wealthy, funny, lucky
     (add -y) note the doubled consonant:
     fun – funny

*note the difference in meaning between the following pairs of adjectives:

*economic*: of or relating to an economy
eg a purely economic decision, the government's economic policy

*economical*: not wasteful, cheap to run or operate
eg an economical car/washing machine

*historic*: famous or important in history
eg an historic event/monument

*historical*: belonging to or typical of the study of history
eg a historical document/film

*sensitive*: describes a person who shows understanding of people's needs, problems or feelings; sensitive about something: easily worried or offended when someone talks about it

*sensible*: describes an action or decision which is based on reason rather than emotions; a person who behaves in this way

*funny* (adj): amusing

*fun* (n): if something is fun, it is enjoyable; to have fun means to have a good time

Note: *sensitive* and *sensible* appeared in Unit 6; *fun* and *funny* in Unit 8.

## Speaking 1: FCE Part 3 — Collaborative task
Page 114

Refer students to the instructions and information in their books. Students should underline the key words in the question before they start to ensure that they follow each part of the instructions:

*Talk to your partner about* <u>each</u> *of the suggestions below and say how they might appeal to* <u>different people</u> *and then choose* <u>two</u> *that you think would be* <u>most popular</u>.

Before they begin, students complete the Useful language exercise.
**Note:** see Unit 5 for Useful language for this part of the Speaking exam.

**Useful language**

**1**  When students have completed the phrases, practise the intonation.

## Answers

| 1 | 1 | couldn't it? | 4 | would they? |
|---|---|---|---|---|
|   | 2 | will it? | 5 | wouldn't it? |
|   | 3 | don't they? | 6 | shall we? |

**2**
**Positive:** colourful, impressive, enjoyable, exciting, inexpensive, entertaining, spectacular, lively, thrilling, cheerful, bright

**Negative:** dull, costly, impractical, uninspiring

## Speaking 2: FCE Part 4 — Further discussion
Page 115

In the Speaking exam, the interlocutor would ask questions like these. Remember that Part 4 questions are always linked thematically with the discussion in Part 3. Students discuss the questions together in pairs or groups of three as they will do in the exam.

## Writing 1: FCE Part 2 — Informal letters
Page 115

In this section, students read and analyse a model letter about a traditional festival in Britain. (The origins and nature of the festival are explained in the letter in the Coursebook.)

**1–2**  Students read the instructions and underline key words in the question.

## Answers

'You attended an event <u>last weekend</u> to celebrate a <u>traditional festival in your country</u>. Write a <u>letter</u> to your English-speaking <u>penfriend</u>, describing the event. <u>Briefly</u> explain the <u>origins</u> of the festival to your penfriend, then <u>describe what happened</u> and <u>say whether you enjoyed yourself</u>.'

**3**  Students read the letter, making sure they understand it all.

**4**  Students analyse the organization of the letter.

## Answers

Yes, the writer has answered all parts of the question.
a  The origins of the festival are explained in paragraph 1.

**b** He describes what happened in paragraphs 2 and 3.

**c** He says whether he enjoyed himself in paragraph 3: *excellent food, delicious, the mulled wine\* kept everyone smiling.*

*\*'mulled wine' is hot wine with spices, popular in very cold weather.*

**5** Ask students to read the model again and find examples of the different features.

## Answers

**Phrasal verbs**
(see phrasal verbs list on pages 122 and 123 of the Workbook)
*give off* — produce and send
(appears in this unit) — into the air
*put on* — organize an event
*make up for* — compensate for
(appears in unit 8)

**Adjectives**
impressive, welcome, chilly, disappointing, costly, excellent, delicious

**Linking words**
so, and, As you can imagine, Unfortunately, but, Anyway, Well

**Relative clauses**
... 1605, when Guy Fawkes ...   ... heat, which is very welcome ...   ... Fawkes, which is burnt on top ...

**Useful expressions for informal letters**
Sorry it's taken me so long to write, but ...
Well, that's all from me.
Let me know what you've been doing recently.
All the best,

Before students write their own letters,
- elicit names of their festivals on to the board
- give students five to ten minutes to prepare what they want to say about the festival's origins and their personal experience of it
- put students into groups to exchange and share information.

Students should now be ready to write their letter. Remind them to keep within the word limit.

## Sample answer

Dear Maria Luisa

Sorry it's taken me so long to write but you know I'm very bad at writting letters.

I wrote after enjoying one of the numerous fiestas there are in Spain. It's name is Las Fallas and takes place in Valencia. Las Fallas begins on 21 of March and commemorates the fiestas that ancient people did. They used to burn piles of wood and danced around these fires.

Nowadays instead of piles of wood, valencianos burn sculptures called ninots, these ninots ridiculize politicians and local customs. Las Fallas takes a week and has a bonfire every day.

I spent a wonderful week, although I think I drank more than enough some days, but everything I did was worth going to Valencia.

Well, I send you my email, since I think it'll be more confortable and quicker to talk.
All the best
Kisses
Arturo Mendoza Fernández

143 words

**Examiner's comment**
**Content:** The candidate describes the whole week rather than one weekend as specified in the question. He also describes what generally happens and does not focus much on his own experience of the festival. The realization of this Part 2 task is therefore just satisfactory.

**Accuracy:** Few mistakes, generally minor: spelling – *writting*, *I spent a wonderful week* as opposed to *had a wonderful week*, *kisses* rather than *best wishes* or similar, etc.

**Range:** Good range of appropriate vocabulary – *takes place in, piles of wood, danced around, bonfire.*

**Organization and cohesion:** Adequate.

**Style and format:** Consistently friendly.

**Target reader:** The target reader would have some idea of the origins of the festival but would not get a clear idea of how the writer spent his time.

**Mark:** band 3

## Review 9 answers  Page 116

### Word formation

1  thirsty, guilty, stormy, sleepy, cloudy, lengthy, hilly

| 2 | Noun | Adjective |
|---|---|---|
| 1 | finance | financial |
| 2 | commerce | commercial |
| 3 | psychology | psychological |
| 4 | politics | political |
| 5 | anxiety | anxious |
| 6 | variety | various |
| 7 | influence | influential |
| 8 | residence | residential |
| 9 | mystery | mysterious |
| 10 | advantage | advantageous |

Note: You might also ask students to mark the stress (shown in **bold**) on both nouns and adjectives when doing this exercise.

4  Pronunciation changes shown in **bold**

| compare | comparative |
|---|---|
| defend | defensive |
| compete | competitive |
| describe | descriptive |
| receive | receptive |
| represent | representative |
| produce | productive |

### Use of English: Word formation
**FCE Part 3**

| 1 | noisily | 6 | suspicious |
|---|---|---|---|
| 2 | traditional | 7 | amazing |
| 3 | colourful/colorful(AE) | 8 | imprisoned |
| 4 | Surprisingly | 9 | Shortly |
| 5 | Evidently | 10 | mysterious |

### Use of English: Transformations
**FCE Part 4**

1  might not be playing
2  must have been pleased to
3  can't/couldn't have phoned
4  might have stolen your purse
5  may have given
6  give away a secret/give a secret away, would
7  'd/had better give/hand
8  gave a nervous laugh

### Writing 2:  Short stories
**FCE Part 2**

Refer students to the question and advice in their books. If your students have few ideas, do the planning stages in class, putting their ideas on the board. If they work through the planning stages together they will have an extra opportunity for speaking, too.

## Workbook answers

### Reading: Multiple matching  Page 66

| 1 | 1 D | 2 H | 3 B | 4 F |
|---|---|---|---|---|
| | 5 A | 6 G | 7 C | E not used |

**2**

| a | struck (infinitive: strike) | | b | tricking |
|---|---|---|---|---|
| c | account for | d glow | e | cited |
| f | log | g flows | h | hover |

**3**

| 1 | tricked | 2 | cited | 3 | hovering |
|---|---|---|---|---|---|
| 4 | struck | 5 | accounted for | 6 | flows |
| 7 | glow/glowing | 8 | log | | |

### Vocabulary  Page 68

**A Phrasal verbs**

| 1 c | 2 e | 3 a | 4 g | 5 b | 6 d |
|---|---|---|---|---|---|
| 7 f | | | | | |

**B Expressions with *give***

| 1 | example | 2 | lift |
|---|---|---|---|
| 3 | hand | 4 | permission |
| 5 | impression | 6 | call |
| 7 | idea | | |

**C Collocations**

| 1 | blank | 2 | broad |
|---|---|---|---|
| 3 | nervous | 4 | piercing |
| 5 | deep | 6 | full |
| 7 | impressive | | |

**D Revision: *Get***

| 1 down | 2 over | 3 away | 4 by |
|---|---|---|---|

## Language focus   Page 69

### A Modal verbs of speculation

1  1   might have left
   2   correct
   3   could/may/might have gone away
   4   correct
   5   correct
   6   may/might not be the right size
   7   can't/couldn't be going out with Sue
   8   correct
   9   He must have decided
   10  correct

### 2 Possible answers

1  He can't have slept very well.
   He must have been working very hard.
   He might have been driving all day.
2  She could be on a diet.
   She may have split up with her boyfriend.
   She might not be feeling very well.
3  The bus and train drivers might be on strike.
   Everyone must have decided to drive to work today.
   There may be a special event taking place.
4  It must be too hot for them.
   You can't have watered them enough.
   They might have some kind of disease.
5  Their son must have got into trouble again.
   They might have caught the burglar that broke into their house.
   They may have been looking for someone.
6  He might have found a job.
   He must be going out with someone.
   He could have won the lottery.
7  They might be drunk.
   They may be having an argument.
   Someone might have been robbed.
8  You must have parked it somewhere else.
   Someone may have stolen it.
   The police might have taken it away.

### B Question tags

1  has he                    2  aren't I
3  doesn't he                4  wouldn't you
5  didn't she                6  will you
7  will/would/can you        8  shall we
9  did it                    10  do they

## Use of English   Page 70

### Multiple-choice cloze

1  A        2  C        3  A        4  D
5  C        6  B        7  A        8  C
9  D        10 B        11 B        12 A

### Word formation

1  1   humorous      humorously
   2   ambitious     ambitiously
   3   beneficial    beneficially
   4   hungry        hungrily
   5   anxious       anxiously
   6   original      originally

2

| | Verb | Noun | Adjective + | Adjective – |
|---|---|---|---|---|
| 1 | attract | attraction | attractive | unattractive |
| 2 | decide | decision | decisive | indecisive |
| 3 | excite | excitement | exciting/ed | unexciting/ed |
| 4 | imagine | imagination | imaginative | unimaginative |
| 5 | obey | obedience | obedient | disobedient |
| 6 | offend | offence | offensive | inoffensive |
| 7 | please | pleasure | pleasant | unpleasant |
| 8 | succeed | success | successful | unsuccessful |
| 9 | think | thought | thoughtful | thoughtless |
| 10 | tolerate | tolerance | tolerant | intolerant |

3

1  unattractive          2  decisions
3  excitement            4  imaginatively
5  disobedient           6  offence
7  pleasures             8  successfully
9  thoughtful            10 intolerant

## Writing   Page 72

### A Model

1  opinion      2  think       3  However
4  argument     5  extent      6  hand
7  Moreover     8  although    9  conclude

The words used to introduce the three examples are:
such as Carnival, like the 'Fallas',
For example, Bonfire Night

### B Organization

The writer follows plan B.

### C Ideas

A  1, 5, 7, 11  all agree
B  2, 4, 9, 12  all disagree
C  3, 6, 8, 10  all disagree

## First Certificate Paper 2

### Writing Part 1

**Part 1**   Emails
**Part 2**   Questions

Starting with an introduction of the different types of writing that students can expect to find in the exam, the unit then moves on to explore writing extracts from different sources. It then outlines what students need to be aware of when considering style.

Students evaluate two sample answers to a Part 1 question and look at the categories used by First Certificate examiners when marking writing answers, before writing their own Part 1 email. Students are then given an example of each type of Part 2 question. They are encouraged to decide which ones they think they could answer in the exam and are provided with a short checklist of questions to help make sure that they answer the questions appropriately. They are then asked to write one or more Part 2 answer.

This unit of the Teacher's Book includes detailed evaluations of the sample material in the Coursebook, as well as a breakdown of the marking scheme.

### Introduction                              Page 118

This is a brief summary of what Paper 2 consists of. You could:
- elicit the information
- have students brainstorm what they already know about this paper, then check in their books or
- give them time to read through the information.

### Extracts                                  Page 118

Refer students to the instructions in their books. They could either work individually and compare their answers with a partner, or work with a partner to discuss their ideas.

### Answers

The writing in **bold** indicates the unit or units in which this writing type has so far been seen.

1  b  Informal letter or email (Replying to a letter) – informal
   **Units 1** (informal letters) **and 9**
   Linker: *Anyway*
   Phrasal verb: *put you up* (for the night)
   Contraction: *you're*
   Punctuation: dash
   Other language: *if you want* (would like); *let us know* (inform)

2  d  Essay – neutral/formal
   **Units 3 and 8**
   Linkers: *therefore, However*
   No phrasal verbs or contractions. Note also *Some people feel that* and *others argue that* as typical language for introducing different views.

3  c  Article – fairly informal
   **Units 2 and 8** (describing a place)
   Questions: direct, addressing the readers to engage them from the start. Note use of contraction *it's* suggesting a less formal style.

4  a  Formal letter or email (requesting information) – formal **Unit 2**
   No contractions or phrasal verbs and the questions are indirect; *I would be grateful if you could tell me* is a typical way of introducing a polite request.

5  g  Short story – neutral/informal **Units 4 and 9**
   Note typical narrative elements:
   Time linker: *As soon as*
   Tenses: past perfect and past simple
   Phrasal verb: *head for*
   Adverb: *desperately*
   Contraction: *wasn't*

6  f  Review – neutral **Unit 4**
   Vocabulary of the theatre: *musical, cast, stage*
   Opinion: *But my favourite moment of all was*

7  e  Report – formal
   **Unit 7 (Teacher's Book page 163)**
   Linkers: *To sum up, although*
   No contractions or phrasal verbs
   Other language: *of the highest quality* (very good/excellent), *offers a greater selection of dishes* (has more dishes), *provides its customers with* (gives its customers)

**8** h Description – neutral/informal **Unit 6**
(Descriptive short story)
Contraction: *he's*
Phrasal verb: *look up to*
Linker: *Despite*
Language of description: *cheerful, his piercing blue eyes … light up when he smiles*

**9** i Background reading text – semi formal/neutral **Unit 14**
No contractions or phrasal verbs
Linker: *To begin with*
Other language: references to set text

Note: Words or expressions in brackets indicate a contrasting register.

## Formal or informal? Page 119

Students focus on the features of language which conveys formality and informality.

### Answers

| | | |
|---|---|---|
| 1 | d | informal |
| 2 | e | formal |
| 3 | a | informal |
| 4 | c | formal |
| 5 | b | formal |

## Answering questions Page 119

### Part 1: Emails

For the purposes of the First Certificate examination, emails are very similar to letters. Answers must be grammatically correct with accurate spelling and punctuation and in a style which is relevant to the target reader and the situation. Abbreviated language such as that used in text messages is not appropriate. An email box will be printed at the top of the answer page.

**1** Refer students to the question and sample answers in their books. Before moving on to 2, ask students for their impressions of the two answers A and B on page 120.

**2** Draw students' attention to the instructions and categories used when marking answers. Students analyse the sample answers in the light of these categories either in pairs or individually.

The second is better in most respects except paragraphing (see below for more detailed analysis).

### Answers

**Email A**
**Content**
**a** All the points are included, although the writer does not develop them by adding points of his/her own.

**b** The opening is not relevant to the body of the email. Three sentences (over 40 words) are spent talking about the friend's relationship with Marco. This looks like a piece of pre-learnt material, reproduced here in order to include some phrasal verbs (*fall out* and *make it up*) and an idiomatic expression (*you were made for each other*). Examiners would not be impressed.

**Organization and cohesion**
**a** The paragraphing is clear and logical.

**b** Linking words have been used, sometimes appropriately (eg *Anyway, this summer …*), sometimes not (eg the formal *Furthermore*).

**c** The opening is inappropriate (*Dear friend:*) and the continuation irrelevant (see Content). The ending is appropriate despite the errors (*I must to go now* and *think in*) although it is spoiled further by inconsistent register (*do not hesitate to contact me*) and the final *Kisses*.

**Range and accuracy**
**a** The writer shows reasonable control of indirect questions (*I would be grateful if you could to tell me which fruit it is picked in July*) though the register is inappropriately formal. Other language and structures are used reasonably well with similar non-impeding errors (see last paragraph). Other errors: *I am thinking in going, you have worked in the same place last year, wether*

**b** *I would be grateful if you could (to) tell me* is used twice, as is *Anyway*.

**c** The sentence beginning *I know you have worked.* is copied (incorrectly) from the rubric.

## Style and format

**a**  See above for comments on register, which is inconsistent.

**b**  It is clearly set out as an email. (Note incorrect use of colon after *Dear friend:*)

## Target reader

The reader would be reasonably well informed, although the intention behind the question *I would be grateful if you could tell me wether you earned enough money?* is not entirely clear. The formal questions would not sound very friendly.

**Mark:** 3.1 (See below for notes on marks.)

## Email B
### Content

**a**  All the points are included.

**b**  The content, including the opening paragraph, is relevant to the question. The writer builds on the notes with relevant additions:

| July/which fruit days off? | *when my exams have finished* *I really want to go sightseeing in London* |
| travel the next | *I'm thinking of setting off on a month's tour of England* |
| any more advice? | *such as suggestions on how to get there and what clothes to take.* |

Note that the length of the email is slightly over 150 words (155). This is not serious but it serves to show students that adding points of their own should not be done at the expense of other criteria, namely writing within the word limit and covering all the points.

## Organization and cohesion

**a**  The email is written in one paragraph. This would be penalized.

**b**  Good use of (informal) linking words: *but, when, so, then, after, anyway*. Ideas logically organized.

**c**  Opening and ending both appropriate.

## Range and accuracy

**a**  Good variety of structures to express plans, intentions and preferences:
*I hope to, I (really) want to, I'd like to, I'm planning on, I'm thinking of*

Appropriate use of informal expressions for emails:
*That's all for now, Hope to hear from you soon, All the best*

Other vocabulary:
*go sightseeing, setting off on a month's tour, Let me know*

**b**  No unnecessary repetition. Notice techniques for avoiding it:
*like you did last year* (went fruit picking)
*in that month* (July)
*do you think I'd have enough (money) to do that* (go on a month's tour of England)?

**c**  No evidence of 'lifting' (copying whole phrases) from the rubric.

## Style and format

**a**  Register appropriately and consistently informal.

**b**  Clearly an email, though paragraphing would make it clearer.

## Target reader

The reader would be fully informed and clear about all the writer's questions.

Mark: 5.2 (See below for marks)

## Note on marking

When assessing Paper 2 answers, Cambridge First Certificate markers award an impression mark, placing the written work in a band between 0 and 5, band 5 being the highest. Within each band there are 3 further subdivisions: for example, a piece of work which is placed in band 3 will be awarded a mark of either 3.1, 3.2 or 3.3.

The criteria for assessment can be consulted in the *Handbook for FCE*, which is obtainable from the Local Secretary in your area or from:

University of Cambridge ESOL Examinations,
1 Hills Road, Cambridge CB1 2EU.
Tel. 01223 553997
www.CambridgeESOL.org

When marking students' work you might like to use this system. If you prefer to award a mark out of 20 here are approximate equivalents:

| Band + subdivision | Mark out of 20 |
|---|---|
| 5.3 | 20 |
| 5.2 | 19 |
| 5.1 | 18 |
| 4.3 | 17 |
| 4.2 | 16 |
| 4.1 | 15 (75%) |
| 3.3 | 14 |
| 3.2 | 13 |
| 3.1 | 12 (60%) |
| 2.3 | 11 |
| 2.2 | 10 (50%) |
| 2.1 | 9 |
| 1.3 | 8 |
| 1.2 | 4 |
| 1.1 | 1 |

**3** Refer students to the question in their books and to the 'Don't forget!' box.

## Answers

Who is the target reader?
an employee of Family Adventure Holidays
Will you use a formal or informal style?
formal
Will your questions be direct or indirect?
indirect

Students could write their letters at home and if appropriate, do exercise 4 in the next class. If you feel that your students would not respond well to 'evaluating' each other's work then tell them to ask themselves the questions in 2 and make any necessary changes before they give in their work to you.

## Sample answer

Dear Sir
When I was watching the news I saw your advertisment, and I found it enjoyable. I thought I could take my family there but before taking that decision I wanted to ask some questions.

Firstly, I wanted to ask you about the activities. I wanted to know if apart from those you put in the advertisement, is it possible to go sailing because everyone who had done sailing told me that it is great fun. I also noticed something in the activities that said parents are encouraged to participate with their children, and does this mean all the time? And finally I saw that the holidays were from Saturday to Saturday but I would like to arrive there on Friday, and my question is, how much will it cost an extra night?

I am waiting for your response
Yours sincerely
Javier Buendía

142 words

**Examiner's comment**
**Content:** The writer has not followed the rubric exactly in that the question states 'you have found the following advertisement' and the writer states *I was watching the news and I saw your advertisement*. Other points are covered except the proposed date of arrival. Normally in Part 1 questions, failure to cover key points in the question results in a maximum mark of 2.3 only. In this letter the date is important but not essential as the writer is asking for information, not actually booking the holiday. In most other respects this is a convincing letter with few errors.

**Accuracy:** Generally minimal errors – *who had done* instead of the use of the present perfect, omission of the subject in *that (it) is great fun*, and word order in *how much will cost an extra night?* (although in other examples the writer forms indirect questions correctly).

**Range:** Although there is some awkwardness of expression – *I am waiting for your response* – there are examples of good handling of vocabulary and grammar: *apart from those, I also noticed something in the activities that said*.

**Organization and cohesion:** Well organized, although the middle paragraph could be divided into two paragraphs.

**Style and format:** Consistently appropriate.

**Target reader:** Would be informed as to the queries the writer has, except the date of arrival.

**Mark:** band 3

**Part 2**                                                     Page 121

Students follow the instructions given in their books.

**How to go about it**

## Answers

**1** Your college magazine has invited you to write an article about a member of your family who helped you in some way. Describe the person and explain what they did that was helpful to you.
**Style:** could range from informal to formal. As with all writing tasks it must be consistent throughout.

**2** You have had a class discussion on the following statement:
*It should be illegal for parents to smack their children*.
Your teacher has asked you to write an essay giving your views on the statement.
**Style:** neutral/formal composition

**3** You recently visited a place which you had not been to for some time. Your cousin, who now lives abroad, also know this place very well. Write a letter to your cousin, describing the changes and your feelings about them. Do not write any postal addresses.
**Style:** informal

**4** You have a part-time job in a games centre, where people can go to play computer games. The owner would like to buy some new software and he has asked you to write a report, suggesting two games for the centre. You should briefly describe each game and explain why you think the customers would enjoy both games.
**Style:** could range from informal (relationship with owner could be very friendly) to formal

**5** Your school's English language magazine has invited readers to write a review of a holiday they spent recently in a seaside resort. You should include information on your accommodation and what there is to do in the resort, and say whether you would recommend the holiday to other people.
**Style:** could range from informal to formal

**6** You have decided to enter a short-story competition. The competition rules say that the story must begin or end with the following words:
*They were sad to leave, but they had no choice*.
**Style:** neutral or informal narrative

Students choose one or more of the questions to write about for homework.

## Content Overview

### Themes

This unit deals with the themes of crime and punishment, and related language.

### Exam-related activities

| | |
|---|---|
| **Paper 1** | **Reading** |
| Part 1 | Multiple choice |
| **Paper 2** | **Writing** |
| Part 2 | Article or story |
| Part 2 | Articles |
| Part 2 | Short stories (Review) |
| **Paper 3** | **Use of English** |
| Part 1 | Multiple-choice cloze (Review) |
| **Paper 4** | **Listening** |
| Part 2 | Sentence completion |
| Part 3 | Multiple matching |
| **Paper 5** | **Speaking** |
| Part 3 | Collaborative task |
| Part 4 | Further discussion |

### Other

Language focus 1: Passives and passive constructions with the infinitive
Language focus 2: Past necessity
Vocabulary: Crime and punishment
Phrasal verbs

## Vocabulary 1: Crime and punishment
Page 122

**A Crimes and criminals**
You could lead in to the theme by mentioning a recent crime that students will have heard of. Refer students to the pictures in their books and elicit or tell students the name of the crime and the person who commits it:

*Shoplifting, shoplifter*
*Vandalism, vandal*

**1–3** Students then follow the instructions in their books for 1, 2 and 3.

## Answers

**1–2**

| | | |
|---|---|---|
| 1 | murderer | murder |
| 2 | smuggler | smuggling |
| 3 | arsonist | arson |
| 4 | pickpocket | pickpocketing |
| 5 | blackmailer | blackmail |
| 6 | shoplifter | shoplifting |
| 7 | kidnapper | kidnap(ping) |
| 8 | hijacker | hijack(ing) |
| 9 | vandal | vandalism |
| 10 | mugger | mugging |

**2**

| | |
|---|---|
| 4 | pickpocketing |
| 6 | shoplifting |
| 10 | mugging |

**3**

| | | | | | |
|---|---|---|---|---|---|
| a | burgle | b | steal | c | rob |

### B Punishment

**1** Below are suggested answers, from the least severe to the most severe, and descriptions of each term. Students may disagree with the order of some of the punishments. If this is the case, ask students to justify their opinions and listen carefully to make sure that they really have understood what the terms mean.

## Answers

**d** to order someone to pay a £200 fine (a penalty of £200 for breaking the law)

**b** to order someone to do 200 hours of community service (instead of going to prison, an offender has to work for the benefit of the community, eg picking up litter, cleaning walls of graffiti, etc)

**e** to give someone a two-year prison sentence (to send somebody to prison for two years)

**a** to sentence someone to life imprisonment (in Britain, the maximum prison sentence.)

**c** to sentence someone to death (to order that an offender be executed)

**2** Students could discuss the possible punishments in small groups. Encourage them to use the phrases in the shaded box.

**Listening 1:** **FCE Part 2** **Sentence completion**
Page 123

**1** Elicit the students' ideas on the first question. They could discuss the second in pairs.

**2** Remind students to predict the type of information they might hear before they listen for the first time.

## Answers

| | |
|---|---|
| 1 | during the day |
| 2 | less than ten |
| 3 | sell stolen goods |
| 4 | 13/thirteen per cent/% |
| 5 | under the doormat |
| 6 | home alarm system |
| 7 | garage door |
| 8 | fight local crime |
| 9 | elderly *and* disabled |
| 10 | ten million |

---

**Listening 1: Listening script 1.42**

**P = Presenter   O = Police Officer**

**P:** And now it's time for our regular Crimewatch slot and here with us today is Police Officer Richard Woodcock from the Crime Prevention Unit of the Metropolitan Police. Richard, perhaps you could begin by telling us what characterizes a typical burglary?

**O:** Well, burglary is one of the crimes most people worry about, not so much because of the loss of property, but more because of the sense of invasion it causes – the idea that someone has gone through all your personal belongings. Many residential burglaries occur because of common misconceptions. For example, while people typically worry about night-time thefts, nearly 50 per cent of residential break-ins happen during the day, when homes are vacant because owners are out working. What's more, robbing a house takes less time than many people think. Most burglars get in and out in less than ten minutes.

**P:** Mm. And how does the police go about combating the problem?

**O:** Police forces all over the country have targeted burglary. Operation Bumblebee, for example, was a major crime-prevention campaign run by the Metropolitan Police and aimed at beating the burglars. The scheme has included raids on criminals who are known to sell stolen goods. At the end of Operation Bumblebee's first year, burglaries fell by 13 per cent, a figure which has to be considered a success.

**P:** Mmm … And what would you say are the most important measures our listeners can take to protect their own homes?

**O:** Most householders are aware of the risk of being burgled, and the majority have already installed locks on doors and windows. What many of these same people don't do, however, is use them! So rule number one is lock up before you go out. And whatever you do, don't leave spare keys under the doormat, thinking that no one is going to find them. It's the most obvious place for a burglar to look and an open invitation to walk in unchallenged. If you have another set of keys, leave them with a trusted neighbour or friend. A home alarm system is another must, and a good deterrent to any would-be burglars, but make sure you have it put in by an installer who works to the British Standard. Your local crime prevention officer can give you advice on how to choose an installer.

And I mentioned locks earlier, but don't forget about the garage door as well. This can provide easy access for burglars, allowing them to gain access not only to your car, but directly into your home if there's an adjoining door.

**P:** Thank you, Richard. Now, many listeners have phoned in asking about Neighbourhood Watch Schemes and how to set them up. What information can you give them?

**O:** Well, the best thing about these schemes is that they bring the community together and provide everyone with the chance to fight local crime. Your neighbours look out for you, your family, your home and your street, and you do the same for them. If you see anyone acting suspiciously near a neighbour's house, you contact the police. It especially enables people to check on vulnerable members of the community, such as the elderly or disabled. The schemes have come a long way since the early view some people held of nosy neighbours interfering in other people's business. There are now more than 155,000 Neighbourhood Watch schemes in the country, with more than ten million residents directly benefiting from them. It's the largest voluntary organization in the country and one of the most effective for beating crime.

**P:** And where should listeners go to ask about starting one?

**O:** The local police station will tell you all about it, or you can phone the National Neighbourhood Watch Association on – and I have the number here – 0207 2723348.

**P:** Thank you Richard. We'll give that number again at the end of the programme …

## Speaking 1:
**FCE Part 3**
### Collaborative task
Page 124

Refer students to the instructions in their books. Encourage them to use expressions from the Useful language section on page 59 of Unit 5.

## Speaking 2:
**FCE Part 4**
### Further discussion
Page 124

Students could discuss these questions in pairs or groups of three.

## Vocabulary 2: Phrasal verbs      Page 124

**1** In this exercise, students read first for general understanding in order to answer the question in their books. They should not focus on the underlined phrasal verbs at this stage but read quite quickly.

**2** Students follow the instructions in their books.

| Answers | |
|---|---|
| **1** *own up to doing something* | to confess to something which you are to blame for |
| **2** *make something up* | to invent (a story) |
| **3** *take somebody in* | to trick or deceive someone |
| **4** *let somebody off* | to give someone a lighter punishment than they expected, or not punish them at all |
| **5** *get away with something* | to avoid being caught or punished for something wrong you have done |
| **6** *find something out* | to discover or hear about something |
| **7** *show off* | to try to impress people by telling or showing them what you are capable of |
| **8** *look into something* | to investigate |

**3** In this exercise students both practise using some of the phrasal verbs in context and prepare a test for their partner. Remind students to use the appropriate form of the verbs in their sentences.

If you have a large group and cannot check that each student's sentences are correct before they test each other, set the task for homework and take it in to check. After checking, redistribute so that students can try each other's exercises.

## Writing 1:
**FCE Part 2**
Page 125

There is a choice of writing type – an article or a story. In the exam students will have to choose: you or the students can decide which is more relevant to them or which is preferred. Both of the titles are related to the theme of 'crime'.

For help and advice about writing the article refer students to the relevant 'How to go about it' boxes in 1 and 2.

## Answers

**Style**

The target readers of the article are other students at your school or language school.

The style could be either formal/neutral because of the topic, or informal to suit the target readers.

When responding to your students' writing, refer to how successfully students have followed the advice given in their books.

**Reading: FCE Part 1**  **Multiple choice**
Page 125

Photocopiable vocabulary exercise on page 166.

**1** Refer students to the pre-reading questions in their books. Students discuss their answers together in pairs.

**2** Students read through the text fairly quickly to compare the ideas with their own answers. Ask pairs to give feedback to the whole class both on their own ideas and those they have found in the text.

The text mentions the following:
*Why might somebody hire a private detective?*
infidelity in a marriage, tracing a missing person, insurance fraud, employee theft, company security
*What image do you have of private detectives?*
The writer tells us, jokingly, that he half expects to see 'a small, dark, smoke-filled room, a single desk with an empty in-tray and a long, scruffy raincoat hanging from a hat stand in the corner' but finds that this is not the case. In addition, at Wright and Wrong, detectives '… always work very strictly within the law – there's no violence, no break-ins, and certainly no guns.'
*What qualities do you think are required to do the job well?*
patience, sensitivity

**3**

### Answers

| | | | |
|---|---|---|---|
| 1 D | 2 C | 3 C | 4 A |
| 5 B | 6 D | 7 C | 8 A |

## Language focus 1: Passives   page 127

**1** Students read the text quickly and answer the questions.

### Answers

**a** Sometimes they bug telephones with parents' consent, though usually they follow the children and film any wrongdoings.
**b** They see it as an invasion of privacy, caused by a lack of communication between parents and children.

**2** Refer students to the instructions in their books.

With a strong group you could tell them to cover the verb forms in the box and let them try the exercise from their own knowledge first before looking at the words in the box.

Point out to students that:
• they will need to complete both passive and active forms
• two of the gaps require two words.

### Answers

| | | | |
|---|---|---|---|
| **1** are | **2** be | **3** has | **4** were |
| **5** have | **6** be | **7** to be | **8** is |
| **9** to be | **10** are | **11** is | **12** was |
| **13** been | **14** being | **15** being | |

**3** As a record of how the passive is formed students complete the box with examples from the summary.

### Answers

| | |
|---|---|
| Present simple | (1) are hired |
| | (8) is not done |
| | (10) are followed |
| | (11) is captured |
| Present continuous | (0) are being used |
| Present perfect | (3) has been caused |
| Past simple | (4) were kept |
| | (12) was interviewed |
| Past perfect | (13) had been caught |
| Future simple | (6) will be published |

| Infinitive | (7) to be bugged |
| | (9) to be (done) |
| Gerund | (14) being subjected |
| | (15) being filmed |

The passive is formed with the appropriate form of the verb *be* + past participle.

**Passive construction with the infinitive**

Ask students to read the extract from the article and its transformation.

**Practice and Transformations**

Students could complete these individually before checking with the whole class.

### Answers

is believed (that) they stole/have stolen £3 million
1 must not be taken
2 is known to have broken
3 is not thought to be
4 will be made to (note use of *to* with *make* in the passive)
5 must have been tapped
6 has not been contacted by

**Further practice: Passives**

In this exercise students are given no help with the form (active or passive) of the verbs needed in each space. Point out to students that, as in the example **(0)**, more than one word is often necessary.

Before students read the text, set them the following questions which ensure that they read the whole text before they start completing the gaps:

*How much are people normally fined for this kind of offence?* (£50)

*Of the £800 that Mr Humphris had to pay, how much was the real fine?* (£400)

### Answers

| | | | |
|---|---|---|---|
| 1 | letting/he let | 8 | do not clean |
| 2 | *was found | | (*will not clean* = |
| 3 | will send/sends | | refusal) |
| 4 | have been fined | 9 | was told |
| 5 | put | 10 | was invited |
| 6 | are fined | 11 | being followed/ |
| 7 | caught | | having been followed |
| | | 12 | being ordered |

*note: not *has been found*. In newspaper reports like this the present perfect tends to be used to introduce the story, and the past simple to give further details.

**Writing 2:** **Articles** Page 129
**FCE Part 2**

In this section, students are introduced to expressions and considerations useful for writing articles.

**1** Refer students to the examples in their books and the substitution exercise.

### Answers

| | | | |
|---|---|---|---|
| 1 | Personally | 5 | Curiously |
| 2 | Astonishingly | 6 | Worryingly |
| 3 | Sadly | 7 | Interestingly |
| 4 | Unfortunately/Sadly | 8 | Happily |

**2** Refer students to the instructions in their books.

**3** Students compare their ideas with those in the model answer. Ask different pairs to give feedback.

**4** Students can continue working in pairs before checking with the whole class.

### Answers

a *A load of rubbish*
(This expression can also be used to express disagreement or criticize something.)
b *I'm sure the people of Brenton don't drop crisp packets and drink cans on the floor in their own home.*
c *So why do so many think it's acceptable to do so on the streets of our town?*
*But surely they, more than anyone, want a town they can be proud of, don't they?*
d *Incredibly, Clearly, Unfortunately, surely*
e *So, And, But*
(Normally, these are used as conjunctions to link two ideas in the same sentence. Here they are used informally at the beginning of a sentence to link the ideas which follow with those in the previous sentence.)
f *But surely they, more than anyone, want a town they can be proud of, don't they?*

**5** Refer students to the instructions in their books. Students can answer these points individually before checking with the whole class.

## Answers

**Paragraph 1**
A criticism of some of Brenton's residents and their tendency to drop litter.

**Paragraph 2**
The serious nature of the problem in Brenton, and the impression left on tourists.

**Paragraph 3**
Suggested solutions.

**Paragraph 4**
A criticism of the council and a reason why they should take action.

**6** Refer students to the Part 2 instructions in their books and if necessary deal with the meaning of *graffiti* by referring to the picture at the bottom of the page. Then refer them to the 'Don't forget!' box. Encourage students to list their paragraph headings and make brief notes under each one. Remind them that they can make up information in their answers, if it is helpful to do so.

Your students may appreciate some help with ideas and/or vocabulary, particularly for the second part of the question. Brainstorm ideas from the whole class and, as you do so, elicit or provide relevant words and collocations. Depending on their suggestions, this might include the following:
*impose stiff fines on offenders*
*order graffiti artists to clean off graffiti/clean up buildings/do community service, provide special/legal graffiti walls*
*remove graffiti as quickly as possible*
*restrict the sale of spray paints/ban the sale of spray paints (to under 18s)*
*install more CCTV cameras*

**Listening 2:** **FCE Part 3**

## Multiple matching
Page 131

**1** Students discuss these questions in pairs or small groups.

**2** Refer students to the instructions in their books.

## Answers

| 1 C | 2 A | 3 F | 4 E | 5 D |
|-----|-----|-----|-----|-----|

**Listening 2: Listening script 1.43–1.47**

**Speaker 1**
My mum gave me nearly £100 in cash to pay for a trip to France with my school. When I went to give the money to the French teacher, I couldn't find it anywhere. I knew my mum would be angry with me for losing it – so I told her I'd been mugged by two boys on the way to school. So she phoned the school, who called the police and when they came to the school to interview me the next day they realized I was lying, because I kept giving different descriptions of my attackers. I've never been told off by so many people – my mum, the teachers, the police. Later that day I realized I needn't have lied after all – I found the money in the bottom of my jacket pocket.

**Speaker 2**
We were just going shopping, not far away, just to the shopping centre in town. And anyway, I was supposed to check that all the windows were closed upstairs in the house – before we left, like. Well, I forgot, didn't I, and when dad asked me if I'd remembered to 'check the windows were closed', I couldn't be bothered to get out of the car and go back to do it. So I said I had. Well, we were only going to be out for a short while, so I thought we didn't need to worry. That morning we were burgled – we lost £3,000 worth of stuff, including my whole music system. I had to own up – I mean it was obvious they got in through the window, wasn't it? And there was no sign of forced entry.

**Speaker 3**

We weren't allowed to have parties in our house when I was a teenager, my mum and dad wouldn't let us. They didn't really approve of our friends – they didn't want them smoking in the house and spilling drinks and stuff on the new carpet. So when they went away for the weekend to celebrate their wedding anniversary, me and my brother decided to have a celebration of our own, with some friends, of course. We would have got away with it – if they hadn't phoned up in the middle of the party. They heard all the music and all our friends and everything. They never let us do anything after that.

**Speaker 4**

I once wrote a note to my teacher, you know, a fake one in my mum's handwriting, so I could get out of doing sport. My mum found out and went mad. I'd written a couple of practice letters before doing the final copy, you know, to practise her writing, and the next day she found them in the bin. I should have burned them or torn them up into pieces. I can still hear her now: 'You've let us down, my boy. We've brought you up to be honest and you've let us down.' She was really upset. I didn't have to do sport, though.

**Speaker 5**

All the time I was growing up I don't think I ever told one lie to my parents. There were things I got up to, you know, things I wasn't supposed to do that I did, like most people. I mean I wasn't an angel, by any means. I smoked the odd cigarette with friends, got into trouble at school for not being polite to teachers, that kind of thing. But if I wanted to do something like go to an all-night party I knew how to get round my dad so he'd let me go. You know, I'd wash his car or offer to do the gardening or something like that. But telling lies? No, I didn't need to do that.

## Language focus 2: Past necessity

Page 131

These structures often cause confusion for learners of English.

Speaker 1 **b**     Speaker 5 **a**

Once the meanings have been established, elicit from students or point out how Speaker 1's structure is formed:

*need (not)* + *have* + past participle

**Practice**

Student complete the sentences individually or in pairs.

If some students are still having problems remembering which form of *need* is appropriate, ask them to write down three things that they did not need to do at the weekend and three things that they need not have done.

Students then tell each other their situations, one by one, and see if their partner can say the sentence that the 'teller' has written down.

| Answers |
|---|
| 1  needn't have written |
| 2  didn't need to set |
| 3  didn't need to go |
| 4  needn't have bothered |
| 5  needn't have worried |

| Review 10 answers Page 132 |
|---|

### The passive

| | |
|---|---|
| 1  has been robbed | 6  will be given/is going to be given |
| 2  were arrested | |
| 3  be made | 7  are currently being looked |
| 4  being burgled | |
| 5  are (being) smuggled | 8  had never been told |

### Vocabulary

**Phrasal verbs**

1

| A | 1 c | 2 a | 3 e |
|---|---|---|---|
|   | 4 b | 5 f | 6 d |

| B | 1 c | 2 f | 3 a |
|---|---|---|---|
|   | 4 b | 5 d | 6 e |

**Use of English:** FCE Part 1  **Multiple-choice cloze**

| 1 D | 2 A | 3 B | 4 C | 5 D | 6 C |
|---|---|---|---|---|---|
| 7 A | 8 B | 9 A | 10 C | 11 C | 12 D |

## Workbook answers

### Reading: Multiple matching   Page 74

**1**

| | | | |
|---|---|---|---|
| **1** E | **2** C | **3/4** A, E in any order | |
| **5** D | **6** E | **7** D | **8** B |
| **9** C | **10/11** A, B in any order | **12** D | |
| **13** E | **14** A | **15** D | |

**2**

| | | | | | |
|---|---|---|---|---|---|
| **1** a | **2** c | **3** e | **4** b | **5** f | **6** d |

**3**

| | | |
|---|---|---|
| **1** snatched | **2** squirt | **3** waving |
| **4** Unaware | **5** stuck | **6** pointed |

**4**

*get* in touch with someone/get lucky/get back (to the hotel)/get out

*hold* one's nose/hold tightly onto the camera

*pick* the wrong person/pick something up

*take* off a jacket/take someone to a place/take a wallet

*make* a mess/make the mistake of doing something

*have* fun/have no idea (what someone is on about)

**5**

| | | |
|---|---|---|
| **1** in touch | **2** tightly on to | **3** them up |
| **4** me to | **5** the mistake | **6** no idea |

### Vocabulary   Page 76

**A Crime**

| | |
|---|---|
| **1** pickpocketing | **2** arson |
| **3** robbery | **4** burglary |
| **5** kidnap | **6** blackmail |
| **7** smuggling | **8** drug trafficking |

**B Phrasal verbs**

**1**

| | |
|---|---|
| **1** take in | **2** look into |
| **3** get away with | **4** make out |
| **5** make up | **6** take up |
| **7** look up to | **8** get up to |

**2**

| | | |
|---|---|---|
| **1** making (it) up | **2** make out | **3** taken in |
| **4** get away with | **5** looking into | **6** getting up to |

### Language focus   Page 77

**A Active and passive**

1 was released, being found, did not commit/had not committed
2 is being repaired, was told, won't/wouldn't be
3 have been asked, haven't prepared
4 happened, were caught, were made, took
5 are produced, are sold, are exported
6 was given, died, stopped, hasn't been fixed
7 is thought, was found, was walking
8 destroyed, didn't do/haven't done, be allowed

**B Revision: Modal verbs**

1 needn't have revised
2 didn't need to pay
3 don't have to go
4 mustn't tell
5 shouldn't have
6 needn't have bought
7 needn't worry/don't need to worry
8 didn't have to go

### Use of English   Page 78

**Transformations**

1 was not/wasn't given
2 is/'s being met
3 was robbed (by thieves) of
4 is being looked into
5 had been made up by
6 is said to be
7 are expected to be announced
8 is believed to have
9 is thought to have known
10 needn't have taken
11 we didn't need to

**Word formation**

| | | |
|---|---|---|
| **1** buildings | **2** residential | **3** amazing |
| **4** reduction | **5** robbery | **6** effective |
| **7** criminals | **8** presence | **9** invasion |
| **10** evidence | | |

**Open cloze**

| | | |
|---|---|---|
| **1** who/that | **2** has | **3** not/never |
| **4** being | **5** such | **6** or |
| **7** the/its | **8** is | **9** take |
| **10** for | **11** are | **12** made |

# 11 What on Earth's going on?

## Writing    Page 80

Student B's answer would be given a higher mark.

**A Analysis**

| | A | B |
|---|---|---|
| 1 | no | yes |
| 2 | yes | yes |
| 3 | no | yes |
| 4 | no | yes |
| 5 | no | yes |
| 6 | no | yes |
| 7 | no | yes |
| 8 | yes | yes |
| 9 | no | yes |
| 10 | no | yes |

**B Accuracy**

a  I **arrived** at the station
**to catch** the train
I **was feeling/felt** sad
I **had finished** my holiday
I **decided** to go
make me **feel**
somebody **had stolen** it
I **felt** sadder

b  **at** the station
because I had finished
I enjoyed the holiday
want to come home
the shop to buy
suitcase **on** the ground
paid the woman
to finish **a** holiday

**C Addressing the reader**

Did you get my postcard from Italy?
You'll never guess what happened to me after I'd posted it to you!
… you know how unfit I am!
You can imagine how relieved I felt.
How about you, Esther? Did anything exciting happen on your holiday? Write and tell me all about it.

## Content Overview

### Themes

In this unit, students read, listen, speak and write about the weather, extreme weather conditions, natural disasters and concerns about the environment.

### Exam-related activities

| | | |
|---|---|---|
| **Paper 1** | **Reading** | |
| Part 3 | Multiple matching | |
| | | |
| **Paper 2** | **Writing** | |
| Part 1 | Formal letters (Review) | |
| Part 2 | Essays | |
| | | |
| **Paper 3** | **Use of English** | |
| Part 2 | Open cloze | |
| Part 4 | Transformations (Review) | |
| | | |
| **Paper 4** | **Listening** | |
| Part 1 | Multiple choice | |
| Part 2 | Sentence completion | |
| | | |
| **Paper 5** | **Speaking** | |
| Part 3 | Collaborative task | |

### Other

Language focus 1: Conditionals
Language focus 2: *So, neither* and *nor*
Vocabulary:       Weather
                  *Put*
                  The environment
Reading:          Christina Tugwell text

## Vocabulary 1: Weather    Page 134

In this section, students extend their ability to describe weather conditions with accuracy. Refer them to the pictures in their books but ask them to cover the vocabulary section for the moment. Either in pairs or as a whole group, students compare the pictures using their existing vocabulary resources. If possible note the words students use to make their descriptions.

**1** In each group of three adjectives, students will probably know at least one or two – enough for them to be able to complete the exercise without help from you or a dictionary.

## Answers

| 1 storm | 2 rain | 3 wind | 4 sunshine |
|---------|--------|--------|------------|
| 5 sea | 6 clouds | 7 showers | |

Elicit from the students the words they do not understand and cannot guess, and write them on the board. Deal with them yourself, going through them one by one.

*overcast sky* – when the sky is covered with grey clouds

*angry-looking clouds* – often just before a storm when the clouds are different shades of grey

*gale (-force wind)* – a strong wind moving at 45 km to 90 km per hour

*choppy sea* – reasonably turbulent or agitated (less so than 'rough')

*torrential rain* – extremely heavy rain

*fine rain* – rain made up of a lot of very small droplets

*scattered showers* – intermittent periods of rain moving over an area of land or sea

**2** Students follow the instructions in their books.

**3** If students have already talked about the photos, as suggested above, then now is a good time to draw their attention to the way they did this. You could write up some of the things students said earlier and elicit other ways of saying them which use some of the word combinations just studied.

Students now describe the pictures at the top of the page using expressions recently seen.

**Reading:** **Multiple matching**
FCE Part 3        Page 134

Photocopiable vocabulary exercise on page 167.

**1** Help students with the correct pronunciation of the different types of conditions:

| *drought* | /draʊt/ |
|-----------|---------|
| *floods* | /flʌds/ |
| *avalanches* | **hur**ricanes |
| **earth**quakes | |
| tor**na**does | /eɪ/ |

Students answer the questions as a lead-in to the reading.

**2** Students read the exam instructions. If necessary, refer them to the 'How to go about it' box in Unit 6 on page 66.

## Answers

| 1 C | 2 A | 3 D | 4/5 A, B |
|-----|-----|-----|----------|
| 6 C | 7 B | 8 A | 9/10 A, C |
| 11 B | 12 A | 13 D | 14 C |
| 15 B | | | |

**Reacting to the text**
Students discuss the questions in pairs or small groups.

## Language focus 1: Conditionals
Page 136

**A Real or imaginary?**
Focus students on the sentence from the text in their books or write it on the board. Students read the explanation and decide what the correct alternatives are from the context of the extract.

## Answers

In this sentence the speaker, Pat Beddows, is referring to a situation in the *past*. The situation she describes is imaginary because we know that the guide *shouted* at them to get out of the way, and that the consequences *were not* tragic.

**B Context**
Discuss the sentences as a whole class activity.

## Answers

**1 and 2**
Zero conditional          text C
present simple, present simple, present simple

First conditional          text A
*will* + infinitive without *to*, present simple

Second conditional          text D
past simple, *would* + infinitive without *to*

Third conditional          text C
past perfect, *would* + infinitive without *to*

Mixed conditional          text B
past perfect, *would* + infinitive without *to*

**C Meaning**

**1–4** Go through exercises 1–4 in this section with the class.

### Answers

1  **a**  third conditional
   **b**  second conditional
   **c**  first conditional
   **d**  mixed conditional
   **e**  zero conditional

**2** Both sentences refer to the future.
In the first sentence (first conditional) the speaker sees it as a real possibility that there will be another tornado. In the second sentence (second conditional) the speaker sees it as unlikely.

3  **1**  **a**  certainty
        **b**  possibility
   **2**  **a**  certainty
        **b**  possibility

4  **a**  *as long as, provided, providing, on condition* can all replace *if* in the sentence.
   **b**  unless

**Practice**

**1** Let students work individually first to give them time to concentrate then they could compare their answers together before formal feedback takes place.

### Answers

1  If you'd asked me, …
2  … if I find out
3  What will you do if she doesn't come …
   **or** What would you do if she didn't come …
4  If I drink
5  I'll never go
   **or** If they lost … I'd …

**2** Refer students to the instructions in their books. This activity provides practice of recognition of form and meaning as well as pronunciation: students will probably have to repeat their sentences to their partner a few times before their partner is able to identify the appropriate halves of the sentences. In this way students drill themselves.

To ensure that students understand exactly what they have to do and that they read out only what they have written, demonstrate with them before they begin to work in pairs.

Note: As in the example given in the Coursebook, there are various possibilities. Let students know that sometimes more than one structure is possible.

## Conditionals: Expressing regret  Page 137

Refer students to the instructions, drawings and example in their books.

### Answers

Suggested answers
1  If I hadn't gone skiing I wouldn't have broken my arm.
2  If I hadn't committed a foul, the referee wouldn't have sent (be sending) me off.
3  If I hadn't been using my mobile phone, I wouldn't have crashed into a tree.
4  If I hadn't gone out of the room, the cat wouldn't have eaten the fish.
5  If I'd worked harder, I would have got a better grade.

Note: In each of the above sentences, *might* can substitute *would* in order to express possibility rather than certainty. The negative auxiliaries *hadn't* and *wouldn't* are usually stressed but in the affirmative they are usually unstressed.

**Personalization of third and mixed conditionals**
Demonstrate the following activity with examples of your own. Write on the board some important dates in your life and names of people who have had some influence over you or decisions you have made. Also write up other less significant information. Talk about the dates and people, using conditional forms where appropriate, eg

   1 *Sonia*     2 *1994*     3 *Angela's Ashes*

*I have a friend called Sonia whom I met in Athens in 1994. We worked together. If I hadn't met Sonia, I wouldn't have come to live in this country. She recommended it to me because she used to work here as well.*

*If I hadn't tried to finish the book 'Angela's Ashes' last night, I wouldn't feel so tired now.*

Students then write down three or four pieces of information about themselves and tell each other about the incidents in a similar way. Encourage them to ask each other 'follow-up' questions.

## Listening 1: FCE Part 2
### Sentence completion
Page 137

**1** Refer students to the questions in their books.

Elicit students' answers to the question in their books, writing their ideas on the board. Through careful prompting, eg
*What special things do rescuers use to hear/locate survivors?*
elicit miniature cameras, microphones and images which recognize body heat. Circle these on the board and elicit or tell students that these are examples of 'special equipment' and write that up.

**2** Refer students to the instructions.

| Answers | | | |
|---|---|---|---|
| 1 | firefighter | 6 | mosquitoes *and* (the) (torrential) rain |
| 2 | find missing people | 7 | four hours |
| 3 | United Nations | 8 | wardrobe |
| 4 | specialist equipment | 9 | bored |
| 5 | volunteers | 10 | safer buildings |

---

**Listening 1: Listening script 2.1**

**I = Interviewer    P = Paul Murphy**

**I:** So Paul, how did you get involved with the International Rescue Corps?

**P:** One of the founder members of the organization lived near me in the East of England. He helped set up the IRC way back in 1981 after the Italian earthquake. Er, he was a friend of mine but also a fellow firefighter. I joined because I've got a skill to offer, and I thought it would be exciting to travel all over the world rescuing people.

**I:** And how many missions have you been on?

**P:** Eight abroad – seven earthquakes and a hurricane – and about ten in the UK. Er, in this country we're often called upon to find missing people, especially in bad weather. Er, if a disaster strikes a foreign country, er, we sometimes make offers of help to the government there via the British Embassy, but, more often than not the country goes to the United Nations and er, asks for rescue teams like ours.

**I:** And what can IRC offer that other agencies can't?

**P:** Er, as well as being able to offer our services free of charge, we carry our own specialist equipment for finding and saving people who are trapped in collapsed buildings. That includes fibre optic probes, er, where we can put a camera into the smallest of holes to see what's happening, microphones to pick up voices or vibrations and er, thermal imaging to detect heat.

**I:** Who pays for you to go?

**P:** Now, IRC is a charity, and none of our members receives any kind of payment. They're volunteers, so they also have to ask for time off work to go abroad.

**I:** What's the worst weather you've worked in, Paul?

**P:** Armenia was freezing cold but Nicaragua was bad because of the heat and mosquitoes, which never stopped biting. And the rain was horrendous, too. When we got there the hurricane had been reclassified as a tropical storm, but we had to suffer torrential rain all the time we were there.

**I:** What's the most amazing survival story you have come across?

**P:** I suppose it has to be the time we went to Japan after the Kobe earthquake. Er, one woman had been trapped for over 40 hours when we discovered she was there, and it took us another four hours to get her out. The remarkable thing about that is that normally, once people have been trapped for 24 hours after an earthquake, not many come out alive. The thing which saved her was a wardrobe, which had fallen on top of her and protected her from the falling debris. She was partly inside it. And I remember the first thing she said when we finally got her out was that she was bored! Not the kind of emotion you'd expect from an earthquake victim, is it?

**I:** Certainly not! And what advice would you give to people if they get caught in an earthquake?

**P:** As soon as you feel the slightest shake, get out of the building and into the open air. That's often easier said than done, of course, especially if you're on the tenth floor when it happens. Um, if it's not possible to get out, then you should take cover in the safest area of the building to stop other things falling on you. But really it's up to the governments of countries in earthquake zones to take the initiative and construct safer buildings. In this way damage is minimized and er, lives are saved.

**I:** Thank you, Paul, and the best of luck on your future missions.

---

The post-listening question could be discussed as a whole class or in pairs/small groups.

## Vocabulary 2: *Put*
Page 138

### A Phrasal verbs with *put*
**1–2** This section looks at different meanings of *put off*, *put on* and *put up* – three very common phrasal verbs. Students are asked to deduce the meanings from context and match them with synonyms or expressions. For **1** and **2** students

follow the instructions in their books. Stop after students have finished each section to check their answers.

### Answers

1  C discourage

| 1 A | 2 B | 3 D |
|-----|-----|-----|

2  **A** The missing word is *on*.

| 1 C | 2 B | 3 A |
|-----|-----|-----|

  **B** The missing word is *up*.

| 1 C | 2 A | 3 B |
|-----|-----|-----|

**B Expressions with *put***

**1**  Ask students to follow the instructions for exercise **1**.

If you feel your students need more help you could write on the board the words needed for each section, but not in the correct order.

### Answers

**Text A**

| 1 | *night* | 4 | risk |
|---|---------|---|------|
| 2 | touch | 5 | cigarette |
| 3 | smoking | | |

**Text B**

| 6 | pressure | 7 | effort |
|---|----------|---|--------|

**Text C**

| 8 | feet | 9 | book |
|---|------|---|------|

**Text D**

| 10 | money | 11 | blame | 12 | position |
|----|-------|----|-------|----|----------|

**2**  Students follow the instructions in their books. Deducing the meaning from context is a skill used naturally in one's first language. It needs to be actively encouraged in a second language as it leads to more efficient reading.

### Answers

**1**  *put her up for the night at my house*
  let her stay at my house for one night

**2**  *put her in touch with my friend*
  give her my friend's address or telephone number so she can make contact

**3**  *put up with anyone smoking*
  tolerate smoking

**4**  *put his health at risk*
  endanger his health

**5**  *put out her cigarette*
  extinguish her cigarette

**6**  *put pressure on me to study*
  strongly persuaded me or forced me to study

**7**  *put more time and effort into it*
  dedicate enough time and effort to

**8**  *put my feet up*
  rest my feet on something or just relax in general

**9**  *can't put the book down*
  keep reading because it is so good

**10**  *putting some money aside*
  saving some money

**11**  *put the blame on me*
  blame me

**12**  *put yourself in my position*
  see the situation from my point of view

## Speaking
Page 139

Refer students to the picture and the instructions. Give students a little time to look back at Units 8 and 9 (Language of speculation) if necessary. This speaking activity serves as a lead-in to the reading task on page 140.

## Reading
Page 140

Refer students to the instructions and the questions which precede the text. If your students tend to worry about every item of unknown vocabulary, set a time limit to prevent them from stopping at every word.

### Answers

She is protesting against a construction company's plans to build luxury houses on an area of woodland.

She and others are camping on the proposed site and they have built underground tunnels.

Her mother worries about her and does not really agree with her methods but she supports her.

**Reacting to the text**

Answers will clearly depend on students' own views. If you choose to ask them the questions yourself, encourage them to give reasons for their answers and to develop what they say as much as they can.

## Language focus 2: *So, neither* and *nor*

Page 141

**1** Refer students to the example sentences from the reading in their books or write the sentences on the board.

### Answers

- *Neither* and *so* are used when something is true for all people referred to in the sentence.
- *Neither* is used with reference to grammatical negatives and *so* with reference to affirmatives.

The auxiliary used in the short reply is the same auxiliary that is needed to form the question or negative.

**2a** Students match the statements in pairs.

### Answers

| | | | |
|---|---|---|---|
| **1** c | **2** e | **3** f | **4** g |
| **5** a | **6** h | **7** b | **8** d |

**2b** Students then change the underlined parts of each statement as instructed.

**2c** This exercise provides meaningful, personalized practice of *so, neither* and *nor*.

Demonstrate the mechanics of the activity to students before they begin so that they know what to do.

### Use of English: Open cloze   Page 141
FCE Part 2

**1–2** Refer students to the question in exercise 1, which aims to get them thinking about what they are going to read before they start on the exam-style exercise. It also opens the way for the gist reading task in exercise 2: it is important that students read through the whole text before attempting to complete the gaps.

**3** Refer students to 'What to expect in the exam'.

### Answers

| | | |
|---|---|---|
| **1** This/The | **2** is | **3** to |
| **4** order | **5** if | **6** part |
| **7** although/though/but | | **8** which/that |
| **9** such | **10** However | **11** has |
| **12** without | | |

**4** As well as asking students to discuss the questions in the book, you could also write the following questions on the board.
*What would your life be like if your family didn't own a car?*
*How would the world be different if the car hadn't been invented?*

### Speaking: Collaborative task
FCE Part 3

Page 142

**1** If possible, put students in groups to work together on the vocabulary and provide a dictionary per group.

### Answers

| Recycling | Keeping cities clean | River and sea pollution |
|---|---|---|
| *recycled paper* | *dog mess* | *toxic effluent* |
| bottle bank | dropping litter | oil slick |
| plastic containers | cigarette butts | dumping waste |

| Traffic pollution | Climate change | Animal welfare |
|---|---|---|
| *carbon monoxide* | *rising sea levels* | *facing extinction* |
| unleaded petrol | global warming | nature reserve |
| exhaust fumes | (the) greenhouse effect | endangered species |

Put the first word of the collocations above onto the board in the next lesson.

 to drop _____            to dump _____
 cigarette _____          greenhouse _____ etc.

Students see how many combinations they can remember. Repeat the same activity in a later class to see if retention is the same or has improved.

**2** Students read the instructions in their books and refer back to Unit 10 for appropriate language they can use when agreeing and disagreeing. Before they start the activity, ask them to identify the key words in the instructions.

*Talk with your partner and decide which three categories are the most important for your local area. Then discuss what ordinary people can do to help.*

### Writing: Essays   Page 142
FCE Part 2

Refer students to the essay title and go through the advice in the 'How to go about it' box point by point.

Further ideas for prompting:

**Recycling**

*If you agree with the statement*

There will always be too much material to recycle effectively.

*If you disagree with the statement*

As time goes on it will be possible to recycle all manufactured materials.

**Keeping streets clean**

*If you agree with the statement*

People do not care enough to change their habits and take their litter home or put it in litter bins provided.

*If you disagree with the statement*

Campaigns on TV and in schools make a big difference to people's behaviour.

**River and sea pollution**

*If you agree with the statement*

Some oil companies may prefer to pay the fines imposed on them than dispose of their cargo properly.

*If you disagree with the statement*

Organizations such as Greenpeace make dumping international news and make people aware of the problem.

**Traffic pollution**

*If you agree with the statement*

Big oil companies and oil producing countries ensure that alternatives to petrol are not a viable alternative.

*If you disagree with the statement*

Traditional resources are not unlimited. Electric cars could be used in cities for short distances.

**Climate change**

*If you agree with the statement*

Historically, the Earth's climate has always had periods of change. It is not a new phenomenon.

*If you disagree with the statement*

Reduction in toxic emissions is now a reality in many parts of the world. This will continue elsewhere.

**Animal welfare**

*If you agree with the statement*

Growth in the world's population leads to destruction of animals' natural habitats.

People not interested in animals – they have other problems.

*If you disagree with the statement*

Government can create more nature reserves. People can stop wearing fur coats.

Students could write the essay at home. As much of the thinking and planning have already been done, ask students to spend a maximum of 45 minutes on writing their essay.

## Listening 2: FCE Part 1 — Multiple choice
Page 143

Photocopiable exercise on page 167.

Note that the question types in this exercise represent most of those which students can expect to find in the exam. The different question words can denote the following areas:

1   Where – location
2   Who – role
3   How – feeling
4   Why – attitude or opinion
5   What/relationship – relationship
6   What – gist
7   What/doing – function
8   What/going to do – intention

Draw your students' attention to this, as knowing what kind of information to listen for will help them with the task.

Refer students to the instructions and the advice contained in the 'What to expect in the exam' box.

| Answers | | | |
|---|---|---|---|
| 1 C | 2 A | 3 C | 4 B |
| 5 C | 6 B | 7 A | 8 A |

---

**Listening 2: Listening script 2.2–2.9**

**One**

I really can't understand why they put it all the way out there. They maintained that if they'd built it in the heart of the city there would have been problems getting out to fires in the rural areas. Too far and too much traffic, they said. But that's exactly why it would have made more sense to build it in the centre instead of on the edge. You know, it takes a fire engine nearly 20 minutes to get from that suburb to the other side of the city.

**Two**

If I was a member of the Council I'd make sure something was done about the mess on the streets. It's an absolute disgrace. Local people need more help to

---

keep them clean, and that help has to come from the authorities. There aren't enough litter bins, for one thing, so the pavements outside my premises are covered with paper, drink cans and cigarette butts. Before I open up in the morning I have to spend about ten minutes sweeping it all up. I wouldn't sell anything if I didn't.

**Three**

You have to remember that some species of plants were facing extinction in the area. People would come out to the countryside for a picnic, see all these beautiful flowers and pick them, without realizing the effect this was having. If we hadn't made this a conservation area and limited the number of people coming in, then we'd have no flowers at all, and people would be really upset. As it is, we can congratulate ourselves on the action we took and look forward to a brighter future for this patch of countryside.

**Four**

**Woman 1:** So what was it like?

**Woman 2:** Marvellous. Just what we were looking for.

**Woman 1:** And what was that?

**Woman 2:** Well, if we'd gone to one of the other islands, we'd have had to put up with busy roads and crowded beaches.

**Woman 1:** So weren't there many tourists where you went?

**Woman 2:** Oh plenty. More than we expected really. But it didn't seem to matter, because with the vehicle restrictions there was almost a total lack of exhaust fumes, no congestion and very little noise. And because the island's so small, you could walk everywhere, anyway.

**Five**

**Man:** I think we should all get together and decide what we're going to do. I can't put up with it any more.

**Woman:** Neither can we. The noise of that boy's music makes the whole house shake. My husband says it's just like being in an earthquake, only worse.

**Man:** Of course it's the parents' fault, but it's no good talking to them. They're no better than he is.

**Woman:** And his teachers can't control him, either. Apparently, he's as rude to them as he is to all of us.

**Man:** So, let's have a meeting of all the residents in the street and we'll decide how to deal with him.

**Six**

Violent storms swept across the south coast today, causing widespread damage to property. Torrential rain and gale-force winds lashed seaside towns and several people had to be evacuated from their flooded homes by rescue services. One man in Bognor narrowly escaped death as the car he was driving was crushed by a falling tree, which had been struck by lightning.

**Seven**

**Woman:** What's the problem, John?

**Man:** Well, we lost a lot of our plants last night.

**Woman:** It wasn't our cat, was it?

**Man:** No, the wind. Pulled up all the roses, it did. Blew down a few bushes, too.

**Woman:** I'm sorry to hear that.

**Man:** Oh, not to worry. I'd be grateful if you'd give me a hand to clear up the mess, though.

**Woman:** I'd be pleased to.

**Eight**

Something's got to be done. These massive petrol tankers should just not be allowed to sail so close to our shores. The oil slick has already killed thousands of birds and the beaches are a disaster area. Demonstrating is all very well, but it's not going to clean up the mess, is it? We can't leave it in the hands of the politicians, so we've just got to get down to the coast and get our hands dirty with the rest of the volunteers. You coming?

## Review 11 answers Page 144

### Vocabulary

**A Weather**

1  1  light *rain/wind/showers*
   2  heavy *rain/storm/showers*
   3  strong *wind*

2  1  gentle *breeze*          6  brilliant sunshine
   2  angry-looking clouds  7  overcast sky
   3  rough sea                 8  tidal wave
   4  torrential rain          9  violent storm
   5  scattered showers      10  gale-force wind

**B Put**

1  down          4  on
2  out           5  in
3  up            6  off

### Conditional sentences

1  stays, 'll probably
2  had known, could have prepared
3  wouldn't do, paid
4  had taken, wouldn't be
5  do, 'll make
6  would have done, hadn't helped
7  am, always watch
8  would go, had

## Use of English: FCE Part 4    Transformations

1  if it wasn't/was not/weren't/were not so/too
2  if I hadn't/had not spoken
3  I would not have written
4  not help you unless you
5  I had/'d remembered to take
6  give up smoking you put
7  to put up with
8  is being put at
9  provided it is
10  as long as you give

## Writing: FCE Part 1    Formal letters

Refer students to page 63 of the Workbook for help
on correcting information.

## Workbook answers

### Reading: Gapped text    Page 82

| 1 | H | 2 | E | 3 | A | 4 G |
|---|---|---|---|---|---|-----|
| 5 | F | 6 | D | 7 | B | C not used |

2  1  developments      2  survival
   3  participants       4  passionately
   5  global             6  anywhere
   7  awareness          8  technological

3  **Verb**              **Noun**
   entertain             entertainment
   refuse                refusal
   assist                assistant
   occupy                occupant
   enjoy                 enjoyment
   replace               replacement
   approve               approval
   deny                  denial
   arrange               arrangement
   inhabit               inhabitant

4  1  inhabitants        2  approval
   3  enjoyment          4  denial
   5  occupants

### Vocabulary    Page 84

**A Crossword: The weather**

**Across**              **Down**
1  drought              2  hail
6  flood                3  clouds
7  gale                 4  tidal

8  severe          5  breeze
9  choppy          6  forecast
11  fine          10  pour
12  struck
13  gust

**B The environment**

1  1  c    2  d    3  f    4  a    5  b
   6  e

2  1  e    2  d    3  a    4  f    5  b
   6  h    7  g    8  c

3
1  exhaust fumes
2  oil slick
3  dog mess
4  greenhouse effect
5  power station
6  nature reserve

### Language focus    Page 85

**A So, neither and nor**

1  1  c    2  e    3  d    4  h    5  g
   6  a    7  b    8  f

2
1  neither can I        2  so is
3  neither/nor does     4  so are
5  so did               6  neither/nor will
7  so has               8  neither/nor would
9  so had

**B Conditionals**

1
1  had, would help
2  will buy, promise
3  hadn't said, wouldn't have got
4  sleeps, is usually
5  had gone, would have met
6  beat, will go
7  press, underlines/will underline
8  were, would go
9  will be, get
10  hadn't taken, would have got

**2 Suggested answers**
2  We would have gone sailing if there had been
   enough wind.
3  If I wasn't afraid of flying, we would go abroad
   on holiday.
4  If he hadn't broken his leg, he could drive.
5  I could have taken some photos if I had
   remembered to pack my camera.
6  If he had a suit, he would go to the wedding.

7 He wouldn't be feeling ill if he hadn't drunk so much last night.

8 She could have gone to university if she'd passed her exams.

9 If they'd watched the news, they would have heard about the earthquake.

**3 Possible answers**

1 I would probably miss my family.

2 I would try to improve the health system.

3 I hadn't come to this school.

4 they gave us an extra week's holiday in summer.

5 I'll spend it on computer games.

6 I wouldn't be able to send emails to my friends in Australia.

## Use of English  Page 87

**Multiple-choice cloze**

| | | | |
|---|---|---|---|
| 1 B | 2 D | 3 C | 4 D |
| 5 B | 6 C | 7 B | 8 A |
| 9 C | 10 D | 11 D | 12 A |

**Transformations**

1 so did

2 put me up

3 put the concert off/put off the concert

4 more time into

5 's/has been raining heavily

6 won't/will not go swimming unless

7 had enough money

8 his brother hadn't/had not told

## Writing  Page 88

**2 Features**

• A relevant title:
  *The highs and lows of mountain weather*

• Questions to involve the reader:
  ... what would be your favourite type of weather?
  Glorious sunshine to sunbathe in?
  Deep snow to ski in?
  And what would you find it hard to put up with?
  Who wouldn't feel bad-tempered by the end of it all?

• A range of vocabulary related to the weather:
  glorious sunshine, deep snow, fine or heavy, spitting or pouring, wet weather, the sun comes out, a shower, wind ... blows

• Elements of informal language:
  it's, there's, wouldn't, I'd
  And, But, put up with

• Examples to illustrate a point:
  Clothes are blown off washing lines, etc

• Adverbs expressing opinion or attitude:
  Surprisingly

**4**

**Extract a**  Writing competition (page 88)
Consistent. An informal style.

**Extract b**  People and places (page 89)
Inconsistent. Begins with a more formal style, but ends informally.

**Extract c**  Competition (page 89)
Consistent. A neutral narrative style.

# 12 Looking after yourself

## Content Overview

### Themes

Food and drink, dieting, the importance of water, ailments and injuries are the themes in this unit.

### Exam-related activities

| | |
|---|---|
| **Paper 1** | **Reading** |
| Part 3 | Multiple matching |
| | |
| **Paper 2** | **Writing** |
| Part 1 | Letters: Givng information |
| Part 2 | Reports |
| | |
| **Paper 3** | **Use of English** |
| Part 1 | Multiple-choice cloze |
| Part 2 | Open cloze (Review) |
| Part 3 | Word formation (Unit and Review) |
| Part 4 | Transformations (Review) |
| | |
| **Paper 4** | **Listening** |
| Part 3 | Multiple matching |
| | |
| **Paper 5** | **Speaking** |
| Part 2 | Talking about photos |

### Other

| | |
|---|---|
| Language focus 1/2: | Countable and uncountable nouns |
| Language focus 3: | Reported speech |
| Language focus 4: | Reporting verbs |
| Language focus 5: | Reported questions |
| Vocabulary: | Health matters |
| Word formation: | Noun suffixes |

### Speaking                                          Page 146

Ask students to discuss these questions in pairs.

### Language focus 1: Countable and uncountable nouns A          Page 146

**1** Refer students to the pictures in their books (*chocolates*/[*some*] *chocolate*, *a cake*/[*some*] *cake*) and the examples given (*plate*[*s*], *some bread*).

> #### Answers
>
> milk, health, spaghetti **U** chocolate **U, C** meal **C** (**U** = animal feed) chicken **U/C** (for a whole one) pepper **C** (vegetable)/**U** (spice) diet, chip **C** cake **U/C**

**2** To see how much your students already know and can remember, ask them how they could describe more precisely the quantities in the pictures. Then refer them to the exercise.

> #### Answers
>
> **1** a piece of cheese, toast, cake, chocolate
> **2** cheese, toast, cake
> **3** spaghetti* (also *plateful*)
> **4** sugar, salt
> **5** salt
> **6** chocolate
> **7** jam
> **8** milk
>
> *notice that 'spaghetti' takes a singular verb in English

#### Further practice and pronunciation

See how much students can remember either immediately after they have checked their answers or later on in the class by calling out the nouns one by one and getting the students to give the whole expressions. Help them with the pronunciation by drilling one or two phrases chorally and individually until students naturally run the words together, eg

*a **car**ton of **milk*** = /kɑːtənəv/
*a **bar** of **cho**colate* = /bɑːrəv/

### Listening: FCE Part 3   Multiple matching   Page 147

**1** Refer students to the discussion questions.

**2** Refer students to the instructions and listening task in their books and give them about 30 seconds to read through the statements. Refer students to the 'Don't forget!' box and deal with any vocabulary that students ask about before they listen.

Play the recording twice and allow students to compare their ideas before they hear it the second time.

> #### Answers
>
> **1** B    **2** E    **3** A    **4** F
> **5** C    D not used

114

## Listening: Listening script 2.10–2.14

**Speaker 1**

I tried crash diets, such as one where you just eat cabbage soup, and another where you drink nothing but lemonade with some salt and pepper for about seven days without any food. They worked temporarily, but after a while I put the weight back on. Then I was introduced to these diet pills and my weight went down to 65 kilos. But I wasn't earning a great deal of money and I simply couldn't afford to keep it up. That's when I decided to save my money and join a gym.

**Speaker 2**

I used to eat a lot of junk food. It was quick, inexpensive and it satisfied my hunger immediately. The problem was, I ate very little fresh food, and this had a serious effect on my health. I became overweight and suffered all sorts of illnesses. The doctor strongly advised me to rethink my attitude to food. If not, he said, the consequences could be very serious. Well, you can't ignore advice like that, can you? So I started to eat more healthily. And now if I get hungry between meals, I have a little cheese or some nuts, just to fill the hole.

**Speaker 3**

I'm under no real pressure to lose weight, but I take care over what I eat, simply because it makes me feel better. When I want to treat myself I have a piece of cake or a few biscuits. I read a lot about dieting, and most nutritionists seem to agree that as long as you eat sweet things after a meal, then there's no problem. So, for example, I only ever eat chocolates after lunch or dinner. And never too many of course – just one or two.

**Speaker 4**

I like eating and I'm not at all interested in dieting. But I do go to see a nutritionist, who helps me maintain a sensible, balanced diet: plenty of fresh fruit and vegetables, meat and fish, carbohydrates such as rice and pasta, several glasses of water a day – and no snacks between meals. She told me to give up cheese, but I ignored her. I enjoy good food and I don't want to deprive myself of the things I love.

**Speaker 5**

A large number of people follow diets, but very few of them are happier as a result. We are constantly under attack from advertising and the media, who tell us that 'thin is beautiful'. I used to believe this and think that I wouldn't find a boyfriend unless I was really skinny, that I had to weigh under 60 kilos for boys to like me. But of course, now I realize that there's more to it than that. Just being yourself is what counts and I don't pay much attention to what others think or say.

**3** Students discuss in pairs or as a class.

## Language focus 2: Countable and uncountable nouns B          Page 147

Refer students to the cartoon in their books and the question.

*Just a few* – refers to a countable noun in the plural: a few *glasses* of sherry.

*Just a little* – refers to an uncountable noun: a little *sherry*.

By saying 'Just a few' she really means that she wants a lot of (glasses of) sherry. Warn students that they have to consider this aspect of grammar when doing the following exercise.

Students have already heard these sentences but have not been specifically listening out for these expressions. This exercise serves as the initial stage of a test-teach-test approach to the language.

Tell students before they start that sometimes various answers are possible and that they should put all possibilities provided they fit the context of the extract. They should not change the words given in any way.

When they have completed what they can, play the recording for them to check, stopping after each answer and writing it on the board so that all students have a record of the correct answers.

| Answers |
| --- |

**Speaker 1**
**a** some     **b** any/much     **c** deal

**Speaker 2**
**d** lot     **e** little     **f** little     **g** some/several

**Speaker 3**
**h** piece     **i** few     **j** no/little     **k** many

**Speaker 4**
**l** plenty     **m** several/many     **n** no/few

**Speaker 5**
**o** number     **p** few     **q** much/any

As a way of grouping the expressions, provide students with a copy of the following, perhaps with some of the expressions removed and written at the bottom. Students have to read and complete.

**Expressions used with countable nouns**

| a few | a number of |
| --- | --- |
| (not) many | several |

**Expressions used with uncountable nouns**

| a little | (not) much |
| --- | --- |
| a piece of | a great deal of |

**Expressions used with both**

| | |
|---|---|
| some | a lot of |
| any | plenty of |
| no | |

### Reading: FCE Part 3 — Multiple matching
Page 148

Photocopiable vocabulary exercise on page 168.

**1** Students answer in pairs, giving reasons where possible. If you choose to ask the questions yourself remember to encourage the students to elaborate on their answers.

**2** Refer students to the task and reading. Students may not know the following vocabulary in the questions. Check before they start.

*consumption* (noun) (question 1) – the amount of food or drink that is eaten or drunk
*provision* (noun) (question 2) – the act of supplying somebody with something that they need
*implementing* (verb) (question 12) – making something start to happen

Tell students to try to deduce the meaning of any other vocabulary they come across while they are reading, as they will have to do this in the exam.

| Answers | | | | |
|---|---|---|---|---|
| **1** A | **2** D | **3** C | **4** B | **5** A |
| **6** E | **7** C | **8** D | **9** B | **10** A |
| **11** C | **12** E | **13/14/15** A, D, E in any order | | |

**Reacting to the text**
Students discuss their answers in groups, pairs, or they can be discussed as a whole group with you leading the activity.

## Language focus 3: Reported speech
Page 149

**1** If possible write the information from the Coursebook on the board to help to ensure that you and the board are the focus of the students' attention.

Elicit the answers directly or let students write them down and compare with a partner before telling you.

| Answers |
|---|
| The verb tense 'steps back' from the present simple (direct speech) to the past simple (reported speech) in this example.<br>*Under what circumstances would the following reported speech version be possible?*<br>If the statement being reported is still true. |

**2** This exercise not only tests students' ability to change tense appropriately but also encourages them to think about changes in time and other expressions.

| Answers |
|---|

**Reported speech**
**b** She said she *had seen* him twice *that* day.
**c** He told me she *had been* living *there* for years.
**d** He said he *had spoken* to her *the previous* week.
**e** He told me he *had been* working *the day* before.
**f** They said they *had asked* her several times.

**3**

| Direct speech | | Reported speech |
|---|---|---|
| **a** present continuous | → | past continuous |
| **b** present perfect simple | → | past perfect simple |
| **c** present perfect continuous | → | past perfect continuous |
| **d** past simple | → | past perfect simple |
| **e** past continuous | → | past perfect continuous |
| **f** past perfect simple | → | past perfect simple (no change) |

Notice how often the past perfect tense is used in reported speech. Draw students' attention to this.

**4**

| Direct speech | | Reported speech |
|---|---|---|
| will | → | *would* |
| would | → | *would* |
| can | → | *could* |
| could | → | *could* |
| should | → | *should* |
| must | → | *had to* |
| may | → | *might* |
| might | → | *might* |
| ought to | → | *ought to* |

**5**

| two days ago | → | two days before/earlier/ previously |
| next month | → | the following/next month |
| tonight | → | that night/evening |
| this morning | → | that morning |
| now | → | then |

**6** In this exercise, emphasize the fact that students should write down the person's real words first. Demonstrate with a couple of examples of your own on the board and use inverted commas and a heading (Direct speech).

Review the uses of *say* and *tell* with your own examples:

| **Direct speech** | **Reported speech** |
| my brother – 'I'm not feeling well' | *Last weekend my brother told me that he wasn't feeling very well.* |
| Steve Batley (footballer) – 'I think I'll be fit for the match on Saturday.' | *Steve Batley said he thought he would be fit for the match on Saturday.* |

Tell students to think about the following people for their own sentences:
*family   friends   teachers   classmates/workmates sportsmen/women   other famous people   yourself*

Students write down the reported speech. When students tell each other or you their sentences, stronger ones can fold back the reported speech column so that they have to remember and think about the structures before speaking rather than reading from the page.

### Speaking: FCE Part 2    Talking about photos
Page 150

These tasks encourage students to speculate about the feelings of the people in the photographs. They should be encouraged to use modal verbs (see Language focus, page 108 in Unit 9 of the Coursebook) as well as other language of speculation (see Useful language, page 98 in Unit 8).

## Language focus 4: Reporting verbs
Page 150

This section reviews and extends students' ability to report what people have said. Students are encouraged to categorize verbs depending on the grammatical patterns that follow them. This exercise focuses on *advise* type verbs, ie verbs that follow the same grammatical pattern as *advise*, and *offer* type verbs.

**1** Students study the example sentences.

**2** Using dictionaries or their own previous knowledge, they decide which column each verb should go into.

| Answers | |
|---|---|
| **advise** (verb + object + infinitive) | **offer** (verb + infinitive) |
| order | refuse |
| urge | threaten |
| persuade | *promise |
| warn | |
| tell | |
| remind | |
| ask | |
| encourage | |
| recommend (and same patterns as suggest) | |

\* can also take an object, eg *He promised me that he would …*

**3** First, ask students to read through the direct speech sentences and identify which reporting verb is needed in each one (see below). Then students work individually or together to complete the transformation-style exercise.

| Answers |
|---|
| 1  refused to clean her room |
| 2  reminded him to take his sandwiches |
| 3  threatened to call the police if I didn't turn my music down |
| 4  warned/advised her not to take the car out (as/ because/since the roads were very icy) |
| 5  ordered/told him to get out of his/her office immediately |
| 6  urged/encouraged/persuaded me to report the theft to the police |

**4** Students follow the instructions given.

### Answers

*Suggest* is not possible with the pattern in the first sentence.

**5** Decide which students are going to be 'A' and which 'B' or tell them to decide that quickly for themselves. Demonstrate the activity with a student to give everyone the idea of what they have to do. Do this by asking a student to tell you one of his/her 'problems' from page 200 or 202. Elaborate on the basic dialogue by asking the student other related questions before finally giving your suggestion – this means that students will have to improvise a little and use their imaginations.

Students then follow the instructions in their books.

## Use of English 1: FCE Part 1 — Multiple-choice cloze
Page 151

**1** Ask students for their answers to this question but do not spend too long on it, as they have already been working on the theme.

**2** Refer students to the questions and set a time limit (about two minutes) for them to read the text. (The 'alternative diet' consists of singing karaoke. It is not very effective – see end of paragraph 3 … *suggesting that karaoke may not be the ideal weight loss programme.*)

**3** Having read the text for the general meaning, students now do the multiple-choice cloze.

### Answers

| 1 B | 2 D | 3 A | 4 C | 5 A | 6 D |
|-----|-----|-----|------|------|------|
| 7 D | 8 B | 9 D | 10 A | 11 A | 12 C |

## Writing 1: FCE Part 2 — Reports
Page 152

Before referring students to the question, do the following activity to prepare them for the theme of the report.

- Tell students to write two lists: 1 the types of restaurants they have gone to/go to with their friends, and 2 with their families.
- Now students write down any similarities and/or differences between the two. They should think about the food, the price, atmosphere, background music, self-service or waiter service, the lighting, etc.
- Elicit their ideas regarding the point above onto the board, circling any which are mentioned by more than one student.
- Ask students for their opinions about what makes restaurants popular with families.

**1–2** Students read the question and the model text and follow the instructions.

### Answers

| 2 | 1 C | 2 F | 3 E |
|---|-----|-----|-----|
|   | 4 A | 5 B | D not used |

**3** The restaurant manager is the target reader. The style is semi-formal/formal.

**4a** *Many of those under sixteen, Most parents, a large number of teenagers, 80% of those interviewed, over 90% of those under twelve, Several younger parents*

**b** *those under sixteen, … felt that, Most parents expected to see, 80% … said they, 90% … wanted chips with everything, a large number … thought that*

**c** *recommend + should – I would recommend that the restaurant should …*
*suggest + gerund – I also suggest extending the menu …*

**5a** *The aim of this report is to …, The report is based on a survey of …*
**b** *on the other hand …, whereas …*
**c** *Understandably, Not surprisingly*

**6** If you have time and you want to give your students extra speaking practice the following activity will act as a lead-in to the theme of their writing task.

- Refer students to the question in their books.
- If they are from the same country, put them in pairs to write a list of regional or national dishes and how they could describe those dishes to a visitor from another country.
- Provide dictionaries if possible or move around the room helping with translations.
- Students could then join up with another pair to describe the dishes and see if the other pair can identify which dish is being described.

If students are from different countries, follow the same basic procedure. The students can work individually on their descriptions, using their own bilingual dictionaries, and then come together in pairs or groups to describe their dishes to each other. Encourage them to ask each other more questions about their respective countries and customs if time allows.

**7** Now refer students to the possible plan and the Wordlist on page 205 of the Coursebook. Reassure them that they can invent statistics if they want provided that what they mention sounds reasonable! You might like them to do the vocabulary exercise on page 91 of the Workbook before they write their report.

**8** Students should carefully consider who the target reader is and the style they will need to use. The target reader is the leader of the group of foreign students.

The style could be semi-formal as in the model given or, because of the student connection, informal.

Note: Whatever style the students write in, it must be consistent; they will be penalized in the exam if they mix styles.

## Sample answer

This is a report about the main dishes in my area, especially for young people. The report is based on a survey of 100 people aged between 12 and 20 who live in Asturias and is referred about regional dishes.

The most popular and important dishes are always based on natural food. Although a large number of young people – almost 80% – declare they like fast food in some situations, everybody prefers absolutely their own regional food based on vegetables, beans, meat, pork and, on the other hand, seafruits.

The people of our survey, either boys or girls, give the best qualification to the 'fabada', the most known dish of the Asturias kitchen; it is made with a especial beans – 'fabes' – and pork products such as ham, bacon, blood pudding. Another variations with 'fabes' are too expensive for young people, as for instance, partridges or shellfishes.

The most popular pudding is rice pudding, very famous in Asturias. Young people like it very much.

In the end, there is a lot of natural food dishes for young people in Asturias, though some of them are expensive, especially with seafruits. Of course, if you like fast food you'll get a burger as in any part of the world.

By Emilio Jiménez Aparicio

206 words

**Examiner's comment**
**Content:** Good realization of the task. Rather longer than necessary but it is well expressed and relevant and so is not penalized.

**Accuracy:** Some minor inaccuracies – *is referred about* rather than *refers to* or *is about, prefers absolutely,* etc as well as more obtrusive errors which could cause confusion – *seafruits, the best qualification.*

**Range:** Good range of appropriate expressions for this type of task – *the report is based on, a large number of young people declare, pork products such as ...* The writer also shows good knowledge of food vocabulary.
**Organization and cohesion:** The report is clearly divided into appropriate sections.

**Style and format:** Consistently neutral.

**Target reader:** Would be suitably informed about the culinary possibilities in the region to be visited.

**Mark:** band 4

## Language focus 5: Reported questions
Page 153

**1** Write the sentences in the Coursebook on the board and elicit the original direct questions:

### Answers
1 What facilities should a family restaurant have?
2 Do you think it is important to have a non-smoking area?

**2–3** Elicit the answers from the class as a whole group activity.

### Answers

**2**

- Word order – changes from verb + subject to subject + verb when we report.
- Auxiliary verbs *do*, *does*, *did* – disappear
- Verb tenses – 'step back' a tense unless the question is reported in the same time period
- Yes/No questions – use *if/whether*

**3**

1  what type of food they expected to see on the menu.
2  how important the price of the food was.
3  if/whether they always ate the same things when they went to a restaurant.
4  what other things they would like a restaurant to offer.

## Vocabulary: Health matters    Page 154

**1**  Check that students understand the words in the boxes by pointing to see if the students remember what the words are in English.

Students work on exercises A and B together and then check their answers. Encourage students to look carefully at the context of the sentences. Check that students have understood the vocabulary by asking them to explain or demonstrate the expressions you think they may be unsure about. If they cannot provide explanations, do so yourself.

### Answers

**A**

1  heart attack      3  blood pressure
2  stomach ache      4  ear infection

**B**

1  black eye         3  runny nose
2  sore throat       4  sprained ankle

**2**  Students follow the instructions in their books. Repeat this at the end of class or the beginning of the next class to keep the expressions fresh in the students' minds.

**3**  This exercise is designed to give students vocabulary for the following speaking exercise.

### Answers

1  bandage          4  plaster
2  a plaster        5  injection
3  prescription

**4**  Students work in groups of three in this exercise to provide a variety of responses and experiences. Encourage students to take the initiative by thinking of their own 'follow-up' questions. This is an important feature of interactive communication in Parts 3 and 4 of the oral exam. However, if students are slow to get started or run out of ideas use the questions below.

**Further questions:**

*If you have had any of these accidents, how did they happen?*
*How did you feel?*
*If you were with someone, what was their reaction?*
*Do you know of any remedies for any of the conditions mentioned above?*

## Word formation: Noun suffixes

Page 154

**1**  Either tell students to write down their answers first and then elicit and correct at the board or elicit their answers directly.

### Answers

| treat     | – | treatment    |
|-----------|---|--------------|
| prescribe | – | prescription |
| weak      | – | weakness     |
| severe    | – | severity     |

**2–3**  This next exercise includes *-ance* and *-ence* from Unit 5. Students try doing this exercise from their own previous knowledge and/or by using dictionaries.

### Answers

| Verbs      | Nouns          |
|------------|----------------|
| a'muse     | a'musement     |
| de'cide    | de'cision      |
| ap'pear    | ap'pearance    |
| enter'tain | enter'tainment |
| **ex'plain** | **explan'ation** |
| per'form   | per'formance   |
| **i'magine** | **imagin'ation** |
| de'velop   | de'velopment   |

| Adjectives | Nouns |
|---|---|
| im'portant | im'portance |
| fit | 'fitness |
| sin'cere | sin'cerity |
| 'happy | 'happiness |
| se'cure | se'curity |
| 'evident | 'evidence |
| 'careless | 'carelessness |
| **o'riginal** | **origin'ality** |

The apostrophe ' indicates that the stress falls on the following syllable. Those words marked in **bold** show stress changes to accommodate the following stress rules:

For nouns ending in *-ion* the stress falls on the penultimate syllable.
For nouns ending in *-ity* the stress falls on the pre-penultimate syllable.

If you wish to explore this further with your students, here are some more examples:

| Answers | |
|---|---|
| 'popular | popu'larity |
| 'complex | com'plexity |
| 'flexible | flexi'bility |
| 'personal | person'ality |
| 'curious | curi'osity |
| 'circulate | circu'lation |
| in'hale | inha'lation |
| ob'serve | obser'vation |
| repre'sent | represen'tation |

Note: The words above have been selected for their tendency to appear in FCE exams.

## Use of English 2: Word formation
**FCE Part 3**    Page 155

Refer students to the title and ask them to read, ignoring the gaps, in order to answer the following question:

*Has he completely recovered?*
Answer – no

This is to encourage students to read through the whole text before doing the task. Remind them if necessary that some words may be plurals and that correct spelling is essential.

| Answers | | | |
|---|---|---|---|
| 1 | competition | 6 | complications |
| 2 | ability | 7 | activity/activities |
| 3 | stiffness | 8 | improvement |
| 4 | operation | 9 | movements |
| 5 | majority | 10 | tiredness |

## Writing 2: Letters: Giving information
**FCE Part 1**    Page 155

Refer students to the Part 1 instructions in their books and if necessary deal with the meaning of *health spa* (a resort with medicinal mineral water for drinking and bathing in).

Ask the students to underline the key words in the question, ie what they need to know in order to write a letter in an appropriate style and points they need to cover and can build upon in their answer.

Students could work together to list ways of building on the information given and adding relevant ideas of their own.

Ask students to note down a possible structure for their writing. An example is given below:

Three or four paragraphs
*Opening*: brief response to Trevor's letter, express sympathy about the fact that he is feeling exhausted. Give general impression of your stay at the spa.

*Second (and third)*: mention each point and develop by building on the information given.

*Last paragraph*: final comment encouraging Trevor to go.

Students write the letter for homework.

**Responding to the students' written work**
Comment on how successfully students have incorporated the information and notes given. This will let students know which areas of this particular piece of writing they need to improve the next time they write a 'Giving information' informal letter.

| Sample answer |
|---|
| Dear Trevor |
| I'm glad you stopped thinking that I was crazy when I decided to go to a health spa last year. |
| The first thing I have to tell you is that it is the best place to go if you want to relax after you |

exams. It was very quiet place and I remember going for a walk in the evening because there was a really nice landscape. However, if you prefer not to go out, there was an outdoor thermal pool which temperature was wonderful!

As for food, it was well-cooked and there were lots of vegetable dishes to choose, but a bit small portions.

I don't think you will get bored because there were lots of enjoyable things to do. As well as discos, there was karaoke, which was great fun, and bingo.

I hope you have a good time and I'm sure you will cheer up.

Lots of love
Coral Berriochoa Hausmann

151 words

**Examiner's comment**

**Content:** All content points have been covered.

**Accuracy**: Generally accurate. Errors do not obscure meaning, eg *after you(r) exams, it was (a) very quiet place, pool which (whose) temperature*. Examples of accurate language use in often difficult areas are *stopped thinking, remember going, prefer not to go out*.

**Range:** A reasonably good range of structure and vocabulary for the task. Examples of good vocabulary are *well-cooked, get bored, enjoyable, great fun, cheer up*.

**Organization and cohesion:** The introduction and conclusion are well expressed. The letter is well organized with suitable paragraphs and the writer uses linking expressions, eg *As for food, However, As well as discos*

**Style and format:** The tone is friendly and natural.

**Target reader:** This would have a very positive effect on the reader, whose questions are answered.

**Mark:** Band 5

## Review 12 answers Page 156

**Use of English: FCE Part 2** — **Open cloze**

| | | | |
|---|---|---|---|
| 1 few | 2 when | 3 to | 4 had |
| 5 no | 6 her | 7 where | 8 as |
| 9 so | 10 off | 11 in | 12 not |

**Use of English: FCE Part 4** — **Transformations**

1 Roy if he had bought
2 was such a rapid improvement
3 advised Matt not to go
4 knowledge of English amazes
5 her if she was able
6 offered to give Dawn
7 would not be (very) many
8 suggested eating out the next/following

## Vocabulary: Health matters

| | |
|---|---|
| 1 a black eye | 5 an eye/ear infection |
| 2 a sore throat | 6 a nose bleed |
| 3 a sprained ankle/wrist | 7 a heart attack |
| 4 a runny nose | 8 a stomach ache |

**Use of English: FCE Part 3** — **Word formation**

| | |
|---|---|
| 1 ability | 5 performance |
| 2 relationship | 6 sadness |
| 3 patience | 7 explanation |
| 4 argument | |

### Collocation revision: Units 1–12

| | |
|---|---|
| 1 clothes | 7 town/neighbourhood/area |
| 2 musician | 8 trip |
| 3 device | 9 give |
| 4 film | 10 sentence |
| 5 job/work | 11 wind(s) |
| 6 hair | 12 food |

**Teacher-led revision activity**

Look through the units yourself and write down some examples of collocation seen in the Coursebook so far. Then read the words out one by one and students have to call out what they think the collocation is, eg:

**Teacher:** strong

**Students:** smell, person, beer, cheese (ie possible collocations)

**Teacher:** No, light.

Students make other suggestions.

**Teacher:** Gale-force

**Students:** wind (students call the correct word, which is common to all three adjectives)

Here are some more examples. The numbers refer to the units. The words are read out one by one in the order shown below.

1 _____ angry/ready for school/married (get)
2 perform/mime/sing (a song)
3 solar-powered/electric/microwave (oven)
4 _____ someone's advice/the blame/ a joke (take)
5 _____ long hours/overtime/shifts (work)
6 sparkling/piercing/bright blue (eyes)
7 _____ as a surprise/to an end/up with an idea (come)
8 tourist/skiing/seaside (resort)
9 _____ smile/shoulders/minded (broad)
10 tackle/commit a/confess to a _____ (crime)
11 _____ someone up for the night/ someone's health at risk/ pressure on someone (put)
12 _____ cake/toast/bread (a slice/ piece of)

## Workbook answers

### Reading: Multiple choice   Page 90

1

| 1 C | 2 B | 3 D | 4 B |
| 5 A | 6 C | 7 C | 8 A |

2

| 1 against | 2 in, of | 3 of | 4 on |
| 5 for | 6 with | 7 on | 8 for |

### Vocabulary   Page 91

**A Food**

| 1 *bitter* | 2 greasy | 3 rich |
| 4 savoury | 5 sour | 6 sickly |
| 7 crunchy | 8 spicy | 9 stodgy |
| 10 bland | | |

**B Health**

| 1 damaged | 2 hurting | 3 aches |
| 4 wounding | 5 injuries | 6 pains |

**C *Have, put, give* and *take***

| 1 e | 2 d | 3 g | 4 a | 5 b |
| 6 h | 7 f | 8 c | | |

**D Word formation: nouns**

| 1 involvement | 2 disappearance |
| 3 obligation | 4 seriousness |
| 5 comparison | 6 popularity |
| 7 permission | 8 retirement |

### Language focus   Page 93

**A Countable and uncountable nouns**

| 1 a | 2 a large number |
| 3 Every | 4 suggestion, accommodation |
| 5 bar | 6 few, much |
| 7 no, a few | 8 little |
| 9 any more | 10 another |

**B Reported speech**

1

1 why did you apply/why have you applied for this job?
2 I'm thinking of going
3 I want to have
4 do you have/have you got
5 was (very) useful
6 helped me to understand what it's like
7 What are your main strengths?
8 have a lot of patience
9 I'm a very reliable

2

1 they did to keep fit
2 he was competing in a marathon the next/ following day
3 (that) she did aerobics
4 she was thinking of taking up jogging
5 if/whether they could give us
6 eating/that we should eat/us to eat
7 her students not to eat
8 if they thought diets were
9 he had never needed to go on one
10 she had been on a diet once
11 she would not do it again
12 liked eating

### Use of English   Page 95

**Open cloze**

| 1 few | 2 From | 3 order |
| 4 course | 5 do | 6 which |
| 7 being | 8 it | 9 much |
| 10 to | 11 one | 12 be |

## Transformations

1 had to wear
2 they had been trying
3 where she had bought her
4 warned him not to
5 (that) I (should) lie down
6 not give me very much

## Writing    Page 96

**A Planning**

**1**

| 1 | B | 2 | A | 3 | C |

**B Writing**

| 1 | b | 2 | c | 3 | a |

## First Certificate Paper 4

### Listening

**Part 1**  Multiple choice
**Part 2**  Sentence completion
**Part 3**  Multiple matching
**Part 4**  Multiple choice

This is the fourth of five 'Ready for …' units which focus on the five different skills areas tested in the First Certificate exam: Reading, Writing, Use of English, Listening and Speaking.

See information on page 6 of the Teacher's Book for advice regarding possible approaches to using the material.

*Note:* It is appreciated that students will not have a great deal of time to predict language in the exam before each of the listenings. They may well indeed raise this objection. However, it is important that they do not waste the little but valuable time they are given to prepare themselves mentally before the recording begins.

The intention here is to train them how to use that time profitably, and so increase their chances of understanding correctly.

### Part 1: Multiple choice    Page 158

Follow the instructions given in the Coursebook.

| Answers |
| --- |

**Predicting**

Similarities and differences:
A dress also covers part of the top half of the body like a blouse.
A blouse has **sleeves**, and a dress may do too.
A dress and a blouse may have **collars**, whereas a skirt wouldn't.
A blouse is more likely to have several **buttons** whereas the other two may have just one.
Dresses and skirts can be **short** or **long**, reaching as far as the knees, the ankles, etc.

Answer:   **A** a blouse

**Key words and expressions**
It'll go really well with a skirt I bought last week.
The sleeves are a bit short, but if I wear a jacket over it …

**Distractors**

Cheaper than getting a dress ...

It'll go really well with a skirt I bought last week.

**Listening**

| | | | |
|---|---|---|---|
| 2 C | 3 A | 4 A | 5 C |
| 6 B | 7 B | 8 C | |

---

**Listening Part 1: Listening script 2.15–2.21**

**Two**

These two sides are very well matched. You'll remember they both met in the semi-finals last year, when the game ended in a draw. This year we've had some heavy showers in the last few days and one or two of the players are finding the playing conditions on the pitch more than a little difficult. But it's a throw-in now. Briggs takes it and passes to Duckham. Duckham tries a shot ... and it goes just wide of the post.

**Three**

I thought at first it was some kind of virus, but now I'm wondering if it might be something more serious ... No, it's annoying. I simply can't do any work on it at the moment ... Yes, I phoned them, but they said they'd need to have it for three days before they could give me an answer ... Well, I was wondering if you wouldn't mind having a look at it for me ... Could you come round after work? ... No, that's great; the sooner the better as far as I'm concerned, as long as your boss doesn't mind.

**Four**

**Man:** Lots of room for the legs, that's nice.

**Woman:** Mm, and so comfortable. It's like my favourite armchair. I could go to sleep here and now.

**Man:** Yes, we should've had a coffee after the meal to keep us awake.

**Woman:** We'd never have got a ticket to see this if we had.

**Man:** That's true. The queue was enormous.

**Woman:** Anyway, wake me up when it starts, won't you?

**Five**

You can't fault the food, really. Even my husband was impressed and he's always the first to complain if it's not cooked properly. No, I just felt a little uncomfortable; silver cutlery, antique furniture and everyone dressed as if it was a wedding, including the waiters. And the way they spoke to us! It was 'Sir' and 'Madam' every sentence. I suppose I'm just not used to it, that's all.

**Six**

**Woman:** Just look at that. It's incredible.

**Man:** What do you mean?

**Woman:** Well, there must be about 20 different types of butter in this section. Low-fat, high-fat, Irish, Dutch, Australian – you name it, they've got it.

**Man:** Confusing, isn't it?

**Woman:** No, that's not the point. I'm sure a lot of people will be disappointed there aren't 20 types of carrots and 60 different varieties of cheese. I just don't see why we need them all. And when you think of the transport costs and the fuel needed to import all this stuff and the effect this has on the environment. It makes my blood boil.

**Seven**

The play finishes at about 11 ... Well, I had at first thought of coming back on the train straight afterwards, but the last one's at 11.05, so I probably wouldn't make it. ... Are you sure you don't mind? ... I could always stay in a hotel. There are plenty of cheap ones in that part of town ... OK, well, if you're going to put me up for the night, then you'll have to let me take you out for a meal ... No, I insist.

**Eight**

We all know juvenile crime's on the increase. The police do all they can with very limited resources and then it's up to people like ourselves to sort the problem out. In this school alone we have more than 20 youngsters with a criminal record and we get virtually no support from the parents. Social services come in occasionally to give us advice on how to deal with them, but once they've gone and we close the classroom door, we're very much on our own.

## Part 2: Sentence completion   Page 159

### 1–2 Possible procedure

Students could work together or you could ask students the questions in the style of a quiz, eliciting different answers and reasons from the students. Make sure you clarify what the correct answers are and that students copy those answers into their books so that they have a permanent record.

| | Answers | |
|---|---|---|
| **1** | False | All parts of the listening paper are heard twice. |
| **2** | True | |
| **3** | True | |
| **4** | False | The maximum number of words you need to write is normally three. |
| **5** | False | It is not necessary to rephrase the words you hear. |
| **6** | False | You do usually hear the answers in the same order as the questions. |
| **7** | False | If you are having difficulty with a question, move quickly onto the next. You may miss later answers if you spend too long on one answer. |

8   True   Spelling errors are accepted, but if the word is so badly spelt it is unrecognizable, then it may be marked wrong.

**Listening**

1  tea house
2  several hundred
3  isolated
4  farmers
5  (local) Indians
6  beautiful valley
7  song and dance
8  (groups of) teachers
9  (Welsh) flags
10 chocolate cake

---

**Listening Part 2: Listening script 2.22**

Argentina is a country known internationally for the tango, gaucho cowboys and premium quality beef. To many people, therefore, it comes as some surprise to discover that in certain parts of Patagonia, in the south of the country, one of the 'musts' for any tourist is a visit to a Welsh tea house, a place where you can sip tea and enjoy delicious cakes, baked according to traditional Welsh recipes. Perhaps even more surprising, though, is the fact that some of the locals can actually be heard speaking in Welsh. Exactly how many native Welsh speakers there are in the region is not known, but most estimates put the figure at several hundred, a relatively high number, given that there are just under 600,000 speakers of the language in Wales itself.

But how did these Welsh speakers come to be there? The first wave of settlers arrived from Wales in 1865. Unhappy with conditions at home, they were looking for an isolated area to set up a colony, a place where their language and identity would be preserved intact and not assimilated into the dominant culture, as had already happened in the United States. The 153 colonists who landed on the east coast of Argentina included carpenters, tailors and miners, but no real doctors and just one or two farmers. This was rather worrying, since the Chubut valley where they settled was virtually a desert, and what they needed most of all were agricultural skills.

Against all the odds, though, they survived, overcoming droughts, floods and a succession of crop failures. They were also quick to establish friendly relations with the local Indians, who helped the Welsh through the hard times and taught them some of their ways, how to ride and how to hunt. Twenty years after their arrival some of the settlers moved up into a green fertile region of the Andes mountains, an area which they named Cwm Hyfryd, meaning 'beautiful valley'. Indeed, quite a number of places in Patagonia still bear Welsh names:

Bryn Gwyn which means 'white hill', Trevelin, meaning 'milltown' and Trelew or 'Lewistown', named after Lewis Jones, one of the founders.

The Welsh have left their mark in other ways, too. Their windmills and chapels can be found throughout the region and there are a number of cultural activities, such as poetry readings, male voice choirs and the annual Welsh song and dance festival, a smaller version of the International Eisteddfod held in Wales each year. All of this helps to keep the language and traditions alive in a small corner of the world, 8,000 miles from the homeland. And so too does the fact that every year, as part of a programme administered by the National Assembly for Wales, groups of teachers come to Patagonia to teach the language to the growing number of people who are interested in learning it.

And then, of course, there are the Welsh teas. For my afternoon treat, I visit *Nain Ceri*, reputed to be one of the best tea houses in Gaiman, where the streets and houses are adorned with Welsh flags, a reminder to visitors that they are in the self-proclaimed Patagonian-Welsh capital of Chubut. Inside, *Nain Ceri* is decorated with prints and paintings of Wales and the music playing is that of a traditional all-male choir. I sit next to the fireplace and my mouth begins to water as I look at the various cakes on offer. I am about to order the cream-topped apple pie to accompany my tea, when I catch sight of an irresistible-looking chocolate cake and choose that instead. I am not disappointed - it is absolutely delicious. Afterwards, I chat at length to the owner, Ceri Morgan – in Spanish, as she speaks no English and I speak no Welsh. She tells me a little more about the history of …

## Part 3: Multiple matching    Page 160

| Answers |
|---|

**2 Suggested answers**

**E**    is very different from A because it talks about personal qualities rather than academic qualifications.

**B**    This is the only sentence which clearly suggests the person is already doing the job.

**C & D** Both these sentences mention the fact that the person has been told by someone about work or a specific job.

**E**    see example. Both E and C express an opinion: *I disagree with …* and *I think I have …*

**F**    see example. Note the following difference between A, B and F:

**A**    We do not know if the person is studying or not for that qualification.

**B** The person is studying though we do not know if it is relevant to the work they are doing.

**F** The person is studying now and the subject is relevant either to what they are doing and/or what they are going to do.

### Suggested underlinings of key words

Note also the different tenses in A (future), B (present simple), D (past simple) and F (present continuous). Grammatical features such as this may also be relevant.

**A** I will need <u>a specific qualification</u> to do this job.

**B** I <u>combine</u> work with studying.

**C** I <u>disagree</u> with the <u>careers advice</u> I have been given.

**D** I <u>heard about</u> this job from <u>someone in my family</u>.

**E** I think I have the necessary <u>personal qualities</u>.

**F** I am studying a <u>relevant subject</u>.

Words related to *qualification*
degree, 'A' Levels, diploma, certificate

### Further predictions

Students need not necessarily come up with any of this particular language or indeed the language in the recording. This is very much an awareness-raising exercise and a procedure to follow in the 30 seconds which students have to read the questions in the exam.

## Answers

Possible answers:

**B** at the same time, while I am studying, I'm also working/studying

**C** they told me to, they recommended me to, I was advised to, I didn't agree, I thought it was a bad suggestion

**D** a particular relative (eg uncle, sister, father, grandmother etc) + verbs such as *told me*

**E** nouns or adjectives related to personality, eg patient/patience, tolerant/tolerance

**F** alternative words for *relevant* – appropriate, useful, helpful, which I can apply later

### 3 Listening

| 1 B | 2 F | 3 D | 4 A |
|-----|-----|-----|-----|
| 5 E | C not used | | |

---

**Listening Part 3: Listening script 2.23–2.27**

**Speaker 1**
I've been writing for as long as I can remember, and it's something I want to continue to do for a living when I've finished university. I say 'continue' because I've already had one collection of short stories published and I've just started another. I write mostly late at night and at weekends, always after I've finished my course work. I'm doing a maths degree, which has little to do with writing, but I believe in keeping my options open, just in case my creativity runs out.

**Speaker 2**
For some strange reason I want to be a tattoo artist; you know, paint people's bodies. I'm doing a course in graphic design at art college, which I've been told will be useful. The brother of a friend of mine has a studio and he lets me go and watch him work when I'm not studying at the college. It's the only way to learn, as there are no official courses and no specific qualifications for tattoo artists. At least, not as far as I know.

**Speaker 3**
As soon as I leave school I'm going to join the Army. I tried to do it when I was ten but they told me to go back when I was older – so I will! You can learn a trade and do almost any job you want to, and they let you study while you're working. I'd like to work as a physical training instructor, and then maybe later try and get an engineering qualification or something like that. My granddad's an ex-soldier and he always told such good stories that I knew that was what I wanted to do. My parents just think I'm crazy.

**Speaker 4**
I hope one day to be a speech therapist. I'll have to get a degree in speech therapy first, and to do that I'll need to get good grades next year in my 'A' levels. It's a job which involves helping people who have difficulty communicating, and I've always known I wanted to work in one of the 'caring professions'. My uncle's a speech therapist, but I learnt all about it from a TV documentary I saw a few years ago. And that's when I thought; 'I want to do that'. Then last year I did some voluntary work while I was studying for my GCSEs, and I was hooked.

**Speaker 5**
I haven't made up my mind yet, but I'd quite like to go into teaching. Naturally I've had lots of advice from teachers at school about how to go about it and how hard I'll have to work for my exams. But to be honest my decision is based not so much on my academic abilities but rather on the fact that I just feel I'd be right for the job. The teachers I look up to at school are all dynamic, outgoing people and that's precisely how I like to see myself.

## Part 4: Multiple choice

Page 161

**1–2** Refer students to the information and instructions in their books.

**3**

| Answers |
| --- |
| C Underline the whole of the first sentence. |

**4**

| Answers |
| --- |
| **A:** Most of the people he works with are below average height. At one metre 84, he is above the average height of one metre 78 for British men. |
| **B:** We are told that he is taller than most, if not all, of the people in his studio, but we we do not know if he is taller than most people in his profession. |

**5**

| Answers |
| --- |
| **2** B   **3** A   **4** A   **5** B   **6** B   **7** C |

**6**

| Answers |
| --- |
| **2**<br>**A** We are only told that tall people come from all over the country to stay in a hotel.<br>**C** Not mentioned.<br><br>**3**<br>**B & C** are both mentioned as problems but not the biggest.<br><br>**4**<br>**B** People who make comments like 'What's the weather like up there?' think they are funny. Jenny does not.<br>**C** Jenny says that many fellow TPC members take offence, but she is used to it now.<br><br>**5**<br>**A** They stand up straighter as they grow in confidence. No one encourages them to do so.<br>**C** Not mentioned. |

**6**

**A** Not mentioned. Jenny says 'I've never been very good at volleyball, but I always got picked for the university team when I was a student.'

**C** Not mentioned. The word 'job' is mentioned when she says 'you can get things off the top shelf that most other people have a job to reach.'

**7**

**A** Not mentioned. Jenny merely compares the GB and Ireland club with those in America.

**B** No. People decide for themselves if they should join.

---

**Listening Part 4:  Listening script 2.28**

**I = Interviewer  J = Jenny Parfitt**

**I:** Do you consider yourself to be tall, medium or short? At one metre 84 I've always thought of myself as being a little on the tall side, particularly when I stand next to the people I work with here in the *Round Britain* studio. Rather curiously, most of *them* are below the national average height of one metre 78 for men and one 62 for women. But when I popped in yesterday to the annual conference of the TPC - that's the Tall Person's Club of Great Britain and Ireland - I felt decidedly small. I asked one of the organizers, Jenny Parfitt, to tell me about the conference.

**J:** Well, this is the main event in the club's very busy social calendar. <u>Throughout the year we put on a whole number of activities for members in their local area, like barbecues, theatre excursions, walks and so on. And this conference is the highlight of that year.</u> It's a three-day event that gives tall people from all over the country the chance to meet in the comfort of a hotel, where they can chat, eat, dance and go sightseeing with others who are also above average height.

**I:** But there's also a serious side to it as well, I gather.

**J:** That's right, it's not all partying! We discuss a lot of important issues, too. One of the aims of the TPC is to promote the interests of tall people, to change current attitudes. We live in a heightist world, where tall people are discriminated against. Beds in hotels are usually too short for us, and we often have to sleep with our feet hanging off the end. Travelling by bus, train or plane is a major problem too – there's very little leg room and it can feel very cramped. <u>The main difficulty, though, is finding shops that sell long enough trousers or big enough shoes.</u> That can be a real headache.

**I:** I imagine too that the attitudes of other people can be a problem.

**J:** Yes, people do tend to stare at us when we walk into the room, treat us like circus freaks. And some actually laugh out loud, as if something funny has just happened. I think if I weren't so used to it now, I might take offence – I know many fellow TPC members do. But to be honest, <u>I find it a little bit annoying. You get tired of it all,</u> particularly when the fifteenth person in a day says something like 'What's the weather like up there?' And they think it's so funny.

**I:** Yes, not very original, is it? Does the club offer help to tall people who come across attitudes like these?

**J:** Yes, we regularly give advice to victims of insults and bullying at school or in the workplace. But perhaps the greatest benefit of the club is the opportunity to see that as a tall person you are not alone. When people come to their first meeting and walk into a room full of tall people, they start standing up straighter. <u>They lose their shyness and very soon begin to feel less awkward, more comfortable about their height</u>. It's a remarkable transformation.

**I:** You've mentioned some of the negative aspects of being taller than average. But surely there must be some advantages, too?

**J:** Oh yes, there are plenty of them. Erm, for example, <u>you can always see over everyone's head if you're watching something in a crowd or an audience</u>, and if you're in a supermarket you can get things off the top shelf that most other people have a job to reach. And then also you automatically become first choice for sports like basketball, volleyball or rowing. I've never been very good at volleyball, but I always got picked for the university team when I was a student.

**I:** Now, one thing of course we've failed to mention, Jenny, is your height. How tall are you?

**J:** One metre 88. And actually, I'm one of the smaller members at this conference. The tallest woman here is exactly two metres and the tallest man 2 metres 30, that's an incredible 7 foot 6 inches.

**I:** Goodness me!

**J:** Yes, impressive, isn't it? Incidentally, though, <u>you don't need to be above a certain height to qualify as a member of the Tall Person's Club</u>. Unlike some clubs in the USA, which can be difficult to join because of their restrictions, <u>we are very inclusive over here</u>. We believe that people know for themselves whether they are tall or not and <u>it's up to them to decide if they should join</u>.

**I:** Jenny, it's been fascinating talking to you ...

## Content Overview

### Themes

Extreme situations in which people have been successful are the themes of this unit.
The unit title means succeeding in doing something against all expectations.

### Exam-related activities

| | |
|---|---|
| **Paper 1** | **Reading** |
| Part 1 | Multiple choice |
| Part 2 | Gapped text |
| | |
| **Paper 2** | **Writing** |
| Part 1 | Email (Review) |
| Part 2 | Formal letters: An application |
| | |
| **Paper 3** | **Use of English** |
| Part 3 | Word formation (Review) |
| Part 4 | Transformations (Review) |
| | |
| **Paper 4** | **Listening** |
| Part 1 | Multiple choice |
| Part 2 | Sentence completion |

### Other

| | |
|---|---|
| Language focus 1: | Ability |
| Language focus 2: | Verbs + prepositions |
| Vocabulary: | Money |
| | *Make* and *do* |
| | Ways of looking |
| Word formation: | Miscellaneous nouns |

## Vocabulary 1: Money    Page 162

**1** Refer students to the pictures in their books and elicit/teach the vocabulary.

| | |
|---|---|
| a cheque book | currency/cash |
| a credit card | coins |
| calculator | (bank) notes |

Ask students to discuss the advantages and disadvantages in pairs, then give feedback to the class.

**2–3** Elicit the meanings of the phrases in the boxes before students complete the spaces in each exercise.

### Answers

**2** 1 stock market      4 currency
    2 rate of interest    5 rate of exchange
    3 account

**3** 1 for, for      3 in, in
    2 on, on      4 to, to

**4** Before students start discussing the questions, tell them to choose individually which questions are relevant to them.

## Reading 1: FCE Part 1 — Multiple choice
Page 163

Photocopiable vocabulary exercise on page 168.

**Note:** It is important that students should not be helped with items of vocabulary when doing the reading task. At this stage of the course students need to be more independent of the teacher and other sources of help; encourage them to rely on their own language resources, putting into practice the skills of deducing meaning from context that they have been using throughout the course.

**1–2** Refer students to the instructions. As well as encouraging students to read the title and introduction to reading texts, this procedure is designed to get students to read the text through once for an understanding of gist before tackling the multiple-choice questions.

**3** Refer students to the instructions for the multiple-choice task. You might like to set a time limit of 20 minutes, a third of the time they have in the exam to answer questions on three texts (and transfer their answers to the answer sheet).

### Answers

1 C   2 B   3 C   4 A   5 D   6 C   7 D   8 B

**Reacting to the text**
You may wish to leave these questions until after exercise 3. Before students start discussing these questions in pairs or small groups, remind them to develop their answers when possible. Try using the technique of setting a longish time limit which students must try to reach by keeping the

conversation going. If necessary remind them that in the oral exam in stages 3 (and 4) the examiner will not help them if they do not say enough.

## Language focus 1: Ability
Page 165

**1** Students follow the instructions in their books.

### Answers

**a** travel      **d** to get
**b** reaching    **e** setting
**c** to retire

**2** Students read through and write their ideas and answers down, then check with the Grammar reference as instructed.

### Answers

- *can* is not possible in **c** because it does not have an infinitive form.
- *could* is not possible in **d** because this sentence refers to a specific occasion, not a general ability in the past.
- *could* is not possible in **e** because it does not have a participle form.
- We can use the negative form *couldn't* to refer to specific occasions in the past.

**3–4** Students should do the transformations individually.

### Answers

**3** 1 was capable of swimming
    2 finally managed to give up
    3 was unable to finish
    4 succeeded in finding out
    5 be able to find
    6 didn't manage to buy

**4** 1 could     3 couldn't     6 couldn't

**5** Students could write down their ideas first and then ask and tell each other or ask and tell each other without preparation time.

## Vocabulary 2: *Make* and *do*     Page 166

### A *Make* or *do*

This is a notoriously confusing area for learners of English, as in many languages the two verbs *make* and *do* are expressed by just one verb.

**1**  Students follow the instructions in their books.

#### Answers

1  made
2  made
3  do (*make* is also possible with *deals*)
4  doing
5  made
6  make

**2**  This exercise attempts to cut through the seemingly arbitrary nature of the use of the verbs *make* and *do* by grouping their collocates into different categories. Recording the verbs in this way should help students to learn and remember them.

#### Answers

1  damage            5  an experiment
2  an effort          6  an exercise
3  someone a favour   7  progress
4  the beds           8  a job

1  MAKE a plan, an appointment, an arrangement *arranging or planning to do things*
2  DO homework, a course, a degree *all related to study*
3  MAKE up your mind, a decision, a choice *decisions*
4  DO the housework, the washing-up, the ironing *housework*
5  MAKE a speech, a phone call, a complaint *communication*
6  MAKE a film, a cake, a cup of tea *creation*
7  DO badly in an exam, well at school, your best *all refer to how successful or unsuccessful a person is*
8  MAKE a mistake, a mess, a lot of noise *to cause something with a negative result*

| MAKE | DO |
|---|---|
| a profit | business |
| money | the ironing |
| a loss | damage |
| a plan | an experiment |
| an appointment | homework |
| an arrangement | an exercise |
| an effort | a course |
| up your mind | badly in an exam |
| a decision | a degree |
| a choice | well at school |
| the beds | someone a favour |
| a speech | your best |
| a phone call | the housework |
| a complaint | a job |
| a film | the washing-up |
| a cake | |
| a cup of tea | |
| progress | |
| a mistake | |
| a mess | |
| a lot of noise | |

### B Phrasal verbs with *make* and *do*

**1**  In this exercise students are asked to deduce the meaning of the phrasal verbs from the context.

#### Answers

1  fasten it
2  become friends again
3  invent it
4  renovated and decorated it
5  hear properly
6  pretended/feigned
7  need
8  couldn't manage/survive

**2**  This exercise is suitable as written homework or writing in class. Alternatively, students could do it orally in small groups.

### Writing: FCE Part 2     Formal letters: An application Page 167

Begin by asking if any of the students have ever had a grant to study abroad or applied for one. If someone has, ask him/her to tell the class what process he/she had to go through in order to obtain it.

**1** Refer students to the instructions in their books and the questions about the target reader.

### Answers

- The target reader is the Director of St George's House.
- The effect would not be positive. As well as making several requests concerning the school and the class (Manchester, the class size, idiomatic expressions), the applicant gives rather frivolous reasons for wanting to go to England: meeting a relative, going clubbing, using it as a base for travelling. This does not sound like a serious letter from someone asking for money and the application would probably not be successful.

**2** Refer students to the paragraph plan or elicit something similar from them.

**3** Students follow instructions in their books.

### Answers

Examples of other reasons:
- A course in the UK would help you pass FCE.
- Your writing and grammar are fine but you would like to improve your fluency in speaking.
- You are going to study English at university next year.
- You are interested in meeting speakers of English from other countries.
- You will be working for two years overseas for a charity and English is a requirement.

Examples of further details relating to the other three reasons in the Coursebook:
- A period of study in the UK would improve your chances of obtaining a job in your own country.
  *You would like to work in the travel industry but your job applications are repeatedly rejected because of your level of spoken English.*
- A recent illness has caused you to fall behind in your studies.
  *You were absent from school for three months after a car accident and this has affected your chances of passing First Certificate.*
- You are interested in learning about British culture and the British way of life.
  *You believe that knowledge of the culture would increase your enjoyment of the subject and provide an important context for your study of the language.*

Before students start, refer them to the 'Don't forget!' box. In pairs students think of personal relevant information.

Relevant personal information might include:
- level of English
- how long you have been studying the language
- difficulties with the language and other information already mentioned in the *reasons* (eg family moving to England, recent illness).

### Listening 1: FCE Part 2
### Sentence completion
Page 168

**1** In many countries nowadays, blind people have been integrated into society. National organizations are dedicated to education and training programmes to enable blind people to have access to jobs and professions that would not have been open to them a few years ago. In this warm-up activity, students are asked to put themselves in a blind person's position. Most of these jobs can be done by blind people. Students work in pairs or this could be done in an open class format.

Encourage students to answer using appropriate structures, eg
*I wouldn't be able to …*
*I'd find it hard to …*
*… would be easier.*

**2** Consider checking that students understand *partially sighted* (not totally blind), and *bully* (frighten or hurt someone who is smaller or weaker than you).

Play the recording twice, letting students compare together before they hear it the second time.

### Answers

1  one *or* a/one year old
2  left
3  (any) better
4  tunnel
5  normal
6  called names
7  became good friends
8  get a job
9  going on tour/touring
10  shyness

## Listening 1: Listening script 2.29

A = Announcer    G = Grace

**A:** Grace, how long have you had problems with your eyes?

**G:** Well, I was actually born completely blind and my sight didn't develop until I was about a year old. Ever since that age I've only ever been able to see out of one eye. I kind of got used to that, and I thought it was quite normal. Then one day when I was about eight I was having a bit of a laugh with my mum. Just for a joke she covered up my left eye, the good one, and said, 'How many fingers?' and I said, 'I don't know' 'What do you mean you don't know?' she said. She thought I was playing around, but when she realized I wasn't she took me straight down to the doctor. That's when I found out I have an incurable eye disease, which may or may not get worse, but definitely won't get any better.

**A:** And *has* it got worse?

**G:** Not really, no. It's been more or less the same ever since. Though I was having a check-up when I was a bit older and they discovered I had tunnel vision as well.

**A:** What exactly is that?

**G:** It means I only have central view. I don't have any lateral view, so I'm unable to see anything which isn't directly in front of me. Not like most people who can see slightly to the side when they look ahead. It sounds a bit weird, but to me it's normal.

**A:** So did you have to go to a special school when you were younger?

**G:** I was determined to go to a normal school because I was convinced that if I did it would teach me to cope better. I kind of suspected, and my parents warned me, that it wouldn't be easy. You know how cruel kids of eleven and twelve can be to each other. And sure enough they called me names and bullied me and I must have cried every day for a year. And I did get to the point when I wanted to leave, but my dad told me to carry on and see it through. He said it'd get better – and it did. A lot of those who'd called me names became good friends.

**A:** You eventually left school at 16, didn't you?

**G:** That's right. I guess I got to the point where I felt like I knew that all I wanted to do was sing and play the guitar. My dad said I was too young and tried to put me off the idea. But then when he saw how determined I was, he told me I'd need to get a job if I wanted to save up enough money to record a demo. So I did get a job and very quickly managed to get enough money together to do the demo.

**A:** And that led to your first record deal.

**G:** And everything else that went with it – the contacts, the song writing, the touring. I love it all, especially going on tour, though you wouldn't believe the stresses and strains involved. Most people think it's a breeze, like dead easy and no worries. But the way I see it, you have a kind of responsibility when you're up there on stage. Being an entertainer is all about being larger than life and making people feel good.

**A:** So you've come a long way from your schooldays when the other kids made you cry!

**G:** Right. But in a way going through that experience at school helped me get over my shyness. So I don't worry any more what people think about my eyes. I'm far too busy worrying about what they think of my music!

**A:** Well, your first single was a number one hit in America, so you certainly don't seem to have anything to worry about there …

For the final speaking question, students should consider people they know or know of as well as famous people.

## Word formation: Miscellaneous nouns
Page 168

**1** The noun forms of the verbs in the Coursebook are as shown below. Students follow the instructions on where to check their answers.

| Answers | | | |
|---|---|---|---|
| choice | loss | complaint | speech |

**2** Students could do this in pairs or individually.

| Answers | | |
|---|---|---|
| **1** Sales | **2** signature | **3** laughter |
| **4** behaviour | **5** arrival | **6** beings |
| **7** *proof | **8** saying | |
| *uncountable, *proofs* is not possible | | |

## Reading 2: Gapped text    Page 169
**FCE Part 2**

Photocopiable vocabulary exercise on page 169.

**1** Students discuss what they might do in each of the situations.

**2** Students follow the instructions. If necessary, remind them to pay close attention to contextual clues and tell them to underline the clues in the text and the sentences which helped them to make their decisions.

Before you check their answers, let students compare their answers and the clues in the text and sentences which they identified.

| Answers | | | |
|---|---|---|---|
| 1 E | 2 H | 3 G | 4 A |
| 5 F | 6 C | 7 B | D not used |

**Reacting to the text**
Students discuss these questions in pairs, groups of three or open class format.

## Language focus 2: Verbs followed by prepositions
Page 170

**1** Students could try to complete the sentences without looking back at the article.

| Answers | | |
|---|---|---|
| **1** 1 for | 2 for | 3 against |
| **2** 1 *for*, d | 2 for, a | 3 for, f |
| 4 from, b | 5 from, c | 6 on, g |
| 7 on, e | | |

**3** Students discuss the four situations.

**Further practice**
Prepositional expressions need frequent use and review in order to be assimilated. The following are some suggestions:

- Personalization ideas as in number 3 of the Coursebook. Vary the expressions you want students to focus on, write them on the board and ask students to make real sentences or ask legitimate questions using the expressions.
- Say the verb in the expressions and elicit from students (written or spoken) the complete expressions, eg Teacher: *forgive*
  Students: *forgive someone for something*
- Write the expressions on cards with the missing preposition written on the back of the cards. Students test themselves and each other. They can prepare the cards themselves – even more memorable!
- You and/or students prepare wall charts to pin up on the walls. This keeps the expressions always visible and in students' peripheral vision.

## Vocabulary 3: Ways of looking   Page 170
This is another area of confusion for learners.

**1** Give students a short time to think about their answers before eliciting their ideas.

| Answers | |
|---|---|
| **a** | *see* = (the ability) to use your eyes, one of the five senses |
| **b** | *look at* = pay attention to or examine someone or something with the eyes. |
| **c** | *watch* = (usually) to pay attention to someone or something that is moving |

**2–4** Students could do exercises 2 and 3 in pairs. Provide students with dictionaries if possible or teach the vocabulary by demonstration.

| Answers | | | | |
|---|---|---|---|---|
| **2** 1 look at | 2 see | | | |
| 3 watching (the image moves) | | | | |
| 4 seen | 5 Watch | | | |
| **3** 1 d | 2 e | 3 b | 4 a | 5 c |
| **4** 1 peered | | 4 stared | | |
| 2 glanced | | 5 glimpse | | |
| 3 gazed | | | | |

Review this vocabulary by asking some students to mime the actions and the others to guess the appropriate verbs.

## Listening 2: Multiple choice
**FCE Part 1**   Page 171

Refer students to the instructions and the information in the 'What to expect in the exam' box. Read the example together which predicts how the speaker might sound in each situation.

Read out the other situations and the three options one by one, eliciting and helping students to predict how the people might sound.

Now that students are more aware of what to listen for, do the listening task in the usual way, allowing students to compare answers before they hear the recording for the second time.

| Answers | | | |
|---|---|---|---|
| 1 C | 2 A | 3 C | 4 B |
| 5 C | 6 B | 7 B | 8 A |

**Listening 2: Listening script 2.30–2.37**

**One**
Of course, I wasn't very happy about him losing his job. We had a few sleepless nights, I can tell you, what with the mortgage to pay and two hungry kids to feed. But no one was to blame for what happened, and thankfully it all worked out in the end. I'm just glad it's all over now. I don't know how we'd have managed to cope if he hadn't been taken on at the power station.

**Two**
**Woman:** Dave's done well for himself, hasn't he?

**Man:** Yes, well, it's hardly surprising, is it?

**Woman:** Why do you say that?

**Man:** Well, it was the same thing at school. Fortune always smiled on him. He passed exams with the minimum of effort and now he's making money in the same way. He makes a few good decisions, invests in the right companies and bingo! Suddenly he's a millionaire. Still, it couldn't happen to a nicer guy. No one deserves it more than him.

**Three**
**Man:** Looking forward to going rock climbing, Sally?

**Woman:** Well, to tell you the truth, I haven't made my mind up about it. Everyone tells me it's great fun, especially when you realize that you're quite safe, with all the ropes and everything. But what if you get stuck and can't go on? That's what worries me. I can't see I'm going to enjoy myself, clinging to a rock waiting for someone to come and pull me off. Still, I won't know if I don't try, will I?

**Four**
Yes, well, we're very pleased you actually managed to phone us. At least you've done something right. You may have noticed, however, that it is now two o'clock in the morning. … Yes, but you said you would be home by 12. If you can't keep promises then you shouldn't make them … No, we can't come and pick you up. You're old enough to be able to solve your own problems now.

**Five**
Oh come on, you said you'd help me out. I'll pay you back as soon as I get paid. It's just that it's our anniversary and I want to take her somewhere special to celebrate … I can't ask Mum! You know how she is with money. She didn't lend you any that time you were broke, so I don't see why it'd be any different for me.

**Six**
**Woman:** How on earth did you manage to get in such a mess?

**Man:** It's toner from a photocopier. I was changing it and it went all over my clothes.

**Woman:** If your mother could see you now, she'd have a fit!

**Man:** Have you got anything to clean it off with?

**Woman:** No, you'll have to go next door and get something from the shop. But don't take too long about it. I've got a few jobs I want you to do in the sales department.

**Seven**
I'd like to say how flattered I feel to have been invited to open this magnificent sports centre. And I'm particularly proud of the fact that you voted unanimously for my name to be given to the centre. If I think back to all my sporting successes, the medals I've won and the records I've broken, none of them ever gave me as much pleasure as this moment today. As a child growing up in this area, I never dreamed I would one day …

**Eight**
What I like about it is that you're doing things that nobody else has done before, discovering things about yourself as well as the world you live in. I've been to places I never knew existed until I got there, and I've travelled enormous distances without seeing another living soul. It's not whether it's the highest, the hottest or the coldest that matters to me, but being the first person to set foot there. That's why I do it.

## Review 13 answers Page 172

**Use of English: FCE Part 3 — Word formation**

1 saying   2 Advertising   3 signature
4 laughter   5 speeches   6 poverty
7 wealthiest   8 growth   9 success
10 choices

**Use of English: FCE Part 4 — Transformations**

1 blamed Helen for starting/having started
2 apologized for being
3 warned us against/about
4 prevented him (from) coming
5 insisted on seeing
6 did not/didn't succeed in finding
7 didn't/did not manage to get
8 make a complaint

## Vocabulary

**A Make and do**

1 do   5 making
2 do   6 do
3 make   7 make
4 made   8 do

**B Ways of looking**

1 c   2 d   3 e   4 a   5 b

135

## Writing: Email
**FCE Part 1**

At this stage of the course stronger students should be able to do this without the aid of preparation in class time. On the other hand, if you have younger learners you may decide to do some preparation with the students due to the 'financial' nature of the task. Remind students of previous occasions on which they have written informal emails and letters in Units 1, 7, 9 and 12. The email in Unit 7 and the letter in Unit 12 were of a similar type to this, requiring the writer to give information.

## Workbook answers

### Reading: Multiple matching   Page 98

**1**

| | |
|---|---|
| **1/2** C, E in any order | **3** A |
| **4/5** B, E in any order | **6/7** A, D in any order |
| **8** F | **9** C |
| **10/11** A, F in any order | **12/13** D, E in any order |
| **14/15** B, E in any order | |

**2**
1. to put some money to one side
2. Money's a bit tight
3. to make ends meet
4. looking a million dollars
5. hard-up
6. came into
7. have money to burn
8. the jackpot
9. we're made of money
10. money grows on trees

### Vocabulary   Page 99

**A Money**

**1**

| | | | |
|---|---|---|---|
| **1** change | **2** debt | **3** bill | **4** on loan |
| **5** owe | **6** coin | **7** do | **8** sell |

**2**

| | | | |
|---|---|---|---|
| **1** *the receipt* | **2** coin | **3** owe | **4** on loan |
| **5** bill | **6** change | **7** debt | |

**B Revision: Lexical phrases**

| | |
|---|---|
| **1** *taken, given* | **2** made, came |
| **3** took, had | **4** having, getting, do |
| **5** doing, put | **6** come, putting, get |
| **7** gave, made | |

### Language focus   Page 100

**A Ability**
1. correct
2. Trevor was able to/managed to mend/succeeded in mending
3. correct
4. correct
5. correct
6. I've never been able to swim
7. he's incapable of organizing
8. correct
9. she won't be able to come/she can't come
10. They didn't succeed in getting

**B Phrasal verbs and prepositions**

| | | | |
|---|---|---|---|
| **1** off | **2** round | **3** for | **4** up |
| **5** up | **6** for | **7** for | **8** out |
| **9** of | **10** on | **11** for | **12** from |
| **13** for | **14** from | **15** on | |

### Use of English   Page 102

**Multiple-choice cloze**

| | | | |
|---|---|---|---|
| **1** B | **2** D | **3** B | **4** A |
| **5** A | **6** D | **7** B | **8** D |
| **9** C | **10** A | **11** B | **12** A |

**Word formation**

| | | |
|---|---|---|
| **1** highest | **2** amazed | **3** surprisingly |
| **4** injuries | **5** broken | **6** survival |
| **7** disbelief | **8** death | **9** reasonably |
| **10** relief | | |

**Transformations**
1. made up our minds
2. made several telephone calls
3. was a difficult choice
4. no proof of
5. congratulated the players on winning
6. me for forgetting her birthday
7. didn't/did not succeed in reaching
8. 's/is capable of running

## Writing   Page 104

**2**  4  Introduction (or Aim)
   3  Sightseeing
   1  Shopping
   5  Lunch
   2  Conclusion

Different ways of referring to the tourists:
those who would rather go shopping, senior
citizens, the visitors, the group, everyone, a group
of elderly tourists, non-vegetarians

Different ways of making recommendations:
it is to be recommended, visitors can enjoy ...
Non-vegetarians should try ...

Words expressing number or quantity:
wide range of goods, a number of exclusive
gift shops, numerous exhibits, one of several
restaurants, one of the many fresh fish dishes

Words and expressions related to cost:
exclusive gift shops, generous discounts,
reasonably priced lunch

**3  b**  Target reader: the teacher in charge
      Style: formal
      Differences:

| 1 | 3 a |
|---|-----|
| elderly tourists | young foreign students |
| for the morning | for the afternoon and evening |
| sightseeing | entertainment |
| | little money to spend |

**3  c**  Words to describe prices:
      reasonable, affordable, competitive
      Words to describe goods:
      cut-price, inexpensive

      Other words and expressions:
      good bargains, discounts, special offers
      good value for money

## Content Overview

### Themes

The themes in this unit are varied: the Arts, Damien
Hirst and television. Students also talk about
animals and listen to a woman who has swum with
sharks.

The title of this unit is a well-known simile typically
used to describe a little girl. As this unit is about the
Arts the title is also a play on words.

### Exam-related activities

| Paper 1 | Reading |
|---------|---------|
| Part 2 | Gapped text |
| Part 3 | Multiple matching |

| Paper 2 | Writing |
|---------|---------|
| Part 2 | Set books |
| Part 2 | Essays (Unit and Review) |

| Paper 3 | Use of English |
|---------|---------|
| Part 3 | Word formation (Review) |
| Part 4 | Transformations (Review) |

| Paper 4 | Listening |
|---------|---------|
| Part 4 | Multiple choice |

| Paper 5 | Speaking |
|---------|---------|
| Part 3 | Collaborative task |

### Other

| Language focus: | Hypothetical situations |
|-----------------|--------------------------|
| Vocabulary: | The Arts |
| | Animals |
| | Television |
| | Phrasal verbs |
| Word formation: | Adjective suffixes -ible and -able |

## Vocabulary 1: The Arts   Page 174

**1**  Before students look at their books, write
the title *THE ARTS* on the board and *DANCE,
PAINTING, MUSIC, THEATRE* below or around the
title. Students work together to think of and write
down as many associations as they can. Set a time
limit of about three minutes for this. Ask each pair
or group how many words they wrote down. There
is no need to check their vocabulary.

### Answers

| | |
|---|---|
| **1** classical | **4** gallery |
| **2** opera | **5** painting |
| **3** stone | **6** novel |

**2** This exercise can be done as a whole class either eliciting directly onto the board or asking students to write their ideas first, then tell you.

### Answers

| | |
|---|---|
| *music* | musician, composer, conductor, orchestra, pianist, violinist, etc |
| *literature* | novelist, writer, author, publisher |
| *art* | artist, painter, art collector |
| *opera* | opera singer, tenor, soprano, cast |
| *ballet* | ballet dancer, ballerina, choreographer |
| *sculpture* | sculptor |

Students check their answers in the Wordlist on page 205 of their books.

**Reading 1:** FCE Part 2    **Gapped text**    Page 174

Photocopiable vocabulary exercise on page 169.

**1** Refer students to the picture and the questions in their books. You could encourage a wider discussion of the topic by asking some of the following questions:
*Why is this considered a work of art?*
*Can you think of any other examples of unusual works of art?*
*Is there anything that couldn't be used in a work of art?*
*Do you think modern art is more or less interesting than traditional art?*
*What skills are needed to create modern art?*

Alternatively (or in addition), you might like to set up a roleplay based around the artwork in the photograph. This could be done either before or after students have read the text and completed the task. Students work in pairs, A and B.

**Student A** works for an art gallery and is trying to sell the artwork to their partner, who is looking for something to decorate the reception area of a building (eg company headquarters, hospital, hotel, sports centre, town hall etc). Student A should point out the advantages of having such an artwork on display in the building.

**Student B** is responsible for the interior decoration of the building. He or she is unsure whether the artwork will be suitable for display in the reception area and expresses those doubts by pointing out the disadvantages of having such an artwork there.

When they have finished, and Student B has decided whether or not to purchase the artwork, students could change roles and use a photograph of a different work of modern art.

**2** Refer students to the instructions.

### Answers

| | | | |
|---|---|---|---|
| **1** C | **2** G | **3** D | **4** A |
| **5** H | **6** E | **7** B | F not used |

**Reacting to the text**
Students discuss in pairs, groups or as a whole class.

## Language focus: Hypothetical situations    Page 176

**A Wishes**
**1** Students at this level may have come across this area of language before. If you think this is the case with your students, instead of referring them to their books, write up the sentence from the text and elicit from the students what the real situation is:
*I wish I could be an artist.*
I don't have the ability to be an artist
I would like to have that ability but it's not possible.

**2** Students follow the instructions in their books. Students may make mistakes at this stage, but once their answers are checked they will have a record of the form and meaning of the three structures.

### Answers

**2**   **a** the past simple
    **b** *would* + base form
    **c** the past perfect

**3a** I wish I ~~would~~ give up smoking.
        **could**
    *I wish I would* is not normally said.

  **b** *I wish she could come to my party on Saturday.*
    The speaker <u>knows</u> that she cannot come.
    *I hope she can come to my party on Saturday.*
    The speaker <u>does not know</u> if she can come or not.

Students check their answers and read more about expressing wishes in the Grammar reference on page 217 of their books.

## Practice

Students should do these exercises individually before checking with a partner and the whole class.

| Answers | | |
|---|---|---|
| **1** **1** could | **2** didn't | **3** hadn't bought |
| **4** would | **5** you'd listened | |
| **2** **1** were | **2** would stop | **3** had gone |
| **4** had | **5** would make | |

### B *It's time* and *would rather*

*I'd (would) rather* expresses preference.
*It's time* expresses the idea that the speaker thinks something should happen immediately.

| Answers |
|---|
| **1** I'd rather you *didn't* bring a mobile phone to school. |
| **2** It's time you *went* to bed now. |

Note: both sentences are expressed with the past simple tense but refer to present time.
Students read the Grammar reference as indicated in their books.

## Practice

You might like to teach your students the expression *to get something off your chest* (to be honest about things that are troubling or worrying you) before they start this exercise.

Students follow the instructions in their books or at the last stage where they compare sentences, the listener should try to guess who the sentences are about.

Expand the activity in the Coursebook into a roleplay. The partner takes on the various roles and 'defends' him or herself, eg
(to a neighbour)
**A:** I wish you would keep your dog quiet at night. We have problems sleeping.
**B:** You think you have problems! We can't sleep ourselves.

## A follow-up activity for next class

Students complete the following sentences and then tell each other and discuss:
*I wish I had* + past participle
*I should've/shouldn't have* + past participle
*I regret* + gerund (see Unit 2)

If you or they feel that they have spoken about themselves enough you could change this by writing on the board the names of famous people. Include some historical characters too. Each student completes the sentences for one of the famous people and their partner guesses which one.

## Word formation: Adjective suffixes *-ible* and *-able*           Page 177

This exercise tests students' knowledge of various prefixes and suffixes.

| Answers |
|---|
| **1** **un**predict**able** |
| **2** reason**ably** |
| **3** **im**poss**ibility** |
| **4** incred**ibly**, comfort**ably** |
| **5** valu**ables**, responsib**ility** |
| **6** **un**bear**ably** |
| **7** **in**access**ible** |
| **8** consider**ably** |

**2** Students follow the instructions in their books.

 **Collaborative task**
**Speaking:** FCE Part 3
Page 177

Refer students to the instructions. Put them in pairs or a group of three if you have an odd number of students in your class. You could mix up pairs after they have done the task. In this way, they could compare their ideas, and see if they agreed on the same three places or events.

## Vocabulary 2: Animals           Page 178

**1** Refer students to the pictures in their books and the similes that they illustrate. Find out if these kinds of expressions exist in the students' first language and how similar or different they are from English.

Check students understand the animal vocabulary by using dictionaries, or by putting students into groups to share their knowledge and ask you for any words they do not understand. Deal with unknown vocabulary by translating where appropriate, pictures, drawings and/or descriptions.

| Answers | | |
|---|---|---|
| **1** a bat | **2** a bee | **3** a mouse |
| **4** a fox | **5** a mule | **6** an owl |
| **7** a peacock | | |

**2** Students can probably guess most of the following expressions from the context.

| Answers | | |
|---|---|---|
| **1** fly | **2** horse | **3** fish |
| **4** cat, dog | **5** bear | **6** frog |

**3** Students can use dictionaries if necessary. Encourage them to use language of speculation when they are matching the animals to the groups of nouns.

| Answers | | | |
|---|---|---|---|
| **a** bird | **b** fish | **c** cat | **d** horse |

**4** Students discuss as instructed in their books, giving reasons for their answers.

## Multiple choice

Page 179

Photocopiable vocabulary exercise on page 170.

**1** Students discuss the questions in pairs or groups before sharing ideas with the whole class. Do not give any answers at this point: the purpose of this stage is to generate interest in the theme before students listen to the recording (which contains many of the answers to the questions).

**2** Give students enough time to read through the instructions and questions before playing the recording twice, stopping before the second listening to enable students to compare their answers together.

| Answers | | | |
|---|---|---|---|
| **1** C | **2** A | **3** B | **4** B |
| **5** A | **6** C | **7** B | |

**3** Students discuss the post-listening questions in groups or as a whole class.

**Prompts to stimulate discussion**
Consider:

- Animals are sometimes illegally caught and exported for sale.
- Some animals sold as pets may be endangered species.
- Moving animals from their natural habitat can harm them.
- Children get a lot of pleasure, and can learn a lot, from having pets.
- If animals are well kept, they can live comfortably as pets and may survive much longer than they would in the wild.

---

**Listening: Listening script 2.38**

**P =** male **Presenter**
**S = Sally**, a middle-aged pet shop owner

**P:** Ants, spiders, snakes and rats may not sound like ideal house companions, but as Sally Jefferson can confirm, they have become the pets of choice for an increasing number of pet-lovers in the Radio Carston area. Sally is the owner of *Animal Crackers*, a large pet shop in the centre of Carston. Sally, why the move away from cats and dogs?

**S:** Well, primarily, I think the trend reflects changing lifestyles. Cats and dogs need a lot of looking after, whereas insects and spiders, for example, are very low-maintenance – they more or less take care of themselves. And that's perfect for busy working couples who are out of the home most of the day and can't afford to spend a great deal of time on the more traditional kinds of pets. And, er, and then of course, there's the so-called educational pet, ants in particular.

**P:** Yes, I was surprised to hear that you sell a lot of them in your shop.

**S:** That's right, leaf-cutter ants mostly. You can create your own colony in an ant farm that's a glass box like a big fish tank filled with clean sand or soil. You can watch them in their nest, digging tunnels and cutting leaves, all collaborating to achieve a common goal. It's a great lesson in the benefits of teamwork, especially for

---

children. And for that reason a lot of parents come in and buy them.

**P:** And do the kids *like* them?

**S:** Yes, most do – after all, ants are fascinating creatures to watch close up. But of course, they're not furry or cuddly, and children can't interact with them in the same way that they can with a cat or a dog. If you pick them up or try to play with them, they can give you quite a nasty bite. So inevitably some children start to grow tired of them, pay less attention to them.

**P:** Right. And how about spiders? You were telling me before the programme that you sell tarantulas - can *they* be handled?

**S:** It's not advisable, but in this case it's more because of the risk involved to the tarantula than to the owner. They do bite, of course, and as we've seen in films, sometimes with fatal results. But a bite from the species *we* sell is rather like being stung by a bee. No, the main problem is that they are fragile creatures and if they run around when they're on your hand or arm, there's a danger they'll fall off and hurt themselves very badly. So best not to get them out of their cage too often.

**P:** No, indeed. Now let's move on to another type of pet that seems to be in fashion these days – snakes. Do they need a lot of care and attention?

**S:** That really depends on the species you buy – different species have different requirements. What's common to the corn snakes and ball pythons that *we* sell is that they can sometimes go for months without eating. So if you're going on holiday you don't have to worry about finding someone to feed them while you're away. However, it's important to realize that many snakes have a lifespan of more than 20 years – so you need to be aware that you are making a long-term commitment when you buy one.

**P:** And what sort of things do they eat?

**S:** Mice, mainly, and perhaps rats or even rabbits for some of the larger species. It's better to give them pre-killed animals, which can be bought frozen at reasonably little cost from pet stores. It's more humane for the mice and rats and so on, and also safer for the snakes. A rat can seriously wound a snake when it's acting in self-defence.

**P:** Interesting that you mention rats, because of course, they too are kept as pets nowadays, aren't they?

**S:** That's right. They make very *good* pets and they don't bite quite as readily as most people think. You need to bear in mind, though, that they like being with other rats, so they really need to be kept in pairs or even groups, and in a large cage, too. Technically, of course, they're nocturnal animals but they will adapt to their owners' schedules and are happy to come out and play when people are around during the day.

**P:** You don't feed them to the snakes, do you, Sally?

**S:** No, don't worry, we never do that ...

Students discuss the post-listening questions in groups or as a whole class.

## Writing 1: FCE Part 2 — Set books  Page 180

The next section of the Coursebook is only relevant to those students who have read one of the set books. Apart from the language benefits students gain from the reading itself, doing a set text with your students can provide a welcome change of pace and focus. In the exam, it gives students an extra choice in Paper 2 Writing. If necessary reassure students that the examiner's judgement is based on the student's control of language in a specific context and is not based on literary criticism.

### Preparing students for this question

Here is a possible plan to follow, much of which students can do on their own with an occasional class discussion based on different features of the book. Ideally, students should read the book three times.

**1** Tell your students to read the book quite quickly the first time to understand the general storyline and familiarize themselves with the story and characters. They should use their dictionary very little, if at all, at this stage.

**2** The second time they should read it more carefully and take notes under headings

eg **events, setting, characters and relationships, ideas**

They should also write down short, easily remembered quotations. They should use their dictionary for the words they cannot guess from context. Students could compare and discuss these notes in class.

**3** They should read the book quickly a third time before the exam, together with the notes they have made at stage 2.

**1** Refer students to the instructions and the eight exam-style questions. Once students have ranked them, ask them to compare their list with their partner's, giving reasons for their choices.

**Optional task**

Instead of, or in addition to the task in exercise 1, you might like to ask your students to do the following.

For each question **1–8**, in exercise 1 of the Coursebook, decide which of the following, **A–F**, you are being asked to write about.

A  the book in general
B  the overall story
C  individual events in the story
D  the setting
E  a character
F  a relationship

### Answers

1  A and any one or more of B–F
2  B and C
3  C
4  E
5  B and D
6  B and C
7  B and D
8  F

**2**  The sample answer about *Animal Farm* by George Orwell answers question 7.

**3**  Students work together to answer questions.

### Answers

*Has the writer answered both parts of the question satisfactorily?*
The writer has answered both parts satisfactorily. The description of the place is brief (no more is given in the book itself) and the reader is fully informed of its importance in the story.
*What is the purpose of each of the paragraphs?*
1  A brief description of the farmhouse and the animals' initial reaction to it.
2  How the farmhouse comes to show the inequality between the pigs and the other animals.
3  How the leader in the farmhouse separates himself from his subjects.

**4**  The final scene in the farmhouse and its importance to one of the themes of the book.
*Which words are used to link ideas?*
Paragraph 1: After, at the beginning, and
Paragraph 2: However, while, As (in Jones's time), whereas
Paragraph 3: Furthermore, In this way
Paragraph 4: At the end, then, (Note also the use of 'It is … that … ' to create emphasis.)

*Has the writer quoted directly from the text?*
Yes – 'the unbelievable luxury'. The quotation is short and relevant.

**4**  The writing can be done at home or in class under exam conditions.

## Vocabulary 3: Television    Page 181

**1**  First, ask students to look at the list and mark any that they do not know. In pairs, see if they can help each other by giving examples as instructed in their books.

**2**  Students discuss the questions about favourite and least favourite programmes in groups of three.

## Reading 2: FCE Part 3    Multiple matching    Page 181

**1**  Pre-teach/check the expression 'a challenge' (invitation or obligation to take part in a contest or test of some kind).

**2**  Students discuss the challenge in pairs.

Students now read on paying special attention to the advice in the 'Don't forget!' box.

### Answers

| | |
|---|---|
| **1** D | **2/3** C, E in any order |
| **4** A | **5** B |
| **6/7** A, F in any order | |
| **8** C | **9/10** D, E in any order |
| **11** F | **12** B |
| **13/14** A, F in any order | **15** C |

## Reacting to the text

Note that these questions will be useful for the writing task later. Stress that students should not just give examples of programme titles in their own language; they should mention what type of programmes they are referring to.

Students discuss in groups or as a whole class in the style of a debate if possible.

## Vocabulary 4: Phrasal verbs    Page 183

**1** Elicit the meaning of each verb from the class.

| Answers |
|---|
| stop (the habit of watching television) accept |

**2** Students deduce the meaning from the context of the sentences. The ones in bold are phrasal verbs which appeared earlier in the book.

### Answers

| | | | |
|---|---|---|---|
| 1 d | 2 e | 3 h | 4 b, f |
| 5 i | 6 c | 7 a | 8 g |

### Writing 2: FCE Part 2    Essays    Page 183

Refer students to the question in their books and give them time to read through the 'How to go about it' box. Students can either do this as a timed essay in class (40 minutes) or for homework.

### Review 14 answers Page 184

#### Use of English: FCE Part 3    Word formation

1 peacefully
2 remarkable
3 originally
4 including
5 responsibility
6 retirement
7 appearance
8 proof
9 seasonal
10 unreliable

## Vocabulary

**A The Arts**
1 portrait
2 sculptures
3 novel
4 open-air
5 priceless
6 playwright
7 composer
8 exhibition

**B Animals**
1 a lion

**C Phrasal verbs**
1 clear up/throw away
2 take over
3 eats up
4 get on with
5 got through

### Use of English: FCE Part 4    Transformations: Hypothetical situations

1 wish I lived
2 wish I hadn't told
3 rather you didn't wear
4 time we went
5 wish I could go
6 only you had brought
7 wish you wouldn't speak
8 wish I knew/could know

### Workbook answers

#### Reading: Gapped text    Page 106

**1** 1 C   2 G   3 E   4 A   5 F   6 H   7 D   B not used

**2**
1 set up
2 take over
3 cut off
4 get over
5 look after
6 come up with

**3**

| Adjective | Noun | Verb | Noun |
|---|---|---|---|
| cruel | cruelty | treat | treatment |
| pregnant | pregnancy | adopt | adoption |
| intelligent | intelligence | survive | survival |
| healthy | health | inspire | inspiration |

## Vocabulary    Page 108

### A Crossword: The Arts

| Across | | Down | |
| --- | --- | --- | --- |
| 1 | sculptor | 1 | stage |
| 4 | play | 2 | priceless |
| 6 | scene | 3 | orchestra |
| 7 | house | 4 | portrait |
| 8 | landscape | 5 | composer |
| 10 | exhibition | 7 | hall |
| | | 9 | cast |

### B Phrasal verbs: Revision

1  a  take up     b  put off      c  do up
   d  make out    e  get on with  f  make up
   g  put up

2  1  do up       2  get on with  3  taking up
   4  made out    5  put off      6  make up
   7  putting up  8  fall for

## Language focus    Page 109

1  1  had              2  wouldn't make
   3  had brought      4  knew
   5  would stop       6  didn't tell
   7  go               8  bought

2  Suggested answers
   1  *started revising for my exams*.
   2  bought a watch.
   3  came round after the film has finished.
   4  would stop interrupting me.
   5  the FCE exam were on a different day.
   6  I'd insured the video camera.
   7  the bus would hurry up and come/I'd caught the train.
   8  I'd got someone to water the plants.

## Use of English    Page 110

### Word formation

1  sculptures        2  best
3  considerable      4  decision
5  possibly          6  daily
7  residents         8  sight
9  irresponsible     10 beneficial

### Open cloze

1  some      2  their    3  many
4  it        5  for      6  be
7  as        8  which    9  No
10 Although  11 there    12 in

### Transformations

1  generosity impressed us very
2  a full recovery
3  had no choice (about) where
4  despite the late arrival/the lateness of
5  he had/has no intention of
6  of/about the exact depth

## Writing    Page 111

### Language preparation

a  1  aim of this report
   2  looking forward to
   3  have no experience of
   4  that struck me
   5  pleased to hear
   6  sum up
   7  I like most about her
   8  express an interest
   9  obvious choice
   10 main difference

b  1  3      2  1      3  2      4  4      5  1
   6  3      7  4      8  2      9  5b     10 5a

# 15 Mind your language

## Content Overview

### Themes

'Mind your language' is a play on words. This expression can be used as a warning to someone who is swearing (using bad language) and is also an appropriate title for the unit, which is based around the theme of language (learning languages, multilingualism, North American English).

### Exam-related activities

| Paper 1 | Reading |
|---------|---------|
| Part 1 | Multiple choice |
| Part 2 | Gapped text |

| Paper 2 | Writing |
|---------|---------|
| Part 2 | Articles |

| Paper 3 | Use of English |
|---------|---------|
| Part 1 | Multiple-choice cloze (Review) |
| Part 4 | Transformations (Review) |

| Paper 4 | Listening |
|---------|---------|
| Part 3 | Multiple matching |

### Other

| Language focus: | Expressing purpose |
|-----------------|--------------------|
| Vocabulary: | Phrasal verbs with *turn* |
| | Compound adjectives |
| | Abbreviations |
| | American English |
| | Education |

## Listening:
### FCE Part 3

## Multiple matching
Page 186

**1** Refer students to the phrases on either side of the photo in the Coursebook. Tell students that the phrases all say the same thing, but in different languages. Can they work out what the phrase would be in English?

answer – *excuse me*

Students can then discuss the questions in the Coursebook in pairs or threes.

## Answers

afedersiniz – Turkish
disculpe – Spanish/Castilian
entschuldigen Sie – German
mi scusi – Italian
permisi – Indonesian
ursäkta mig – Swedish
elnézést – Hungarian
excusez-moi – French

**2** Refer students to the instructions for listening and the task and give them about 30 seconds to read through before they listen for the first time. Let students know that Speaker 4 is from Wales and has a Welsh accent. Allow students to compare their answers before they hear the recording a second time.

## Answers

| 1 C | 2 E | 3 F | 4 B |
|-----|-----|-----|-----|
| 5 A | D not used | | |

### Listening: Listening script 2.39–2.43

**Speaker 1**
I never had time to go to the German classes my company arranged for us at work, so I used to put tapes on in the car on the way in every morning and just let the language wash over me. I was completely immersed in it for the whole journey. Then I'd listen to the same section on the way home and that was enough to ensure I learnt what I'd heard in the morning. When I go to Germany on sales trips now I have very few problems understanding people. Business seems to be improving, too.

**Speaker 2**
I went to Spain twice when I was studying languages at university; once on holiday and the next year to work in a bar. The holiday was a disaster in terms of language learning. I spent most of the time with my English friends and hardly learnt a thing. When I went back there to work, though, I spoke Spanish all day and my speaking and understanding really improved. That experience working abroad helped me pass my final exams just as much as studying, I'm convinced. Oh, and I'm getting married this year to my Spanish girlfriend.

**Speaker 3**
I spent three years teaching English in Poland with my boyfriend back in the early 90s. It took us both quite a long time to learn any Polish in the beginning, partly because of laziness, but mostly because we were working long hours teaching and speaking English all day. Things got better, though, once we eventually got to know a few Polish people and we had more chance

to speak the language. We both became much more integrated after that. We even saw a few films in Polish at the cinema.

**Speaker 4**

Here in Wales everyone can speak English, but more and more young people are learning Welsh, the real native language. My mum and dad both came to Wales from England, so I only ever spoke in English till I came to this school. But all lessons are in Welsh, see? Right from day one everything has been in Welsh and I've learnt really quickly. So now I've got the two languages. I speak in Welsh with my friends and I speak it at home, too, with my brother. It's great, 'cause we can talk about things in front of my mum and dad and they've got no idea what either of us is saying – really useful sometimes!

**Speaker 5**

When I left university I desperately wanted to work abroad, but all three French-owned companies that I applied to turned me down at the interview stage. I'd only ever learnt grammar when I was at school so when I had to speak French in the interview I couldn't understand the questions and I'm sure the interviewers couldn't understand a word of what I was saying. So I signed up for a two-month course in Paris and when I came back I got the first job I applied for.

## Vocabulary 1 | Page 186

**A Phrasal verbs with** *turn*

**1** Discuss the question with the whole class. *To turn someone down* is to refuse their application, offer, proposal, etc.

**2–3** In this exercise, students have to match sentence beginnings with appropriate endings. To do this they have to look carefully at the context and grammar of each one. Do one or two examples with the students if necessary then let them continue individually. Check their answers before moving on to exercise 3. In later lessons students could cover up the sentence endings in the right-hand column and see how many of the sentence beginnings they can complete.

### Answers

| 2 | 1 g | 2 c | 3 e | 4 a |
|---|-----|-----|-----|-----|
|   | 5 f | 6 b | 7 d |     |

3　a　turn into something
　　b　turn something up
　　c　turn out that
　　d　turn up
　　e　turn off something
　　f　turn back
　　g　turn something off

**B Compound adjectives**

**1–3** Follow the order of stages set out in the Coursebook. Refer students to the explanations and examples given before 1.

**Common mistakes**

*1,000-words report, an eleven-years-old girl*, etc. Draw students' attention to the following in their books '… and that a noun used with a number to form an adjective is singular.' (This is because the noun is acting as an adjective and adjectives can not be made plural in English.)

Students now complete the sentences.

### Answers

| 1 | 1 | English-speaking | 5 | American-educated |
|---|---|------------------|---|-------------------|
|   | 2 | five-minute | 6 | one-hour |
|   | 3 | Italian-born | 7 | Irish-made |
|   | 4 | 1,000-word | 8 | 11-year-old |

2　1　a five-pound (bank) note
　　2　a twelve-hour shift
　　3　a ten-man team
　　4　a three-course meal
　　5　a two-week holiday

3　Possible answers
We have six 50-minute lessons a day.
It was a 10-day holiday in Majorca. We had a two-hour flight from London.
It's a twenty-minute car journey/a five-kilometre bus ride/a 15-minute walk
a fifteen-unit/a 217-page book

 **Reading 1:**
**FCE Part 2**

## Multiple choice
Page 188

Photocopiable vocabulary exercise on page 170.

**1** Refer students to the questions in their books. This can be conducted as a whole group or students could discuss their answers in pairs and then report back to you.

**2** Refer students to the advice in the 'Don't forget!' box. If necessary, give students a time limit of about four minutes to read through and check their ideas from exercise 1. Students then look at the questions and read the text again thoroughly to answer them.

## Answers

1 C   2 D   3 A   4 C   5 D
6 B   7 B   8 A

### Reacting to the text

Mandarin Chinese and Spanish are often considered the likeliest languages to replace English as the dominant language of business, because of the large numbers of people who speak these languages and the potential for dramatic growth in China and Latin America.

## Vocabulary 2: Abbreviations    Page 189

**Note**: students are required to know the basic abbreviations for the First Certificate exam. These may appear in the input material for the Part 1 Writing question.

**1–3** Students follow the instructions in their books for this section, working individually or in pairs.

## Answers

1 Professor
  United Kingdom

2 The original Latin terms are in brackets.
  1 eg        for example (exempli gratia)
    etc       and so on (et cetera)
  2 ie        that is (id est)
  3 NB        please note (nota bene)
    www       World Wide Web
  4 PS        postscript
    ASAP      as soon as possible
  5 PTO       please turn over
3 British Broadcasting Corporation
  United Nations
  compact disc
  Member of Parliament
  Federal Bureau of Investigation
  European Union

## Language focus: Expressing purpose
Page 190

**A  *In order to, so as to* and *so that***
**1–2**  In this section, students work with four different ways of expressing purpose.

Students study the sentences and the explanations.

Students then check their answers in the Grammar reference and read more about expressing purpose.

## Answers

*so that* + present simple/*can*/*will* = future
*so that* + *could*/*would* = past

### Practice

**1**  Encourage students to use all the forms to complete the sentences, both in the positive and in the negative.

## Answers

**Possible answers**
1  she can call us if she needs help.
2  to get a good seat near the front/not to miss it/to see the team arrive.
3  as to increase my chances of getting a job/ that I can concentrate on my other studies/ I can prove my level of English/my parents will be happy.
4  as not to have to do sport/I wouldn't have to take the exam/I could stay at home and watch television.
5  to find information about cheap flights.
6  to avoid waking anyone up.
7  I can go out afterwards/I don't forget what we studied in class/I can enjoy the rest of the evening.

**2**  Students work in pairs or groups and think of three reasons for each of the situations given.

**B  *In case***
Comparing *in case* with *if*
Write the following sentences on the board:

1  I'll take my umbrella *if* it rains.
2  I'll take my umbrella *in case* it rains.

Then refer students to the explanations in their books and elicit from them or point out the difference in meaning:

1  *I'll take my umbrella only if it is raining when I leave the house.*
2  *I'll take my umbrella as a precaution, even if it is not raining when I leave the house.*

Note: *if*, *in case*, and *when* are all followed by the present simple or continuous when referring to the future.

**Practice**

| Answers |
|---|
| **Possible answers** |
| 1  the other one runs out of ink/you need to use a different colour. |
| 2  it broke down again/there was heavy traffic on the roads. |
| 3  you are burgled/there's a fire/you break something valuable. |
| 4  I have to do overtime. |
| 5  I saw something good for my dad's birthday present. |
| 6  we lock ourselves out/they need to borrow anything/there's a fire. |

**Roleplay: Expressing purpose**

**1** Put students into pairs and ask each pair to decide who is going to be Student A and who will be Student B. Each student then follows the relevant instructions in the Coursebook. With a weaker class, group A students in small groups and B sudents in small groups to brainstorm ideas for a few minutes. They will then be better prepared to work in A–B pairs for the roleplay itself.

**2** You could round off the roleplay by asking for feedback from the whole class.

 **Articles**  Page 191

You could ask students to speak together and compile a list of pieces of advice on preparation for the exam *throughout* the course.

Then ask them to compare with the ideas in the 'How to go about it' box in their books.
- Find out how many were the same and different.
- Remind them that they will have to select which ideas to mention.

Students then write the article in class or for homework.

 **Gapped text**  Page 191

Photocopiable vocabulary exercise on page 171.

**Information regarding the American High School system**

| Age | Year | Title |
|---|---|---|
| 13/14 | 9th grade | freshmen |
| 15/16 | 10th grade | sophomore |
| 16/17 | 11th grade | junior |
| 17/18 | 12th grade | senior |

Exploit the photo in the students' books and Question 1. Pre-teach/check vocabulary, eg *lockers*, *extra-curricular activities*, *peer*, *to hang out* (also in Unit 10), *frisk someone for something*.

Alternatively, because students are near the end of their course, do not pre-teach any vocabulary and see how students manage for themselves.

**1** The questions should generate a lot of discussion. Some of your students may have personal experience of a US high school if they have been on exchange programmes. If so, ask them to tell the rest a little about their time there.

**2** Refer students to the instructions and if necessary set a time limit of about 15 minutes for the task.

| Answers | | | |
|---|---|---|---|
| 1 H | 2 A | 3 G | 4 D |
| 5 F | 6 B | 7 E | C not used |

**Reacting to the text**

Students discuss in pairs, groups or you could lead the discussion in a whole class format.

Note: the phrasal verbs *come up* and *put something on* first appeared in Units 7 and 9 respectively.

## Vocabulary 3  Page 193

**A American English**

**1** This section takes typically American expressions seen in the reading text and extends to other American expressions and their British equivalents.

**Note:** US English, both vocabulary and spelling, has a great influence on British English, and more and more Americanisms are being borrowed and used.

**2–4** Refer students to the instructions in their books.

## Answers

**2**  **1** *b*    **2** a    **3** g    **4** d
   **5** f    **6** e    **7** c

**3**  **1** underground (or tube)
   **2** petrol station (or filling station)
   **3** motorway
   **4** holiday
   **5** railway
   **6** car park
   **7** return ticket

**4**
**1** She took the *rubbish* out to the *dustbin* in the *garden* (*Yard* might be possible in British English, depending on what is referred to).
**2** The *lorry* driver slowed down and pulled into the *petrol* station on the *motorway*.
**3** 'I can't find my *trousers* anywhere, *Mum*!' 'Try looking in the *wardrobe*, *darling*.'
**4** No *biscuits* or *sweets* for me thanks. I'm on a *diet*.
**5** It was early *autumn*. The *pavements* in the *neighbourhood* were covered with leaves of different shapes and *colours* and the summer *holiday* was just a distant memory.

## B Education

**1** Exercise 1 deals with vocabulary which is easily confused by many learners of English and which they may need to use in Part 1 of the Speaking exam.

Give students time to think of the differences for themselves before conducting feedback.

## Answers

**1** **nursery school** – for young children aged between 2 and 5
**primary school** – for children aged between 5 and 11

**2** **a state school** – one which is controlled and funded by the government or a local authority
**a public school** – a private school; pupils' parents pay fees for their child to attend

**3** **a grammar school** – a secondary school for children (aged 11–18) with a high academic ability

**a comprehensive school** – a secondary school for children of all abilities; the majority of secondary schools in Britain are comprehensive schools

**4** **a degree** – a course of study at a college or university; the qualification you are given when you pass the course, eg
   *I'm doing a degree in chemistry.*
   *I got a degree in French.*
**a career** – an occupation or profession

**5** **a teacher** – in a school, for example
**a professor** – the most senior teacher in a university department

**6** **a qualification** – an exam you have passed, eg First Certificate in English; the degree, or certificate which you are awarded for this, eg *What qualifications do you need for the job?*
**a title** – the name of a book, film, etc; *Mr, Mrs, Ms, Lady, Lord* are all titles.

**2** Students follow the instructions in their books.

## Review 15 answers Page 194

### Use of English: FCE Part 1 — Multiple-choice cloze

**1** C   **2** B   **3** A   **4** D   **5** D   **6** A
**7** C   **8** C   **9** B   **10** D   **11** B   **12** A

### Vocabulary

**A Abbreviations**
**1** eg   **2** etc   **3** ie   **4** NB
**5** www   **6** PS   **7** ASAP   **8** PTO

**B Compound adjectives**
**1** clock   **5** composition
**2** shift   **6** lesson
**3** baby girl   **7** holiday
**4** meal   **8** note

**C American English**
**1** pants   **5** freeway
**2** trashcan/garbage can   **6** truck
**3** closet   **7** parking lot
**4** yard   **8** sidewalk

## Use of English: Transformations
**FCE Part 4**

1 in order not to get
2 so as not to miss
3 in case it doesn't/does not
4 so that she would not
5 turned down an/the offer
6 did Mike (eventually) turn up

## Workbook answers

### Reading: Multiple choice    Page 114

1  1 C    2 A    3 D    4 D
   5 C    6 C    7 B    8 A

2  1 communication    2 anxiety
   3 anger            4 irritation
   5 ability          6 alertness
   7 self-awareness   8 confidence
   9 weight          10 subtlety/subtleties

3  1 weakness         2 variety
   3 credibility      4 certainty/certainties
   5 persistence      6 complication
   7 complaint        8 hunger

### Vocabulary    Page 116

**A Word grid: Education**
1 primary        2 resit
3 open           4 fail
5 education      6 subjects
7 state          8 Oxford
9 revise        10 professor

**B Phrasal verbs with *turn***
1 down      2 up       3 into
4 on        5 out      6 off

**C Expressions with *turn***
1 c    2 e    3 a    4 b
5 h    6 g    7 d    8 f

**D Compound adjectives**
1 *a British-trained doctor*
2 a Spanish-made car
3 a Russian-speaking guide
4 a London-based company
5 a French-owned supermarket chain
6 a ten-day cruise
7 a 29-year-old woman

8 a 650-page book
9 a four-hour film
10 a three-day conference

### Language focus    Page 117

**Expressing purpose**
1  1 c    2 e    3 a    4 f    5 h
   6 i    7 b    8 g    9 d

2
2 so that she wouldn't/so as not to/in order not to
  speak any Spanish.
3 in case it was cold there.
4 in case she didn't understand any English.
5 in order to see/so as to see/so that she could see
  the rest of the country.
6 so that she could read/in order to/so as to (be
  able to) read about the different places before
  visiting them.
7 so that her parents wouldn't worry about her.
  (in case her parents were worried about her.)
8 so that she doesn't/won't forget/in order not to
  forget/so as not to forget everything she learnt.
9 in case she decides to go back to Ireland next
  year.

### Use of English    Page 118

**Transformations: Grammar revision**
**A Units 1–5**
1 get used to living
2 feel like going
3 time the film starts
4 sing as well as he
5 such good English (that)
6 'd/had better not tell
7 don't/do not let us wear

**B Units 6–9**
1 not old enough to
2 had the house painted
3 it was raining heavily
4 to watch rather than play
5 first time I've/I have seen
6 aren't/are not likely to get
7 might have seen

**C Units 10–15**
1 he was being followed by
2 is said to be
3 had not broken down
4 if/whether he had been behaving

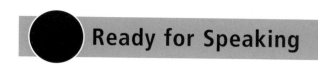

5  offered to carry his mother's
6  didn't/did not succeed in completing
7  I had not spent
8  so as not to/so that he wouldn't/would not

**Open cloze**

| | | | | | |
|---|---|---|---|---|---|
| 1 | is | 2 | Each/Every | 3 | their |
| 4 | where | 5 | order | 6 | have |
| 7 | so | 8 | would | 9 | a/one |
| 10 | If | 11 | this | 12 | to |

**Word formation**

| | | | | | |
|---|---|---|---|---|---|
| 1 | inaccessible | 2 | written | 3 | suspicious |
| 4 | researchers | 5 | imprisoned | 6 | political |
| 7 | disappearance | 8 | fewer | 9 | unlikely |
| 10 | knowledge | | | | |

## First Certificate Paper 5

### Speaking

**Part 1**  Interview
**Part 2**  Talking about photographs
**Part 3**  Collaborative task
**Part 4**  Further discussion

In this unit students go through the various stages of the oral exam, finding out exactly what happens in each stage, how long each stage lasts and looking at useful strategies and language they can employ. The classroom management should correspond with the instructions given in the Coursebook in order to make the practice activities as authentic as possible for the students. If you have only one student then you, the teacher, should take on the roles of examiner and candidate where possible!

A note about correction of students' oral work. The aim of this unit is to inform students and give them help and practice. Depending on how near to the exam date you are, you may decide not to focus too much on correction in order to boost students' morale.

However, it is a good idea to make students aware of any basic mistakes they make in response to Part 1 questions, as these are not intended to be difficult and students at this level should be able to answer with reasonable accuracy.

It is probably better to deal with corrections at the end of a practice stage rather than interrupt students while they are speaking. In the exam they will have to rely on themselves.

Photocopiable vocabulary exercise on page 171.

### Introduction                                     Page 196

**1**  Either follow the instructions in the Coursebook or tell the students to close their books and lift the information off the page by giving the students an illustrated mini-lecture using the board or OHP. This provides the students with useful listening practice and the chance to ask questions for clarification when their doubts are still fresh.

| Answers | |
|---|---|
| **Part 1** b | **Part 2** d |
| **Part 3** a | **Part 4** c |

**2** Refer students to the instructions.

## Answers

### Part 1

**a** No. Certainly, students should avoid trying to give over-complicated answers which cause them to become confused and so make unnecessary mistakes. However, very short one-word answers are usually inadequate and do not give the examiners a sufficient sample of language to assess. Students should therefore answer questions with appropriate detail.

**b** No. Long, pre-prepared answers are usually obvious to the interlocutor and will be interrupted. As well as sounding unnatural they are often inappropriate to the question asked and do not therefore form part of effective interactive communication, one of the criteria for assessment in the speaking exam. Students may practise for this part of the test, but they should not try to prepare and learn long answers.

**c** Yes. Students will be nervous at the beginning but this part of the test is designed to relax them by asking questions on areas which are familiar to them.

### Part 2

**a** No. Students are not required to describe the photographs in detail. They should therefore listen carefully to and follow the instructions given to them by the interlocutor.

**b** Yes, as long as the student has tried to address both parts of the question. It is better to fill the minute and be interrupted than to run out of things to say before the allotted time finishes.

**c** Clearly the student should focus on the instructions that the interlocutor gives, though exam nerves often cause students to miss part of the instructions and it is perfectly acceptable for students to ask for them to be repeated. However, this should not be necessary as the second part of the interlocutor's instructions is printed in the form of a question alongside the photographs.

### Part 3

**a** Good that the student had a lot to say. However, it seems that he/she may not have been respecting the rules of turn-taking, an aspect of interactive communication, mentioned above. If students are paired with quiet, more reticent candidates, they should invite them to take part in the discussion by asking questions such as 'What do you think?' or 'What would you do?' Attempts to dominate the conversation will be penalized.

**b** No. As with Part 2, students should aim to fill the time allotted and not reach their decision too soon. Students are penalized if they run out of things to say. The aim is not to find a solution in the shortest time possible: rather, students should be aiming to provide enough relevant and appropriate contributions for the examiners to assess their English accurately.

**c** Yes. This student and his/her partner has clearly made full use of the time available. Students do not necessarily have to complete the task, as long as it is clear that they are at least trying to reach a decision. See Unit 5 for Useful language, which will be useful later in this unit when students practise Part 3.

### Part 4

**a** Yes. Candidates should certainly be speaking more than the examiner! The implication here also seems to be that the candidates have been responding to each others' comments, something which is actively encouraged by examiners in Part 4 and which is part of interactive communication.

**b** No. It is not only what you say but how you say it which is important throughout the exam. 'Nonsense, you must be mad' sounds rude and is not the best way to disagree with someone in a discussion such as this. Alternative expressions of agreeing and disagreeing are given on page 123 in Unit 10.

**c** No. Students should respond to questions appropriately and not try to divert the discussion to their favourite topic of conversation.

## Part 1: Interview                    Page 197

**1** Students follow the instructions in their books. Try to move around the room to check they have formed the questions correctly. If you have a very large class this may not be possible. In this case you could check the questions of a few of the students. Try to vary whose work you check each time you do this.

**2** Once students are in pairs, set a time limit of three minutes so that students become aware of how long or short three minutes can be. Before they start draw their attention to the advice contained in the 'Don't forget!' box.

**3** Refer students to the questions in the Coursebook. Note that Christina and Paolo are fairly strong candidates. The questions in the Coursebook address the issue of exam technique.

For further work on the recorded Part 1 example, see the photocopiable exercise on page 171 of this book.

### Answers

**2** Christina has obviously come with a prepared speech. The interlocutor asks her about her home town, and having answered the question, she begins to talk about her family. The interlocutor will interrupt if a student does this in the exam.

**3** He should develop his answers more, particularly in relation to his home town and his interest in football.

---

**Part 1:  Listening script 2.44**

**I:** Good morning. My name is Allan Reeves and this is my colleague Teresa Riley. And your names are?
**C:** Christina.
**P:** My name is Paolo.
**I:** Can I have your marksheets, please? Thank you. First of all we'd like to know something about you. Where are you from, Paolo?
**P:** From a small town near Ravenna.  In Italy.
**I:** And you Christina?
**C:** I'm from Corinth, in Greece. I have lived there all my life. I live there with my three sisters and my parents. I am in my last year at school. My mother works in a shop and my …

**I:** Thank you, Christina. What do you like about living in Corinth?
**C:** Ah well, yes. Erm, it is by the sea, so we can go swimming. Also there are parks, er, and lots of bars and things to do in the evening, so, er, it is very lively, especially in summer. In winter it is more quieter. But it is very interesting to live there. It is very ancient.
**I:** And what about you Paolo?
**P:** My town?
**I:** Yes.
**P:** It is a little boring. I mean, I don't really like living there. There's more to do in Ravenna.
**I:** OK, Christina, what subjects do you enjoy most at school?
**C:** Well, I like languages very much, but my favourite subject is mathematics. I always like it, since I was very young. It is something I can do, working with numbers and usually I get very good marks. I wish my English would be as good!
**I:** Paolo, do you work or are you a student?
**P:** I work in my uncle's computer business.
**I:** And how important is English for your work?
**P:** Well, yes, it's very important. I have to read a lot of things about computers in English, and sometimes I must talk to foreign customers.
**I:** Now, let's move on to what you do in your spare time. Paolo, what kind of sports are you interested in?
**P:** Er, I play football, tennis, and, er, I go swimming.
**I:** And how often do you play football?
**P:** Once a week. Yes, every Saturday. I play in a team. It's good fun.
**I:** And Christina, do you have any hobbies?
**C:** Well, not really hobbies, but in my free time I like to go to the cinema, going out with my friends and things like that.
**I:** Which sort of films do you like to watch?
**C:** Oh, I like action films. I like films where many things happen. I don't like romantic films or historical films. I think they are a little bored.
**I:** Now, thinking about the future, Christina. What do you hope to do in the next few years?
**C:** Well, I want to go to the university and study business studies first. Then after that, if it is possible I'll work in a big company, as an accountant or something like that. Maybe, in the future I can use my English and find a job in another country. That would be very exciting.
**I:** And what kind of job do you hope to be doing in ten years' time, Paolo.
**P:** Well, ten years is a long time, so I'm not sure what will happen. First, I want to help my uncle expanding his business and then maybe in the future, I could set up my own business.

## Part 2: Talking about photographs

Page 198

Refer students to the useful language box in the Coursebook. If your students are shortly going to sit the oral exam, these fillers can be extremely useful. One worry that students often have is that they will go blank in the exam and be unable to think of anything to say. These fillers give them a chance to gather their thoughts and can help students to feel more confident.

Draw students' attention to the 'Don't forget!' box. It is extremely important that students listen to the interlocutor carefully and address both parts of the instructions. The instructions always take the format *Compare these photographs and say … .*

Once your students have completed the speaking task in pairs, refer them to the question concerning Christina and Paolo and the recorded Part 2 task.

For further work on the recorded Part 2 example, see the photocopiable exercise on page 171 of this book.

### Answers

Christina compares the photographs very well, using language such as *both pictures* and *whereas*. Paolo does not compare them.

### Part 2: Listening script 2.45–2.46

**I:** In this part of the test, I'm going to give each of you two photographs. I'd like you to talk about your photographs on your own for about a minute, and also to answer a short question about your partner's photographs. Christina, it's your turn first. Here are your photographs. They show grandfathers with their grandchildren. I'd like you to compare the photographs, and say how important grandparents can be in situations like these. All right?

**C:** Yes, er, in the first picture the girl is playing the piano with her grandfather whereas in the other one the man is teaching his granddaughter to ride a bicycle. In both pictures everybody is smiling and seems to be enjoying themselves. Er, what else? Yes, in the first picture they are indoors whereas in this one they are outside and the girl is wearing a special hat for protect her head if she falls over. I can't make out how old is the man in this picture, but I think he is

younger that the other grandfather. Er, let me see, well, I think grandparents can help a lot, especially nowadays, because parents are very busy and often they don't have the time to be with their children. Grandparents can look after the grandchildren, during the school holidays, er, cook for them and make sure they are not in danger. They can even play with them, like in these pictures. Children can learn many things from their grandparents, maybe not things like use the computer, but more traditional activities, such as riding a bike or making things, er ..

**I:** Thank you, Paolo, has an older relative taught you to do something?

**P:** Yes, my uncle taught me to play golf.

**I:** Thank you.

**I:** Now, Paolo, here are your photographs. They show people in an emergency situation. I'd like you to compare the photographs, and say how serious you think each of the situations looks. All right?

**P:** OK. In this picture I can see a television journalist interviewing a policeman. They must be in America because the policeman's uniform is the typical one you see in films and on TV. Also the writing is in English. It's not obvious what has happened but maybe there's been an accident or there might have been a crime, even. Perhaps a murder or something, I don't know. Er, in this picture it looks as if they are in an ambulance, because the woman's wearing a thing on her face for air, for oxygen, and the man's writing down the details about the woman. Er, it's difficult to say which is more serious, we don't really know what's happened. In the first picture the television camera is there, and nobody is allowed to cross the, the, line, so it must be quite important. It's not just an ordinary crime or accident. In the second one, the woman looks quite relaxed, well, not relaxed, maybe, but she isn't panicking, so I think this situation isn't very serious.

**I:** Thank you. Christina, do you think you could be a policewoman?

**C:** Oh, no. I think it is a very difficult job. It's maybe good to meet lots of people and work outside, but it's too dangerous – I wouldn't like to do it, no.

**I:** Thank you.

## Part 3: Collaborative task

Page 199

Give students time to read through the instructions and the information in the 'How to go about it' box. Either give a minute or two to think of some ideas before they begin or treat the practice as if it were the exam and tell them to start immediately.

**How to go about it**
Words with a similar meaning:

## Answers

interesting eg fascinating, enjoyable, good fun, appealing

boring eg dull, uninteresting, monotonous, tedious

good eg ideal, excellent, marvellous, wonderful, suitable

Once your students have completed the speaking task in pairs, refer them to the questions concerning Christina and Paolo and the recorded Part 3 task.

For further work on the recorded Part 3 example, see the photocopiable exercise on page 171 of this book.

## Answers

1 They both agree on the medieval fair. Christina's second choice is cave-painting whereas Paolo's is the Megascreen.

2 Christina summarizes their decision at the end, but they more or less decided on the medieval fair in the first half of the conversation as they discussed it.

3 Christina asks Paolo questions to encourage him to speak.

*Which one shall we start with?*

*It could be fun, don't you think?*

*Now, what do you think about the concerts?*

*And children love doing that, don't you agree?*

*How about the cave painting?*

*What do you think, Paolo?*

*What do you think of the fashion shows?*

Note that Paolo uses tag questions to invite Christina's opinion: *don't they? would it? Can't you?*

### Part 3: Listening script 2.47

**I:** Now I'd like you to talk about something together for about three minutes. I'd like you to imagine that the History Museum in your town would like to attract more visitors. Here are some ideas for improving the museum. First, talk to each other about the proposals saying how they might appeal to different people. Then decide which two would be the most successful in attracting new visitors. All right?

**C:** Which one shall we start with?

**P:** Er, let's talk about the interactive computer programme first. In my opinion it will appeal to a lot of people, because computers are so important in our lives today. Most people know how to use a computer now, don't they?

**C:** Well, no everyone, no, I don't agree. And anyway, I don't think the people go to the museums to use a computer. They can do that at home or at work. A medieval fair would be something very different, though. That would be interesting for people of all ages. It could be good fun, don't you think?

**P:** Yes, that's true. The visitors could take part in different activities and eat medieval food. And if the organizers dressed up in costumes, that would make history very colourful and realistic. It sounds like a great idea.

**C:** So that could be one of the two things we choose. Now, what do you think about the concerts? Visitors to the museum would like to listen music. People who work could come in their lunch break and have a relaxing moment.

**P:** Yes, but I really don't think it would attract many people who work, particularly if the museum is in a city – everyone is busy all day. Retired people would probably appreciate it and have more time to enjoy it, but that wouldn't increase the number of visitors very much, would it?

**C:** No, I suppose you're right.

**P:** Personally, I think we need to have activities which appeal to children, because if children want to come, their parents will have to come too.

**C:** Yes, I agree. So, let's have a look for something. Well, children could enjoy coin-making, but it wouldn't make parents say, "we really must take our children to the museum"!

**P:** You're right. It's a bit dull.

**C:** But how about the cave painting? That sounds really enjoyable for children. If they have to paint like prehistoric man, then I imagine they will have to use their hands, and make a mess. And children love doing that. Don't you agree?

**P:** Yes, I do. They would enjoy themselves very much. But let's look at the others before we decide. Er, the exhibition of kitchens is nothing special. I mean, you can see things like that in lots of places, can't you?

**C:** Yes, it isn't the most fascinating idea. I don't know who would want to see that. Maybe some adults, but not many. And the Megascreen, well, that's like the computers. Nobody will go to a museum to see a film. What do you think, Paolo?

**P:** I completely disagree. To my mind that's the kind of thing that will make it different to other museums and would appeal to all types of different people. And the screen would be very big, so it's not the same that watching it on television or at the cinema.

**C:** Well, I'm really keen on films, but I rather go to a real cinema. I prefer the atmosphere there. And historical films are old and a bit boring, especially for children, so not many people would go.

**P:** Well, I think that should be one of the two things we choose, personally. I think it would bring people who don't normally go to museums or even who have never been.

**C:** OK, well we agree on the medieval fair, but not on the Megascreen. I think the cave painting is a better idea. What do you think of the fashion shows?

**P:** Oh no. I don't know anyone who is interested in fashion shows.

**C:** Really?

**I:** Thank you

## Part 4: Further discussion
Page 199

In order to remove the predictability of both students being able to see all the questions, you could make copies of the questions and cut them into strips, giving each student in a pair three of the six questions. Tell them not to show their partner their questions but to ask as though they were the examiner. They should of course also participate by responding naturally to what their partner says. Alternatively, and if appropriate to your classroom size and design, you could copy half of the questions onto two different sheets of paper large enough for the students to see. Seat them in a line down the middle of the room facing each other and pin each sheet on opposite walls in order that each member of each pair can see one of the sheets of paper with the three questions. Students ask and answer, developing the answers where possible. Before they start, remind them about the advice in the 'Don't forget!' box.

Once the students have finished the discussion, refer them to the questions regarding the recorded example Part 4 speaking task.

### Answers

1 When answering the first two questions they do not interact at all, failing to respond to what each other says. Rather than a discussion, there is a series of short monologues. Students should be referred to the interaction patterns at the beginning of this unit. They interact much better in the second half of Part 4.

2 In the second half Christina helps the interaction by asking questions to involve Paolo: *What do you think Paolo? Don't you agree?* and *Do you really think we will have robots?* and Paolo responds accordingly.

For further work on the recorded Part 4 example, see the photocopiable exercise on page 172 of this book.

### Part 4: Listening script 2.48

**I:** Christina, what do you think makes a good museum?

**C:** I don't know really. I suppose that, I think that, in general the museums are a little bored. You only look at objects which are in, in, erm, how do you say? Erm, well, like boxes, in glass boxes or cupboards, so there is nothing to do. I think if you could touch the things in an exhibition, that would make it more interesting, a more enjoyable experience.

**I:** Uh huh. Paolo?

**P:** I think ideas like the medieval fair are good because they help you to have a better idea of life in the past. The last year I went to a museum where people in costumes explained how different things were used. Even they cooked with some old saucepans and things. Perhaps they weren't real, but it doesn't matter. The important is that you can imagine how people lived before.

**I:** How could the teaching of history in schools be improved?

**C:** I'm not quite sure, but, well, er, at school we just sit and listen the teachers, listen to the teachers, and write what they say. In Greece there are so many ancient monuments so perhaps we could visit more and not just read and write about them all the time.

**I:** What do you think, Paolo?

**P:** Er, when I was at school we just listened to the teachers. I think history was the worst subject for many people. I think we need better teachers who are good at making a subject more interesting for pupils. I don't know, but I think it depends on the teacher.

**I:** What was the most important moment in the history of the twentieth century?

**C:** Er, I haven't thought about it before, really, but, er, perhaps it was, yes, I think it was when the first man landed on the Moon. I have seen pictures of this, and I think it should, it must have been something quite incredible at the time. Now, going into space is quite normal, but that moment was very different. What do you think, Paolo?

**P:** Well, I think the landing on the Moon was important, but travel in space would not be possible if we did not have computers. The invention of the computer, for me, was the most important moment. It changed the way we live ...

**C:** You only say that because you like computers!

**P:** No, but almost everything we do needs computers nowadays. Aeroplanes, industries, banks, companies – they all need to have computers. And if the computers break down, there are always many problems for these things. We cannot survive without computers.

**C:** Maybe, but I think there are more important things that happened in the last century. Things with people and not machines. For example, when people started to think about the environment more. The planet is in a bad condition, and if organizations like Greenpeace didn't exist, it would be worse. Don't you agree?

**P:** Yes, you're right, but even organizations like Greenpeace need computers to do their work!

**I:** Paolo, what items from our lives today will be in the history museums of the future?

**P:** That's a difficult question. Possibly, some things we have in the house, some domestic ap, er, domestic applications? No, well, it doesn't matter, domestic machines we use for cooking or other jobs, things like the cooker, the vacuum cleaner or the iron. I think some of these things will be replaced for robots which do not need people to use them.

**C:** Do you really think we will have robots?

**P:** Yes, we already have them now. In only a few years, I think we will be able to use them in the home for doing simple things.

**C:** Well, I think one thing in the museums of the future will be the money. I think the credit cards will be the only thing we use. Already now, some people never pay for things with cash. In only a few years I think they will stop making the money.

**I:** Thank you. That is the end of the test.

# Photocopiable exercises

## Unit 1

**Reading: Handle with care**           Page 4

**A**  Match each of the nouns in the box with one of the definitions **1–5**.

| booking | itinerary | catwalk |
|---|---|---|
| fashion shoot | cover | |

1  the narrow, raised area which models walk along at fashion shows
2  the plan of a journey, including the places you will visit
3  the front page of a magazine
4  a session during which a series of photographs are taken of a model
5  a reservation for a hotel room, a show, a table in a restaurant, etc

**B**  Match each of the verbs in the box with the situation in **1–5** which best illustrates its meaning.

| reassure | encourage (someone to do something) |
|---|---|
| humiliate | cheer someone up    complain |

1  Look at Mark, everyone! Have you ever seen such unfashionable clothes before?
2  When I bought this coat you told me it was waterproof. Well it isn't, and I'd like my money back.
3  He looked a little depressed so I bought him a nice new tie to make him feel better.
4  There's no need to worry, sir. Your suit will be ready in time for the wedding on Saturday.
5  It'll be cold in the mountains. Believe me, you'll be much more comfortable if you wear a hat and scarf.

**C**  Complete each of the gaps with one of the words in the box.

| of | after | for |
|---|---|---|

Bookers are people who
1  care _____ models.
2  take care _____ models.
3  look _____ models.

## Unit 2

**Reading: Going to extremes**           Page 19

**A**  Complete each gap with an adjective from the box.

| brittle | custom-built | state-of-the-art |
|---|---|---|
| steep | thrilling | tough |

1  A _____ **person** is strong and able to deal with difficult situations.
2  A _____ **hill** rises quickly and is difficult to climb.
3  _____ **ice** is ice which can easily break into pieces.
4  A _____ **sport** is an extremely exciting one.
5  A _____ **car** is one which is designed and built for one particular person.
6  _____ **equipment** uses the newest and most advanced ideas and features.

**B**  Match each of the underlined verbs in sentences **1–8** with one of the meanings **a–h**.
1  A dog ran out in front of the car and I had to <u>brake</u> suddenly.
2  It's very difficult to <u>steer</u> a car with one hand and speak into a mobile phone at the same time.
3  Skiiers were <u>hurtling</u> down the slopes at speeds of up to 80 miles an hour.
4  We <u>clambered</u> up the hill with our heavy rucksacks.
5  It was Shakespeare who <u>coined</u> the phrase 'All the world's a stage'.
6  We should <u>do away with</u> exams and just have continuous assessment throughout the year.
7   These new tyres <u>grip</u> the road firmly and help prevent accidents.
8  He <u>shifted</u> his weight nervously from one foot to the other.

**a**  climb with difficulty
**b**  get rid of
**c**  move your body or part of your body slightly
**d**  stop or slow down a vehicle
**e**  use a word or phrase that no one has used before
**f**  move or travel very quickly, often in a dangerous way
**g**  hold a surface tightly
**h**  control the direction in which a vehicle moves

© Macmillan Publishers Ltd.  This page may be photocopied and used within the class.

# Unit 3

## Reading: The convenience society, or con for short
Page 27

**A** Match each of the following items of vocabulary **1–6** with the correct picture **a–f**.

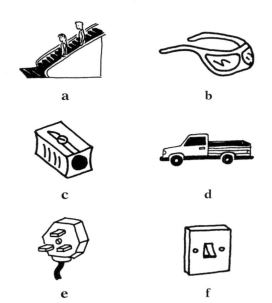

a            b

c            d

e            f

1 plug _____
2 pencil sharpener _____
3 pickup truck _____
4 switch _____
5 goggles _____
6 escalator _____

**B** Complete each of the gaps with a noun from the box. You may need to use the plural form.

> tip    blade    hurry    stream
> wrinkle

1 I can't stop – I'm in a _____ . I'm late for work already.
2 You obviously haven't ironed that shirt, have you? It's full of _____ .
3 Pick the knife up by the handle, not the _____ . You don't want to cut yourself, do you?
4 I wanted to become a ballet dancer, but I could never stand on the _____ of my toes.
5 We've had a constant _____ of phone calls since we put the job advertisement in the newspaper.

# Unit 3

## Listening 2: Multiple choice
Page 34

Decide which answer (**A**, **B**, **C** or **D**) best fits each gap in these sentences from the listening. Then listen to the recording again or read the listening script on page 220 of the Coursebook to check your answers.

1 Keith's company, *ELA Robotics*, _____ the news last year with their *Home Help* robot.
   **A** appeared  **B** hit      **C** stroked  **D** beat

2 We've all been given our instructions and signed an agreement not to _____ anything away until it actually comes onto the market.
   **A** give       **B** say       **C** tell       **D** let

3 We'll look forward to that. In the _____ , perhaps you could tell us what you think are the most important applications of robots in our lives.
   **A** moment    **B** duration  **C** actuality  **D** meantime

4 That's not an exhaustive list, but it gives you an idea of the _____ of different uses they have.
   **A** range      **B** whole     **C** reach     **D** limit

5 They might feel happy for example that they have _____ out a domestic task particularly well.
   **A** worked    **B** done      **C** carried    **D** performed

6 Yes, unfortunately, robots do get rather a bad _____ sometimes, don't they?
   **A** fame       **B** rumour   **C** reference **D** press

7 There is actually an ethical code which _____ out what we can and can't do in robot design.
   **A** puts       **B** sets       **C** gives     **D** writes

8 If we _____ intelligent robots do all of our thinking for us, there is a danger we won't be able to make any of our own decisions.
   **A** permit    **B** let        **C** allow     **D** tolerate

9 If you _____ back to just twenty-five years ago, few of us then would have predicted that we'd soon have a personal computer in our home.
   **A** see        **B** remind  **C** think     **D** wonder

10 When they eventually become _____ available, people will be ready for them.
   **A** widely    **B** deeply   **C** highly    **D** shortly

© Macmillan Publishers Ltd.  This page may be photocopied and used within the class.

PHOTOCOPIABLE

## Unit 4

**Reading: The exam**                                    Page 48

**A** Match each of the underlined verbs in sentences **1–6** with one of the meanings **a–f**.

1   She <u>blushed</u> when I told her how pretty she looked.
2   I'm sorry I'm late. My car <u>broke down</u> and I had to call a mechanic.
3   Anyone caught <u>cheating</u> in the exam will be disqualified and asked to leave.
4   You shouldn't <u>stare</u> at people; you know it's rude.
5   You must not start until I have <u>handed out</u> all the examination papers.
6   It wasn't my fault. I was just <u>carrying out</u> your instructions.

**a**   behave in a dishonest way
**b**   look for a long time
**c**   become red in the face
**d**   stop working
**e**   do what you are asked to do
**f**   distribute/give to everyone

**B** Complete each of the gaps with one of the adjectives in the box.

| bearable   dull   ingenious   rough |
|---|

1   A/An _____ method is a very clever one involving new ideas.
2   _____ paper is used for making notes on in an exam.
3   A/An _____ job is neither interesting nor exciting.
4   A/An _____ job is one which you can tolerate.

## Unit 5

**Reading: Home is where the school is**

Page 55

**A** Match each of the underlined verbs in sentences **1–5** with one of the meanings **a–e**.

1   They decided to <u>withdraw</u> their daughter from the school because she wasn't making enough progress.
2   Fewer graduates seem to <u>opt for</u> a career in teaching these days.
3   Stop talking please, and <u>carry on</u> with your work.
4   The other children in Sally's class are much slower than she is, and this is <u>holding</u> her <u>back</u>.
5   Children must be <u>supervised</u> in the library by an adult at all times.

**a**   prevent from making progress
**b**   remove from; stop sending to
**c**   be in charge of somebody and check they are behaving or working correctly
**d**   continue
**e**   choose one thing in preference to others

**B** Complete each of the gaps with one of the adjectives in the box.

| abrupt   infectious   rigid   voracious |
|---|

1   A/An _____ **reader** reads a lot and often quickly.
2   A/An _____ **disease** can be caught by being near a person who is suffering from it.
3   A/An _____ **timetable** is not flexible and cannot be changed.
4   A/An _____ **end** is sudden and often unexpected.

PHOTOCOPIABLE

© **Macmillan Publishers Ltd.**  This page may be photocopied and used within the class.

# Unit 5
## Listening 2: Sentence completion    Page 60

Decide which answer (**A**, **B**, **C** or **D**) best fits each gap in these sentences from the listening. Then listen to the recording again or read the listening script on page 221 of the Coursebook to check your answers.

1 Potential recruits do have to undergo a short educational test _____ at assessing basic literacy and numeracy.
   **A** designed  **B** intended  **C** aimed  **D** meant

2 If they get through this stage, they _____ on to the next one, the practical awareness day.
   **A** continue  **B** go      **C** do      **D** work

3 Firefighters are obviously _____ call 24 hours a day.
   **A** on       **B** in       **C** at      **D** under

4 A firefighter works two nine-hour day shifts, _____ by two 15-hour night shifts.
   **A** combined          **B** followed
   **C** proceeded         **D** continued

5 It's essential that this and everything else is maintained in perfect working _____ .
   **A** state   **B** situation  **C** operation  **D** order

6 And then after that, if we're not _____ out to a fire, there's the routine work which is programmed into the day.
   **A** gone     **B** asked    **C** called  **D** phoned

7 Fitness of course is extremely important, so we also have a kind of mini gym where we _____ out every day.
   **A** work    **B** train    **C** exercise  **D** run

8 It's worth pointing out that the fires themselves often take only minutes to _____ out.
   **A** get      **B** take     **C** do      **D** put

9 Any firefighter who said that he had never felt frightened would be _____ himself and you.
   **A** lying            **B** fooling
   **C** mistaking        **D** disbelieving

10 There's also the camaraderie which goes with working as _____ of a team.
   **A** member           **B** collaborator
   **C** part             **D** participant

# Unit 6
## Reading: Family feuds – or just lunch?
Page 67

**A** Match each sentence **1–5** with a sentence **a–f** which expresses a similar idea.

1 It didn't strike them as surprising.
2 It didn't matter to them.
3 They didn't always see eye to eye.
4 They had a terrible row.
5 They hardly ever moaned.

a They sometimes disagreed with each other.
b They had a big argument.
c They didn't find it strange.
d They rarely complained.
e They didn't mind.

**B** Match each of the underlined verbs in sentences **1–4** with one of the meanings **a–d**.

1 There's no need to <u>rush</u>; we've got plenty of time.
2 I've just got time to <u>grab</u> a coffee before the meeting starts.
3 He <u>wandered in</u> to work at 9.30, and made no effort to explain why he was late.
4 The police <u>interrogated</u> him for eight hours until he admitted he had stolen the money.

a to enter in a casual, relaxed way
b to hurry
c to ask a lot of questions to obtain information
d get quickly

© Macmillan Publishers Ltd.  This page may be photocopied and used within the class.

# Photocopiable exercises

## Unit 6

### Listening 1: Multiple matching
Page 70

**A** Write each adjective from the box next to its definition.

| | | | |
|---|---|---|---|
| outgoing | plain | sensitive | shy |
| spiteful | tough | | |

A person who ...

1 ... is nervous and embarrassed in the company of other people. _____
2 ... deliberately tries to upset someone or cause problems for them. _____
3 ... is confident and determined to get what they want. _____
4 ... is friendly and enjoys meeting and talking to people. _____
5 ... becomes angry or upset easily. _____
6 ... is not very attractive.

**B** **1** Complete each gap with the correct form of a verb from the box. You will need to use some verbs more than once.

| get | have | look | let | make | see | tell |
|---|---|---|---|---|---|---|

1 I _____ my hair cut short and wore clothes that _____ all the neighbours talking.
2 Mum and Dad used to _____ really mad about the way she lived her life, but I'd always _____ excuses for her. And if she ever _____ into trouble, I never _____ them the whole truth. I don't think they know half of what she _____ up to.
3 She's always been very tough, my sister – determined to _____ on with her life without _____ anyone or anything else bother her, and I've always _____ up to her for that.
4 When people _____ us fighting, they immediately think we don't _____ on with each other, but nothing could be further from the truth.
5 She used to _____ fun of me because I was so plain and unconcerned about my appearance.

**2** Listen to the recording again or read the listening script on page 222 of the Coursebook to check your answers.

## Unit 7

### Reading: Shopping: a curable disease?
Page 84

**A** In **1–5** below, decide which alternative, **A** or **B**, expresses the meaning of the underlined word(s).

1 I've decided to <u>splash out</u> on a new dress for the wedding. After all, it's not every day your daughter gets married, is it?
   **A** buy something which costs a lot of money
   **B** avoid paying a lot of money for something

2 As soon as she got paid, she <u>went on a shopping binge</u>, and then had to borrow money from her parents to get through the rest of the month.
   **A** went into lots of shops without buying anything
   **B** spent an excessive amount of money in shops

3 The school is <u>making a purchase</u> of 15 new PCs, so there will be a computer in every classroom.
   **A** buying
   **B** selling

4 They've just <u>launched trials</u> of a new drug to cure baldness. If the trials are successful, the drug should be available in the shops by next year.
   **A** started selling
   **B** started testing

5 When she was ill in hospital I sent her some flowers to <u>cheer her up</u>.
   **A** make her like me more
   **B** make her feel happier

**B** Match each of the underlined nouns in sentences **1–4** with one of the meanings **a–d**.

1 He was filled with <u>remorse</u> when he realized how much suffering his crimes had caused.
2 She suffers from low <u>self-esteem</u> and has no confidence in her own abilities.
3 It was very expensive but I just couldn't resist the <u>urge</u> to buy it.
4 It gave me a real <u>thrill</u> to see so many famous people in one place.

**a** strong desire
**b** strong feeling of guilt and regret
**c** feeling of great excitement
**d** the opinion you have of yourself

162

© Macmillan Publishers Ltd.  This page may be photocopied and used within the class.
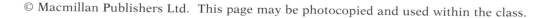

# Unit 7
## Writing FCE Part 2: Reports    Further practice

**1** Read the following question for Part 2 of the Writing Paper.

The consumers' association which you work for is planning to publish an information leaflet describing local shopping facilities. You have to write a report for your boss comparing two supermarkets in your area. You should compare the products on sale, the layout and the facilities, and comment on any particularly good or bad points.

**2** Read the following model answer. For questions **1–15**, underline the correct alternative.

Introduction
**(1)** *The/Some* aim of this report is to compare two supermarkets in the area, Madison's and Pricerite.

Products
**(2)** *Both/Two* shops offer a wide range of products. The selection of fresh fish is particularly impressive in Pricerite, **(3)** *while/however* the main attraction in Madison's is the delicatessen counter, **(4)** *which/that* sells a variety of salads and home-made patés. Pricerite's own brands are slightly better value for money than **(5)** *those/them* in Madison's.

Layout
The aisles in Madison's are spacious, enabling customers to shop in comfort. **(6)** *Despite/However*, the top shelf in some sections is **(7)** *too/enough* high for many shoppers to reach. There are several express checkouts in Pricerite, **(8)** *which/what* is useful for **(9)** *they/those* who only require a few items.

Facilities
**(10)** *Neither/None* supermarket has its own parking facilities, **(11)** *although/because* Madison's is planning to build a car park soon. It has **(12)** *also/too* recently introduced a supervised play area, where parents can leave their children **(13)** *during/while* they do their shopping.

Conclusion
To sum up, **(14)** *either/both* supermarkets are popular with local people. Madison's is the larger of the two, and has more facilities, **(15)** *whereas/despite* Pricerite is generally cheaper.

**3** Look back at the model report in exercise 2 and answer the following questions.

Who is the target reader?
Is the style of this report more formal or informal?
What is the purpose of each paragraph?
Why are headings used?
Which words and structures are used for comparing and contrasting?

**4** Read the following Part 2 instructions. What differences are there between this question and the one in exercise 1?

The consumers' association which you work for is planning to publish a leaflet describing local shopping facilities. You have to write a report for your boss comparing two shopping districts in your town. You should compare the types of shops and places to eat, as well as parking and other facilities, and comment on any particularly good or bad points.

Write your **report** in **120–180** words.

**5** Plan and write your answer to this question. See the Wordlist on page 204 of the Coursebook for a list of shops.

**Notes/Plan**

PHOTOCOPIABLE

# Photocopiable exercises

## Unit 7
### Listening 2: Multiple choice    Page 87

**A** **1** Use the words in the box to complete the phrasal verbs in sentences **1–5**. The verbs are all used in the recording.

| into | off | on | out | up |
|------|-----|----|----|----|

1 He irritates his neighbours by driving along with all the windows open and loud music **blaring** _____ of the car stereo.
2 Thieves **broke** _____ the school and took five computers from the IT department.
3 At Christmas the local authorities usually **put** _____ extra buses to take shoppers into the town centre.
4 I told my husband we could have children, but that I wasn't prepared to **give** _____ my career to stay at home and look after them.
5 Stay here with me children – don't **wander** _____ on your own!

**2** Write the infinitive of each phrasal verb in exercise 1 next to the correct definition **a–e**.

**a** sacrifice something; stop doing one activity in order to do another_____
**b** enter a building by force, especially in order to steal things _____
**c** provide a means of transport for people to use _____
**d** make a loud and unpleasant noise _____
**e** move away from a place where people expect you to be _____

**B** Complete the expressions in bold by writing a noun in each gap. Then check your answers in the listening script on page 224 of the Coursebook.

1 When I first went to London, I used to love **the hustle and** _____ of the place.
2 I feel I have to **keep an even closer** _____ **on** my two kids than before.
3 Everyone seems to **know everyone else's** _____ in the village.
4 I know at that age I would have been **bored out of my** _____ !
5 Naturally, I'd prefer to stay in the village and work at home rather than **do a nine-to-five** _____ in an office.
6 We'd be prepared to move back to London if we felt it was **to our** _____ .

## Unit 8
### Reading 1: Wish you were here?    Page 94

**A** Complete each of the gaps with one of the words in the box.

| sweat | foresee | dizzy |
|-------|---------|-------|
| debris | drawback | lack |

1 After dancing round in circles for five minutes I started to feel _____ and had to sit down.
2 The only _____ to living here is the noise. Apart from that, it's marvellous.
3 It was so hot in the room I started to _____ and my whole face was wet.
4 The only reason I can't go on holiday with you is a _____ of money.
5 It's impossible to _____ what will happen in the future – we just don't know.
6 Several people were killed by flying _____ from the explosion.

**B** Complete each of the gaps with either *in*, *to* or *into* and then match each expression in **bold** with one of the meanings **a–d**.

1 We're going to **treat ourselves** _____ a weekend in a five-star hotel.
2 She tried to **tempt me** _____ going on holiday with her to Spain.
3 Having considered the advantages of air travel, let's now **turn our attention** _____ the problem of overbooking.
4 Roadworks on the A27 this morning will **result** _____ long delays between Chichester and Portsmouth.

**a** begin to do, think or talk about something different
**b** persuade someone to do something
**c** buy or arrange something special
**d** cause

**164**  © Macmillan Publishers Ltd.  This page may be photocopied and used within the class.

PHOTOCOPIABLE

# Unit 8
## Reading 2: Travel narrows the mind

Page 100

**A** Complete each of the gaps with a word in the box.

| warming | source | summit |
|---------|--------|--------|
| charter | dump | mess jet |

1 A **rubbish** _____ is a place where rubbish is taken and left.
2 If tourism is a major _____ **of income** for a country, the country earns a lot of money from tourism.
3 _____ **lag** is the tiredness you feel after a long journey by aeroplane (especially when travelling between places with a large time difference).
4 **Global** _____ is the increase in the earth's temperature.
5 To _____ **a plane** is to hire it for your own use.
6 If you **make a** _____ of something, you spoil it or do damage to it.
7 The _____ **of a mountain** is the top of it.

**B** Match each of the adjectives in the box with the sentence **1–4** which best illustrates its meaning.

| unwise | remote | restless |
|--------|--------|----------|
| energy-hungry | | |

1 Their house is ten miles from the nearest village.
2 He can't sit still for five minutes; he always has to be doing something.
3 I don't think you should take the car; the roads are in a terrible condition.
4 Because of its size the engine uses up a lot of petrol.

# Unit 9
## Reading 1: UFOs – have we been visited?

Page 106

**A** Complete each of the gaps with one of the words in the box.

| reported | practical | blinding |
|----------|-----------|----------|
| molten | intense | high-pitched |

1 We had to stand back from the fire because of the _____ **heat**.
2 With the explosion there was a _____ **light**, and I covered my face to protect my eyes.
3 _____ **metal** is metal in a liquid state.
4 There have been several _____ **sightings** of aliens but we have no definite proof that they really exist.
5 The children changed the time on all the classroom clocks as a _____ **joke**.
6 We heard a _____ **noise**, like the sound of a young child screaming.

**B** Complete each of the gaps with the correct form of one of the verbs in the box.

| glow | boil | spit | melt |
|------|------|------|------|

1 The sun came out and caused the snow to _____ .
2 When the water _____ , turn the heat down and cook the potatoes for 20 minutes.
3 The only light came from the two cigarettes, which _____ like cat's eyes in the dark.
4 He painted a picture of a dragon _____ flames from its mouth.

© Macmillan Publishers Ltd. This page may be photocopied and used within the class.

PHOTOCOPIABLE

## Unit 9
### Reading 2: The trouble with Hallowe'en
Page 112

**A** Match each of the underlined verbs in sentences
1–6 with one of the meanings **a–f**.

1 With great skill he <u>carved</u> the piece of wood into
the figure of a bird.

2 Casterton <u>clutched</u> the bag to his chest as he
walked through the crowd.

3 The beer's <u>run out</u>. Can you go to the shop and
get some more?

4 We had to <u>dip into</u> our savings to pay the gas
and electricity bills this month.

5 Everyone <u>rejoiced</u> at the news that the war had
finally ended.

6 I remember how I <u>shrieked</u> with pain when I
broke my leg.

**a** be used up; finish

**b** express great happiness

**c** give a short, loud, high-pitched cry

**d** hold something tightly

**e** make an object by cutting it out of material such
as stone

**f** pay for something with some of the money
which was intended for a different purpose

**B** Complete each of the gaps with a word or
expression in the box.

> Provided     Considering
> Needless to say     Indeed

1 It was a really funny film. _____ , I
laughed so much I cried.

2 _____ they didn't have some of their
best players today, I thought they played really
well.

3 _____ you behave yourself this
afternoon, we'll let you watch the film on TV
tonight.

4 He broke his arm at the weekend.
_____ , he won't be able to drive for a
few weeks.

## Unit 10
### Reading: Private investigators investigated
Page 126

**A** Complete each gap with an adjective from the
box.

> dull     rewarding     scruffy
> spacious     tight

1 _____ **laws** are strict laws.

2 A _____ **job** is a satisfying one.

3 A _____ **job** is a monotonous one.

4 A _____ **room** is a large one with a lot of
space.

5 A _____ **coat** is dirty or untidy.

**B** Complete the compound adjectives, nouns and
verbs by writing the correct particle from the
box in each gap. Then match the compound
words with their meanings in **a – f**.

> in     in     off     over     to     up

1 How did people survive in those **far-____** days
before washing machines?

2 Politicians are familiar faces on our television
screens, but their **day-____-day** work is far
from glamorous.

3 The file is still in my ____ **-tray**; I'll deal with it
as soon as I can.

4 There was a police car outside the chemist's at
three o'clock this morning – I think there must
have been a **break-____**.

5 *The History of Modern Europe* has been
____**dated** to include the events of the last five
years.

6 Close the door – I don't want anyone to
____**hear** our conversation.

**a** a container on a desk where you keep
documents that are ready to be read

**b** hear what is said by others who do not know
you are listening to them

**c** add the most recent information to something
such as a book or document

**d** happening every day as part of ordinary life

**e** happening a long time ago

**f** illegal entry into a building using force,
especially to steal things

© Macmillan Publishers Ltd. This page may be photocopied and used within the class.

PHOTOCOPIABLE

# Unit 11
## Reading: Lucky to be alive          Page 135

**A**  Match each of the following items of vocabulary **1–7** with the correct picture **a–f**.

**1**  kite  _____

**2**  branch (of tree)  _____

**3**  candle  _____

**4**  debris  _____

**5**  to board up  _____

**6**  dustbin bag  _____

**7**  tidal wave  _____

**B**  Match each of the underlined nouns in sentences **1–5** with one of the meanings **a–e**.

**1**  He cut off a large <u>chunk</u> of meat and threw it to his dog.

**2**  The hurricane brought chaos and <u>devastation</u> to the area.

**3**  She suffered a number of <u>misfortunes</u>, including the loss of her job and a near-fatal car accident.

**4**  The <u>tremor</u> could be felt throughout the city, though fortunately no lives were lost.

**5**  There was a tremendous sense of <u>camaraderie</u> after the earthquake, with everyone working together, helping each other.

**a**  small earthquake

**b**  thick piece

**c**  unlucky events

**d**  feeling of friendship and solidarity

**e**  severe damage and destruction

# Unit 11
## Listening 2: Multiple choice          Page 143

Complete each gap in these sentences from the recording with an auxiliary verb or a modal verb. You may need to use a negative form. When you have finished, check your answers in the tapescript on pages 227 and 228.

**One**

They maintained that if they'd built it in the heart of the city, there _____ _____ been problems getting out to fires in the rural areas.

**Two**

If I was a member of the Council, I _____ make sure something _____ done about the mess on the streets.

**Three**

If we _____ made this a conservation area and limited the number of people coming in, then we'd have no flowers and people _____ be really upset.

**Four**

If we'd gone to one of the other islands, we _____ _____ had to put up with busy roads and crowded beaches.

**Five**

Man: I can't put up with it any more.
Woman: Neither _____ we.

**Six**

One man in Bognor narrowly escaped death as the car he was driving _____ crushed by a falling tree, which _____ _____ struck by lightning.

**Seven**

Woman: It wasn't our cat, _____ it?
Man: No, the wind. Pulled up all the roses, it _____.

**Eight**

These massive petrol tankers _____ just not be allowed to sail so close to our shores.

© Macmillan Publishers Ltd.  This page may be photocopied and used within the class.

PHOTOCOPIABLE

# Photocopiable exercises

## Unit 12
### Reading: Water: are you drinking enough?

Page 148

**A** Use the suffixes in the box to form nouns from the verbs **1–5** and adjectives **6–10**. You will need to use two of the suffixes more than once. Some words require further spelling changes. The first one has been done for you.

| -ion | -ness | -ance | -al | -ity | -y |
|------|-------|-------|-----|------|-----|

**Verb**      **Noun**

**1** consume     _consumption_
**2** dehydrate    _____
**3** perform      _____
**4** deny         _____
**5** provide       _____

**Adjective**     **Noun**

**6** irritable      _____
**7** vain         _____
**8** aware        _____
**9** generous     _____
**10** difficult     _____

**B** In **1–5** complete each gap with a noun from the box.

| water | health | problem | needs |
|-------|--------|---------|-------|
| message | action | | |

**1** The tap water in this region is unsafe and drinking it could seriously **jeopardize your** _____ .

**2** Governments need to **take** _____ now to **address the** _____ of climate change.

**3** If grapefruit juice is **diluted with** _____ , the taste is not so strong and it's easier to drink.

**4** The government has launched an advertising campaign in an attempt to **get the** _____ **across to** parents that fast food can cause obesity.

**5** The library does not **meet the** _____ **of** the disabled, as there are no lifts to the first floor.

## Unit 13
### Reading 1: Life in the fast lane

Page 163

Complete each of the gaps **1–7** with a word in the box which has the same meaning as the definition in brackets.

| potential | showroom | entrepreneur |
|-----------|----------|--------------|
| stock | sales | cash in    set up |

Successful **(1)** _____ (person who starts his/her own company), Les Dawes, aged 21, has made a fortune from selling cars powered by electricity. He saw the **(2)** _____ (possibility of success) for the business when **(3)** _____ (the quantity sold) of conventional cars fell as a result of increased petrol prices.

In order to raise the necessary money to **(4)** _____ (start) the business, Les decided to **(5)** _____ (exchange for money) some investments he had, in addition to taking out a loan from his bank. He rented a **(6)** _____ (place where goods are displayed) in the high street of his home town, Newhaven, and within a month his initial **(7)** _____ (amount of goods for sale) had all been sold.

PHOTOCOPIABLE

## Unit 13
### Reading 2: My river hero                    Page 169

In **1–7** below, decide which alternative, **A** or **B**, expresses the meaning of the underlined word or expression.

1  Maradona has been <u>hailed</u> as one of the greatest footballers of all time.
   A  recognized publicly
   B  criticized

2  Beethoven's 9th Symphony is my favourite piece of music; it always <u>sends a shiver down my spine</u> when I hear it.
   A  makes my back ache
   B  makes me feel excited

3  She never panics in a crisis; she's so wonderfully <u>level-headed</u>.
   A  shy and reserved
   B  calm and sensible

4  When the champagne had been served everyone <u>drank a toast</u> to the bride and groom.
   A  had a quick snack
   B  wished them luck by drinking

5  Jacobson calmly picked up the phone and called his wife. 'I've been arrested,' he said <u>matter-of-factly</u>.
   A  without showing emotion
   B  in a worried voice

6  The violent storms <u>made the front page</u> of the newspaper, together, of course, with the General Election results.
   A  appeared on the first page of the newspaper
   B  was the main story in the newspaper

7  He always <u>put other people before himself</u> and regularly gave up his weekends to do charity work.
   A  he was selfish
   B  he was unselfish

## Unit 14
### Reading: The most successful living artist
                                    Page 175

A  Match each of the underlined verbs in sentences **1–8** with one of the meanings **a–h**.

1  The painting by Van Gogh <u>fetched</u> over a million dollars.
2  The Earth <u>spins</u> once a day from west to east.
3  We <u>pickle</u> the cucumbers in summer and eat them through the winter.
4  The bedroom furniture company has <u>branched out</u> and now sells kitchen products.
5  Columbus was <u>ridiculed</u> for believing the world was round.
6  If we don't pick the fruit now it will start to <u>rot</u>.
7  She <u>took on</u> the challenge of climbing the highest mountain on each continent.
8  The composer died in 1843 but his memory will <u>live on</u> forever in his music.

a  survive
b  accept
c  be sold for
d  turn round and round
e  start doing something new or different
f  be destroyed gradually by natural processes
g  make fun of somebody in an unkind way
h  preserve food in vinegar or salt water

B  Complete each gap with a word from the box and match the expressions in **bold** with the meanings **a-d**.

| face | breath | string | time |
|------|--------|--------|------|

1  The Swedish group Abba **had a** _____ **of** hits including 'Dancing Queen' and 'Mamma Mia'.
2  The Rolling Stones are often **mentioned in the same** _____ **as** The Beatles, but their musical styles are very different.
3  With his good looks and unique playing style, Björn Borg **changed the** _____ **of** tennis.
4  **Only** _____ **will tell** whether he made the right decision to move to Spain.

a  speak about two things together because they are considered similar
b  we will not know until some time in the future if something is true or correct
c  have a series of similar or connected events
d  alter the way that something looks or appears

# Photocopiable exercises

## Unit 14
### Listening: Multiple choice
Page 179

When you have completed the following two exercises, listen to the recording again or read the listening script on page 232 to check your answers.

**A** Complete each gap with the correct form of one of the verbs from the box. Use the words in bold to help you make your choices.

| | | | | |
|---|---|---|---|---|
| bear | go | keep | look | make |
| move | pay | pick | take | |

1 Cats and dogs need a lot of _____ **after**, whereas insects and spiders, for example, are very low-maintenance – they more or less _____ **care of** themselves.

2 If you _____ them **up** or try to play with them, they can give you quite a nasty bite. So inevitably some children start to grow tired of them, _____ less **attention to** them.

3 Now, let's _____ **on to** another type of pet that seems to be in fashion these days – snakes.

4 What's common to the corn snakes and ball pythons that we sell is that they can sometimes _____ **for months without** eating.

5 Interesting that you mention rats, because of course, they too are _____ **as pets** nowadays, aren't they?

6 That's right. They _____ **very good pets** and they don't bite quite as readily as people think. You need to _____ **in mind** though that they like being with other rats.

**B** Complete each gap in these sentences from the recording with one of the word combinations from the box.

| | |
|---|---|
| a great deal | an increasing number |
| a long-term commitment | little cost |

1 Ants, spiders, snakes and rats .... have become the pets of choice for _____ of pet-lovers in the Radio Carston area.

2 And that's perfect for busy working couples who .... can't afford to spend _____ of time on the more traditional kinds of pets.

3 Many snakes have a lifespan of more than 20 years – so you need to be aware that you are making _____ when you buy one.

4 It's better to give them pre-killed animals, which can be bought frozen at reasonably _____ from pet stores.

## Unit 15
### Reading: Two languages good, three languages even better
Page 188

Match each of the underlined verbs in sentences **1–8** with one of the meanings **a–h**.

1 They've <u>enrolled</u> their three-year-old daughter in a ballet school.

2 I <u>picked up</u> a few Greek phrases when I was on holiday in Corfu.

3 He <u>opted</u> not to have school dinners; he takes his own sandwiches instead.

4 Katie has <u>outgrown</u> her school uniform so we'll have to buy her a new one before she starts back in September.

5 As a student I <u>gained</u> a great deal from living away from home; it made me far more independent for one thing.

6 The Prime Minister <u>conceded</u> that mistakes had been made and that action would be taken to resolve the situation.

7 It was a one-month intensive course, so we had to <u>absorb</u> a lot of information very quickly.

8 After retiring from boxing, Higgins went on to <u>wrestle</u> professionally under the name of Big Bad Bill.

**a** make a choice or decision from a range of possibilities

**b** put somebody's name on the official list of students

**c** get a benefit or advantage for oneself

**d** fight by holding and pushing someone but without hitting them

**e** learn without making a deliberate effort

**f** learn and understand new facts, so that they become part of your knowledge

**g** admit that something is true

**h** be unable to wear clothes because you are now too big for them

© Macmillan Publishers Ltd. This page may be photocopied and used within the class.

PHOTOCOPIABLE

# Unit 15
## Reading 2: American high          Page 192

**A** Match each of the nouns in the box with one of the definitions **1–8**.

| | | | |
|---|---|---|---|
| buzzer | buzzword | pass | locker |
| clique | period | peer | nerd |

1 document, card or ticket which allows you to do something, go somewhere or use a particular form of public transport
2 person of the same age or social position as other members in a group
3 electrical device which makes a continuous sound when pressed and is used, for example, to attract attention
4 a word or expression that has become fashionable among a group of people
5 a group of people who spend a lot of time together
6 an informal word for someone who is considered stupid or socially awkward
7 a lesson or time for private study
8 a small cupboard in a school or sports centre, for example, in which you can keep your personal things

**B** Match each of the underlined verbs in **1–4** with one of the meanings **a–d**.

1 She ran out of the room angrily, <u>slamming</u> the door as she went.
2 The police <u>frisked</u> him and found a knife in his pocket.
3 She <u>cherishes</u> the watch her grandmother gave her before she died.
4 I never intended to become an actor – I just <u>drifted into</u> the profession, really.

**a** to search someone with your hands in order to find hidden objects
**b** to enter gradually or casually
**c** to close something noisily and with force
**d** to be fond of and take care of something which is important to you

# Ready for Speaking          Pages 196–199
## Part 1: Interview

Listen to Part 1 again and note down any mistakes you hear Christina or Paolo make.
Can you correct the mistakes?

## Part 2: Talking about photos

**1** Listen to Christina again and note down any 'fillers' she uses.

**2** Listen to Paolo again and note down any expressions that he uses to speculate about what is happening/has happened.

## Part 3: Collaborative task

Listen to Part 3 again and make a note of the following:

**1** The different expressions which Paolo uses to introduce his opinion, eg In my opinion …

**2** The different expressions which both Paolo and Christina use to agree or disagree with each other, eg Yes, that's true.

**3** Any words they use as alternatives to interesting, boring and good, eg good fun

## Part 4: Further discussion

Listen to Part 4 again and answer the following questions.

**1** What expressions does Christina use while she is thinking how to answer the first three questions?

**2** Christina does not know the word for 'showcase' and Paolo forgets the word 'appliances'.
How do they solve these problems?
What words do they use?

© Macmillan Publishers Ltd.  This page may be photocopied and used within the class.

PHOTOCOPIABLE

# Photocopiable exercises

## Answers to photocopiable exercises

### Unit 1

**Reading: Handle with care**

**A**  1 catwalk  2 itinerary  3 cover
   4 fashion shoot  5 booking

**B**  1 humiliate
   2 complain
   3 cheer someone up
   4 reassure
   5 encourage someone to do something

**C**  1 for  2 of  3 after

### Unit 2

**Reading: Going to extremes**

**A**  1 tough   2 steep     3 Brittle
   4 thrilling  5 custom-built  6 State-of-the-art

**B**  1 d 2 h  3 f  4 a  5 e  6 b  7 g  8 c

### Unit 3

**Reading: The convenience society, or con
for short**

**A**  1 e  2 c  3 d  4 f  5 b  6 a

**B**  1 hurry  2 wrinkles  3 blade  4 tips  5 stream

**Listening 2: Multiple choice**

1 B    2 A    3 D    4 A    5 C
6 D    7 B    8 B    9 C    10 A

### Unit 4

**Reading: The exam**

**A**  1 c  2 d  3 a  4 b  5 f  6 e

**B**  1 ingenious  2 Rough  3 dull  4 bearable

### Unit 5

**Reading: Home is where the school is**

**A**  1 b  2 e  3 d  4 a  5 c

**B**  1 voracious  2 infectious  3 rigid  4 abrupt

**Listening 2: Sentence completion**

1 C aimed   2 B go    3 A on    4 B followed
5 D order   6 C called  7 A work  8 D put
9 B fooling  10 C part

### Unit 6

**Reading: Family feuds – or just lunch?**

**A**  1 c  2 e  3 a  4 b  5 d

**B**  1 b  2 d  3 a  4 c

**Listening 1: Multiple matching**

**A**  1 shy      2 spiteful    3 tough
   4 outgoing    5 sensitive   6 plain

**B**  The words shown in brackets are also possible
   answers.
1  had (got), got (had)
2  get, make, got, told, got
3  get, letting, looked
4  see, get
5  make

### Unit 7

**Writing FCE Part 2: Reports**

2  1 The   2 Both    3 while     4 which
   5 those  6 However  7 too      8 which
   9 those 10 Neither 11 although 12 also
   13 while 14 both     15 whereas

3  The target reader is 'your boss'.
   The style of the report is formal.
   Paragraph 1 tells the reader what the purpose
   of the report is.
   Paragraph 2 describes the products available
   in each supermarket.
   Paragraph 3 describes the layout of each
   supermarket.
   Paragraph 4 talks about the facilities at each
   supermarket.
   Paragraph 5 summarizes and concludes the
   report.
   Headings are used to help structure the report
   and make it easy to read/refer to.
   Words used for comparing and contrasting:
   *compare, both, while, better ... than, however,
   neither, although, larger, cheaper.*

4  The question asks for a report comparing
   two *shopping districts* rather than two
   *supermarkets*. The specific areas it requires to
   be compared are the types of shops and places

© Macmillan Publishers Ltd.  This page may be photocopied and used within the class.

to eat and the parking facilities as well as the general facilities and particular good and bad points as mentioned in the first question. It does not require a detailed comparison of the products available.

## Unit 7

### Reading: Shopping: a curable disease?

**A** 1 A 2 B 3 A 4 B 5 B

**B** 1 b 2 d 3 a 4 c

### Listening 2: Multiple choice

**A**
1 1 out 2 into 3 on 4 up 5 off
2 a give up b break into c put on
d blare out e wander off

**B** 1 bustle 2 eye 3 business
4 mind 5 job 6 advantage

## Unit 8

### Reading 1: Wish you were here?

**A** 1 dizzy 2 drawback 3 sweat
4 lack 5 foresee 6 debris

**B** 1 to, c 2 into, b 3 to, a 4 in, d

### Reading 2: Travel narrows the mind

**A** 1 dump 2 source 3 Jet 4 warming
5 charter 6 mess 7 summit

**B** 1 remote 2 restless 3 unwise
4 energy-hungry

## Unit 9

### Reading 1: UFOs – have we been visited?

**A** 1 intense 2 blinding 3 Molten
4 reported 5 practical 6 high-pitched

**B** 1 melt 2 boils 3 glowed/were glowing
4 spitting

### Reading 2: The trouble with Hallowe'en

**A** 1 e 2 d 3 a 4 f 5 b 6 c

**B** 1 Indeed 2 Considering 3 Provided
4 Needless to say

## Unit 10

### Reading: Private investigators investigated

**A** 1 Tight 2 rewarding 3 dull 4 spacious
5 scruffy

**B** 1 off e 2 to d 3 in a 4 in f 5 up c
6 over b

## Unit 11

### Reading: Lucky to be alive

**A** 1 b 2 d 3 a 4 f 5 g 6 c 7 e

**B** 1 b 2 e 3 c 4 a 5 d

### Listening: Multiple choice Page 143

1 would, have 2 'd (= would), was
3 hadn't, would 4 'd (= would), have 5 can
6 was, had, been 7 was, did 8 should

## Unit 12

### Reading: Water: are you drinking enough?

**A** 2 dehydration 3 performance 4 denial
5 provision 6 irritability 7 vanity
8 awareness 9 generosity 10 difficulty

**B** 1 health 2 action, problem 3 water
4 message 5 needs

## Unit 13

### Reading 1: Life in the fast lane

1 entrepreneur 2 potential 3 sales
4 set up 5 cash in 6 showroom
7 stock

### Reading 2: My river hero

1 A 2 B 3 B 4 B 5 A 6 A 7 B

## Unit 14

### Reading: The most successful living artist

**A** 1 c 2 d 3 h 4 e 5 g 6 f 7 b 8 a

**B** 1 string c 2 breath a 3 face d 4 time b

### Listening: Multiple choice

**A** 1 looking, take 2 pick, pay 3 move
4 go 5 kept 6 make, bear

**B** 1 an increasing number 2 a great deal
3 a long-term commitment 4 little cost

© Macmillan Publishers Ltd. This page may be photocopied and used within the class.

PHOTOCOPIABLE

## Unit 15

### Reading: Two languages good, three languages even better

**1** b  **2** e  **3** a  **4** h  **5** c  **6** g  **7** f  **8** d

### Reading 2: American High

**A**  **1** pass  **2** peer  **3** buzzer  **4** buzzword
**5** clique  **6** nerd  **7** period  **8** locker

**B**  **1** c  **2** a  **3** d  **4** b

## Ready for Speaking

### Part 1: Interview

Christina
*In winter it is more quieter.* (In winter it is quieter.)
*I always like it, since I was very young.*
(I have always liked it, since I was very young.)
*I wish my English would be as good!*
(I wish my English were as good!)
*I think they are a little bored.*
(I think they are a little boring.)
*I want to go to the university.*
(I want to go to university.)

Paolo
*Sometimes I must talk to foreign customers.*
(Sometimes I have to talk to foreign customers.)
*I want to help my uncle expanding his business.*
(I want to help my uncle expand his business.)

### Part 2: Talking about photos

**1** *what else?  let me see  well*

**2** *They must be in America.  Maybe there's been an accident or there might have been a crime.  Perhaps a murder. It looks as if they are in an ambulance … … it must be quite important … the woman looks quite relaxed*

### Part 3: Collaborative task

**1** *In my opinion  I really don't think … Personally, I think … To my mind … I think …*

**2** Agree: *Yes, that's true* (P), *I suppose you're right* (C), *Yes, I agree* (C), *You're right* (P)
Disagree: *I don't agree* (C), *Yes, but …* (P),

*I completely disagree* (P)

**3** *good fun, dull, enjoyable, fascinating*

### Part 4: Further discussion

**1** *I don't know really …*
*I'm not quite sure, but … well …*
*I haven't thought about it before, really, but …*

**2** They both paraphrase the words successfully.
*showcase:* glass boxes or cupboards
*appliances:* domestic machines we use for cooking or other jobs

© Macmillan Publishers Ltd.  This page may be photocopied and used within the class.

# Progress test 1: Units 1–3

## Reading FCE Paper 1

### Part 3 Multiple matching

You are going to read a magazine article in which various musicians are interviewed. For questions **1–15**, choose from the people (**A–E**). The people may be chosen more than once. When more than one answer is required, these may be given in any order.

**Which of the musicians states the following?**

| | | |
|---|---|---|
| I didn't listen to others' advice. | 1 | |
| I thought I'd be famous one day. | 2 | 3 |
| My taste in music was different from everyone else's. | 4 | |
| I was training for a non-musical profession. | 5 | |
| I regretted a decision I made. | 6 | |
| I sometimes found it difficult to concentrate. | 7 | |
| The more confident I became, the better I performed. | 8 | |
| I perform my own material. | 9 | 10 |
| My family was more important to me than music. | 11 | |
| I'd like to live a more stable life. | 12 | |
| I enjoyed all the attention I received. | 13 | 14 |
| Someone's misfortune was my good luck. | 15 | |

© Macmillan Publishers Ltd. This page may be photocopied and used within the class.

# Making music

**Getting into the music business isn't easy. We asked five different musicians to tell us about their experiences.**

**A**

**Martin**   Country and western singer
17 years old

I always used to sing along to my granddad's old country and western records, and when I got a guitar for my eighth birthday, they were the first tunes I played. My mates were all into Madonna and Michael Jackson so, of course, they thought I was a bit strange. At the age of ten I began writing songs and when I was 13 I started taking part in talent contests. Things didn't go too well at first, partly because audiences didn't know the words to the songs I'd written, but mostly because of nerves. I gradually lost them, though, as I got used to being on stage, and so my playing and singing improved. I won my first contest when I was 15 and I've just signed a record deal.

**B**

**Natasha**   Violinist   34 years old

When I was just seven I was accepted into a music conservatory in Moscow and had to spend four or five hours a day practising. That's a long time for someone of that age to keep their mind on something as intense as that, and I didn't always succeed. Friends and family tried to put me off becoming a professional musician because it's such a hard life. They're right of course, but I'm glad I ignored them. Now, as I get older, I want to move away from performing and the constant tours, and start composing my own music. It'll also be easier to start my own family if I have a more permanent home.

**C**

**Pete**   Guitarist and singer   50 years old

When I was 16 I played lead guitar in a band, doing versions of songs by The Beatles and The Stones. The other guys in the group seemed to think our chances of success were slim, but I took no notice. I was confident I'd make a name for myself one day, with or without the rest of the band. I left when I was 20 to become a session musician, which was a mistake, I realized afterwards, as it took me away from the one place I wanted to be – the stage. Then my wife and I had two children and I decided to put them first and got a more stable job in a bank. Now they've both grown up, I've started performing again – songs I write myself, this time. I play the local pubs and clubs at weekends only, which is enough for me at my age!

**D**

**Jake**   Rap singer   19 years old

I remember when I was five and I sang a couple of songs on the karaoke machine at my uncle's 30th birthday party. When I finished everyone cheered and came up and gave me hugs and kisses. 'This is good,' I thought, 'I could get used to this!' Then at school I performed in plays and musicals – always the lead part, of course – and once again the audience's reaction made me feel good. I think I knew at that stage I was going to be a star. It was just a question of time.

**E**

**Sonia**   Guitarist   24 years old

I was a student nurse at the time. My sister was a guitarist in an all-girl band called Femme and they were booked to play on a kid's TV programme. The day before the recording my sister broke her arm and she asked me to go on instead of her. It was dead easy, really; I knew how to play the guitar, and we were miming anyway, so no one noticed if I was playing the right notes or not. Then all the kids came up and asked me for my autograph, which was brilliant! I formed my own band soon afterwards, and we've just signed a deal with a record company.

PHOTOCOPIABLE

© Macmillan Publishers Ltd.  This page may be photocopied and used within the class.

# Use of English FCE Paper 3
## Part 4 Transformations

For questions **1–8**, complete the second sentence so that it has a similar meaning to the first sentence, using the word given. **Do not change the word given.** You must use between two and five words, including the word given.

Here is an example (**0**).

*Example:*

**0**   I don't usually see him at the weekend.

   **rare**

   It *is rare for me to* see him at the weekend.

---

**1**   My parents never took me anywhere when I was a child.

   **used**

   My parents _____ me anywhere when I was a child.

**2**   She asks boring questions all the time.

   **keeps**

   She _____ boring questions.

**3**   If you can't do it yourself, ask Helen for help.

   **get**

   If you can't do it yourself, _____ you.

**4**   How much will she earn in her new job?

   **get**

   How much will she _____ in her new job?

**5**   Could you tell me your date of birth, please?

   **when**

   Would you mind _____ born, please?

**6**   I can't wait to finish these exams.

   **forward**

   I'm _____ these exams.

**7**   I haven't got enough money for a car.

   **afford**

   I _____ buy a car.

**8**   Steven is friendlier than David.

   **as**

   David _____ Steven.

© Macmillan Publishers Ltd.  This page may be photocopied and used within the class.

PHOTOCOPIABLE

## Part 3 Word formation

For questions **1–10**, read the text below. Use the word given in capitals at the end of some of the lines to form a word that fits in the gap **in the same line**. There is an example at the beginning **(0)**.

### Tennis

| | |
|---|---|
| The **(0)** _earliest_ form of tennis was played in the thirteenth century, when | EARLY |
| (1) _____ hit the ball with their hands, instead of racquets. French | PARTICIPATE |
| monks were enthusiastic (2) _____ of the game, but the Pope at the | PLAY |
| time strongly (3) _____ of it, and it was banned for being too | APPROVE |
| frivolous. The religious authorities, however, were (4) _____ to prevent | ABLE |
| the growing (5) _____ of the game and by the sixteenth century it had | SUCCEED |
| evolved into the sport of Real Tennis, which was played on an indoor court. | |
| The first tennis balls were filled with hair and small stones – a (6) _____ | PAIN |
| experience for anyone who was hit by one. (7) _____ , balls are now | LUCK |
| significantly (8) _____ , consisting of two half shells of rubber covered | LIGHT |
| with cloth. They are also more (9) _____ than before; bright yellow is a | COLOUR |
| lot (10) _____ to see on our TV screens than the traditional white. | EASY |

# Listening FCE Paper 4
## Part 2 Sentence completion

You will hear a woman talking on the radio about African dance classes. For questions **1–10**, complete the sentences.

In her first African dance class the speaker had to dance like [_____ **1** ] .

Throughout the class [_____ **2** ] is played.

You don't need to have good rhythm or [_____ **3** ] to enjoy the dance classes.

Unlike aerobics, in African dance you do not have to [_____ **4** ] of an instructor.

The age range of those who attend the classes is from [_____ **5** ] to pensioners.

In the last [_____ **6** ] of the class participants perform everything they have learnt.

Regular attendance at classes will improve [_____ **7** ] .

Correct positioning of the feet helps prevent your [_____ **8** ] from being injured.

Sixty minutes of African dance will burn off [_____ **9** ] calories.

This activity should lead to a dramatic increase in your [_____ **10** ] .

PHOTOCOPIABLE

© Macmillan Publishers Ltd.  This page may be photocopied and used within the class.

## Vocabulary

Decide which answer **A, B, C** or **D** best fits each space and underline it.

*Example:*

I wish you'd get _____ of these old books – you never read them any more.

**A** away     **B** out     **C** <u>rid</u>     **D** lost

---

1   _____ should not open their exam papers until told to do so by the invigilator.

   **A** Candidates     **B** Participants     **C** Competitors     **D** Takers

2   My mum's just knitted me a lovely _____ sweater.

   **A** high-heeled     **B** long-sleeved     **C** second-hand     **D** ankle-length

3   Most of the people in the _____ were friends or family of the actors and actresses.

   **A** public     **B** spectators     **C** audience     **D** viewers

4   By the time we _____ to the station the train had already left.

   **A** arrived     **B** reached     **C** got     **D** found

5   These jeans don't _____ me any more; they're too tight round the waist.

   **A** suit     **B** fit     **C** match     **D** go with

6   Do you mind if I _____ that track again? I really like it.

   **A** put     **B** listen     **C** play     **D** touch

7   Johnny Strummer's the _____ vocalist and the bass guitarist sings the backing vocals.

   **A** first     **B** front     **C** lead     **D** head

8   The hotel is situated next to an 18-hole golf _____ .

   **A** course     **B** court     **C** field     **D** pitch

9   Alan's never been very _____ on football.

   **A** fond     **B** interested     **C** enthusiastic     **D** keen

10  I couldn't _____ laughing when he fell in the pool with all his clothes on; it was so funny!

   **A** give up     **B** afford     **C** stand     **D** help

11  The sales assistants are so _____ ; they spend more time chatting to each other than serving customers.

   **A** helpless     **B** unhelpful     **C** helping     **D** helped

12  You can leave the vegetables but eat as _____ of the meat as you can.

   **A** much     **B** more     **C** most     **D** many

13  The device is conveniently small, but _____ it isn't particularly easy to use.

   **A** on the contrary     **B** on the other side     **C** on the other hand     **D** in addition

14  My brother's _____ taller than me.

   **A** bit     **B** slightly     **C** more     **D** something

15  Take your umbrella, just in case – it's better to be _____ than sorry.

   **A** sure     **B** secure     **C** safe     **D** sound

© **Macmillan Publishers Ltd. This page may be photocopied and used within the class.**

PHOTOCOPIABLE

# Writing FCE Paper 2
## Part 1 Email

You are interested in going to a tennis school in England in summer and you have seen this advertisement in an international magazine. Read the advertisement and the notes you have made. Then write an email to the John Taylor Tennis School using **all** your notes.

Write your answer in **120–150** words in an appropriate style.

---

For professional tennis coaching
in a perfect setting, come to the

# JOHN TAYLOR
# TENNIS SCHOOL

**Our one-week courses run this year from
April 4th to September 16th.**

All coaching takes place between 9 and 1 o'clock
each day on the finest quality grass courts.

Individual and <u>group</u> coaching sessions available.
Accommodation in single or double rooms.

*For further details contact:*
**Robin.Connor@jtts.co.uk**

*ask about costs
– cheaper in
September?*

*what about the
afternoon?*

*and if it rains … ?*

*more information
please. Important
because …*

Write your **email**. You must use grammatically correct spelling and punctuation in a style appropriate for the situation.

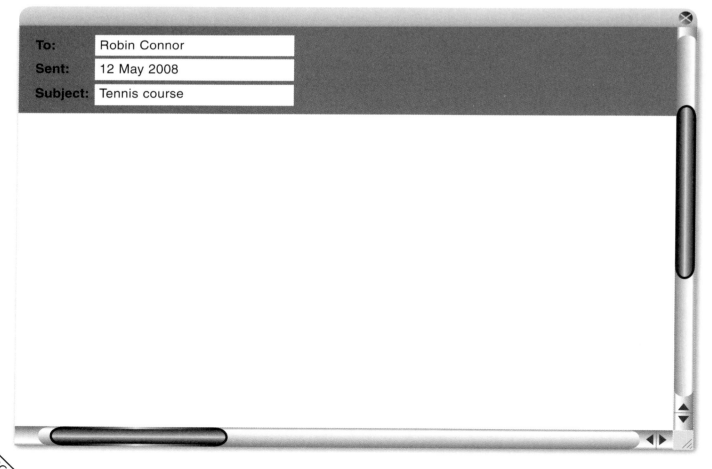

| To: | Robin Connor |
|---|---|
| **Sent:** | 12 May 2008 |
| **Subject:** | Tennis course |

© Macmillan Publishers Ltd. This page may be photocopied and used within the class.

PHOTOCOPIABLE

# Progress test 2: Units 4–6

## Reading FCE Paper 1
### Part 2 Gapped text

You are going to read a newspaper article about a trainee male nanny. Seven sentences have been removed from the article. Choose from the sentences **A–H** the one which fits each gap **(1–7)**. There is one extra sentence which you do not need to use.

## Male enters the home of nannies

Norland College, which has turned out the cream of the world's nannies since 1892, has admitted its first male student, 22-year-old Katsuki Yuzawa. Mr Yuzawa, who has experience of child care at a nursery run by his parents in Tochigi in Japan, will take a one-year International Diploma course.

'I am here because I like children and I like this job taking care of them,' he says. 'I enjoy their company.' Mr Yuzawa applied for the place at the college in Hungerford, Berkshire after his mother visited it during a tour of training colleges in England.

Norland nannies are among the most highly prized in the world, earning salaries of over £250 a week plus perks such as their own accommodation and car. **1** [ ] The nannies' main employers nowadays are pop stars, celebrities and rich professional couples.

**2** [ ] 'Our nurseries are different because we have sand outside for the children, not grass, and when we enter the room, we take off our shoes and put on our slippers,' he explains. 'We don't have harnesses to keep hold of the children. We put them in a big pushchair.'

**3** [ ] The college has its own purpose-built nursery school, where working parents leave their children aged two months to eight years for £50 a night while they are away on business or holiday. The students spend one week working in the nursery school and the next in lessons. **4** [ ]

Mr Yuzawa spends most of his time at the college, but travels to a local primary school once a week where the children help him with his English. He took a course at Richmond College to learn English before applying to the nanny college. After graduating he plans to return to Japan to use his Norland training at his parents' nursery.

Louise Davis, principal of the college, said an equal opportunities policy had been in place since 1992, but only one male applicant had approached Norland since then. **5** [ ]

'We look for exactly the same in a man as we do in a woman. **6** [ ] We would very much like to have more male applicants. Mothers on their own sometimes feel it is good for children not to have an all-female environment.'

**7** [ ] They wear Norland regulation brown dresses, supplied exclusively by Harrods. He wears a blazer, tie and grey trousers.

---

**A**  As well as receiving a broad training in childcare, Norlanders are taught cookery skills and a number of traditional crafts such as knitting and toy making.

**B**  Under a new scheme, less well-off students pay only half of the £25,000 fees for a two-year residential course.

**C**  Practical experience is one of the main features of the course at Norland.

**D**  They are traditionally employed by royalty and wealthy families, and often travel the world, staying in exotic resorts to look after children of the holidaying rich.

**E**  Being a male is not the only thing which makes Mr Yuzawa different from the 80 other students.

**F**  All our nannies must have a liking for children, an interest in their development and education, a good sense of humour and a good education.

**G**  In Japan, where male nannies are more common, the theory of child care is much the same, says Mr Yuzawa, though there are practical differences.

**H**  'The only reason he was not accepted was because he did not satisfy the selection requirements,' she said.

© Macmillan Publishers Ltd. This page may be photocopied and used within the class.

# Use of English FCE Paper 3

## Part 1 Multiple-choice cloze

For questions **1–12**, read the text below and decide which answer (**A, B, C** or **D**) best fits each gap. There is an example at the beginning (**0**).

*Example:*

**0**   **A** rose          **B** gave          **C** <u>came</u>          **D** took

## A wedding consultant

The idea for the business **(0)** _____ to me when I was preparing for my own wedding in the **(1)**_____ 1990s. At the time I was doing a **(2)** _____ in business studies at university and I had **(3)** _____ difficulty concentrating on both things at once.

Almost immediately after graduating I borrowed some money from the bank and **(4)** _____ up the wedding consultancy.  My work **(5)** _____ organizing everything from pre-wedding stag and hen parties to the booking of venues, caterers, photographers and cars. Some **(6)** _____ have neither the time nor the inclination to make any of the necessary arrangements for their wedding and they ask me to take **(7)** _____ of absolutely everything. For many clients I **(8)** _____ the role of big sister, guiding them through the whole process, giving advice on different aspects of the wedding and reassuring them that everything is under control.

I can be working on as **(9)** _____ as five weddings at the same time, and as each big day approaches I need to work very long **(10)** _____ to ensure things go smoothly.  Naturally, everyone wants their wedding to be special and nearly all want something **(11)** _____. I've organized weddings in monasteries, weddings in castles and even weddings on boats or trains. Making people's dreams come true is a wonderful way to **(12)** _____ a living.

| | | | | |
|---|---|---|---|---|
| 1 | **A** first | **B** beginning | **C** soon | **D** early |
| 2 | **A** career | **B** title | **C** degree | **D** study |
| 3 | **A** considerable | **B** large | **C** grand | **D** important |
| 4 | **A** got | **B** set | **C** made | **D** formed |
| 5 | **A** involves | **B** consists | **C** pretends | **D** contains |
| 6 | **A** pairs | **B** partnerships | **C** couples | **D** doubles |
| 7 | **A** mind | **B** attention | **C** care | **D** guard |
| 8 | **A** do | **B** make | **C** play | **D** give |
| 9 | **A** many | **B** several | **C** various | **D** numerous |
| 10 | **A** time | **B** day | **C** turns | **D** hours |
| 11 | **A** unique | **B** single | **C** unlike | **D** only |
| 12 | **A** win | **B** take | **C** do | **D** earn |

PHOTOCOPIABLE

© Macmillan Publishers Ltd.  This page may be photocopied and used within the class.

## Part 4 Transformations

For questions **1–8**, complete the second sentence so that it has a similar meaning to the first sentence, using the word given. **Do not change the word given**. You must use between two and five words, including the word given.

Here is an example **(0)**.

*Example:*

**0**  It was such a good book, I couldn't put it down.

  **so**

  The _book was so good (that)_ I couldn't put it down.

---

**1**  Shall I look after your cats while you're away on holiday?

  **care**

  Would you like _____ your cats while you're away on holiday?

**2**  You didn't have to come on this trip.

  **made**

  Nobody _____ on this trip.

**3**  You shouldn't go to bed late tonight – tomorrow's going to be a busy day.

  **better**

  You _____ early tonight – tomorrow's going to be a busy day.

**4**  I can't work because there's too much noise.

  **me**

  It's _____ work.

**5**  They are installing central heating in our flat next week.

  **installed**

  We _____ in our flat next week.

**6**  You can't see that film because you're still too young.

  **enough**

  You're _____ that film yet.

**7**  I was so frightened by the film, I had to cover my eyes and ears!

  **such**

  It _____ that I had to cover my eyes and ears!

**8**  I wasn't very interested in what he was doing.

  **take**

  I _____ in what he was doing.

© Macmillan Publishers Ltd.  This page may be photocopied and used within the class.

## Part 2 Open cloze

For questions **1–12**, read the text below and think of the word which best fits each gap. Use only **one** word in each gap. There is an example at the beginning (**0**).

## The double life of Stephen King

Stephen King is one of the (**0**) _most_ successful and popular authors in history. He has sold hundreds of millions of books. More (**1**) _____ 75 of his novels and stories have been (**2**) _____ into TV programmes or blockbuster films (**3**) _____ *The Shawshank Redemption*, *Dreamcatcher* and *The Green Mile*. No one knows how much he has earned from his writing, but as long (**4**) _____ as 1989 King was paid $35 million for four books by his publisher Viking. In many respects he is the definition of the successful writer. But even this publishing phenomenon has seemed unsure (**5**) _____ his own abilities, describing (**6**) _____ as 'the literary equivalent of a Big Mac and Fries'.

Interestingly, although his early novels had been well received, King then decided (**7**) _____ write several books under the invented name Richard Bachman. It seems he wanted to see if his books (**8**) _____ still sell without his famous name. For many years King kept up the pretence (**9**) _____ Bachman was a real author and even produced a detailed biography of his life. Eventually a bookshop assistant discovered (**10**) _____ truth, and King staged the death of Bachman in 1985.

In a final twist, King's novel *Blaze*, released (**11**) _____ June 2007, was published under Bachman's name. King claims to (**12**) _____ discovered the manuscript in an attic. In reality it is an early Stephen King story rewritten for his many millions of loyal fans.

## Vocabulary

For each of the definitions **1–12**, write an adjective beginning with the letters given. You should write one letter for each space. There is an example at the beginning (**0**).

Example:

**0**  a m _u_ _s_ _i_ _n_ _g_                          a person or story which makes you laugh or smile

**1**  a s _ _ _ _ _ _ _ _ _ _                  something, such as a piece of news, which is very surprising

**2**  b _ _ - t _ _ _ _ _ _ _              someone who is not cheerful and often gets angry

**3**  c h _ _ _ _ _ _ _ _ _ _            a job which is difficult, but in an interesting and enjoyable way

**4**  d i _ _ _ _ _ _ _ _ _ _ _ _        a book or film which is not as good as you expected it to be

**5**  e x _ _ _ _ _ _ _ _                      a person who is extremely tired

**6**  f l _ _ _ _ _ _                              hair which is long and hangs freely

**7**  i r _ _ _ _ _ _ _ _                        someone who is annoyed

**8**  m o _ _ _ _ _ _ _ _ _ _            a job which is boring and always the same

**9**  r e _ _ _ _ _ _ _ _                        a person you can trust and depend on

**10**  t e _ _ _ _ _ _ _ _ _ _          a film which makes you feel very frightened

**11**  u n _ _ _ _ _ _ _ _ _            someone or something that's not very nice

**12**  w r _ _ _ _ _ _ _                      skin which is old and has many lines in it

© Macmillan Publishers Ltd.  This page may be photocopied and used within the class.

PHOTOCOPIABLE

# Listening FCE Paper 4
## Part 1 Multiple choice

You will hear people talking in eight different situations. For questions **1–8**, choose the best answer, **A**, **B** or **C**.

1   Listen to this man talking about a
    film he has just seen.
    What does he say about the film?

    **A**  It was better than he expected.

    **B**  It was quite short.

    **C**  It was too serious.

2   You hear a woman talking to a man
    about her holiday.
    What is the woman going to do?

    **A**  go somewhere by herself

    **B**  go back to the same place as last year

    **C**  go somewhere with her friends

3   You hear this woman talking to a friend.
    What is she describing?

    **A**  a vacuum cleaner

    **B**  a television

    **C**  a microwave oven

4   At the end of a football match you hear
    two people talking.
    What did the man feel about the match?

    **A**  He was annoyed.

    **B**  He was bored.

    **C**  He was impressed.

5   You hear this man talking on his mobile
    phone at the airport.
    Who is he talking to?

    **A**  his boss

    **B**  his father

    **C**  his brother

6   You hear a woman talking to her husband
    about some concert tickets.
    What is she doing?

    **A**  complaining to him

    **B**  suggesting something

    **C**  explaining something

7   You hear this teenager talking about
    his homework.
    What problem did he have?

    **A**  He found it too difficult.

    **B**  He took the wrong books home.

    **C**  He did the wrong exercise.

8   You hear a woman talking to a man.
    Who is she?

    **A**  an interview candidate

    **B**  an interviewer

    **C**  a secretary

© Macmillan Publishers Ltd.  This page may be photocopied and used within the class.

PHOTOCOPIABLE

# Writing FCE Paper 2

## Part 2

Write an answer to **one** of the questions **1–3** in this part. Write your answer in **120–180** words in an appropriate style.

---

1 You have decided to enter a short story competition. The competition rules say that the story must begin with the following words:

*I'll always remember the first time I …*

Write your **story** for the competition.

2 You see this notice in an international magazine for young people.

> ## TRUE FRIENDSHIP
>
> We are looking for articles on the following question:
>
> ### What makes a good friend?
>
> Write an article telling our readers what you think the qualities of a true friend are.
>
> The best article will be published in our magazine.

Write your **article** for the magazine.

3 Last weekend you saw a film at the cinema which you enjoyed very much. Write a letter to your penfriend telling him or her about the film and saying why you liked it so much.

Write your **letter**. Do not write any postal addresses.

---

### Notes/Plan

---

PHOTOCOPIABLE

© Macmillan Publishers Ltd. This page may be photocopied and used within the class.

# Progress test 3: Units 7–9

## Reading FCE Paper 1

### Part 1 Multiple choice

You are going to read an article about the Lost City of Atlantis. For questions **1–8**, choose the answer (**A**, **B**, **C** or **D**) which you think fits best according to the text.

# The Search For Atlantis

The location of the Lost City of Atlantis is a mystery which has puzzled humanity for thousands of years. Since Plato first told the story of this fabulous island city more than 2,000 years ago, historians and archaeologists have continually debated whether or not the story was true and where the island may have been located. In recent years an international investigation team began searching waters off the south coast of Spain in an attempt to establish once and for all the true location of Atlantis.

The story of Atlantis begins in 360 BC, when Plato wrote two short works, *Critias* and *Timaeus* which mentioned a great civilisation based on an island in the Atlantic. In Plato's account, a large number of people lived on this huge island which he called Atlantis, and they developed an almost perfect society. They built a wonderful city surrounded by circular canals and protected at each entrance by huge gates and towers. After fighting wars against Europe and North Africa, the Atlanteans were eventually defeated. Some time later, according to Plato, 'there occurred violent earthquakes and floods; and in a single day and night the island of Atlantis disappeared in the depths of the sea.'

This may seem an unlikely tale, but many people believe even today, that while Plato undoubtedly invented some of the story, parts of it are based on historical fact. And like all the best stories, it has been retold many times in different forms. A number of other ancient historians described similar island civilisations and the tale of Atlantis was passed down through generations, although it then appears to have been largely forgotten for many years. However, in the late nineteenth century there was a huge resurgence of interest in Atlantis, particularly after the American writer Ignatius Donnely wrote a book suggesting that all the major ancient civilisations were influenced by the Atlantean Empire.

This controversial work inspired many different theories in the years that followed, including one that suggested that Atlantis was an island located in the Caribbean whose inhabitants used fantastical ships and even aircraft. Edgar Cayce, who developed this theory, also suggested that parts of Atlantis would rise from the sea in 1968 or 1969. As if to confirm his theory, a major underwater geological formation was in fact discovered in the Caribbean in 1968. Some people believe this to be the true location of Atlantis and it is still being explored today.

In trying to locate Atlantis, historians have often given close consideration to one particular issue. Plato described the destruction of the island as taking place 9,000 years before his time, in other words roughly 11,000 years ago. However, modern archaeologists and historians do not believe that highly developed civilisations existed so long ago.

Some people believe that Plato may have mistaken his dates and was actually describing events that happened 900, not 9,000, years before his time. This would mean that Atlantis disappeared around the same time that the Greek island of Thera, now known as Santorini, was partially destroyed by a volcanic eruption. So perhaps Atlantis is Santorini? There is some evidence of a well-developed ancient society on this island, but as yet no proof that it is the same place that Plato referred to as Atlantis.

If we assume that Plato didn't get his dates wrong, and that other details of his story are factually accurate, then Atlantis must be located somewhere in the Atlantic. But the Atlantic is, of course, a vast ocean, and where do we begin to look? Plato also referred to the Pillars of Hercules in his story and said that Atlantis was 'in front of the straits'. Many historians now believe that these Pillars are in fact the Straits of Gibraltar, in the western Mediterranean.

A number of islands, such as the Azores and the Canaries have been suggested as possible locations. The most recent expeditions have focused on a mud bank submerged beneath the sea, known as Spartel Island. But still no absolute proof has been found. Despite all of our modern technology and scientific knowledge, Atlantis stubbornly continues to remain one of the great unsolved mysteries of human civilisation.

© Macmillan Publishers Ltd. This page may be photocopied and used within the class.

PHOTOCOPIABLE

1   The story of the Lost City of Atlantis

    **A** was first told by an archaeologist.

    **B** is set on an island near Spain.

    **C** has led to some disagreement.

    **D** was in Plato's first book.

2   According to Plato, the Atlanteans

    **A** lived in large buildings.

    **B** built city defences.

    **C** kept detailed records.

    **D** lost many battles.

3   According to the text, why are there many different versions of the story of Atlantis?

    **A** because it's such a good story

    **B** because historians can't agree

    **C** because it was forgotten for so long

    **D** because Plato made up the story

4   What did Edgar Cayce believe?

    **A** Atlantis wasn't a true story.

    **B** Aircraft were used a very long time ago.

    **C** Atlanteans couldn't have used ships.

    **D** The sea level would rise in the 1960s.

5   Why do some people say that Plato's dates were wrong?

    **A** because he was not an archaeologist

    **B** because he failed to consider one important issue

    **C** because he used a different numbering system from ours

    **D** because complex societies are thought to have developed later

6   What do we learn about Santorini?

    **A** An ancient civilization lived there.

    **B** Part of the island collapsed into the sea.

    **C** The people of Thera destroyed it.

    **D** Plato lived there when he wrote about Atlantis.

7   What is the belief of some modern historians?

    **A** The Pillars of Hercules are in the middle of the Atlantic.

    **B** Atlantis cannot be found in such a large ocean.

    **C** Plato's story is completely inaccurate.

    **D** Atlantis may be located near the Straits of Gibraltar.

8   Where was the latest search for Atlantis carried out?

    **A** on an underwater island

    **B** in the Azores

    **C** in the Canaries

    **D** at a number of different locations

PHOTOCOPIABLE

**188**

# Use of English FCE Paper 3
## Part 2 Open cloze

For questions **1–12**, read the text below and think of the word which best fits each space. Use only **one** word in each space. There is an example at the beginning **(0)**.

### Noise pollution

Studies carried **(0)** _out_ in Britain recently **(1)** _____ shown that day-to-day noise levels can have a serious effect **(2)** _____health and well-being.

The main source of noise-related problems comes **(3)** _____ neighbours: shouting, television, playing musical instruments and noisy parties are among the **(4)** _____ common complaints to police and local authorities. In many cases, once a complaint has been **(5)** _____, the complainant is asked to keep a diary, in **(6)** _____ they note down the times excessive noise is made, the type of noise it is, as **(7)** _____ as a comment about the volume. Health officers will then be sent **(8)** _____ measure the noise level and if the local Department of Environmental Health feels the complaint is justified, they will make certain recommendations. **(9)** _____ may include a total ban on noise between 11 pm and 7 am or a limit as to the number of parties the noisy neighbours can give **(10)** _____ year.

Although this usually goes some way to satisfying those people who have **(11)** _____ to suffer excessive noise, for a few it is much **(12)** _____ late: depression, nervous disorders and even divorce have all been blamed on the stress caused by noisy neighbours.

## Part 3 Word formation

Use the word given in capitals at the end of each line to form a word that fits in the space in the same line. There is an example at the beginning **(0)**.

### Exploration

In 1979 the **(0)** _explorer_ Sir Ranulph Fiennes entered an area of Antarctica | **EXPLORE**
**(1)** _____ than Great Britain where no human being had set foot before. | **BIG**
'It was an **(2)** _____ experience,' he says, 'knowing that we were | **EXCITE**
mapping the area for the first time. Now, of course, satellites can do the same job
far more **(3)** _____ .' Technology, it seems, and the growth in adventure | **EASY**
tourism, may soon see the end of **(4)** _____ exploration, as fewer and | **TRADITION**
fewer human challenges remain. There are now **(5)** _____ expeditions | **NUMBER**
every year to places like Everest, where keen but **(6)** _____ climbers | **EXPERIENCE**
are virtually pulled up the mountain by their guides. **(7)** _____ , the | **FORTUNATE**
increase in this new trend of tourism is **(8)** _____ the natural beauty of | **THREAT**
even the remotest parts of the globe, as **(9)** _____ and other adventurers | **MOUNTAIN**
leave **(10)** _____ of their visit in the form of oxygen bottles and other rubbish. | **EVIDENT**

© Macmillan Publishers Ltd. This page may be photocopied and used within the class.

PHOTOCOPIABLE

## Part 4 Transformations

For questions **1–8**, complete the second sentence so that it has a similar meaning to the first sentence, using the word given. **Do not change the word given.** You must use between two and five words, including the word given.

Here is an example (**0**).

*Example:*

**0**  I've never seen her before today.

    **time**

    This *is the first time* I have seen her.

---

**1**  I started living here when I got married.

    **since**

    I _____ I got married.

**2**  I haven't been to the beach for nine months.

    **last**

    It's nine _____ to the beach.

**3**  I don't mind cooking food but eating it is better.

    **prefer**

    I _____ it.

**4**  We'd prefer to go to the cinema rather than the theatre.

    **rather**

    We _____ cinema than the theatre.

**5**  Despite our late arrival we managed to catch the plane.

    **we**

    Although _____ , we managed to catch the plane.

**6**  She told him the truth, although I had told her not to.

    **despite**

    She told him the truth _____ not to.

**7**  I think she's about to end our relationship.

    **point**

    I think she's _____ up with me.

**8**  I'm certain he didn't use the car because his sister had the keys.

    **used**

    He _____ the car because his sister had the keys.

**90**

© Macmillan Publishers Ltd.  This page may be photocopied and used within the class.

# Listening FCE Paper 4
## Part 4 Multiple choice

You will hear two people being interviewed on the radio about Home Exchange holidays. For questions **1–7**, choose the best answer (**A, B** or **C**).

**1** Brian says that people on a Home Exchange holiday

   A can take their pets with them.

   B do not have to pay any bills.

   C can drive each other's car.

**2** One way Brian found out what his exchange family was like was by

   A speaking to them on the phone.

   B asking people who knew them.

   C arranging to meet them.

**3** Susie says her exchange partners

   A did not get on with her neighbours.

   B had access to help if they needed it.

   C got to know many local people.

**4** Susie says the children who stayed in her house

   A were not very well behaved.

   B were not to blame for a breakage.

   C stole something from her house.

**5** Brian says that his exchange partners

   A owned a small house in Los Angeles.

   B did not do any cleaning in his house.

   C were very pleased with the house swap.

**6** Why didn't Brian drive to Mexico?

   A The car did not have appropriate insurance.

   B He ran out of money during the holiday.

   C The car broke down on the way.

**7** Susie says that before she went to Australia

   A she contacted a number of agencies.

   B she had very little time to prepare her trip.

   C she was able to see what the house looked like.

## Vocabulary

Complete each of the gaps with the correct form of one of the verbs from the box.

| give | take | make | put | look | get | come | have |
|------|------|------|-----|------|-----|------|------|

**1** I've always _____ up to Greg because of his enthusiasm and ability to motivate others.

**2** He _____ after his Aunt Agnes; she was just as bad-tempered and intolerant as he is.

**3** The car workers were on strike for three months before management _____ in and agreed to give them a pay rise.

**4** The food on holiday was wonderful, but it didn't _____ up for the terrible weather we had.

**5** I'm not _____ up with your rudeness any more. Go to bed – now!

**6** I was cleaning out the wardrobe yesterday when I _____ across my old school tie.

**7** I think I might be _____ down with flu; several people in my class have already had it.

**8** Jill isn't really interested in boys at the moment. She still hasn't _____ over her break-up with Allan last year.

**9** 'Jensens have announced plans to _____ on 900 new workers at their Walton factory.'

**10** This cheese is _____ off a strange smell. How long has it been in the fridge?

**11** This may _____ as a bit of a shock to you, but Celia and I have decided to get married.

**12** Thomas Cook _____ an enormous influence on travel and tourism in the 19th century.

**13** Before the Olympics he had only _____ part in two other marathons.

**14** In his latest film Perham _____ an impressive performance as an out-of-work gardener.

**15** We're thinking of _____ rid of this old carpet and buying a new one.

© Macmillan Publishers Ltd. This page may be photocopied and used within the class.

PHOTOCOPIABLE

# Writing FCE Paper 2
## Part 1 Letter

You recently wrote to a friend accepting an invitation to go on holiday with her and two other friends during the summer. Read the extract from her reply and the two advertisements, on which you have made some notes. Then write a letter to your friend, using **all** your notes.

Write your **letter** in **120-150 words**. Do not write any postal addresses.

---

Paul, Sue and myself will probably drive down to the coast as we can share the cost of petrol and save money. How will you get there?

*Coach — meet me at the bus station?*

We haven't worked out yet where we're going to stay, so I've sent you a couple of ads for a campsite and a hotel to see what you think.

Write back soon and let me know if you have any questions.

All the best
Lisa

## BELVEDERE CAMPSITE

**Four-star comfort on the coast
only 3 km from the beach**

*a bit far!*

*shop?*

*Facilities include:*

Bar and restaurant

Swimming pool

Children's playground

Barbecue area

Capacity: 320 people

## HOTEL MAR

**a 2-star hotel close to the sea**

single rooms from £75 a night

*expensive!*

sea views

en suite bathrooms

quality fish restaurant

private garden & tennis courts

car park for guests

Tel: 01273 417939

PHOTOCOPIABLE

© Macmillan Publishers Ltd. This page may be photocopied and used within the class.

# Progress test 4: Units 10–12

## Reading FCE Paper 1
### Part 2 Gapped text

You are going to read an article about hygiene and health. Seven sentences have been removed from the article. Choose from the sentences **A–H** the one which fits each gap (1–7). There is one extra sentence which you do not need to use.

## Too clean for our own good?

It's a common and natural assumption that germs and bacteria are bad for us. Cleanliness and good hygiene practices are generally thought to be essential to good health. However, research is beginning to show that we may actually be too clean for our own good.

**1** | We wrap food in Cellophane, treat kitchen equipment with antibacterial products, spray bathrooms with disinfectants and spend only 5% of our time in the dangerous, germ-filled environment outside of the house.

There is good reason for these fastidious habits. **2** | Before we perfected these techniques, conditions such as cholera were killers in the West, and still are in countries without the resources to build protection.

But recent scientific research suggests that there may be a price to pay for safe Western lifestyles. **3** | Not only that, but some of our hygiene habits may be creating problems for the future, causing bacteria to become resistant to our efforts to destroy them. Scientists believe that by limiting the number of germs that children come into contact with, we could also be limiting their ability to build up natural immunity.

The increase in the number of different allergies such as asthma over the past 100 years may be evidence of this. **4** | Furthermore, it was restricted to those people who were rich enough to be able to live hygienically. It now affects one in three people in the UK, while allergies remain rare in less developed countries.

The idea that children need to be exposed to germs early in their lives to develop resistance to bacteria has been supported by three separate studies in Europe. **5** | It would appear that frequent contact with animals leads to frequent contact with bacteria, and this builds up protection against allergy.

So have we gone too far with hygiene? Should we leave our kitchens dirty? **6** | Making a conscious effort to expose ourselves to more germs would be full of dangers, according to microbiologist Professor Tom Humphrey. 'It may be true that a little bit of dirt is good for you, but only as long as you can control the type of dirt it is, and that's very difficult,' he says.

He recommends sensible hygiene routines, which do not always involve spraying antibacterial products. **7** | 'After you have done the chicken, for example, you may need to use a basic antibacterial product to clean work surfaces.'

**A** They have all shown that children brought up on farms containing animals have 60% fewer allergies than those raised in non-farming environments.

**B** Public health experts are in no doubt as to the answer.

**C** Man is the only creature on earth to wash its hands before meals.

**D** Unlike animals, man is able to develop ways to protect himself from the hostile elements of the natural world.

**E** Most germs can be killed with hot water and detergent, although something a little stronger may be necessary after preparing raw meat.

**F** Hay fever was rare when it was first described in 1819.

**G** They go on to recommend a number of products, which, with proper use, prevent the spread of bacterial infection.

**H** In our obsession with cleanliness we have become less capable of fighting germs.

© Macmillan Publishers Ltd. This page may be photocopied and used within the class.

# Use of English FCE Paper 3

## Part 4 Transformations

For questions **1–8**, complete the second sentence so that it has a similar meaning to the first sentence, using the word given. **Do not change the word given**. You must use between two and five words, including the word given.

Here is an example **(0)**.

*Example:*

  **0**   Someone is meeting her at the airport.

     **is**

     She *is being met* at the airport.

---

  **1**   Someone has vandalized all the phone boxes in our street.

     **vandalized**

     All the phone boxes _____ in our street.

  **2**   My grandfather gave me this watch.

     **by**

     I _____ my grandfather.

  **3**   They do not think his condition is serious.

     **thought**

     His condition _____ serious.

  **4**   We can only go if you give us a lift.

     **unless**

     We _____ give us a lift.

  **5**   It's a good thing you reminded me about the programme or I would have missed it.

     **if**

     I would have missed the programme _____ me about it.

  **6**   'I'm going away next weekend,' she said.

     **following**

     She said she _____ weekend.

  **7**   'Have you been smoking again?' he asked his daughter.

     **had**

     He asked his daughter _____ again.

  **8**   He has made very little progress this year.

     **not**

     He _____ progress this year.

PHOTOCOPIABLE

© Macmillan Publishers Ltd.  This page may be photocopied and used within the class.

## Part 1 Multiple-choice cloze

For questions **1–12**, read the text below and decide which answer (**A**, **B**, **C** or **D**) best fits each gap. There is an example at the beginning (0).

*Example:*

**0**   **A** <u>come</u>          **B** gone          **C** been          **D** brought

---

# Life in the age of the virtual burglar

We have entered an age of high-tech communication, and with it has **(0)** _____ a whole new wave of previously unimagined high-tech crime. Gregory Straszkiewicz, 24, **(1)** _____ became the first person in the UK to be found guilty of stealing **(2)** _____ else's wireless broadband connection.

This crime has highlighted a new threat to householders. Wireless broadband **(3)** _____ out a signal from a box somewhere in the house so that a computer can be **(4)** _____ to access the internet from anywhere within the house. But of course, the signal doesn't simply stop when it **(5)** _____ the outside wall of the house. It may in fact travel **(6)** _____ metres beyond the house. We generally **(7)** _____ our windows and lock our doors to protect our possessions from theft, but how do we prevent somebody from stealing an electronic signal which has escaped **(8)** _____ the wall?

As well as using your broadband, it might also be possible for these 'virtual burglars' to access private **(9)** _____ stored on your computer. Police suggest two simple **(10)** _____ to avoid becoming a victim of this type of crime: set up a password to access the broadband, and **(11)** _____ your wireless box in the centre of the house, not **(12)** _____ an outside wall.

|    |               |               |               |                |
|----|---------------|---------------|---------------|----------------|
| 1  | **A** newly     | **B** freshly   | **C** lately    | **D** recently   |
| 2  | **A** anyone    | **B** someone   | **C** no one    | **D** one        |
| 3  | **A** makes     | **B** comes     | **C** sends     | **D** moves      |
| 4  | **A** made      | **B** handled   | **C** used      | **D** achieved   |
| 5  | **A** reaches   | **B** gets      | **C** arrives   | **D** goes       |
| 6  | **A** few       | **B** several   | **C** various   | **D** plenty     |
| 7  | **A** finish    | **B** join      | **C** fix       | **D** close      |
| 8  | **A** in        | **B** through   | **C** along     | **D** for        |
| 9  | **A** knowledge | **B** news      | **C** record    | **D** information |
| 10 | **A** means     | **B** roads     | **C** ways      | **D** arrangements |
| 11 | **A** place     | **B** decide    | **C** find      | **D** work       |
| 12 | **A** close     | **B** around    | **C** near      | **D** within     |

© Macmillan Publishers Ltd.  This page may be photocopied and used within the class.

## Part 3 Word formation

For questions **1-10**, read the text below. Use the word given in capitals at the end of some of the lines to form a word that fits in the gap **in the same line**. There is an example at the beginning **(0)**.

### Wildlife in danger

One of the major **(0)** _environmental_ concerns in today's world is                     **ENVIRONMENT**

the growing list of **(1)** _____ plants, birds and animals. The        **DANGER**

**(2)** _____ threat of all to wildlife is, of course, Man, who must    **BIG**

take action now to prevent the **(3)** _____ of these species.          **APPEAR**

Whales, tigers and elephants all require greater **(4)** _____ ,        **PROTECT**

as **(5)** _____ threaten to drive them to extinction. Similarly,       **HUNT**

more **(6)** _____ measures are required to stop global warming,        **EFFECT**

which has led to the loss of important **(7)** _____ habitats. Fish     **NATURE**

too, are **(8)** _____ at risk from high levels of river and sea        **INCREASE**

**(9)** _____ , caused by oil spills and toxic effluent. Stricter       **POLLUTE**

government controls will help in the fight to save our wildlife, but so

too will a greater public **(10)** _____ of the issues involved.        **AWARE**

# Listening FCE Paper 4

## Part 3 Multiple matching

You will hear five different people talking about experiences with weather. Choose from the list **A–F** what each speaker says about their experience. Use the letters only once. There is an extra letter which you do not need to use.

**A**   The weather made me ill.

Speaker 1 [        ]

**B**   The weather stopped me from working.

Speaker 2 [        ]

**C**   The weather was unusual for the time of year.

Speaker 3 [        ]

**D**   I wanted the weather to change.

Speaker 4 [        ]

**E**   The weather kept changing all the time.

Speaker 5 [        ]

**F**   The weather ruined our holiday.

PHOTOCOPIABLE

© Macmillan Publishers Ltd.  This page may be photocopied and used within the class.

# Vocabulary

Decide which answer **A, B, C** or **D** best fits each gap and underline it.

***Example:***

The _____ ordered the pilot of the plane to fly to Venezuela.

**A** mugger      **B** kidnapper     **C** hijacker      **D** blackmailer

---

1  Jewellery worth over £1 million was _____ from a house in Wimbledon last night.
   **A** robbed        **B** burgled        **C** stolen        **D** mugged

2  Because it was the first time he'd been in trouble with the police, he was let _____ with a warning.
   **A** down        **B** off        **C** out        **D** away

3  The whole class will stay here until the person who broke the chair _____ up.
   **A** admits        **B** confesses        **C** tells        **D** owns

4  You'll need to put more effort _____ your work if you want to pass the exam.
   **A** on        **B** into        **C** through        **D** at

5  Tomorrow we can expect to see an end to the _____ rain in the region, but it will remain cloudy.
   **A** heavy        **B** hard        **C** strong        **D** rough

6  There will also be _____ to moderate winds blowing from the north.
   **A** light        **B** fine        **C** thin        **D** calm

7  Sea levels are expected to _____ considerably in the next few decades.
   **A** lift        **B** raise        **C** arise        **D** rise

8  I was wondering if you could _____ me up at your place for the night.
   **A** give        **B** live        **C** put        **D** take

9  He put his own life at _____ in an attempt to save his dying friend.
   **A** danger        **B** threat        **C** hazard        **D** risk

10  Heavier fines should be imposed on those people who _____ litter.
   **A** drop        **B** dump        **C** throw        **D** waste

11  You only need to put a _____ of salt in the mixture, not a whole teaspoonful!
   **A** piece        **B** drop        **C** pinch        **D** little

12  He was _____ an injection in his arm.
   **A** put        **B** given        **C** had        **D** treated

13  You have very high blood _____ , Mr Woolgar.
   **A** tension        **B** infection        **C** pressure        **D** level

14  I've decided to go _____ a diet.
   **A** on        **B** to        **C** for        **D** by

15  He _____ me to do more exercise.
   **A** suggested        **B** offered        **C** recommended        **D** said

© Macmillan Publishers Ltd. This page may be photocopied and used within the class.

# Writing FCE Paper 2
## Part 2

Write an answer to **one** of the questions **1–3** in this part. Write your answers in **120–180** words in an appropriate style.

1   Each week your local English-language newspaper publishes an article on environmental issues. You have been asked to write an article on what is being done in your area to help the environment.

Write your **article**.

2   You have been doing a class project on healthy eating. Your teacher has asked you to write an essay giving your opinions on the following statement:

*There should be a strict limit to the number of fast food restaurants in each town.*

Write your **essay**.

3   You are studying English at a language school in Britain. Recently there have been a number of thefts in the school, both of students' possessions and school materials. You have been asked to write a report for the director of the school, giving details of the thefts and suggesting ways in which similar crimes can be prevented in the future.

Write your **report**.

### Notes/Plan

© Macmillan Publishers Ltd.  This page may be photocopied and used within the class.

PHOTOCOPIABLE

# Progress test 5: Units 13–15

## Reading FCE Paper 1

### Part 1 Multiple choice

You are going to read an article about an unusual artist. For questions 18, choose the answer (**A**, **B**, **C** or **D**) which you think fits best according to the text.

---

# What is art?

What is art? And what is an artist? These are common questions in the world of modern art, where a pile of bricks or a pool of oil can become works of art when they're placed in a gallery. Traditional sculpture, for example, refers to images, often of people, frequently made from stone or metal; but modern sculpture can be a very different thing. The British artist, Andy Goldsworthy makes sculptures in the open air out of sticks, stones, leaves and even ice.

Currently, Goldsworthy is setting up the largest exhibition he has ever produced in a special sculpture park in Yorkshire, in the north of England. The show features some important new and previously unseen works and some reworkings of sculptures he first created some years ago. Outdoors there are sculptures made from fallen oak trees, enclosed by neat stone walls. Inside there are enormous egg-shaped sculptures made from tree branches and a curtain made from more than 10,000 chestnut leaves pinned together.

The sculptures are designed for people to get close to them. They are quite unlike works of art in a traditional gallery, where the public are obliged to keep a respectful distance. Here people are encouraged to touch the sculptures, climb inside them, and even lie on them. For this particular artist, art is something very physical and one of the things he enjoys most is getting his hands dirty.

From the age of 13 Goldsworthy lived and worked on a farm, so he's no stranger to tough, and messy, outdoor work. He always wanted to be an artist, but the farm work had a significant effect on the type of art he chose to produce. The stone walls, the lines of the ploughed fields, huge bales of straw stacked high – all these shapes and textures figure prominently in his sculptures. And in everything he produces there is a close connection to the land and to nature.

In the 1970s, Goldsworthy left art college to make sculptures on a windswept sandy beach. He describes this as a new awakening: 'I splashed in water, covered myself in mud, went barefoot and woke with the dawn.' His early works involved arranging piles of stones into neat towers and bringing huge snowballs down to London from Scotland and letting them melt. In the years that followed he made sculptures from human hair and mud, from ice and sand, from practically anything he found.

The use of colour and light is an interesting feature of the artist's work. Rather than squeezing colours out of a tube, as a painter does, Goldsworthy collects his colours directly from the natural materials he finds around him. The effect can be very striking, as for example when he filled a rock pool with bright red leaves. In another case he built a three-kilometre path through a forest, using white limestone. During the day it looked quite ordinary, but at night under the moonlight it suddenly became brightly illuminated.

The choice of working tools is another area which makes Goldsworthy unusual. Whereas some sculptors use heavy machinery to work stone or metal, Goldsworthy mostly uses his bare hands, his teeth, or sometimes a stick that he finds lying nearby.

Perhaps the most distinctive feature of the work, and one which makes it quite unlike the work of traditional sculptors, is that it can be extremely temporary. Some pieces made from leaves or other soft materials last until they rot away, unless they are blown away first. Others made from frozen ice may only last for a few minutes. Often they are created wherever Goldsworthy finds the materials – out in a field, on a beach or up a mountain. The only lasting record of many of these works is the photographs he takes of them.

Art galleries have shown increasing interest in Goldsworthy's work, but most of his sculptures have been made specifically for the great outdoors. He has created artworks in places as varied as the Australian outback, the Northern Territories of Canada, New York, Japan and the North Pole. But for now he's come home to Yorkshire; back to the place where he grew up, a landscape he really deeply understands, and a place where his unique sculptures are truly at home.

© Macmillan Publishers Ltd. This page may be photocopied and used within the class.

1   According to the text, modern sculpture

    **A**   is often made from metal or stone.

    **B**   always uses natural materials like stones or leaves.

    **C**   is often nothing like traditional sculpture.

    **D**   is never found in an art gallery.

2   The exhibition in Yorkshire

    **A**   is a special outdoor event in a former park.

    **B**   includes items that have never been displayed before.

    **C**   features sculptures made from stone, cloth and food.

    **D**   is the largest ever shown in a sculpture park.

3   What is different about this type of exhibition?

    **A**   The public can talk to artists about their work.

    **B**   The public are encouraged to get their hands dirty.

    **C**   The public are allowed to handle the works of art.

    **D**   The public have to get close in order to see the sculptures.

4   How did working on a farm affect Goldsworthy later in life?

    **A**   He disliked the tough work and so he decided to become an artist.

    **B**   His art was influenced by the physical features of the landscape.

    **C**   He chose to produce a series of sculptures made from straw.

    **D**   The messy work made him realize he should take up painting.

5   How does Goldsworthy view the time he spent working on a beach?

    **A**   He didn't enjoy it because he got so wet and dirty.

    **B**   It was a new experience because he stayed awake all night.

    **C**   It wasn't a good idea to leave art college early.

    **D**   It was the start of something completely different in his life.

6   How does Goldsworthy work with colour and light?

    **A**   He gets all his colours out of a paint tube.

    **B**   He shines bright lights on the sculptures to illuminate them.

    **C**   He works with what nature provides.

    **D**   He avoids using bright colours like red or orange.

7   According to the writer, a very significant aspect of Goldsworthy's work is that

    **A**   it often doesn't last for a long time.

    **B**   it always gets blown away by the wind.

    **C**   it is made of ice and snow.

    **D**   it is preserved in the form of a photograph.

8   Why does the writer suggest that Goldsworthy's sculptures are 'truly at home' in Yorkshire?

    **A**   because the artist has brought the sculptures back to his home town

    **B**   because the artist has always lived and worked in Yorkshire

    **C**   because the sculptures have a strong connection with the environment of Yorkshire

    **D**   because the sculptures aren't suitable for exhibition in other countries

PHOTOCOPIABLE

© Macmillan Publishers Ltd.   This page may be photocopied and used within the class.

# Use of English FCE Paper 3
## Part 1 Multiple-choice cloze

For questions **1–12**, read the text below and decide which answer **A, B, C** or **D** best fits each gap. There is an example at the beginning (**0**).

***Example:***

**0**　**A** arise　　**B** rise　　**C** <u>arouse</u>　　**D** raise

## Fur clothes

The use of animal fur in the making of clothes will always (**0**) _____ strong feelings in people. Whilst some will (**1**) _____ admiringly at a fur coat in a shop window, others will grow angry at the thought of the animals which have (**2**) _____ so that it could be produced.

In many countries, animal rights campaigners have (**3**) _____ for a ban on the farming of animals for their fur, claiming that it is (**4**) _____ to breed and kill animals purely for fashion. They have also (**5**) _____ pressure on designers and (**6**) _____ to convince some not to use fur for their clothes.  They argue that the fashion industry can do (**7**) _____ fur, as artificial alternatives are equally warm and attractive.

Supporters of fur say that it is a matter of personal choice and people should be allowed to (**8**) _____ up their own minds about what they wear.  In addition, they point out that many people earn their (**9**) _____ from the fur trade and to ban it would cause thousands to become unemployed.

Some people, then, are prepared to (**10**) _____ a fortune for the latest trend, but it is the animals that are the real fashion victims. Even if some countries stop fur farming, international trade rules (**11**) _____ governments from banning the importing of clothes made from fur. So as (**12**) _____ as there is a demand for fur, animals will continue to be sacrificed.

| | | | | | | | |
|---|---|---|---|---|---|---|---|
| **1** | **A** glimpse | **B** gaze | **C** examine | **D** peer |
| **2** | **A** injured | **B** wounded | **C** hurt | **D** suffered |
| **3** | **A** demanded | **B** requested | **C** intended | **D** called |
| **4** | **A** severe | **B** violent | **C** cruel | **D** strong |
| **5** | **A** turned | **B** put | **C** given | **D** done |
| **6** | **A** arrived | **B** succeeded | **C** managed | **D** got |
| **7** | **A** away | **B** without | **C** off | **D** up |
| **8** | **A** make | **B** form | **C** decide | **D** give |
| **9** | **A** work | **B** job | **C** living | **D** life |
| **10** | **A** pay | **B** buy | **C** spend | **D** invest |
| **11** | **A** prevent | **B** avoid | **C** hold | **D** stay |
| **12** | **A** soon | **B** long | **C** well | **D** much |

© Macmillan Publishers Ltd.  This page may be photocopied and used within the class.

PHOTOCOPIABLE

## Part 2 Open cloze

For questions **1–12**, read the text below and think of the word which best fits each gap. Use only **one** word in each gap. There is an example at the beginning **(0)**.

### A new life in colour

All the time he was growing **(0)** __up__ , colour did not exist for Londoner Brian Langridge. Brian **(1)** _____ born with a very rare eye defect, affecting only one in a million people, which meant he **(2)** _____ only see things in black and white.

Then, **(3)** _____ the age of 21, he heard about some revolutionary new contact lenses developed by British scientists, and he decided to save **(4)** _____ the £600 needed to buy a pair. In **(5)** _____ to raise the money, Brian had to work overtime in his job at a local supermarket. But he was careful **(6)** _____ to build his hopes up too high. 'The opticians had always told me that nothing could be **(7)** _____ to help me because I was so severely colour blind,' says Brian. 'Consequently, I didn't get too excited about the lenses in **(8)** _____ they didn't work for me.'

He needn't **(9)** _____ worried, though: as soon as he put them on he began to see the world in all its colour. 'I had to get a friend to spend the first day with me **(10)** _____ that he could tell me which colours were which, because I had absolutely **(11)** _____ idea. It was just amazing.' Now, as a result of being **(12)** _____ to distinguish between different on-screen colours, Brian has begun a new career working with computers.

# Listening FCE Paper 4
## Part 2 Sentence completion

You will hear an interview with an Australian firefighter. For questions **1–10**, complete the sentences.

Frank Williams works in a [_____ **1** ] area of Victoria.

Bushfires are also known as [_____ **2** ] fires or wildfires.

Bushfires are particularly likely to occur in the [_____ *or* _____ **3** ] period.

There are more bushfires in the [_____ **4** ] of Australia than in the rest of the world.

The Victoria fire service has more than [_____ **5** ] unpaid firefighters.

Their equipment includes firetrucks, planes and [_____ **6** ].

Very large bushfires cannot be controlled with [_____ **7** ].

The firefighters [_____ **8** ] anything that could burn in order to establish 'control lines'.

Frank agrees with the interviewer that backburning can be [_____ **9** ].

Frank says backburning can go wrong if you're not certain about the [_____ **10** ].

PHOTOCOPIABLE

© Macmillan Publishers Ltd. This page may be photocopied and used within the class.

## Vocabulary

For questions **1–15**, complete each of the gaps with **one** word.

*Example:*

**0**  Now that I've started work my parents have stopped giving me _pocket_ money every week.

---

**1**  I'd like to make an _____ to see Doctor Dart, please.

**2**  We made a _____ of ten thousand pounds on our house; we bought it for eighty thousand and sold it for ninety.

**3**  She only caught a brief _____ of her attacker, but she was able to give a full description of his face to the police.

**4**  Do your coat _____ properly; it's very cold outside.

**5**  Your handwriting is so small; I can't make _____ what you've written.

**6**  They automatically give you a credit card when you open an _____ at the Central Bank.

**7**  The current _____ of interest on a personal loan is 8%.

**8**  All four of the cat's _____ were white, giving the impression it was wearing trainers.

**9**  He applied for the job but was _____ down because of his lack of experience.

**10**  I wouldn't trust him if I were you; he's as cunning as a _____ .

**11**  We visited four museums and three art _____ when we were in London.

**12**  Westbrook Street is my favourite television _____ opera. I've watched every episode on Tuesdays and Thursdays for the last three years.

**13**  They're talking of building a new opera _____ in the city.

**14**  She gave the waiter a twenty-pound _____ and told him to keep the change.

**15**  A _____ school is one for young children who are not old enough to go to primary school.

© Macmillan Publishers Ltd.  This page may be photocopied and used within the class.

PHOTOCOPIABLE

# Writing FCE Paper 2

### Part 1 Letter

You have received a letter from a friend, Rita, asking you about a language school. Read the extract from Rita's letter and an advertisement for the school, on which you have written some notes. Then write a letter to Rita, using all your notes.

so I'm thinking of going to England to study English this summer. How did you get on at that language school you went to last year?

Could you write and let me know what you thought of it, and whether you'd recommend it?

Many thanks

Rita

*Study English this summer at*

# COASTLINE LANGUAGE SCHOOL

*on one of our Summer Intensive Courses*

- 20 hours a week
- £400 for 2 weeks
- £150 per week for host family accommodation

*Fully qualified teachers, friendly atmosphere, well-equipped classrooms, self-study facilities, full social programme.*

*My teachers were …*

*For example …*

*Some students not happy, because …*

*Give details*

Write your **letter** in **120-150 words**. Do not write any postal addresses.

© Macmillan Publishers Ltd. This page may be photocopied and used within the class.

# Final test

## PAPER 1   READING  (1 hour)

### Part 1

You are going to read a magazine article about an internet search engine. For questions **1–8**, choose the answer (**A**, **B**, **C** or **D**) which you think fits best according to the text.

## Big Brother Google Is Watching You

When Google first started up, in summer 1998, it quickly established itself as the internet's best, most efficient search engine. In less than ten years it had become a $150 billion organization.

5   Not bad for a company set up by two university students in a friend's garage. But Google is changing. Now it wants to know everything - all the knowledge contained on the world wide web, and everything about you as a computer user,
10  too. The world's biggest search engine is setting out to create the most comprehensive database of personal information ever assembled, one with the ability to tell people how to run their lives.

In recent statements that suggest it may become
15  like an internet version of George Orwell's Big Brother, Google has revealed details of how it intends to organize and control the world's information. The company's chief executive, Eric Schmidt, has said that Google is just beginning
20  to build up detailed information on private individuals: 'The goal is to enable Google users to be able to ask questions such as "What shall I do tomorrow?" and "What job shall I take?" '

Privacy protection campaigners, however, are
25  concerned that this type of sophisticated internet tracking and the building up of a giant database represents a real threat to personal freedom. That concern has been reinforced by Google's $3.1 billion bid for DoubleClick, a company
30  that helps build a detailed picture of someone's behaviour by combining its records of web searches with the information from DoubleClick's 'cookies', the software it places on users' machines to record which sites they visit.

35  Ross Anderson, chairman of the Foundation for Information Policy Research, said there was a real issue with 'lock in', where Google customers are obliged to keep using the search engine because of its close links with other Google
40  services, such as iGoogle, Gmail and YouTube. He also said internet users could no longer effectively remain anonymous as Google software tracks and stores information on all users.

'A lot of people are upset by some of this. Why
45  should a teenager who subscribes to MySpace have their information dragged up 30 years later when they go for a job as say editor of the *Financial Times*? But there are serious privacy issues as well. Under data protection laws, you
50  can't take information that may have been given incidentally, and use it for another purpose.'

Peter Fleischer, a Google lawyer, said the company intended only doing what its customers wanted it to do. He said Mr Schmidt was talking
55  about products such as iGoogle, where users volunteer to let Google use their web histories. 'This is about personalized searches, where our goal is to use information to provide the best possible search for the user. If the user doesn't
60  want information held by us, then that's fine. We are not trying to build a giant library of personalized information. All we are doing is trying to make the best computer guess of what it is you are searching for.'

65  Privacy protection experts have argued that governments or police forces – in certain circumstances – can force search engines and internet service providers to hand over information. One expert has been quoted as
70  saying, 'The danger here is that it doesn't matter what search engines say their policy is because it can be overridden by national laws.'

So the big question now is whether the positive ideas with which Google began can survive in the
75  modern business world where information is not just an intellectual ideal, but also a political issue involving privacy and freedom of speech. One of their most famous slogans is, 'You can make money without doing evil.' Does that extend
80  to signing deals with individual governments allowing them to interfere in a private citizen's internet searches? Google's activities clearly relate to some of the major philosophical questions of our society. Because of its power
85  and importance in our modern digital age, the actions of this multi-billion dollar company will significantly affect how society approaches the answers to those questions.

© Macmillan Publishers Ltd.  This page may be photocopied and used within the class.

PHOTOCOPIABLE

1  In what way is Google becoming different from before?

   **A** It is becoming the biggest search engine.

   **B** It is controlling people's lives.

   **C** It is collecting detailed facts about individuals.

   **D** It is no longer based in a university.

2  Who or what does the word *one* in line 12 refer to?

   **A** a search engine

   **B** a database

   **C** personal information

   **D** a computer user

3  According to Eric Schmidt, what is Google aiming to do?

   **A** help people to plan parts of their lives

   **B** organize people into different groups

   **C** store information about different companies

   **D** ask specific questions about people's daily lives

4  DoubleClick is a company that

   **A** carries out web searches for businesses.

   **B** stores information about internet users.

   **C** converts information into pictures.

   **D** sells software to the public.

5  Ross Anderson is concerned that

   **A** Google doesn't provide enough services.

   **B** people won't be able to access the search engine in 30 years' time.

   **C** people's personal details may be used in the wrong way.

   **D** the MySpace website may be taken over by Google.

6  Peter Fleischer maintains that Google is trying to help its customers

   **A** by improving its search facilities.

   **B** by opening a new library.

   **C** by deleting their personal information.

   **D** by carrying out searches for them.

7  According to some experts, the problem with search engines is that

   **A** they sometimes give out too much information.

   **B** they cannot control how their information is used.

   **C** they often break the laws of some countries.

   **D** the service they provide is not very good.

8  What does the writer conclude about Google?

   **A** It will always work closely with individual governments.

   **B** It will play a major role in our future.

   **C** It will become a billion-dollar company.

   **D** It won't continue to make a lot of money.

PHOTOCOPIABLE

© Macmillan Publishers Ltd. This page may be photocopied and used within the class.

**Part 2**

You are going to read an article about a couple who are travelling round the world. Seven sentences have been removed from the article. Choose from the sentences **A–H** the one which fits each gap (**9–15**). There is one extra sentence which you do not need to use.

# Round the world – what's the rush?

'Wait a minute. You mean, you're going to travel all the way round the world, without taking a plane?' This was the usual reaction when Ed Gillespie told people about his plans for a somewhat unusual circumnavigation of the globe. After a little consideration, though, some of them found the adventure intriguing. After all, when you stop to think about it, the idea of travelling through so many different countries and cultures at a gentle pace, with time to reflect, and to actually communicate with the people living there, is quite appealing.

So is Ed Gillespie a fanatical environmentalist or just a reflective traveller? **9** He's the director of a climate change company, Futerra, which teaches people about ways to protect the environment. However, he admits that he's done plenty of flying in his time. In his former career as a marine biologist he worked in Australia and Jamaica, so long-haul travel was a necessity.

Recently he came to the decision that the flying had to stop. 'Four years ago, I took my last holiday flight to visit friends in Malaga in southern Spain. Now I find it increasingly difficult to justify the environmental impacts of flying purely to indulge myself.' **10** 'You travel through a landscape, not just over it,' he points out, 'and see first-hand the transition of scenery, culture, language and people that flying robs you of when it dumps you dazed and disorientated on the other side of the world.'

When their journey is complete, Ed and his girlfriend Fiona King will have travelled to 20 different countries, covering 65,000 kilometres by a variety of sea and land transport. **11** A round-the-world air ticket could be found for less than a fifth of that amount.

Clearly, saving money is not what this trip is about. **12** Another is the sheer pleasure of moving through the world and appreciating its subtle changes as you go, rather than simply flying over it. More importantly, they feel they're making a real statement about the futility of modern air travel in this age of falling oil supplies.

The first leg of the journey is now over and it has lived up to expectations in many ways. **13** Next, the train sped them to the ferry port of Portsmouth: journey time 1 hour 50 minutes. So far, so good. At Portsmouth, however, they hit the first setback of the trip, perhaps the first of many. The ferry to Bilbao, they were informed, was delayed by three hours due to bad weather at sea.

Eventually, they boarded the ferry and as the ship pulled out into the open sea, they quickly discovered that the pleasant cruise advertised in the brochures was about to turn into a lurching, rolling, seasickness-inducing ordeal. **14** Was this really any worse than being stuck in an overcrowded airport lounge for 24 hours while air traffic controllers take a day off to press for higher wages?

Ultimately, Ed and Fiona arrived safely in Spain, where they jumped on a train and are currently heading east across Europe. Next stop Singapore. **15** From Singapore, they will travel by container ship to Australia, a yacht will speed them on to New Zealand and a cargo ship will take them to Los Angeles. Then it's on to Costa Rica, where a banana boat should be waiting to take them home to England. It will have been a wonderful adventure for Ed and Fiona, but above all they hope it will show the world that it is possible to travel widely without doing major damage to the environment.

**A**  Not a great start perhaps, but then any type of travel has its difficulties.

**B**  The total cost of this little adventure will be about £5,000 per person.

**C**  So these days he does most of his holiday travel the slow way: by boat or train.

**D**  We don't have to do everything at the speed that modern technology allows.

**E**  One advantage, according to Ed and Fiona is the greater flexibility of routes.

**F**  Well, probably a bit of both.

**G**  The journey time is expected to be about four months.

**H**  From their flat in Brixton, London, they caught a bus to Waterloo station: journey time 15 minutes.

© Macmillan Publishers Ltd.  This page may be photocopied and used within the class.

PHOTOCOPIABLE

## Part 3

You are going to read a series of articles about money. For questions **16–30**, choose from the people (**A–D**). The people may be chosen more than once.

---

**Which person**

| | |
|---|---|
| sent back items that they had bought? | **16** ☐ |
| mostly buys things that have already been used? | **17** ☐ |
| suggests ways of making money last? | **18** ☐ |
| likes the unpredictable nature of shopping? | **19** ☐ |
| paid more than they were expecting for an item? | **20** ☐ |
| couldn't stop themselves from buying things? | **21** ☐ |
| mentions a time when they had very little money to spend? | **22** ☐ |
| talked to the things they bought? | **23** ☐ |
| didn't use to like shopping for food? | **24** ☐ |
| believes that the money they spend is helping other people? | **25** ☐ |
| advises against eating fast food | **26** ☐ |
| checks different prices for items before buying them? | **27** ☐ |
| likes the variety of goods available in some shops? | **28** ☐ |
| orders the same things more than once? | **29** ☐ |
| shops for somebody else as well as themselves? | **30** ☐ |

PHOTOCOPIABLE

© Macmillan Publishers Ltd. This page may be photocopied and used within the class.

# How we spend our money

**A**  **Sandra Jensen** does practically all her shopping in charity shops. 'All the money goes to a good cause, and I don't mind wearing second-hand clothes, or reading old books that other people have already left their mark on. Of course, it saves me money too. There's an incredible range of goods for sale in most charity shops: from antique cameras to vintage watches, faded T-shirts to designer dresses.'

And you may even pick up an unexpected bargain. 'I recently heard about a man in America who bought an old document in a charity shop for $2.48. It turned out to be a rare copy of the Declaration of Independence, made in 1823. Apparently, it's now been valued at about $250,000! I've certainly never found anything like that – and I'm not expecting to. I just like the fact that it can be a bit of a random experience. When I go out shopping I never know what I'm going to come home with.'

**B**  Online Shopping is becoming increasingly popular. **Joe French** lets his computer take the strain. 'I do the weekly food shopping online. My wife works very long hours, and it was always my job to trail round a crowded supermarket on a Friday night. I hated it! Now, I spend five minutes typing in our order and the groceries get delivered straight to our door.

We use eBay a lot too. You're not just buying from other people, there are thousands of businesses operating from within the site. It's the best way to get a good deal on things because you can compare prices so easily. There are so many advantages to shopping online, although I have had one bad experience. Last year, I bought a flat-screen TV from a company in Germany. It was on a website I'd never used before, but it was such a good price, I couldn't resist it. It arrived OK, and we were really happy with it, but when I checked my credit card statement, I discovered I'd been billed for more than twice the amount that was advertised.'

**C**  **Robbie Fullerton** gives a few tips about how to survive on a student grant. 'In my last year at university I had £40 per week to live on, after paying my rent. It's really not much, but there are ways to make it stretch.

Transport is an area where costs can be high, but there is plenty of scope for saving money. Because students generally have more time than money, travelling by coach rather than train is a sensible option. Don't even think about buying a "cheap car" – they don't exist, not once you've added in road tax, insurance, petrol and servicing. Get a student bus pass, or better still, ride a bike or use your own personal built-in transport system. Yes, walking is good exercise and, of course, it's free.

Eat vegetables. Lots of them. They're cheap, especially if you can buy them in a big wholesale market. If possible, avoid take-aways completely otherwise your week's budget will quickly disappear.

Finally, get some part-time work. You shouldn't neglect your college essays, but a bit of paid work will take away the stress of worrying about money and leave you free to concentrate on your studies.'

**D**  **Lucille Schenk** bought $20,000 worth of jewellery a year ago, plunging herself into debt and despair. She knew something was wrong but couldn't help herself. For hours each day, she watched a jewellery channel and the Home Shopping Network, until the salespeople felt like family.

She did most of her binge buying late at night. Often, after her purchases arrived, she returned them, knowing she could not afford them. Then she would see the same items on TV and send for them again.

When Schenk finally sought help, New York psychologist April Lane Benson advised her to have a 'conversation' with the jewellery before she made her next purchase, as a way to put some distance between herself and her compulsion.

'I would say, "You are so beautiful, I can't live without you; I love the way you sparkle," ' recalled Schenk, 62, in an interview. 'The jewellery would say back, "You need me. You look pretty when you wear me." I would say, "I do need you. I can't possibly think of being without you. But something has to change. I need to stop this. I can't afford a penny more." '

© Macmillan Publishers Ltd. This page may be photocopied and used within the class.

PHOTOCOPIABLE

# PAPER 2 WRITING (1 hour 20 minutes)

## Part 1

You **must** answer this question. Write your answer in **120–150 words** in an appropriate style.

1    You have seen an advert for a college in Britain and are interested in attending a summer course there. Read the advert and the notes you have made. Then write an email to the college principal, using all your notes.

Can I start on a Wednesday?

How far from the school?

What else? Tennis, football, etc?

How many?

Need more details

## The Activity English Centre

*At Activity English in Edinburgh we offer great English tuition and much more.*

Students study from Monday to Friday mornings, with highly experienced teachers in our fully-equipped school. We have the latest language-learning materials and a state-of-the-art computer room. Our special outdoor activity programme will keep you busy each afternoon. We offer sailing, windsurfing, horse-riding, mountain walking, and more.

- **Students study in small groups.**
- **All language levels catered for.**
- **Courses from 1 week to 1 month.**
- **Stay with a local family.**
- **Very competitive prices.**

*Contact the principal, Sally Jenkins:*
principal@activityenglish.co.uk

Write your **email**. You must use grammatically correct sentences with accurate spelling and punctuation in a style appropriate for the situation.

| To: | Sally Jenkins |
| Sent: | 18 April 2008 |
| Subject: | Language course |

PHOTOCOPIABLE

© Macmillan Publishers Ltd. This page may be photocopied and used within the class.

## Part 2

Write an answer to **one** of the questions **2–5** in this part. Write your answer in **120–180** words in an appropriate style.

---

**2**   You saw this notice in an English-language magazine called *Arts Review*.

> Have you been to a live music event recently? If so, could you write a review of the concert you saw? Include information on the venue (concert hall, festival site, etc), the crowd, the atmosphere and the band's performance and say whether you would recommend the concert to other people.
>
> The best reviews will be published in the next magazine.

Write your **review**.

**3**   Your teacher has asked you to write a story for a competition. Your story must end with the following words:

*Tim decided he would never do anything so stupid again.*

Write your **story**.

**4**   You have seen this announcement in your local newspaper.

> ### Where I live
> What's special about the area you live in? Tell us about it. What are its interesting features and why would somebody want to visit it?
>
> *We will publish the most interesting articles in a special edition of the newspaper.*

Write your **article**.

**5**   Answer **one** of the following two questions based on your reading of **one** of the set books.

   **(a)**  What is your opinion of the ending of the book? Write an essay describing the ending and explaining how it relates to the rest of the story.

Write your **essay**.

   **(b)**  Write a letter to an English-speaking friend describing the book you read. Explain what you liked and didn't like about it. Do not write any postal addresses.

Write your **letter**.

© Macmillan Publishers Ltd.  This page may be photocopied and used within the class.

PHOTOCOPIABLE

## PAPER 3  USE OF ENGLISH  (45 minutes)
### Part 1

For questions **1–12**, read the text below and decide which answer **A**, **B**, **C** or **D** best fits each space. There is an example at the beginning **(0)**.

*Example:*

| **0** | **A** known | **B** <u>famous</u> | **C** discovered | **D** public |

---

## The Leaning Tower of Pisa

One of Italy's most **(0)** _____ landmarks is the bell tower of the cathedral in Pisa. This 55-metre-high tower leans at an angle of 5.5 degrees. This may not **(1)** _____ like much, but it means that the **(2)** _____ of the tower is more than 4 metres out of position!

Many people **(3)** _____ that it only began to lean after it was built, but in fact the tower started to sink during the **(4)** _____ stages of construction due to poor foundations. In an effort to compensate for the tilt, the engineers built the higher **(5)** _____ with one side taller than the other. This made the tower begin to lean in the other **(6)** _____ . Because of this, the tower is actually curved.

There are a **(7)** _____ of interesting historical tales associated with the tower. The famous astronomer and physicist Galileo Galilei was **(8)** _____ to have dropped two cannonballs of different sizes from the top of the tower to prove a principle of physics. In the 1930s, Italian leader Benito Mussolini **(9)** _____ that the tower be straightened. Concrete was poured into the foundations, but the only **(10)** _____ was that the tower sank further into the ground. In 1990, the tower was declared unsafe and **(11)** _____ to tourists. It reopened in 2001, after the tower had been straightened **(12)** _____ to a safer angle and it has now been declared safe for the next 300 years.

| | | | | |
|---|---|---|---|---|
| **1** | **A** appear | **B** be | **C** seem | **D** view |
| **2** | **A** top | **B** summit | **C** point | **D** peak |
| **3** | **A** understand | **B** assume | **C** propose | **D** acknowledge |
| **4** | **A** beginning | **B** former | **C** immediate | **D** early |
| **5** | **A** grounds | **B** layers | **C** floors | **D** sheets |
| **6** | **A** point | **B** route | **C** course | **D** direction |
| **7** | **A** quantity | **B** sum | **C** number | **D** set |
| **8** | **A** said | **B** talked | **C** spoken | **D** told |
| **9** | **A** made | **B** forced | **C** threatened | **D** ordered |
| **10** | **A** finish | **B** result | **C** conclusion | **D** answer |
| **11** | **A** blocked | **B** ended | **C** locked | **D** closed |
| **12** | **A** narrowly | **B** hardly | **C** slightly | **D** lightly |

PHOTOCOPIABLE

© Macmillan Publishers Ltd.  This page may be photocopied and used within the class.

## Part 2

For questions **13–24**, read the text below and think of the word which best fits each space. Use only **one** word in each space. There is an example at the beginning **(0)**.

## Sailing against the odds

Sailing can **(0)** ___be___ an expensive business. British yachtswoman Ellen MacArthur saved her school dinner money for three years **(13)** _____ buy her first boat and then spent several years living in a small shed in a boatyard **(14)** _____ another craft was being built. When she first tried to get sponsors to help with the enormous cost **(15)** _____ building a serious racing boat, she sent out 250 letters and got just two replies. Eventually a home-improvement company called Kingfisher came up **(16)**_____ the money after she had sailed across the Atlantic alone at the age of 22.

Next she took on the very tough Vendee Globe race, **(17)** _____ involved sailing nonstop round the world single-handed. Racing against older and far **(18)** _____ experienced sailors she came second and became the youngest person and the fastest woman ever to sail alone round the world. She became a celebrity overnight, and immediately began to plan her **(19)** _____ trip. In 2005, she once **(20)** _____ sailed round the world on her own. Her time of just under 72 days set a new record for the fastest ever solo round-the-world voyage.

It hasn't **(21)** _____ easy for her. Whilst sailing MacArthur has burnt herself badly trying to fix a generator and she has had to climb to **(22)** _____ top of a 27-metre mast in 50-kilometre-per-hour Antarctic winds in **(23)** _____ to carry out repairs. But something still drives this young woman on to further success. Perhaps it's her simple philosophy: 'the **(24)** _____ important thing is being happy, and I'm happy sailing, any boat, anywhere.'

© Macmillan Publishers Ltd. This page may be photocopied and used within the class.

PHOTOCOPIABLE

## Part 3

For questions **25–34**, read the text below. Use the word given in capitals at the end of some of the lines to form a word that fits in the gap **in the same line**. There is an example at the beginning (**0**).

# Growing up in a big family

(**0**) _Unlike_ most people I have ever met, I grew up in a family of eight     **LIKE**
children. As the eldest, I suppose I inherited a position with some benefits
but also quite a few (**25**) _____ . I never had a room of my own – so     **ADVANTAGE**
(**26**) _____ space is something I've little experience of. On the other     **PERSON**
hand, our house was often so (**27**) _____ , with children running in all     **CHAOS**
(**28**) _____ , that we were able to get away with a lot. Also, with seven     **DIRECT**
brothers and sisters on hand there was always the (**29**) _____ of     **POSSIBLE**
something different to do.

Needless to say, it was often (**30**) _____ difficult for Mum or Dad to get     **EXTREME**
our (**31**) _____ . Sometimes if Mum wanted some help she would just call     **ATTEND**
out all eight names, (**32**) _____ of who she really wanted, just to see who     **REGARD**
came running.

As children we often had (**33**) _____ , but now that we're adults we get on     **ARGUE**
(**34**) _____ whenever we meet up.     **FANTASTIC**

PHOTOCOPIABLE

214

© Macmillan Publishers Ltd.  This page may be photocopied and used within the class.

## Part 4

For questions **35–42**, complete the second sentence so that it has a similar meaning to the first sentence, using the word given. **Do not change the word given.** You must use between **two** and **five** words, including the word given. Here is an example (**0**).

*Example:*

**0** The climber was too weak to carry on to the top of the mountain.

**strong**

The climber *wasn't strong enough* to carry on to the top of the mountain.

---

**35** Kate, please could you tell me how much your new dress cost?

**mind**

Kate, _____ me how much your new dress cost?

**36** I have been driving for much longer than Simon.

**nearly**

Simon hasn't been driving for _____ I have.

**37** Will you look after the dog while we're away on holiday?

**take**

Will you _____ the dog while we're away on holiday?

**38** I really don't think you should climb on that wall.

**ought**

I really think you _____ climb on that wall.

**39** We haven't been abroad for a holiday since we bought the caravan.

**time**

The _____ abroad for a holiday was before we bought the caravan.

**40** What are you going to do when you finish university?

**on**

What are you _____ when you finish university?

**41** We didn't go to the beach because it was raining.

**have**

If it hadn't been raining we _____ to the beach.

**42** 'Don't put your feet up on the chair, please, Jack.'

**told**

His father _____ his feet up on the chair.

© Macmillan Publishers Ltd. This page may be photocopied and used within the class.

PHOTOCOPIABLE

# PAPER 4   LISTENING  (approximately 40 minutes)
## Part 1

You will hear people talking in eight different situations. For questions **1–8**, choose the best answer, **A**, **B** or **C**.

1   You turn on the radio and hear a man being interviewed about his work.
    Who is he?

    **A** an architect

    **B** an artist

    **C** a photographer

2   You overhear this man talking about a film he went to see recently.
    What does he say about the film?

    **A** It was disappointing.

    **B** It was very funny.

    **C** It was frightening.

3   You hear this woman talking to her friend on the phone.
    What is she doing?

    **A** encouraging her

    **B** criticizing her

    **C** giving her advice

4   Listen to this woman talking to her husband.
    What does she want him to do?

    **A** do some housework

    **B** go to the shops

    **C** repair something

5   You hear this woman telling her friend about the hotel she stayed in on holiday.
    Where was the hotel?

    **A** in the mountains

    **B** on the coast

    **C** in a town

6   You hear this man talking about a pullover.
    What is he going to do with it?

    **A** take it back to the shop

    **B** offer it to someone else

    **C** keep it

7   You are in a school when you hear this teacher talking to someone.
    Who is she talking to?

    **A** the head teacher

    **B** a parent

    **C** a secretary

8   You hear this man talking to a friend about a football match.
    Why was the match postponed?

    **A** because of bad weather

    **B** because of the poor condition of the pitch

    **C** because of illness

PHOTOCOPIABLE

       © Macmillan Publishers Ltd.  This page may be photocopied and used within the class.

**Part 2**

You will hear part of a radio interview with John Burgeon, an actor. For questions **9–18**, complete the sentences.

The name of John Burgeon's latest film is [ **9** ] .

One of his favourite photographs shows him at the top of [ **10** ] .

As a teenager he would often go rock climbing with his [ **11** ] .

For his part in the new film John had to learn [ **12** ] .

He was also told to [ **13** ] .

John studied [ and **14** ] at university.

His father was [ **15** ] when John took up acting.

John's first acting jobs were in [ **16** ] .

The film *Sleepy Willow* won [ **17** ] awards for 'Best Film'.

John wants to [ **18** ] for a few months.

**Part 3**

You will hear five different people talking about their work, which is in some way connected with music. For questions **19–23**, choose from the list **A–F** who each speaker is. Use the letters only once. There is one extra letter which you do not need to use.

**A**   a songwriter

Speaker 1 [    ]

**B**   a singer

Speaker 2 [    ]

**C**   a disc jockey

Speaker 3 [    ]

**D**   a shop owner

Speaker 4 [    ]

**E**   a journalist

Speaker 5 [    ]

**F**   a conductor

© Macmillan Publishers Ltd.  This page may be photocopied and used within the class.

## Part 4

You will hear an interview about the different people who have lived in a house. For questions **24–30**, choose the best answer, **A**, **B** or **C**.

24　The Rayners bought the house because

**A** it had been modernized.

**B** it was the right size for them.

**C** it wasn't too expensive.

25　Reginald Cornford was

**A** a gardener.

**B** a photographer.

**C** a greengrocer.

26　What do we learn about Annie as a child?

**A** She was very lonely.

**B** She used to play in the attic.

**C** She had many friends in the neighbourhood.

27　When did Annie move out of the house?

**A** when she got married

**B** after the death of her husband

**C** after she had an accident

28　The Averys sold the house

**A** in order to make money.

**B** because it was in very poor condition.

**C** because they wanted to live abroad.

29　What changes did the Robertsons make to the house?

**A** They increased the number of rooms.

**B** They knocked down one of the walls.

**C** They made one of the rooms smaller.

30　What does Liz say about the garden?

**A** She likes working in it.

**B** It helps to create a good working environment.

**C** She'd like to spend more time in it.

PHOTOCOPIABLE

 © Macmillan Publishers Ltd.  This page may be photocopied and used within the class.

# PAPER 5  SPEAKING (approximately 14 minutes)
## Part 1 (3 minutes)

The examiner asks the two candidates questions about themselves. Possible questions include:

> What do you like about living in your town or village?
>
> Do you plan to continue studying? What would you like to study in the future?
>
> Do you like playing sport? Why?/Why not?
>
> Do you prefer listening to music or reading? Why?
>
> Imagine that you could travel around the world? Where would you go?
>
> What sort of things do you use the internet for?

## Part 2 (4 minutes)

1 | The first two photographs show people taking part in different outdoor activities.

**Student A**

Compare the photographs, and say why you think people take part in this kind of activity. (You have approximately one minute to do this.)

**Student B**

Which activity would you prefer to try? (You have approximately 20 seconds to do this.)

2 | The second two pictures show people in different work environments.

**Student B**

Compare the photographs, and say what are the advantages of working in each of these environments? (You have approximately one minute to do this.)

**Student A**

Which place would you prefer to work in? (You have approximately 20 seconds to do this.)

## Part 3 (3 minutes)

> Imagine that a new park is going to be built in your village or town. The planners want to make it suitable for all age groups. Here are some of the suggestions they are considering.
>
> First, talk to each other about how successful these suggestions might be. Then decide which two you think would attract most people.

## Part 4 (4 minutes)

The examiner asks the candidates to discuss some questions which relate to the theme in Part 3.

© Macmillan Publishers Ltd.  This page may be photocopied and used within the class.

## Part 2 (4 minutes)

**1** | Why do people take part in these kinds of activity?

PHOTOCOPIABLE

Text © Macmillan Publishers Ltd.  This page may be photocopied and used within the class.

**Part 2 (4 minutes)**

**2** What are the advantages of working in each of these environments?

Text © Macmillan Publishers Ltd.  This page may be photocopied and used within the class.

## Part 3 (3 minutes)

- How successful might these suggestions be?
- Which two would attract most people?

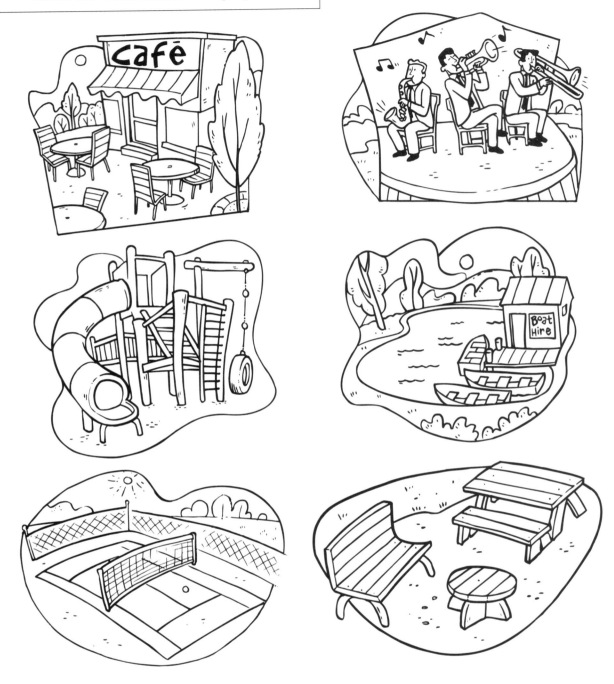

## Part 4 (4 minutes)

Do you like spending time in your local park?

How do you think your local park could be improved?

If your local park was being improved would you be willing to help without being paid?

How important do you think it is for young people to spend time doing outdoor activities?

Do you think that there is generally enough for young people to do when they are out?

Why do you think young people and older people like to do different things? Then decide which two would atttract most people.

PHOTOCOPIABLE

222                © Macmillan Publishers Ltd.  This page may be photocopied and used within the class.

## Progress test 1: Units 1–3

# Reading FCE Paper 1

### Part 3: Multiple matching

| | | | | |
|---|---|---|---|---|
| 1 | B | | 2/3 | C and D in any order |
| 4 | A | | 5 E | 6 C | 7 B |
| 8 | A | | 9/10 | A and C in any order |
| 11 | C | | 12 B | 13/14 D and E in any order |
| 15 | E | | | |

# Use of English FCE Paper 3

### Part 4: Transformations

1 never used to take
2 keeps (on) asking
3 get Helen to help
4 get paid
5 telling me when you were
6 (really) looking forward to finishing
7 can't afford to
8 isn't/is not as/so friendly as

### Part 5: Word formation

| | | | | | |
|---|---|---|---|---|---|
| 1 | participants | 2 | players | 3 | disapproved |
| 4 | unable | 5 | success | 6 | painful |
| 7 | Luckily | 8 | lighter | 9 | colourful |
| 10 | easier | | | | |

# Listening FCE Paper 4

### Part 2: Sentence completion

| | | | |
|---|---|---|---|
| 1 | a bird | 6 | half hour |
| 2 | live music | 7 | strength and balance |
| 3 | co-ordination | 8 | back |
| 4 | follow the steps | 9 | (about) 800 |
| 5 | teenagers | 10 | self-confidence |

# Vocabulary

| | | | | | | | |
|---|---|---|---|---|---|---|---|
| 1 | A | 2 | B | 3 | C | 4 | C |
| 5 | B | 6 | C | 7 | C | 8 | A |
| 9 | D | 10 | D | 11 | B | 12 | A |
| 13 | C | 14 | B | 15 | C | | |

---

**Listening script: Part 2 Sentence completion**

There are moments in life when you question how you came to be doing a certain thing at a certain time. This happened to me recently in my first African dance class, when I was called upon to dance like a bird. In a room full of other would-be birds, I flapped my arms wildly, more in the manner of an excited chicken than a graceful flamingo.

The minute you start the warm-up it becomes clear that African dance offers a more unusual route to fitness than an average gym session. The class I attended was led by dancers Mona Daniel and Big Joe Lartey from the Adzido troupe, which became famous with its performance of 'Under African Skies'. We danced to the beat of live music throughout the 90-minute class. The African drums, a room full of gyrating bodies and a furiously fast pace is a combination that makes any other class seem mundane in comparison.

In gyms across America there is an increasing interest in ethnic dance classes – last year, members at the trendy New York Sports Club voted African dance the most popular of all classes on offer. Surprisingly perhaps, good rhythm and co-ordination are not essential requirements for African dance, which is good news for people like me who have neither of these qualities. There are an increasing number of classes like this one in which the emphasis is on feeling the way your body moves rather than simply having to follow the steps of an aerobics instructor. African dance allows for freedom of movement because there is no right or wrong way to do it. It is a great way of working out, but more importantly it leaves you feeling both physically and mentally fulfilled.

At the Adzido classes the mix is roughly half men, half women, of all ages, from teenagers to pensioners, some of whom travel long distances to attend the evening sessions. Mona and Big Joe explain the origin and meaning of each traditional move before we try it, then in the final half hour of the class, there's an enthusiastic, and rather untidy performance of everything we've been taught.

By the end of the evening, Joe tells me, members of the class will have used most of the big muscles in their body and over time, if you attend regularly, it will improve strength and balance.

There are other fitness advantages to this unique art form. In spite of the effort it involves, it is largely a low-impact activity and the feet are nearly always kept parallel with the knees, taking stress off the joints and this helps protect the back from injury. Besides this, many of the steps require you to remain flat-footed so that ankles do not suffer strain. And if calorie-counting is important, well, you can burn off about 800 calories in a one-hour African dance class, provided you don't stop too often. This compares with 600 if you did conventional aerobics for the same length of time.

But African dance is really about more than sweating to reduce the size of your bottom. It is about getting rid of inhibitions and getting back in touch with your body's natural rhythms, something most of us haven't done since early childhood. However strange you feel at first, you will eventually get over the uneasiness of moving dynamically and freely in front of a crowd of strangers, and you should find your self-confidence increases dramatically. Believe me, if you can dance like a chicken, anything else is easy.

## Reading FCE Paper 1

### Part 2: Gapped text

1 D  2 G  3 C  4 A  5 H  6 F
7 E  B not used

## Use of English FCE Paper 3

### Part 1: Multiple-choice cloze

| 1 D | 2 C | 3 A | 4 B |
|---|---|---|---|
| 5 A | 6 C | 7 C | 8 C |
| 9 A | 10 D | 11 A | 12 D |

### Part 4: Transformations

1 me to take care of
2 made you come
3 'd/had better go to bed
4 too noisy for me to
5 're/are having central heating installed
6 not old enough to see
7 was/is such a frightening film
8 didn't/did not take much interest

### Part 2: Open cloze

| 1 than | 2 made/turned | 3 like/including |
|---|---|---|
| 4 ago | 5 of/about | 6 himself |
| 7 to | 8 would/could | 9 that |
| 10 the | 11 in | 12 have |

## Vocabulary

| 1 astonishing | 7 irritated |
|---|---|
| 2 bad-tempered | 8 monotonous |
| 3 challenging | 9 reliable |
| 4 disappointing | 10 terrifying |
| 5 exhausted | 11 unpleasant |
| 6 flowing | 12 wrinkled |

## Listening FCE Paper 4

### Part 1: Multiple choice

| 1 B | 2 A | 3 A | 4 B |
|---|---|---|---|
| 5 C | 6 C | 7 C | 8 B |

### Listening script: Part 1 Multiple choice

1 **Man:** I was quite surprised really. I mean, the only reason I went to see it was because Julia Robbins was in it – she's usually really good and knows how to choose her films. So, you know, I expected better. But once I realized it wasn't supposed to be taken too seriously I just sat back and laughed at the really awful bits. Luckily it only lasted an hour and a quarter, which is unusual these days, and it meant we had time to go for something to eat afterwards.

2 **Man:** Booked your holiday yet, Sal?

**Woman:** Just about to.

**Man:** You're going to Spain again, aren't you?

**Woman:** My friends are, but I had such a good time last year that I thought going back might spoil the memory. Also, the thought of spending two weeks with the same group of friends didn't really appeal. So, I'll pack a few books and see if I can survive ten days of my own company somewhere. You never know, I might meet the man of my dreams.

3 **Woman:** No, it's not very heavy. It's about the same size as a portable TV and it weighs a little less, if anything. I usually plug it in in the kitchen and then run an extension lead out to the car. It only takes a few minutes to do the seats and the floor. It's like having a new car all over again.

4 **Woman:** They played much better today, didn't they?

**Man:** I suppose so.

**Woman:** What do you mean?

**Man:** Well, they defended well, and the goalkeeper had a good game. But there wasn't much happening in the attack, was there?

**Woman:** You can't expect them to take too many risks. They're too near the bottom of the table.

**Man:** I realize that. All I'm saying is that it wasn't my idea of an exciting afternoon's entertainment, that's all.

5 **Man:** Listen, Graham, I'm going to be a bit late, I'm afraid … Well, the plane's been delayed and we're only just about to get on it … Listen, would you mind phoning Dad to let him know what's happened … Thanks, I'll see you at Heathrow … Oh, are you going to bring my new nephew with you, too? … Great – see you later.

6 **Man:** But these tickets you've got are at the back. I thought you were going to try to get some near the front.

**Woman:** That's right, but then someone at work told me that the acoustics in the first few rows weren't very good. Apparently you can't appreciate the full sound of the orchestra down the front. She said it was better to sit near the back, so I got row 15.

7 **Teenage boy:** So I sat there for about ten minutes looking at it, wondering why she'd told us to do that particular exercise. I mean, it didn't have anything to do with what we'd done in class. Anyway, I did it in the end – it was a bit tricky, but OK. Then of course I realized I'd been looking at the right page but in the wrong book, so I had to start all over again.

8 **Man:** How's it going?

**Woman:** Not too bad I suppose. But people do ask such silly questions. I used to think it was a good sign if they wanted to know when the company was formed, how many employees there were, and so on. But that's really the kind of thing you should find out before you come for an interview. Let's face it, it's the kind of thing you can ask the secretary while you're waiting in reception.

## Progress test 3: Units 7–9

## Reading FCE Paper 1

### Part 1: Multiple choice

| | | | |
|---|---|---|---|
| 1 C | 2 B | 3 A | 4 B |
| 5 D | 6 A | 7 D | 8 A |

## Use of English FCE Paper 3

### Part 2: Open cloze

| | | | |
|---|---|---|---|
| 1 have | 2 on | 3 from | 4 most |
| 5 made | 6 which | 7 well | 8 to |
| 9 These | 10 each/every/a/per | | 11 had |
| 12 too | | | |

### Part 3: Word formation

| | |
|---|---|
| 1 bigger | 2 exciting |
| 3 easily | 4 traditional |
| 5 numerous | 6 inexperienced |
| 7 Unfortunately | 8 threatening |
| 9 mountaineers | 10 evidence |

### Part 4: Transformations

1 have lived/have been living here since
2 months since I last went
3 prefer eating food to cooking
4 'd/would rather go to the
5 we arrived late
6 despite me/my telling her
7 on the point of splitting/breaking
8 couldn't/can't/won't have used

## Listening FCE Paper 4

### Part 4: Multiple choice

| | | | |
|---|---|---|---|
| 1 C | 2 A | 3 B | 4 B |
| 5 C | 6 A | 7 C | |

## Vocabulary

| | | | |
|---|---|---|---|
| 1 looked | 2 takes | 3 gave | 4 make |
| 5 putting | 6 came | 7 coming | 8 got |
| 9 take | 10 giving | 11 come | 12 had |
| 13 taken | 14 gives | 15 getting | |

### Listening script: Part 4 Multiple choice

**Interviewer:** In our travel slot today we take a look at Home Exchange. With us in the studio we have two people who've taken part in this increasingly popular holiday option. Brian and Susie, what exactly is Home Exchange?

**Susie:** Well, it's a remarkably simple concept. While you spend your holiday living in someone else's house, they come and live in yours. To some extent you take over each others' lives.

**Brian:** Yes, and that can include any pets you might have, the car, and of course the bills – gas, electricity and so on.

**Susie:** That's right. It wouldn't be fair if I had to pay for someone else's phone calls, just because they were made in my home … and vice versa, of course.

**Interviewer:** Isn't there a risk in all this, that damage may be done to your house? You are after all inviting complete strangers into your home.

**Brian:** If you're worried you can ask for references from previous people your exchange partner has swapped houses with. That wasn't possible in our case, because it was the first time our partners had done an exchange. But we got a pretty good idea about them from phone calls we made and letters we received when we were organizing it all.

**Susie:** And you can always ask a neighbour to call round and see that everything's OK. We got ours to meet the family when they arrived, which made them feel very welcome from day one. It also of course provides the exchange partner with a useful local contact if they need help of any kind.

**Interviewer:** And did things work out alright for you? Were there any problems?

**Susie:** Not really, no. The family we exchanged with from Australia had two young children, so we made a point beforehand of moving anything fragile or valuable out of the way to prevent it from getting broken. Unfortunately, a couple of vases we'd left out fell off a shelf, but apparently that was the cat's fault. The family offered to pay, but we refused.

**Interviewer:** And Brian, you went to California, didn't you? How was that?

**Brian:** Marvellous. We did very well out of the whole thing. Merrill and Jackie, the couple we exchanged with, chose our house because they wanted somewhere smaller than their own which didn't require too much cleaning. So we swapped our two-bedroomed flat in the centre of Manchester for a smart detached house in the suburbs of Los Angeles. They were delighted and so were we.

**Interviewer:** And you mentioned a car earlier?

**Brian:** Yes, we had the use of their petrol-hungry Cadillac for the two weeks we were there. It was expensive to run, but that didn't stop us from going almost everywhere we wanted. A holiday with a house exchange is just so much cheaper than a normal holiday, so we could afford to travel about. The car wasn't insured to be driven in Mexico, so we couldn't cross the border, which was a shame, but we may do that when we go back next year.

**Interviewer:** And Susie, how did you go about exchanging with the family in Australia? How did you set it all up?

**Susie:** We went through one of the agencies on the Internet. Agencies generally charge a membership fee, which enables you to put your property on their database, and have access to details of all the homes which are already on it. Most of these, including the one we chose, have photos of the house, which is very useful in helping you decide which people to contact. And that can be done by email of course, so it takes very little time to organize everything.

**Interviewer:** And are you going back next year, like Brian?

**Susie:** South Africa next year. We want to see as many different places as possible.

## Progress test key

### Progress test 4: Units 10–12

## Reading FCE Paper 1

### Part 2: Gapped text

| | | | |
|---|---|---|---|
| 1 C | 2 D | 3 H | 4 F |
| 5 A | 6 B | 7 E | |

## Use of English FCE Paper 3

### Part 4: Transformations

1 have been vandalized
2 was given this watch by
3 is not thought to be
4 can't/cannot go unless you
5 if you had not/hadn't reminded
6 was going away the following
7 if/whether she had been smoking
8 has not made (very) much

### Part 1: Multiple-choice cloze

| | | | |
|---|---|---|---|
| 1 D | 2 B | 3 C | 4 C |
| 5 A | 6 B | 7 D | 8 B |
| 9 D | 10 C | 11 A | 12 C |

### Part 3: Word formation

| | | |
|---|---|---|
| 1 endangered | 2 biggest | 3 disappearance |
| 4 protection | 5 hunters | 6 effective |
| 7 natural | 8 increasingly | 9 pollution |
| 10 awareness | | |

## Listening FCE Paper 4

### Part 3: Multiple matching

| | | | |
|---|---|---|---|
| 1 B | 2 D | 3 A | 4 F |
| 5 C | E not used | | |

## Vocabulary

| | | | |
|---|---|---|---|
| 1 C | 2 B | 3 D | 4 B |
| 5 A | 6 A | 7 D | 8 C |
| 9 D | 10 A | 11 C | 12 B |
| 13 C | 14 A | 15 C | |

### Listening script: Part 3 Multiple matching

**Speaker 1**

It was the first time we'd had snow as deep as that. The kids were delighted, of course – they'd just started their Christmas holidays so they had lots of time to play in it. I was a sales representative for a frozen food company at the time, but for a couple of days the roads were blocked and there was no way I could drive anywhere to visit my clients. So I just stayed at home and made snowmen with the kids.

**Speaker 2**

I think we must have gone nearly two months without a drop of rain. At the beginning, of course, everyone was really pleased; it was really nice to get so many days of sunshine and high temperatures in a row. By the end of the second month, though, I was getting sick of it, and like most people, I was really looking forward to seeing the rain again.

**Speaker 3**

It poured with rain every day for about two weeks. We had floods and everything down in this part of the country. It's not very unusual, mind, but ... I remember it because I got so wet and cold I came down with flu or something. I had a really high temperature, anyway. It didn't stop me going to work, though. I had my own building company then and I couldn't afford to stay at home.

**Speaker 4**

The tent was blown down by the wind on the first night, and on the second night it started letting in the rain. We were so fed up by the end of the week we decided to come home early. It was such a shame, because the campsite was really calm and peaceful and it was in a beautiful setting in the mountains. It seems we chose the wrong month of the year – apparently it's always like that there in July.

**Speaker 5**

It only lasted a week or so, but it was wonderful. We had glorious sunshine and temperatures as high as 25 degrees – better than when we were on holiday. You just don't expect it to be like that in November. And then, of course, it was a real shock to the system when it changed – we went from one extreme to the other in just a few days. The temperatures dropped to about four or five degrees and there was thick fog.

## Progress test 5: Units 13–15

### Reading FCE Paper 1

**Part 1: Multiple choice**

| | | | |
|---|---|---|---|
| 1 C | 2 B | 3 C | 4 B |
| 5 D | 6 C | 7 A | 8 C |

### Use of English FCE Paper 3

**Part 1: Multiple-choice cloze**

| | | | |
|---|---|---|---|
| 1 B | 2 D | 3 D | 4 C |
| 5 B | 6 C | 7 B | 8 A |
| 9 C | 10 A | 11 A | 12 B |

**Part 2: Open cloze**

| | | | |
|---|---|---|---|
| 1 was | 2 could | 3 at | 4 up |
| 5 order | 6 not | 7 done | 8 case |
| 9 have | 10 so | 11 no | 12 able |

### Listening FCE Paper 4

**Part 2: Sentence completion**

| | | |
|---|---|---|
| 1 rural | 2 forest | 3 summer, autumn |
| 4 south-east | 5 fifty thousand/50,000 | |
| 6 helicopters | 7 water | 8 clear away |
| 9 risky | 10 wind direction | |

### Vocabulary

| | | |
|---|---|---|
| 1 appointment | 2 profit | 3 glimpse |
| 4 up | 5 out | 6 account | 7 rate |
| 8 paws | 9 turned | 10 fox | 11 galleries |
| 12 soap | 13 house | 14 note | 15 nursery |

---

**Listening script: Part 2 Sentence completion**

**Interviewer:** As many of you may know, Australia recently experienced the worst bushfires for 70 years with firefighters battling the odds in the most difficult of circumstances. Our next guest is Frank Williams who is a firefighter in the Australian state of Victoria. Frank, welcome to the programme.

**Frank:** Thank you.

**Interviewer:** Now, Frank, you're based in a rural area, and I gather you spend most of your time fighting bushfires. Can you explain to the listeners what exactly a bushfire is?

**Frank:** Sure. A bushfire is simply what we Australians call any fire in open countryside - whether that's a forest or an area of grassland, or whatever. You might call them forest fires, or in America they call them 'wildfires'. They're usually started by lightning strikes, or occasionally by people being careless with matches. Of course, they tend to be most common in summer or autumn, and especially after long periods without rain. Australia is currently suffering from some of the longest and worst droughts in recent history, so bushfires are an increasing danger.

**Interviewer:** And I believe you're in one of the most dangerous spots in Australia?

**Frank:** You could say that, yeah. South-east Australia is the place with the highest incidence of bushfires of anywhere in the world. It just needs a few hot, dry days and a strong northerly wind and we're in danger.

**Interviewer:** And, of course, Australia is an enormous country with huge areas of open ground. How do the fire service deal with a problem on this scale?

**Frank:** Well, the bush fire service is largely a volunteer force. In the state of Victoria we have over 50,000 volunteers, who do it for nothing supported by about 400 career firefighters. In a big bushfire, we'd work alongside Park Rangers from the National Parks and professional firefighters from the big cities like Melbourne. We use firetrucks, of course, but we also have various planes and helicopters we can call in for a big fire. These guys can get in to places the ground crews can't reach and they can drop an enormous amount of water on a blaze. We call it firebombing. There's one plane – the Erickson, which is nicknamed Elvis – it can drop 9,000 litres of water.

**Interviewer:** Yes, that's pretty impressive. But still, it must be difficult to deal with really big fires or a lot of fires breaking out at the same time in different locations.

**Frank:** Well, yeah, it is. In Victoria, you're talking about an area of about 150,000 square kilometres. And when a really big fire gets going, it's impossible to control the whole fire directly with water. What we do then, instead of trying to put the fire out, is try to take control of where the fire spreads.

**Interviewer:** That must be quite difficult.

**Frank:** Well, it isn't always easy, but there are ways of doing it. One way is to set up what we call 'control lines' round the fire. This means we go in with bulldozers and hand tools and clear away all the burnable material - grass, shrubs, trees, whatever - to create a line that the fire can't cross. It's heavy work – hard and dirty - but it's the only way to stop that fire. Of course, it doesn't always work, because you can get a burning tree falling across the control line, or if the wind suddenly picks up the fire can just simply jump the line. Another technique we use is 'backburning'.

**Interviewer:** And what's that exactly?

**Frank:** It's where you burn off an area deliberately, so that there's nothing left for the fire to feed on.

**Interviewer:** That sounds a bit risky. Starting a fire to put out another fire.

**Frank:** It can be, yes. Ideally, you direct the backburning towards the front of the bushfire, and when the two fires meet they're starved of oxygen and materials, so they just die out. But you really have to be sure of the wind direction, or you can get in real trouble.

**Interviewer:** Well, thank you, Frank. You've given us a very interesting insight there. And I hope you won't have to deal with too many bushfires this summer.

# Final test key

## Paper 1 Reading

**Part 1**

| | | | | | | | |
|---|---|---|---|---|---|---|---|
| 1 | C | 2 | B | 3 | A | 4 | B |
| 5 | C | 6 | A | 7 | B | 8 | B |

**Part 2**

| | | | | | | | |
|---|---|---|---|---|---|---|---|
| 9 | F | 10 | C | 11 | B | 12 | E |
| 13 | H | 14 | A | 15 | G | | |

**Part 3**

| | | | | | | | |
|---|---|---|---|---|---|---|---|
| 16 | D | 17 | A | 18 | C | 19 | A |
| 20 | B | 21 | D | 22 | C | 23 | D |
| 24 | B | 25 | A | 26 | C | 27 | B |
| 28 | A | 29 | D | 30 | B | | |

## Paper 3 Use of English

**Part 1**

| | | | | | | | |
|---|---|---|---|---|---|---|---|
| 1 | C | 2 | A | 3 | B | 4 | D |
| 5 | C | 6 | D | 7 | C | 8 | A |
| 9 | D | 10 | B | 11 | D | 12 | C |

**Part 2**

| | | | | | | |
|---|---|---|---|---|---|---|
| 13 | to | 14 | while/whilst/as/where | 15 | of | |
| 16 | with | 17 | which | 18 | more | 19 | next |
| 20 | more/again | | | 21 | been | 22 | the |
| 23 | order | 24 | most/only | | | | |

**Part 3**

| | | | | |
|---|---|---|---|---|
| 25 | disadvantages | 30 | extremely |
| 26 | personal | 31 | attention |
| 27 | chaotic | 32 | regardless |
| 28 | directions | 33 | arguments |
| 29 | possibility | 34 | fantastically |

**Part 4**

35 would you mind telling
36 nearly as long as
37 take care of
38 ought not to
39 last time we went
40 planning on doing
41 would have gone
42 told Jack not to put

## Paper 4 Listening

**Part 1**

| | | | | | | | |
|---|---|---|---|---|---|---|---|
| 1 | B | 2 | C | 3 | B | 4 | C |
| 5 | A | 6 | B | 7 | A | 8 | C |

**Part 2**

| | | | |
|---|---|---|---|
| 9 | *Another Mountain* | 10 | a tree |
| 11 | cousin | 12 | to ski |
| 13 | lose (some) weight | 14 | economics and drama |
| 15 | disappointed | 16 | the theatre |
| 17 | two | 18 | have a break |

**Part 3**

| | | | | | | | |
|---|---|---|---|---|---|---|---|
| 19 | D | 20 | E | 21 | A | 22 | B |
| 23 | F | | C not used | | | | |

**Part 4**

| | | | | | | | |
|---|---|---|---|---|---|---|---|
| 24 | B | 25 | B | 26 | A | 27 | C |
| 28 | A | 29 | A | 30 | B | | |

---

### Listening script

**Part 1**

1 **Interviewer:** James, you're clearly very interested in buildings. Tell us how you go about transferring them to canvas. Do you work from photos?

**James:** That would certainly be the easy option, wouldn't it? But I feel it tends to produce rather lifeless and uninteresting results. No, I usually get up early on a Sunday morning, when there's no one around, and make a fairly detailed pencil sketch of the building, adding a touch of colour here and there to represent the light and shade at that moment. Then … it's back to the studio, where I shut myself away for a few days with my brushes and oils.

2 **Man:** We only went to see it because of the reviews it was getting, but we weren't really expecting it to be that good. The thing is, we've been disappointed in the past by Miller's films, but we decided to give him just one more chance. Well I have to say I found this one really quite scary – so much so, in fact, that in some parts I covered up my face with my hands and watched it through my fingers. Of course, my wife thought this was hilarious and she's been laughing at me about it for days.

3 **Woman:** And you were doing so well with your diet, Sally … But you must have been encouraged by all the comments from everyone. We all agreed you looked so much better … But we did warn you to wait a while before you went away on holiday – it's so difficult to control what you eat when you're staying in a hotel, especially if the food's so good. Really, Sally. If only you'd taken our advice – now you're right back to where you started from.

4 **Woman:** Roger, would you do something for me?

**Man:** What is it this time?

**Woman:** Don't worry, I'm not going to ask you to clean the house or anything.

**Man:** Well that's a relief.

**Woman:** I just need you to have a look at the iron.

**Man:** What's wrong with it?

**Woman:** The same thing as the last time you had to fix it.

**Man:** Oh, right. I'll have to go and get my tools, then. I'll be back in a sec.

5 **Woman:** Well it's only a very small island, but there were various options open to us. Derek insisted on being able to go swimming every day, so it had to have a pool or a nearby beach. And I wanted to be well away from any built-up areas – I needed a holiday without the noise of other people and cars. Anyway, we chose a lovely little place inland, all on its own about 2,000 metres up, with some quite spectacular views of the coastline.

**6 Man:** Look at that, will you. One wash and all the colour has come out of it.

**Woman:** You should take it back to the shop and complain.

**Man:** I would if I'd kept the receipt. Anyway, it's my fault – I didn't read the washing instructions carefully enough.

**Woman:** Oh Peter!

**Man:** I suppose I could let one of the boys have it. It would fit David, wouldn't it?

**Woman:** Probably. There's not much point keeping it, is there? It would just take up more space in the wardrobe.

**Man:** True. I'll ask him when he comes in, then.

**7 Woman:** I've spoken to him time and time again about his behaviour in class, but it doesn't seem to do any good. I think it's time we sent a letter out to his parents asking them to come in and have a word with us. I could write the letter myself, but I think it would look better if it had your signature on it. They might take more notice of it if it came from the top.

**8 Man:** We didn't play in the end. We all decided it was better to postpone it for a week. Can't say I'm sorry, mind. The pitch didn't look too good after all that heavy rain we had on Friday night. We'd still have played, though, even if there were large puddles everywhere. The problem was that half our team had come down with flu, so we only had eight men who were fit enough to play. Hopefully, they'll have recovered by next week, and with a bit of luck the pitch will have dried out, too.

### Part 2

**Interviewer:** With us today on 'Star Turn' we have one of the most talked about people at the moment, actor John Burgeon. John, you've just finished working on a new film about the legendary mountaineer, Edward Brice. What's the title of the film and how did you come to be chosen for the role of Brice?

**John Burgeon:** Yes, the film's called *Another Mountain*, which are thought to have been Edward Brice's last words before he died at the age of 67. Brice's whole life was devoted to mountaineering, and as soon as he'd finished one climb, he would immediately start to plan the next. My involvement in the film came about as a result of my own interest in climbing, which really began when I was about nine. I've got this marvellous photo of me at that age, sitting at the top of a tree which I'd just climbed in my grandmother's garden. It's certainly one of my favourite photographs – I look so pleased with myself in it. Then, as soon as I was old enough, about 14 or 15, I started rock climbing and I often used to go at weekends with my cousin, who was five years older than me and already an experienced climber.

**Interviewer:** So it is actually you we see climbing in the film or did you use a double?

**John Burgeon:** No, that's really me you see there hanging from the rope! The director, David Brett, was very keen for me to use my climbing skills in the film. He also got me to learn to ski before filming started: Edward Brice was a competent skier and they wanted a few shots of me on the slopes. It was great fun. And because Brice was such a fit, athletic man David made me lose some weight as well – that wasn't quite so easy, but I did manage to get rid of four or five kilos by the time shooting began.

**Interviewer:** When you were younger, John, did you ever consider devoting your life to mountaineering like Brice?

**John Burgeon:** Goodness me, no! The shock would have been too great for my father. He didn't like the fact that I was spending so much of my time rock climbing and he forced me to give it up and concentrate on my studies. It was because of him that I went to university to study economics: he said it would help me get a decent job. While I was there though, I also studied drama – as a subsidiary subject. That's when I began to realize what I really wanted to do in life.

**Interviewer:** And how did your father react when you decided to take up acting as a career?

**John Burgeon:** Naturally, he was disappointed when he heard. He felt acting as a profession was far too unstable, and certainly not suitable for someone with an economics degree. However, he relaxed a little when I started to get work, particularly as it was in the theatre; I think he felt quite proud to be able to say his son was a 'theatre actor' rather than someone who worked on TV or in cinema. It all seemed so much more respectable to him. And then by the time I eventually appeared in my first film, *Sleepy Willow*, he'd forgotten about the economics and was very pleased for me.

**Interviewer:** Particularly, I imagine, as it was so successful.

**John Burgeon:** Yes, it won several awards in different film festivals around the world, including two for 'Best Film'. I also picked up three myself for 'Best Supporting Actor'. And ever since then, I've never really had any problems finding work.

**Interviewer:** And what are your plans now, John?

**John Burgeon:** Now that I've finished the Edward Brice film, I'd very much like to have a break for a few months. It's been quite a tiring experience, not only because of the acting, but also all the physical effort that was involved.

**Interviewer:** Yes, it sounds as though you deserve it. Now, if I could ask you …

### Part 3

**Speaker 1 (male)**
We don't usually play music that's in the charts at the moment – people hear that enough on the radio. We tend to alternate between the latest sounds that have just been released and older records that came out some time ago. That way, when people come in, they might say: 'That track sounds good. I'd like to hear more,' or 'I remember that one. I think I'll get that.' I feel a bit like a disc jockey at times, but the purpose is to sell more records, of course.

**Speaker 2 (female)**
During the course of a normal week I listen to … well over 50 new releases, though I usually only write reviews on three or four of them. Email means I can work from home, but I actually spend most of my time travelling up and down the country, or even abroad, to concerts and music festivals. I take a small laptop with me so I can work on the train or in my hotel room, and then send in my articles to the office when I get back home.

**Speaker 3 (male)**
I've always been surrounded by music, ever since I was born, really. My mother was a fairly successful jazz singer and my father a well-respected session musician. I suppose it was inevitable I'd follow them into the music business, but being rather shy I was reluctant to go on stage in front of an audience. I'm much happier working on my own in the background but I get tremendous satisfaction from hearing other artists perform my material, particularly if they're good.

**Speaker 4 (female)**
I always find the most exhausting part of the job is the promoting of a new album. If we didn't do it, of course, we might not sell so many records, so I do appreciate how important it is. But the constant round of newspaper interviews, radio appearances and TV chat shows wears me out. I never seem to stop talking. Coming from someone who earns a living from their voice that must sound strange, but it's different, isn't it?

**Speaker 5 (male)**
The nervousness I always feel comes not so much from the presence of an audience, since I have my back to them during the performance and can shut them out, but rather from the fact that I am working with some of the finest musicians in the world. I feel a tremendous sense of responsibility to them, because if things go wrong, it's very probably my fault – as the music critics are only too quick to point out the next day in the newspapers.

**Part 4**

**Interviewer:** Have you ever wondered who lived in your house before you bought it? Liz Rayner did, and she's come in today to tell us what she found out. What sort of house do you live in, Liz?

**Liz:** Well, it's an old Victorian semi-detached house, built in 1885. It's been modernized since then, of course, which is a shame really because some of the original features which are still there are beautiful. But we needed a place with four bedrooms and there aren't too many large houses like that in our area. So when it went up for sale two years ago we decided to buy it, even though it was a little more expensive than we expected.

**Interviewer:** And quite a lot more than it originally cost, isn't that right?

**Liz:** Yes, the original owners, Reginald and Maude Cornford paid just £125 for it! Unlike us they had quite a large family, but it seems they were also very keen on gardening, and Reginald in particular used to love spending time working in the garden after a long day's work in his photography studio. Maude would then sell the vegetables they grew to a local greengrocer's in order to earn some extra money.

**Interviewer:** Goodness! How did you find all this out?

**Liz:** From their daughter Annie's diary. The last owner came across it one day when he was converting the attic into a playroom for his children. It's absolutely fascinating, but also quite sad, really. Apparently, her parents were always far too busy to pay any attention to her and her three older brothers didn't have much to do with her, either. She desperately wished she had other children her own age to play with and talk to, but that wasn't the case, so she wrote down all her thoughts in a penny exercise book.

**Interviewer:** So how long did Annie live in the house?

**Liz:** Well, I'm sure she would have moved out sooner if she'd found a husband to take her away. But the man she was going to marry was unfortunately killed in the First World War and she ended up staying until she was well into her eighties. She fell down the stairs one day and her nephews and nieces felt that she'd be better off in a home.

**Interviewer:** And who came next?

**Liz:** A young couple, Fred and Gwen Avery, bought it from Annie in 1973. It was in a bit of a sorry state by then, so they did it up, getting rid of the Victorian fireplaces and changing the old window frames for new PVC ones. They sold it two years later to a young family, the Robertsons, who had immigrated here from Australia. The Averys had always intended to stay in the house longer but they were offered such a good price for it that they couldn't refuse. Made quite a large profit, apparently.

**Interviewer:** Did the Robertsons last longer than the Averys?

**Liz:** Considerably longer, yes. When they moved in they had just the one son, Richard, but by the time they sold it to us, Richard had four brothers and a sister! Richard's grandparents also came to live with them, and they had to add an extension to the back of the house so they could fit everyone in! Even then three of the boys had to share one of the bedrooms - so what is really quite a large house must have seemed very small to them.

**Interviewer:** And it was two years ago that you and your husband moved in. What do you do with all those bedrooms?

**Liz:** Well, both Peter and I are writers, so we use two of them as studies. Both rooms overlook the back garden that Reginald and Maude Cornford used to so enjoy working in, and although we probably spend far less time looking after it than they did, it does provide us with a pleasant visual stimulus and the peace and tranquillity we need to get on with our writing. We certainly have no intention of moving out in the near future.

## Macmillan Readers

**Jurassic Park**
Michael Crichton

The Phantom of the Opera
Gaston Leroux

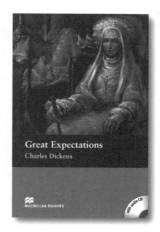

Great Expectations
Charles Dickens

Many of the Macmillan Readers are suitable for FCE students.
Visit **www.macmillanenglish.com/readers** to see the rest of our comprehensive range of graded readers.

www.macmillanenglish.com/readers

simply read

**MACMILLAN READERS**

---

# MACMILLAN EXAMS

Macmillan has a fantastic range of supplementary titles for students studying for FCE.

CHECK YOUR VOCABULARY FOR
**FCE** ✓
Rawdon Wyatt
*All you need to pass your exams!*
MACMILLAN

*First Certificate*
Language Practice
Michael Vince
with Paul Emmerson
*English Grammar and Vocabulary*
MACMILLAN

**First Certificate Testbuilder**
WITH ANSWER KEY
**Tests that teach!**
Tony D'Triggs
MACMILLAN

SKILLS FOR FIRST CERTIFICATE — *Reading*

SKILLS FOR FIRST CERTIFICATE — *Writing*

SKILLS FOR FIRST CERTIFICATE — *Listening and Speaking*

SKILLS FOR FIRST CERTIFICATE — *Use of English*

**www.macmillanenglish.com/exams**

opportunity /ˌɒpə(r)ˈtjuːnəti/ noun ★★★

THE LEARNING CENTRE
HAMMERSMITH AND WEST
LONDON COLLEGE
GLIDDON ROAD
LONDON W14 9BL

The second edition of the award-winning learners' dictionary now has a special focus on writing skills, designed to help learners to become more confident writers in academic and exam situations:

- Get it right boxes for accuracy
- Improve your Writing Skills sections for fluency
- Exercises for writing practice
- Expand your Vocabulary section and a thesaurus for vocabulary building

"....ideal for those attempting examinations, motivating for those engaged in self-study, clear and much more informative than anything I have seen in any other dictionary... Teachers will find that a huge number of their problems have been solved for them."

H. A. Swan, ELT Professional, UK

Open up your world

www.macmillandictionaries.com